Politicization of the Civil Service in Comparative Perspective

One of the persistent claims made about the public sector over the past several decades has been that the public service has become more politicized. Addressing this important area of debate within public administration, this book discusses conceptions and measurements of politicization, as well as some of its causes and consequences.

Using a comparative framework, the authors collected here confront the issue of politicization, identifying the nature and extent of political involvement and assessing the real impact of any changes on the legitimacy and effectiveness of the political system. The book addresses issues such as:

- compensation
- appointments made from outside the civil service system
- anonymity
- partisanship
- systems to handle appointees of prior administrations.

This invaluable study contains case studies of the USA, Canada, Germany, France, Sweden, Denmark, the UK, New Zealand, Belgium, the Netherlands, Spain and Greece. It will appeal to all those interested in public administration and the civil service in particular.

B. Guy Peters is Maurice Falk Professor of American Government at the University of Pittsburgh, USA. **Jon Pierre** is Professor of Political Science at the University of Gothenburg, Sweden.

Routledge studies in governance and public policy

Politicization of the Civil Service in Comparative Perspective

The quest for control

Edited by B. Guy Peters and Jon Pierre

Routledge
Taylor & Francis Group

LONDON AND NEW YORK

First published 2004
by Routledge
11 New Fetter Lane, London EC4P 4EE

Simultaneously published in the USA and Canada
by Routledge
29 West 35th Street, New York, NY 10001

Routledge is an imprint of the Taylor & Francis Group

Typeset in Baskerville by Wearset Ltd, Boldon, Tyne and Wear
Printed and bound in Great Britain by MPG Books Ltd, Bodmin

British Library Cataloguing in Publication Data
A catalogue record for this book is available from the British Library

Library of Congress Cataloging in Publication Data
Politicization of the civil service in comparative perspective : the
quest for control / edited by B. Guy Peters and Jon Pierre.
    p. cm.
Includes bibliographical references and index.
1. Civil service–Political activity. 2. Civil service ethics. 3. Patronage,
Political. I. Peters, B. Guy. II. Pierre, Jon.
JF1673 .P65 2004
352.6'3–dc22

                                                                2003019136

ISBN 0–415–70025–6

Contents

Figures

Tables

Contributors

Jørgen Grønnegård Christensen is Professor of Public Administration at the University of Aarhus, Denmark.

Guido Dierickx is Professor of Political Science at the University of Antwerp, Belgium.

Robert Gregory is Associate Professor of Public Policy at Victoria University of Wellington, New Zealand.

Rachel Locke is a Project Co-ordinator at the Carnegie Council on Ethics and International Affairs, USA.

Salvador Parrado Díez is Professor of Public Administration, Human Resources Management and Local Government at the Universidad Nacional Educación a Distancia, Spain.

B. Guy Peters is Maurice Falk Professor of American Government at the University of Pittsburgh, USA.

Jon Pierre is Professor of Political Science at the University of Gothenburg, Sweden.

Luc Rouban is Director of Research at Centre d'Étude de la Vie Politique Française, France.

Charlotte Sausman is Nuffield Fellow in Health Policy and Fellow of Lucy Cavendish College, University of Cambridge, UK.

Donald J. Savoie holds the Clément-Cormier Chair in Economic Development at the Université de Moncton, Canada.

Eckhard Schröter is Lecturer in Political Science at University of California, USA.

Dimitri A. Sotiropoulos is a Lecturer in Political Science at University of Athens, Greece.

Frits M. van der Meer is Associate Professor in Comparative Public Administration at the University of Leiden, the Netherlands.

Acknowledgements

The original idea to launch a comparative research project on the politicization of the senior civil service came from the late Vincent Wright. Vincent being Vincent, he quickly defined the key issues, identified participants, and secured funding for a conference. We are very sorry indeed that he never got to see the completion of the project which he shaped in many different ways. We dedicate the book to his memory.

The conference in late 1999 when first drafts of the papers were discussed was organized under the auspices of the University of Gothenburg. Stephanie Wright at Nuffield College has been helpful with the administrative details of the project. Bob Gregory, Donald Savoie, and Eckhard Schröter kindly offered to write chapters to add breadth to the project although they could not participate in the conference.

Sheryn Peters and Monika Pierre probably care less about politicization of the civil service than they do about the presence of their spouses. We realize that our being on the road now and then means that they have to cover for us at home and it is now official that we plan to make up for it as soon as this book is published.

Once again, our thanks to the staff at the Royal Wing Lounge at Schiphol Airport in Amsterdam for providing opportunities for secluded conversations about matters of significance and consequence.

B. Guy Peters and Jon Pierre
Pittsburgh and Gothenburg

1 Politicization of the civil service

Concepts, causes, consequences

B. Guy Peters and Jon Pierre

One of the persistent claims made about the public sector over the past several decades has been that the public service has become more politicized. The exact meaning of that term is often not specified, but the general sense is that members of the public service must now pay greater attention to politics than they did in the past. In addition, it appears that politicians in elective offices are investing greater time and energy in ensuring that the members of the public service are compatible with their own partisan and policy preferences. Even in countries such as the United States that have for some time permitted a good deal of latitude for political appointment to administrative positions there is a sense that these political control structures over the bureaucracy continue to "thicken" (Light, 1996). These changes reflect a retreat from the institutionalized merit system that has (or had) been the standard way of organizing employment in the public sector, in the United States (Ingraham, 1995) and elsewhere.

The purpose of this chapter is to discuss alternative conceptions and measurements of politicization, as well as some of its causes and consequences. There appears to be a sense among practitioners as well as academic analysts that some politicization has been occurring, but the evidence supporting that belief is often subjective, anecdotal, and rather diffuse. This chapter therefore will be not so much a firm mapping of the terrain as a set of road signs along the way toward a better understanding of the concept. It will therefore admit several conceptions of politicization, and indeed will welcome various lenses through which we can approach that concept.

Definitions of politicization

Before we begin to try to measure the phenomenon of politicization of the public service we should first attempt to define it. Politicization has appeared in a number of recent discussions of the public service (Meyers, 1985; Rouban, 1998; 1999; Clifford and Wright, 1997; Derlien, 1996), but often has been discussed using rather different interpretations and definitions. At the most basic level, by politicization of the civil service we mean *the substitution of political criteria for merit-based criteria in the selection, retention, promotion, rewards, and disciplining of members of the public service.* Unlike the use of patronage appointments in many less developed countries (World Bank, 2001), politicization in the industrialized democracies implies attempts to control policy and implementation, rather than just supply jobs to party members or members of a family or clique.[1]

The public service is inherently a political creation, and also inherently involved in politics, simply because it is the structure that delivers *services publiques* to the citizens – it plays a role in determining who gets what from the public sector. That said, however, the pattern of political development has been to shield the civil service from overt political control in order to enhance its efficiency and to ensure its fairness in dealing with citizens (Torstendahl, 1991). While any institution so inherently concerned with issues of governing can never be made fully apolitical, it has been removed from the more direct forms of partisan control.

The definition of politicization advanced above is broad, and requires some ramifications. The first point is that almost all civil service systems have some level of political involvement in personnel matters that is considered appropriate.[2] There are a large number of appointed officials in the American bureaucracy that are manifestly political and those appointments have been available to presidents and cabinet secretaries for decades. Likewise the "political civil servants" in Germany have a known party affiliation but the administrative system provides means of permitting that political involvement, while at the same time maintaining the merit basis of their initial appointment (Derlien, 1996). The more recent concern about politicization, therefore, implies a sense that those bounds of acceptability are being breached.

A second point to consider is that the nature of the political criteria being employed when the public service is being politicized may vary. We usually think of these as being partisan political loyalties, but attempts at politicization may also reflect policy and even stylistic issues, as they are manifested in the activities of public servants. For example, during the Thatcher years in the United Kingdom it was often argued that politicization was occurring less on the basis of allegiance to the Conservative Party and more on the basis of being "one of us," i.e. being committed to a program of radical reform of the public sector (Clifford and Wright, 1998). The support for reform may have been correlated with Conservative Party membership, but commitment was more important by far than partisanship. The longer a party remains in power, the more this form of politicization appears to manifest itself, as it did with the Social Democratic Party in Sweden (Rothstein, 1986). In the extreme case civil servants may be selected and deselected on the basis of their personal, almost clientelistic, loyalties to ministers and other political leaders as well as partisan allegiance.

A third point is that the manner in which the political criteria are employed may matter for the performance of the administrative system. For example, permitting merit criteria to dominate the selection and promotion of public servants for most of their careers, with the political criteria being used primarily to remove very senior officials and to replace them (particularly after a change of government), is less destructive of the principles underlying merit systems than is more overt selection of civil servants throughout their careers. Likewise, the focus on policy goals as opposed to partisan allegiance mentioned above may be less destructive to democratic values than would be strict partisanship in selection.

Fourth, politicization may also mean that public servants begin to take on tasks that formerly (and formally) might have been considered to be political. There is some evidence that ministers find it increasingly diffi-cult to separate their political roles from their governmental roles, and require civil servants to perform tasks that might be better performed by political aides, or by political party personnel (Savoie, 1999). There is some truth in the argument that the political and the governmental are difficult to separate in the life of a minister. That having been said, he or she conventionally has been considered to have an obligation to err on the side of not using public employees for political purposes, and to main-tain the probity of public office. As we will point out below, however, par-liaments and other public institutions may be forcing these political roles onto public servants, and civil servants themselves find it difficult to refuse functions assigned to them.

Fifth, increased politicization in the partisan sense may imply depoliti-cization in other senses. One target of would-be politicizers in many coun-tries has been the close connection of social and economic interest groups with ministries, and with individual civil servants. For that functional, corporatist relationship, concerned politicians would substitute a partisan or political loyalty. The commitment of bureaucrats to the values and interests of the policy area is generally seen as just another reason for the difficulties that ministers encounter when attempting to manage their programs and their departments. This is especially true for parties that come to office after some period in opposition and find that there are working relationships in place that they do not favor. Still, substituting the influence of political parties and politicians means that other political actors, the interest groups, will be less influential.

A final consideration arising from this definition of politicization is that in some ways political criteria may be more important for ensuring demo-cratic values in governing than are conventional merit values. One stan-dard critique (see Rose, 1976) of conventional bureaucracies is that the permanent, career public service is not sufficiently responsive to changes in the priorities of their political leadership.[3] They are argued (somewhat stereotypically) to persist in their own conceptions of appropriate policies, regardless of what their ministers want. Replacing those permanent employees with more responsive, if politicized, public employees may actually improve the correspondence between electoral results and policies (see Peters, 2000). Despite that possibility, the term politicization has a generally negative connotation in democratic societies.

Following from this last point, we must ask whether the classic notion of "neutral competence" (Kaufman, 1956) is really the most important dimension of competence for the public service. That is, should governments really be content with civil servants who have few commitments to policy, or even to the government? This is a more normative than empirical point about governing, but it does raise interesting questions about the importance of political appointment of public servants. The "responsive competence" of public servants is especially important for political systems attempting to implement basic changes within the administrative system. Thus, the models of civil service neutrality exported from the Western democracies may not be as suitable for the countries of central and eastern Europe that are attempting to overcome decades of economic stagnation and deterioration of public services.

Targets of politicization

The above definition implies that there is no single way of achieving politicization, and that there are numerous targets that might be addressed. For example, politicization is usually discussed in terms of the *employees of the public sector*. The assumption is that the best way to gain control over the public bureaucracy is to have the capability of appointing one's own faithful to positions that influence or control public policy. There are, of course, numerous examples of those appointees "marrying the natives" and becoming simply new components of the machinery they were meant to direct, but politicians generally persist in the view that appointing personnel into the bureaucracy is a crucial mechanism of control. Public organizations are very good at capturing any new members of their nominal leadership, given that the careerists tend to control information and to control contacts with interest groups in society.

Actual appointment of partisan loyalists to those positions in the bureaucracy may not be so crucial if the political leaders are able to influence the *behavior* of the personnel already in those positions. Indeed, this is a much less expensive strategy, in terms of the political capital required, and in terms of the wastage of personnel resources in government.[4] If the same goals can be achieved by winning over the career bureaucracy, then everyone may be better off. This desired effect on the behavior of public servants may be achieved in several ways. One strategy is to use ideology and leadership to mobilize the public service – this can be seen in Tony Blair's success with the British civil service, as well as in many mobilization regimes in the Third World. Fear (of loss of employment, demotion, transfer, etc.) is, of course, another and much less positive means of achieving those same behavioral ends.

Following closely from the strategy of changing behavior is a political strategy of attempting to change the *attitudes and culture* of the public service. As intimated above, this strategy has some positive democratic connotations if the purpose of the proposed change is to have the bureaucracy follow the election results, and to consider that their task is to be more than grudging executors of government policy. That said, however, changing the component of civil service culture that supports detachment from the politics of the day in favor of a more responsive and political conception of the role may not have entirely positive consequences for government, or for the public service.[5]

Some aspects of the "New Public Management" (NPM) have been directed at changing the culture of the public service into a more business-like set of beliefs and values, but it is not clear that these changes would in fact make the bureaucracy more responsive to politicians. The actual effect of these changes may be to make civil servants responsive to a different set of internal motivations and values, but still largely self-directed rather than responding to their political masters as the motivation for greater politicization would suggest. Indeed, some of the mantras of the NPM, such as "let the managers manage," may provide civil servants with a justification for disregarding the requests of their nominal superiors.

As well as addressing the people within government – themselves as employees, their values and their behaviors – politicization can also manifest itself in *structural* terms. In this instance the strategy is that if the public service cannot be made to respond to political pressures, and its staff cannot be replaced, then there must be some way of working around them to achieve the goals that the politicians were elected to implement. The structural solutions tend to involve duplicating or supplementing the career service with a cadre of more political officials. For example, in a number of cases politically responsive "chiefs of staff" have been appointed to supplement the work of the career head of the civil service within a department, e.g. the Deputy Minister in Canada (Savoie, 1994). The recent controversy over the role of politically appointed "spin doctors" in British ministries represents another example of duplicating career officials with politicized appointments (Webster and Webster, 2002). In other cases there have been attempts to create analogues of the *cabinet* systems found in France and Belgium.

Somewhat related to the structural solution is the idea of politicians attempting to change the arenas in which decisions are made as a means of achieving goals. This strategy is especially effective in federal or quasi-federal regimes in which the different levels of government have a good deal of autonomy. So, for example, conservatives in the United States often attempt to move decisions down to state and local levels in order to produce solutions that are less likely to involve substantial levels of government expenditure, and that are also likely to be more conservative ideologically.[6] Or the political leader may simply attempt to find a government that is controlled by members of his or her party. Within the European Union moving decisions to Brussels may involve different sets of bureaucrats and political interests, and perhaps having policy proposals receive a more favorable reading.

A particular example of changing venues for decision-making is moving decisions out to quasi-public organizations, such as the famous "quangos" in the United Kingdom and analogous bodies elsewhere. A priori, there may be no particular reason to expect these organizations to be any different politically from the central government. What may make quangos a particularly attractive strategy is the capacity of a sitting government to control appointments to the boards running them. In the United Kingdom, for example, it is estimated that there are now over 70,000 political appointments in quangos and other non-departmental public bodies that are available to politicians who seek to control public policy (Skelcher, 1998). There has been a similar growth in these quasi-public organizations in other democracies (Greve, 1999).

Finally, and perhaps most importantly, politicians may politicize the public service in order to change policy. It is often argued by ministers that when they assume their post in a ministry they are confronted by a cadre of public servants, often from top to bottom of the structure, who are committed to a certain way of doing things. The capacity to make at least some appointments is a means of addressing this problem and of perhaps being able to put a particular stamp on policy.

In summary, we should be careful not to think that so long as political leaders do not have the capacity to appoint whomever they wish to public bodies, there is no politicization of the public service. There are a variety of strategies that these political leaders can employ to produce much the same effect as was available in the more traditional forms of responsibility. These alternative strategies have the great advantage that they are not so overt as the firing and hiring of personnel and hence are less likely to generate a political controversy.

Why politicize?

Politicians are, the literature (both popular and academic) argues, investing more time and energy in politicizing the civil service now than in the recent past. For example, the articles contained in a special issue of *Revue Française d'Administration Publique* (1998) all indicated that there had been an increase in political meddling in administration, even in the northern European countries with reputations for more effective systems of merit appointment (see also Dudek and Peters, 1999). If we assume that these observations are correct, then we must wonder why these politicians are willing to do this when for many citizens the practice has very negative connotations.

The most obvious reason, as already mentioned above, is that politicians want to be able to control what their government organizations do; the usual complaint about the bureaucracy is that the decisions taken by ministers simply trickle into the sand. If there are loyal party members administering public programs, so it has been argued, there will be less deflection of policy directions than in a system dominated by the career public service. That concern about the career public service is an old story, so why is there so much expansion of interest in using political appointments to administrative posts?

One answer is that the process of administrative reform so common during the past several decades has tended to remove the controls that previously helped to control the actions of the bureaucracy. This has at once necessitated introducing some additional form of control and presented the opportunity for using political means to achieve that control. For example, "Next Steps" in the UK and analogous deconcentrations of the public sector have purposefully freed major parts of the public sector from direct ministerial control. This greater freedom in turn imposes a need for some form of control over policy and administration. The managerialist perspective inherent in these reforms assumes that the managers should manage, and by extension that controls over those managers are not desirable. Likewise, the tendency to "deregulate government" (see Peters, 1998) also removes a whole range of mechanisms for controlling the civil service and its behavior in office.

Part of the problem faced by ministers and other politicians in these settings is that even though they may have nominally been removed from a position of direct accountability for policy, the public may not accept that. When they identify a failure in transport they rather naturally assume that the minister of transport should be held accountable. Attempts to deny that responsibility may only heighten an already well-developed sense of cynicism among the public. When faced with this problem of control, ministers often attempt to substitute political controls for more conventional forms of control.

There has been some interaction between changes in the ways in which ministers understand their accountability and the politicization of the public service. The old conventions, even if honored in the breach as much as in the practice, were that ministers were responsible for everything that transpired within their ministry. They were deemed to be responsible even if they had no direct part in the decision. As this norm is changing and parliaments are questioning civil servants as well as ministers publicly about their decisions, ministers find that they need civil servants who are in agreement with their stances and who are personally loyal, if not necessarily partisans. There is a need for civil servants willing to put the right "spin" on a set of facts when called upon to do so in parliament or the media.

The shift in accountability systems may become even more pronounced as conventional political modes of accountability are augmented by performance-based systems. While citizens and politicians may want a government that performs well, changes in accountability systems make the exercise of political controls problematic. This, in turn, may accentuate the drive on the part of the politicians to add more loyalists to the organizations administering the programs.

We would also hypothesize that politicization is a more likely reaction to problems of control when there are more rapid and more extreme changes in control of government. In a case in which the parties are relatively similar in their policy goals and their styles of governing, politicization may make little sense. So, for example, the British civil service was able to maintain its depoliticized status during the post-war years of consensus politics. The Thatcher years and the attempts at fundamental change of policy produced a perceived need for a change in the civil service (Kavanagh, 1990).

Following from the above, it can be argued that attempts at very fundamental reforms in the public sector are likely to engender an interest in politicizing the public service. While the administrative reforms of most industrialized democracies have been important and, in terms of the historical persistence of administrative forms, quite dramatic, the more fundamental changes in the post-socialist and democratizing countries are certainly more basic. These changes may be expected to generate an even greater interest in changing the civil service (see Verheijen, 1999). The problem being faced in these cases is that there is a limited supply of qualified people, and a decision to replace an official may mean (in the short term at least) appointing someone with fewer technical or even political capabilities.

Consequences of politicization

Just as there are a number of assumptions about the causes of politicization, so too are there a number of assumptions about the consequences of those changes in the manner of selecting public employees and in the manner in which these employees are managed. As already noted, the majority of those consequences are assumed to be negative. In terms of administrative criteria a politicized administrative system is assumed to be less efficient than the neutral competence associated with the merit system. As noted, that assumption may be contingent on the nature of the political system or even the particular policy area, but it is certainly a dominant assumption. This may, however, be as much a normative as an empirical statement about the effects of politicization.

The political consequences of politicization are also assumed to be negative, and to be primarily loss of confidence in the fairness of government institutions. In most industrialized democracies the bureaucracy continues to be regarded more positively than the more political institutions of government (see Listhaug and Wiberg, 1996), although that may be damning with faint praise given the generally poor assessment of politicians and political institutions. Still, if partisan politics has a more negative connotation than does the bureaucracy, then the increasing utilization of political criteria can only undermine the legitimacy of the bureaucracy – something that few administrative systems can afford.

The final consequence of politicization is that the accountability of public bureaucracy may become more limited. To some extent politicians were a part of the accountability system for the bureaucracy, but as the two may be pushed toward becoming closer allies that objectivity becomes minimized.[7] As a result of the NPM, accountability is being more professionalized and more based on objective quality standards. On the one hand, that change may make political leaders even more content, given that the bureaucracy, rather than themselves, are likely to be the formal targets of such a form of accountability. On the other hand, potential loss of direct engagement with service delivery is not likely to make politicians any less responsible in the minds of the public. Thus, there may be public accountability without real control.

Plan of the book

The remainder of this book will be a series of studies of politicization in twelve industrialized democracies. This "sample" of countries excludes perhaps the most extreme cases of politicization encountered in many less developed political systems, with dominant political parties attempting to impose their control over the political system. Even in this more limited sample of political systems, however, there is a good deal of variation, both in general styles of public administration (see Peters, forthcoming) and in the degree and variety of politicization. Further, these countries have been affected to differing degrees by the ideas of the NPM which, as we have pointed out above, may have a pronounced influence on the way in which political and public servants interact (Peters and Pierre, 2001).

Four of the countries in this group – the United Kingdom (Sausman and Locke), New Zealand (Gregory), Canada (Savoie), and the United States (Peters) – come from the Anglo-American tradition of administration, with a history of political neutrality for the civil service. All of the Anglo-American systems have been affected heavily by the ideas of NPM but the United Kingdom appears to have begun a process of politicization well before those ideas became popular, and fully implemented. These two systems also differ in the extent to which the politicization of the public service has been overt, as opposed to more subtle attempts to shape the attitudes and beliefs of the public servants.

There are also two cases drawn from the heart of the Napoleonic tradition of administration included in this sample. These countries traditionally have been more accepting of political influence over appointments to the public service than have the Anglo-American systems, but they also have strong legal norms of administrative impartiality. The chapters on France by Rouban and on Spain by Salvador Parrado Díez are excellent treatments of the contrasting nature of politicization in these countries and the changes that have occurred with changes in regimes and changes in managerial ideas. In addition to those two cases Greece has been influenced by the French tradition, as well as reflecting its own distinctive approach to public administration. Dimitri Sotiropoulos demonstrates the pervasiveness of patronage and politicization in Greek public administration and shows important contrasts with the other cases.

We also have two Scandinavian cases. Jørgen Christensen provides the most extensive quantitative treatment of politicization in his study of Denmark. He approaches the question of politicization by examining not only who is appointed, but also how people leave the public service, arguing that if senior public servants end their careers earlier, especially around the time of elections, it may indicate that the positions had become more politicized. Jon Pierre takes a somewhat broader perspective when examining politicization in Sweden, and points to the range of cultural, political, and structural influences on politicization of the public service. Further, more than the other authors, he discusses the normative implications of this phenomenon in government.

The Netherlands and Belgium represent the intersection of two major administrative traditions. There are some aspects of the German tradition and some identifiable features of the Napoleonic tradition. These two cases also represent rather different styles and degrees of politicization of the civil service. On the one hand Belgium has had more of the French style of a political civil service, especially the use of ministerial *cabinets* composed of manifestly politically committed public servants. Guido Dierickx points out the rather marked degree of politicization in Belgium and argues that the multiple dimensions of cleavage in the Belgian system exacerbate the politicization of the system. The Netherlands has had a less overtly political public service, but as Frits van der Meer demonstrates there are still a number of ways in which politics creeps into the selection and management of public officials. As in the two Anglo-Saxon countries, administrative reforms appear to have had a substantial influence on the degree and manner of politicization in the Netherlands.

We have pointed out that the top civil service in Germany has long offered opportunities to the "political civil servant," a senior official who is publicly associated with a political party but who will have worked up through the career system on a merit basis. That version of politicization is well established in the system, and Eckhard Schröter demonstrates the persistence of that model as well as the subtle changes that have been

occurring. As in the Danish chapter, Schröter demonstrates the importance of turnover in civil service positions after elections as a clear indicator
of the changing level of politicization in government. Thus, even in a
country that is often cited as having a political civil service, at least at the
upper echelons, there has been some increase in the role of politics in
appointments.

Conclusions

The increased politicization of the public service is one of the truisms of
contemporary government in the industrialized democracies. Many scholars, journalists, and politicians are quite certain that the phenomenon
exists, but identifying and measuring it is substantially more complicated,
and more contentious. This project has been an attempt to initiate some
more systematic and analytic thinking about the nature of politicization.
That systematic exploration is especially important in comparative
context, given that the (presumed) separation of politics and administration, and the normative basis of that separation, differ cross-nationally,
Further, the comparison of politicization needs to be conducted across
time as well as across countries, as the numerous changes in the nature of
public administration have altered rather fundamentally the possibility,
and even the meaning, of politicization.

It is also important to consider the potentially positive features of
politicization of the public service. The connotations of the term are
almost always negative, bordering on corruption, but we have attempted
to point out that there may also be some functional aspects of shifts
toward a more committed bureaucracy – it may be more than a necessary
evil. In particular, greater political commitment may energize the public
service in a way that may not be possible with a more neutral public
service. Therefore, when we confront the issue of politicization we not
only have the empirical challenge of identifying the nature and extent of
political involvement, we must also assess the real impact of any changes
on the legitimacy and effectiveness of the political system.

Notes

1 Also, we are not directly concerned with the actions of public servants who
  themselves seek out involvement in partisan politics. The only relevant part of
  that activity would be if those civil servants believed that political activity was the
  best way to achieve career advancement.
2 This is less true for traditional Westminster systems than for other types of political systems; in some instances, e.g. the United States under the Hatch Act, civil
  servants were not supposed to engage in any political activity other than voting.
3 The *Yes Minister* television series is a humorous, if sometimes a little close to the
  bone, portrayal of that tendency in career public servants.
4 The "temporary retirements" in the German system, for example, mean that a

number of highly skilled civil servants may be tending their dahlias rather than working for government.

5 For example, the Thatcher and Major governments were said to have so changed the culture of the civil service that they could no longer serve a Labour government (*IPMS Bulletin,* 1996). The prediction turned out to be radically incorrect, but it did point to the potential problems of politicizing by changing culture.

6 This outcome is in part a function of the difficulties that sub-national governments may encounter in raising revenue. Further, many state and local governments (especially in the south and west) will indeed be more conservative than the modal decisions taken at the federal level.

7 In some ways this may be a return to the "village life" model described by Heclo and Wildavsky (1974) in the British public service, but in this version the basis of the village may be partisan politics rather than a common commitment to governing.

References

Clifford, C. and V. Wright (1997) "The Politicization of the British Civil Service: Ambitions, Limits and Conceptual Problems" (unpublished paper, Nuffield College, Oxford).

Derlien, H.-U. (1996) "The Politicization of Bureaucracies in Historical and Comparative Context," in B. G. Peters and B. A. Rockman, eds, *Agenda for Excellence II: Administering the State* (Chatham, NJ: Chatham House).

Dudek, C. M. and B. G. Peters (1999) "Clientelism in Cold Climates" (unpublished paper, Department of Political Science, University of Pittsburgh).

Greve, C. (1999) "Quangos in Denmark and Sweden," in M. V. Flinders and M. J. Smith, eds, *Quangos, Accountability and Reform: The Politics of Quasi-Government* (London: Macmillan).

Heclo, H. and A. Wildavsky (1974) *The Private Government of Public Money* (Berkeley, CA: University of California Press).

Ingraham, P. W. (1995) *The Foundation of Merit: Public Service in American Democracy* (Baltimore, MD: Johns Hopkins University Press).

IPMS Bulletin (1996) "Vote of No Confidence" (May).

Kaufman, H. A. (1956) "Emerging Conflicts in the Doctrine of Public Administration," *American Political Science Review,* 50, 1059–73.

Kavanagh, D. (1990) *Thatcherism and British Politics: The End of Consensus?* (Oxford: Oxford University Press).

Light, P. C. (1996) *Thickening Government: The Federal Government and the Diffusion of Responsibility* (Washington, DC: The Brookings Institution).

Listhaug, O. and M. Wiberg (1996) "Confidence in Public and Private Institutions," in H.-D. Klingemann and D. Fuchs, *Citizens and the State* (Oxford: Oxford University Press).

Meyers, F. (1985) *La Politisation de l'administration* (Brussels: International Institute of Administrative Sciences).

Peters, B. G. (1998) *The Future of Governing* (Lawrence, KS: University Press of Kansas).

Peters, B. G. (2000) "Is Democracy a Substitute for Ethics?," in A. Farazmand, ed., *Public Personnel Management* (Aldershot: Ashgate).

Peters, B. G. (forthcoming) *Administrative Traditions: Understanding Public Bureaucracy in Industrialized Democracies* (Oxford: Oxford University Press).

Peters, B. G. and J. Pierre (2001) *Politicians, Bureaucrats and Administrative Reform* (London: Routledge).

Rose, R. (1976) *The Problem of Party Government* (London: Macmillan).

Rothstein, B. (1986) *Den socialdemokratiska staten* (Lund: Arkiv).

Rouban, L. (1998) "La politisation des fonctionnaires en France: obstacle ou necessité?," *Revue Française d'Administration Publique*, 86 (avril–juin), 167–82.

Savoie, D. J. (1994) *Reagan, Thatcher, Mulroney: In Search of the New Bureaucracy* (Pittsburgh, PA: University of Pittsburgh Press).

Savoie, D. J. (1999) *Governing from the Centre* (Toronto: University of Toronto Press).

Skelcher, C. (1998) *The Appointed State: Quasi-governmental Organizations and Democracy* (Buckingham: Open University Press).

Torstendahl, R. (1991) *Bureaucratization in Northwest Europe, 1880–1985: Dominance and Government* (London: Routledge).

Verheijen, T. (1999) *Civil Service Systems in Central and Eastern Europe* (Cheltenham: Edward Elgar).

Webster, P. and B. Webster (2002) "Spin War Forces No 10 on Defensive," *The Times*, 15 February.

2 Political responsiveness in a merit bureaucracy

Denmark

Jørgen Grønnegård Christensen

As political executives, ministers are dependent on bureaucrats in two important respects. They call on their assistance to develop and present their policies, and they delegate decision-making authority to them to relieve themselves of part of the executive burden. In either case, the ministers are concerned with the political responsiveness of their advisors and administrative executives responsible for implementing policy. The question is whether this assistance is and should be provided by career civil servants recruited on a merit basis or by political appointees. Analytically, this involves two issues: (1) when should we expect political appointments to take place, and when should we expect a merit-based civil service? (2) assuming that political appointees are more responsive to political guidance than career civil servants, can ministers do anything to strengthen the incentives of career civil servants to be responsive to their political guidance?

This chapter presents an analysis of both issues. It is based on a case study of the Danish civil service as it has developed from the mid-1930s to the turn of the century. Central to the analysis is a conception of politicization that focuses on "the substitution of political criteria for merit-based criteria in the selection, retention, promotion, rewards, and disciplining of members of the public service" (Peters and Pierre, Chapter 1 above). Following this lead, the present analysis distinguishes between: (1) the installation of advisory bodies with staff recruited by the minister, who leave their office as the minister leaves his; (2) the appointment of top civil servants, i.e. permanent secretaries and agency heads, according to political criteria defined by the government or the minister in charge.

In operational terms, both types of politicization present difficulties if the government is not compelled to announce publicly that it has made a political appointment. For political appointments to advisory positions in ministerial secretariats, a double indicator is used. Politicization presupposes the existence of a distinct advisory body whose members are replaced when a new minister replaces the incumbent. For political appointments to line positions as top civil servants, the indicator again is that the incumbents leave their posts as the minister is replaced by a minister from another party. In both sets of circumstances, political appointments may take place, even if the appointee is recruited from the career civil service, perhaps from within the department. However, recruitment from outside the civil service, especially among people in political posts, is also used as a subsidiary and strong indicator of politicization in the analysis.

Can merit recruitment satisfy the modern political executive?

Much of the debate over merit vs. political appointment is strongly prescriptive. Since Max Weber, a parallel discussion has focused on the prevalence of merit and political appointments and on the effects of each in terms of advisory or executive behavior. In both cases, the underlying assumption is that ministers expect responsiveness from the bureaucracy, but also that such responsiveness is not given. Consequently, ministers may be expected to have a preference for political appointees whom they select themselves, based on their knowledge of their political and/or policy predilections.

This is only possible if ministers can control individual appointments and if they are legally and politically entitled to practice a political bias. Murray Horn has put forward a sophisticated theoretical argument for merit appointments as the preference of the enacting coalition. This coalition is the legislative majority behind a specific policy designed to safeguard the future administration of its policies, in case a competing coalition takes over. According to Horn, this leads the enacting coalition to prefer a merit bureaucracy to a politicized administration. It further invites it to devise a set of incentives that induce civil servants to be loyal to the policies of the enacting coalition when they make decisions to implement them (Horn, 1995, 95–133). There are limits to this argument. First, it only deals with policy implementation, not with the role of civil servants as policy and political advisors. Second, and more importantly, the empirical referent of Horn's theoretical argument is not very clear. At times he may be referring to political systems of the Westminster type, at other times he seems to refer to the American checks-and-balances system. This is a serious flaw in the argument, as the Westminster principles emphasize the dominant role of the incumbent minister, while the checks-and-balances system produces a set of policy coalitions that are strongly preoccupied with creating commitments to loyal policy implementation. However, contrary to the predictions derived from the theory, the American spoils system by definition contains a stronger dose of political appointments than most west European systems (Ingraham, 1995).

Thomas Hammond has more clearly focused on the political and institutional contingencies that lead to either merit or political appointments. His argument is built up around the notion of institutional equilibrium.

Therefore, whether a political executive will prefer one or the other solution, and whether it will be able to put its preferential solution into practice, is contingent upon institutional and political factors. Institutionally, he hypothesizes that the number of veto points is important, and politically the allocation of power between parties and the length of office-holding is central to his argument (Hammond, 1996, 145–147). This leads to a set of complex but testable propositions.

In the Danish case, this argument highlights the existence of multi-party coalitions, often holding only a minority in parliament, that stay in power for relatively short periods. Thus the prediction is that we should find little politicization of civil service appointments as it would be severely criticized and eventually stopped by a parliamentary veto. This would provide a contrast with systems where one party remains in power over a long period and where there is only one veto point, as was the case during the decades of Social Democratic rule in Sweden. Here, politicization would be expected. In addition to its propositions being testable, the advantage of the Hammond approach is that it draws attention to what happens if a system undergoes change because of shifts in the allocation of power or institutional reform.

If, as argued above, no or little politicization has taken place in Danish central government, ministers have to rely on career civil servants both when they ask for policy advice and when they delegate administrative decision-making authority to them. This raises the question of whether ministers can expect such civil servants to be politically responsive and whether they can do anything to increase this responsiveness. The literature is not entirely clear on this point. In Weber's ideal-type bureaucracy, a merit-based career civil service is a central component (Weber, 1921/1980, 551–579). Weberian theory sees merit recruitment, merit promotion and tenure as elements of an incentive structure that equalizes the incentives of individual civil servants and induces them to base their administration of policy on the law. Thus, merit combined with life-long tenure tends to emphasize civil servants' loyalty toward the institutions of parliamentary democracy and the rule of law rather than their responsiveness to the political expediencies of the incumbent minister. In this interpretation, the implications of merit and tenure are close to the implications proposed by Horn within a more explicit analysis of the incentive structure of merit bureaucracy, although he is much more concerned with political guidance and political constituencies striving to protect their long-term interests.

Weber saw the limitations of his own analysis. He assumed top civil servants to be highly motivated by a desire for power, and feared that information asymmetries ensuing from their monopolization of legal and technical insights (*Dienstwissen*) could be used for this purpose (Weber, 1918/1988, 352). Studies that emphasize the relative protection of a career civil service and its potential as an interest group come to similar conclusions. The argument is that it would be politically costly for politicians to counter these groups. Therefore, the existence of a career civil service is seen as a source of public sector inertia that is stronger than would be the case in a bureaucracy based, to a greater extent, on political appointments (Johnson and Libecap, 1994).

These interpretations overlook the possibility that politicians, and in this case ministers, could manipulate the incentives of civil servants in a way that induces them to respond positively to ministers' requests. This, it will be argued, is the case if promotions to top civil service positions are decided by individual ministers or at cabinet level, and if dismissal or removal from a top-level position is similarly a matter of political discretion. Behind this proposition lies the assumption that civil servants are motivated by concerns for their own career. These concerns are both positive (there are always civil servants striving and competing for promotion) and negative (civil servants who have reached a top position strongly dislike the prospect of being sacked). Empirically, the proposition gets support if it can be shown that, over time, Danish ministers and governments have strengthened their control over promotions and dismissals at the top civil service level.

Politicization

Danish ministers and other leading politicians are highly concerned with the responsiveness of civil servants. The issue has been discussed at short intervals for several decades. This discussion has taken several directions. First, former and incumbent ministers have emphasized their demands for qualified advice. In the mid-1970s, a leading Social Democrat pointed out that ministers needed "capacity to think." His implication was that they should gain this capacity by appointing state secretaries or deputy ministers to whom they could delegate part of the responsibility for the day-to-day management of the department, leaving themselves free to concentrate on policy development and policy planning (Olesen, 1975). Another slightly different phrasing of this demand focuses on ministers' need for policy advice as well as strategic advice, reversing the roles so that ministers increase both their managerial capacity and their capacity as policy makers.[1] Second, two concerns have repeatedly been used to justify the need for a certain politicization of the civil service. At critical junctures, when after a long period the government changed from Social Democratic to Liberal-Conservative or vice versa, the new administration would view the civil service with skepticism. So, in 1968 when, for the first time in 15 years, the bourgeois parties succeeded the Social Democrats on the government benches, rumor had it that they expected to find themselves being served by a bunch of "red mercenaries." In 1982, when these parties took over again after some years of Social Democratic dominance, their fear was that the civil service would play bureaucratic politics, making it difficult for them to get their own radical program through. The Social Democratic leadership had similar feelings when it took over from the Liberal-Conservative government in 1993.

The new government also took steps to strengthen the advisory capacity within the government. With the increase in government subsidies to the political parties, the Social Democratic parliamentary group, like other parties, had set up a secretariat of policy advisors. From this secretariat, the Prime Minister himself recruited a personal advisor, while the Minister of Labor set up a secretariat for labor market policy similarly staffed with people from this secretariat (Finance Committee, 1993, 144).

Similar steps had been taken earlier. During the previous, Liberal-Conservative, government, the ministers of social affairs and labor recruited personal secretaries from their party organizations; later, as the two ministers succeeded each other in the Ministry of Finance, they took them there as their personal secretaries. Other singular cases are found in the 1970s, when both a Liberal and a Social Democratic Prime Minister recruited press advisors from their respective parties as members of their staff.

Three things are important for an evaluation of this experience. First, political appointments to positions as ministerial advisors are rare and exceptional. Second, the appointments hardly constitute a pattern. In all the cases reported above, the positions were closed when the advisors for various reasons left the departments concerned. The partial exception is the Prime Minister who in 1997–98 set up a couple of advisory positions for senior staff recruited from the Social Democratic party organization. Third, policy advice to ministers is mainly a departmental responsibility. This places the permanent secretary in a pivotal position as the minister's principal advisor and coordinator of communication between the minister and the line organization, and as the person responsible for both managing the department and for coordinating the agencies reporting to the department. Within this strict departmental hierarchy, the minister has always had a junior civil servant as his personal secretary. The secretary was recruited from within the department, often by the permanent secretary. It was a position held for just a few years (two to three on average), after which the secretary returned to the line organization with good prospects of speedy promotion. The responsibilities of the secretary were few and narrow, mostly concentrated on organizing the minister's meetings and contacts and acting as a gatekeeper for the minister in his dealings with other politicians and the media.

For many years, the minister's personal staff consisted of a personal secretary and a clerk. This was still the case in 1982 when the Liberal-Conservative coalition was formed. However, since the mid-1980s, these personal staffs have expanded into ministerial secretariats headed by either a chief of secretariat or a chief secretary and employing an additional junior civil servant and often a press officer plus two or three clerks.

With the few and not very consistent exceptions noted above, these secretariats are staffed on a clear merit basis. Still, in contrast to the traditional pattern, ministers have, since the 1980s, been actively involved in the selection of staff members (Betænkning 1354, 1998, 119–126). But unlike the special advisors recruited on their political merits, among other things, these staff members can, and often do, keep their job if the minister resigns.[2]

Setting up advisory bodies staffed by political appointees is just one form of politicization. A more direct form takes place if ministers appoint people to top civil service positions on the basis of political criteria. In operational terms, this form of politicization is hard to prove. However, one important indicator is whether people appointed as either permanent secretaries or agency heads have had a prior political career as members of parliament, ministers, or staff members within the party or an organization affiliated to the party, e.g. an interest organization.

As was the case with advisory positions, there have always been cases of political appointments thus defined, but they have been few and exceptional. Ever since the 1930s, there have been agency heads who were appointed to their position from either a prominent party political position (minister, MP, policy advisor or analyst) or from a similar position in an interest organization. Although political considerations may have been among the criteria for their selection, this form of political recruitment is subtle. In 1974, a Social Democratic MP and deputy chairman of the Metal Workers' Union was appointed chief of the National Labor Inspection; similarly, his successor was recruited from a leading position in the Danish Employers' Association, after a career as personal secretary to a Conservative Minister of Social Affairs who later became Minister of Finance. However, in the former case, the appointing minister was Liberal, in the latter Social Democratic. Likewise, the Social Democratic Minister of Environment and Energy appointed the spokesperson on environmental policy for the Socialist People's Party as head of the Environmental Protection Agency in 1999. Whether seen as ministers' occasional demand for agency heads with direct political and parliamentary experience or as instances of political cooptation, this is clearly not politicization in the strict sense defined above.

With no or few political appointments, the Danish civil service has preserved most of the traits of a career civil service. Top civil servants come to their positions from a civil service career. Up to 1970, the prevailing pattern was that permanent secretaries were selected from another managerial position within their present ministry (see Table 2.1). The pattern has since changed, and increasing numbers have been appointed from a senior position in another ministry. In particular the departments of Finance and Law have served as nurseries for permanent secretaries in other departments. Agency heads are also recruited on merit, though following a different pattern. Prior careers only rarely involve employment

Table 2.1 Career background of Danish top civil servants, 1935–99 (%)

Position	Prior political and/ or interest organization career	Same ministry career	Other ministry	Other public sector	Professions and business	Number of top civil servants
1935						
Permanent secretary	–	81	10	10	–	21
Agency head	3	48	3	39	7	31
1950						
Permanent secretary	–	82	7	11	–	28
Agency head	–	62	2	30	6	47
1960						
Permanent secretary	–	90	10	–	–	30
Agency head	2	65	4	28	2	51
1970						
Permanent secretary	–	74	19	7	–	27
Agency head	–	71	4	21	4	56
1980						
Permanent secretary	–	63	19	19	–	27
Agency head	3	86	2	6	3	65
1990						
Permanent secretary	–	70	22	7	–	27
Agency head	5	75	3	9	8	64
1999						
Permanent secretary	–	60	40	–	–	20
Agency head	2	69	7	10	13	61

Sources: Hof-og Statskalenderen, 1935–99; Kraks Blå Bog 1935–99; www.danmark.dk August 1999.

Note
Information is missing for nine top civil servants.

in other ministries, but the specialized tasks of some agencies earlier led to recruitment of agency heads from public sector positions outside central government. But again, things have changed since the 1970s, as agency heads are to some extent recruited from the private sector, in particular the professions. The socio-professional background of these modern agency heads is hardly unlike that of their predecessors who were selected from public sector careers outside central government.

The political limits to politicization

The presumption behind this analysis is that, *ceteris paribus*, ministers would prefer people they know, who share their basic political attitudes, as both political advisors and as top civil servants to whom they delegate managerial tasks. Neither the recruitment pattern nor the organization of advisory bodies shows any signs of politicization in this direction. Furthermore, with the exception of the rare political advisors, both top civil servants and members of ministers' personal staffs stay in office when a new minister takes over, even after a change of governing party. However, none of this means that ministers would not recruit political appointees if they had the opportunity.

Legally, there is nothing to stop them. Both the Civil Service Act and the collective agreements that cover civil servants with employee status have clauses that could be applied to this situation (Betænkning 1354, 1998, 223–225). Political qualifications, including political affiliation with the appointing minister, may be one among several criteria used when screening candidates for advisory or top positions in central government. Still, political appointments have turned out to be highly controversial. Rumors about political appointments and of the government's use of departmental resources for political campaigning are not only controversial in political reporting but are also subject to intense political scrutiny in parliament. Such debates have taken place repeatedly. In the second half of the 1970s, the Social Democrats initiated the debate mentioned earlier concerning the need for ministers to be relieved of some of their more routine tasks to be able to concentrate more on policy issues. Fully in line with this argument, the then Social Democratic government engaged in a more intense use of departmental staff and information for campaign purposes. However, this triggered political criticism, and the ensuing debate in parliament clearly placed strict limits on the government's use of the administrative apparatus for purposes that the parliamentary opposition of both left and right saw as purely party activities.[3]

The same clear lines of demarcation were laid down on several later occasions. This happened during the more than ten years of Liberal-Conservative rule when the government was accused of using Ministry of Foreign Affairs resources for EU campaign purposes. Similarly, when in

2000 Denmark voted on the adoption of the common European currency, the anti-euro groups accused the now center-left coalition of using the civil service for campaign purposes. When the issue was taken up by parliament in 2001 the pro-euro opposition joined the critics and together they vetoed a parliamentary resolution. A majority, encompassing the left-wing and right-wing opposition, stated:

- that there has been an increase in civil service involvement in activities that were formerly taken care of by the political parties,
- that the involvement of civil servants in the handling of tasks that rather are party political is undermining their trustworthiness,
- that in this context attention should especially be directed toward civil service activities related to electoral campaigning, and thus Parliament calls on the government to specify the limits to ministers' use of the civil service so that the credibility of civil servants does not suffer injury.

(www.folketinget.dk-2000–01 – F 20 16.1.2001)

The resolution is hardly a model of operational clarity, but it sent an unequivocal political signal to the government to be careful in its use of the civil service for party political activities. In spite of this resolution an intense debate is still taking place, involving revelations and counter-revelations of instances where incumbent and former ministers have violated these political limits on the use of civil servants.[4]

Against this background, the reaction to the appointment of political advisors to the Prime Minister and to the Minister of Labor comes as no surprise. As in both cases the appointments presupposed the installation of new positions at a senior service level, the Prime Minister had to submit an application for a supplementary appropriation to the parliament's Finance Committee (Finance Committee, 1993, 144). The application triggered a burst of critical questions from the opposition. The Prime Minister's application was approved, but the debate once more demonstrated how sensitive these issues are and how easy it is for the opposition to exploit them. Exactly the same thing happened in 1998, when the Prime Minister wanted to appoint a young party member to a senior position as his media advisor. This time the situation was even more loaded with political conflict. Contrary to the recommendations from a Ministry of Finance task force, the position had not been marked as party political or even as a 'special' advisor position (Betænkning 1354, 1998, 217–225).

As this analysis shows, political opposition in parliament, combined with and nourished by public sensitivity to issues which can be presented as involving a tint of nepotism and sleaze, places severe constraints on Danish governments and individual ministers when they move clearly beyond the principles of merit-based appointments.

The very sensitivity of the politicization issue also allows for the civil service as well as its main union (the Union of Lawyers and Economists) to operate politically to defend merit principles.[5] The opposition parties are inclined to support them, and nobody will challenge the civil servants' right to bring the issue to public attention. This has happened every time the governing party has opened the issue, intentionally or unintentionally. During the 1970s and 1980s, whenever the government used the civil service for campaign purposes, the issue was brought to public attention by civil servants protesting and thus alarming the opposition in parliament. Similarly, in the second half of the 1970s, when the Social Democratic leadership opened the debate on appointing political state secretaries as deputies to cabinet ministers, the permanent secretaries were alarmed. Through a deft maneuver, they first organized a conference in which the leader of the opposition debated with the deputy Social Democratic leader and then they initiated a study demonstrating the futility of a politicized central administration (Christensen *et al.*, 1979). In the mid-1990s, when the debate on politicization again intensified, a very similar chain of events was initiated. After parliamentary pressure, the Minister of Finance appointed a task force of civil servants, academics, a private attorney, and union representatives to prepare a new report analyzing and evaluating the situation in comparative perspective. Its report, made public in 1998, duly concluded that although completely legal, political appointments, including recruitment of political advisors, would not enhance the quality of ministerial advice and policy-making (Betænkning 1354, 1998).

Government control of the civil service

Allowing for the minor exceptions described above, the Danish civil service has upheld its character of a pure merit system. Given the institutions of parliamentary government and the allocation of power within them, large-scale politicization has not taken place, nor does it seem very likely in the future. The government and its ministers therefore have to get along with a career civil service which is practically closed to both the political world and to the private sector. The persons ministers can rely upon for policy and political advice entered government service after graduating from university. To the extent that ministers delegate decision-making authority to the civil service, the people in charge are permanent secretaries and agency heads with the same characteristics. Given these constraints, do ministers have any opportunity to make civil servants responsive to their demands? Or do they have to rely on the possibility that bureaucratic socialization is not only a strong but also an effective transmitter of norms emphasizing civil servants' loyalty and responsiveness to the incumbent minister? If so, we rule out the possibility not only that responsiveness might run counter to civil servants' interests, but also that there might be competing norms, e.g. departmental policies, professional standards, or established routines.

In fact, Danish civil service law allows political executives strong influence on staffing decisions and personnel policy. In spite of its principles of merit recruitment and its unequivocal character of a career civil service, the system has always emphasized that civil servants operate within a departmental hierarchy where the staff ultimately are subject to ministerial guidance and accountable to the incumbent minister. Staff who enjoy civil service status have tenure and are consequently entitled to a government pension.[6] It also enjoys legal protection. However, this protection is mainly economic. It involves civil servants' pension rights together with their right to compensation at their current salary level for a limited number of years if their position is terminated and the government does not offer them another position at an appropriate level. Other legal provisions specify the judicial and disciplinary procedures to be followed if civil servants are either held accountable for not fulfilling their legal responsibilities or are sacked on unlawful grounds. However, the decisive principle in Danish civil service law is that civil servants are subject to discretionary dismissal. Such dismissal can result from a minister's lack of (political) confidence in a particular civil servant. The only caveats are that the government (the state) is obliged to pay his or her pension and not to order a dismissal on unlawful grounds. Lack of trust and failing cooperation are entirely legal motivations for dismissing civil servants. Therefore, the main protection of Danish civil servants lies in their pension rights, not in their tenure. Policy-makers are fully aware of this legal fact (Betænkning 483, 1969, 23; Betænkning 1354, 1998, 53–55). To increase the intended flexibility of the system, a special Act of 1971 allows for appointment of civil servants for a fixed term of three to six years (Act 173/1971).

Compared with the civil service regulations of Westminster-type systems in particular, this is a highly decentralized system that is under unrestricted political control (cf. Horn, 1995, 97 and Boston, 1999 on New Zealand; Dunn, 1997, 10, 121 on Australia; and Hood, 1998 on Westminster-type systems in general). Staffing is the responsibility of individual departments, and appointments are their responsibility or that of the agencies and institutions under their jurisdiction, rather than that of some centralized corps or central government in general. This decentralization makes individual ministers chiefs of personnel within their own ministry, and they can interfere in these decisions just as they can in any other administrative decision as long as they respect the legal constraints governing the particular type of decision.

The decisive question, then, is to what extent ministers use this authority to first select and later sack top civil servants. The test here is not whether ministers occasionally recruit political appointees, nor whether they occasionally interfere in the procedure for appointing chiefs of section and other medium-level civil servants. It is rather, first, whether they use their strong formal authority to select the people they want as permanent secretaries and agency heads, and, second, whether they dismiss them if they do not meet their requirements for advice or for assistance in decision-making.

There is no unequivocal evidence of how ministers have used their authority historically. On the one hand, it is a fair guess that they have always had a say and that in the end they could make their own choice; on the other hand, there are indications that their choice was heavily circumscribed by bureaucratic concerns (Knudsen, 1995, 278–280; Betænkning 1354, 1998, 23–40). Yet, historically, there has been no tradition for involving ministers in personnel affairs, even in the promotion of civil servants to positions at the level of chief of section, although here ministers were informed of the permanent secretary's choice, could raise objections and formally propose the appointment to the queen.[7] But even in cases where ministers made their own choice, they chose from the civil servants already occupying a high-ranking position within their department (see Table 2.1 above). Still, it is equally clear that during the same period, as leading politicians initiated the debate on the need to strengthen their capacity for executive leadership, the procedure for appointments to top civil service positions was revised in order to strengthen government control over appointments. Thus, in 1977, the Social Democratic government introduced a new procedure according to which individual ministers could no longer present their own (allegedly the department's) single candidate to the council of ministers who would formally ratify the appointment. They would in future have to present a list of three applicants to be screened by a cabinet committee chaired by the Prime Minister before a formal decision on whom to appoint. Among the members of the committee are the Minister of Finance and the relevant departmental minister. As cabinet committees in coalition governments serve as fora for political mediation, ministers representing all parties in the governing coalition have seats on the committee. This procedure remains in force (Christensen, 1985; Prime Minister's Office, 1998).

The introduction of a formal procedure for the selection of top civil servants has been accompanied by a gradual change in practice for other appointments as well. Since the 1980s ministers have shown a keen interest in appointments within their departmental jurisdiction of both chiefs of section and key specialists who do not rank high in the departmental hierarchy but may nevertheless represent key functions in policy-making and administrative decision-making.[8] The change in practice is an indication of the importance that modern ministers attach to the staffing of the departments and agencies of which they are politically in charge. It is also an indication of how ministers, granting full respect to the principles of merit recruitment, place strong emphasis on finding the right appointees in terms of both technical qualifications and personal congeniality.

Political manipulation of incentives

Danish ministers find themselves in an ambiguous position. Due to severe institutional constraints, the use of political appointees is not an option for increasing political control over the civil service. But Danish civil service law allows ministers a lot of discretion both to select people who meet their demands and to get rid of those who might no longer do so. In addition, ministerial organization provides the minister with strong formal powers as regards to intra-organizational personnel and resource management. Finally, since the late 1970s, the procedures that regulate the selection of top civil servants have been strengthened, facilitating government control. As civil servants are part of a hierarchical career system where salary, power, and prestige are strongly related to promotions, it is a fair assumption that there is an ample supply of candidates for positions at the very top of this hierarchy. Within the civil service system, dismissal may not involve severe economic losses; still, loss of social and peer prestige makes it an equally fair assumption that top civil servants would prefer to stay in office until the age of retirement or until they choose to give up their job themselves (see Table 2.2).

For ministers concerned with the political responsiveness of their top civil servants, this creates a favorable situation. Not only do they have the instruments to manipulate the incentives of their civil servants, but they also face a civil service that may be inclined to react positively to these incentives. Do ministers use these instruments, and has the increased concern about political responsiveness led ministers to a more active use of their authority?

One option for ministers who want to strengthen the incentives of their top civil servants as well as prospective candidates for top positions would be to appoint them for a limited period. This option has been open since the early 1970s, but was not in fact used for many years. This has changed to some extent: many agency heads in particular, and other leading officials in agencies, are appointed on fixed-term contracts (Betænkning 1354, 1998, 54–56). More recently, some permanent secretaries have also been employed on the basis of fixed-term contracts. Yet, for two reasons, the change in practice is of little interest in this context. First, the incentives created by the Act on fixed-period appointments are ambiguous as the minister's discretionary authority to dismiss does not apply to these positions (Act 680, 1998, § 3–4). Second, some permanent secretaries insist on a joint understanding that they do not opt for fixed-term appointments, but keep traditional tenured civil service positions.[9] Paradoxically, the existence of such an understanding enhances the flexibility of the system as it leaves it to ministers to end their employment at any time (cf. Betænkning 1354, 1998, 54–55).

The other option is to remove top civil servants who do not meet the demands of the incumbent minister. Such dismissals serve two functions.

Table 2.2 Retirement patterns among top civil servants, 1935–90

Position	Early leavers* as percentage of total	Early leavers' occupation (%)					Number/early leavers
		Retired	Advisor, ambassador, prefect, etc.**	Private business, government corporation	Minister, MP	Promotion or transfer to position at same level	
1935							
Permanent secretary	19	25	50	25	–	–	21/4
Agency head	19	43	14	–	14	29	31/7
1950							
Permanent secretary	29	38	25	–	13	25	28/8
Agency head	19	40	20	–	–	40	47/10
1960							
Permanent secretary	17	40	40	–	–	20	30/5
Agency head	29	40	20	7	7	27	51/15
1970							
Permanent secretary	33	33	44	11	–	11	27/9
Agency head	29	59	18	–	–	24	56/17
1980							
Permanent secretary	56	13	75	13	–	–	27/16
Agency head	38	30	37	4	–	30	64/27
1990							
Permanent secretary	85	4	57	17	–	22	27/23
Agency head	64	35	27	8	–	30	56/37

Sources: See Table 2.1.

Notes
* Early leavers are defined as top civil servants who left their position before the age of 65 and who had not died.
** Includes lower-level positions within the central government hierarchy. In addition to the examples given, it also includes positions in international organizations. The prefect is a more or less empty office at the regional level.

First, they make it possible for the minister to replace permanent secretaries and agency heads with people who meet their requirements. Second, they send a signal to prospective candidates; if they don't demonstrate responsiveness to the political executive, they risk losing their position to a competitor from within the civil service. Since permanent secretaries work much more closely with ministers, the hypothesis is that they are more exposed to discretionary removal from their position than are agency heads.

Table 2.2 shows the dramatic change in central government that has taken place since the 1930s. Within the 1935 population, it was an exception if top civil servants left their office before the age of 65.[10] This continued to be the case for the next 30 years, but since the 1970s a remarkable change has taken place. Among permanent secretaries especially, it has become normal for them to leave their position before retirement age. Indeed, 56 percent of the permanent secretaries belonging to the 1980 population were early leavers according to this definition. Among the 1990 cohort, 85 percent left their posts during the 1990s. For agency heads, the change is not as dramatic, but the trend is exactly the same.

Some early leavers retire from the labor market, while others move to another position at the same or a higher level. While this has always been the case, the real change is that early leavers from the top civil service increasingly move into positions within central government that ensure them a continued high salary and high social prestige, but do not involve any hierarchical authority (see Figure 2.1). These positions are often advisory (e.g. international advisor), but they may also lead to appointments as ambassadors, prefects, or posts in international organizations. Again, the change took off during the 1970s, so that within the 1980 and the 1990 cohorts, 75 and 57 percent of the permanent secretaries leaving their posts early have taken on these sinecure positions. Agency heads exhibit a similar but weaker pattern.

The pattern discussed above indicates a marked change in relations between ministers and top civil servants. While the age at which civil servants reach a top position has remained constant (48–50 years on average), the length of their service has changed dramatically. On average, from the 1920s and up through the 1960s, permanent secretaries could expect to serve in their position for more than 16 years, and agency heads for more than 17 years. But during the 1970s, a change began. Permanent secretaries appointed during this decade only served for 10 years and agency heads for 12 years. This trend has continued, and many permanent secretaries appointed during the 1980s have not only left their posts but also served for less than eight years; for agency heads the pattern is similar. Figure 2.1 demonstrates the strong change in practice over time.

The patterns for the two groups are close to identical. For permanent

A: Department heads

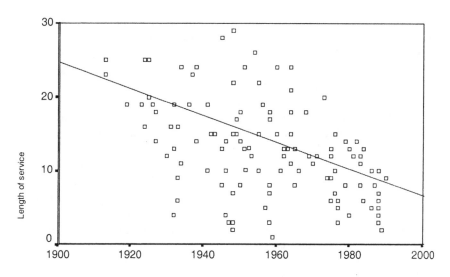

Year of appointment

Note: R^2 0.24; Standard error 6.0837; β-coefficient –0.490; Sig. 0.000; N = 161

B: Agency heads

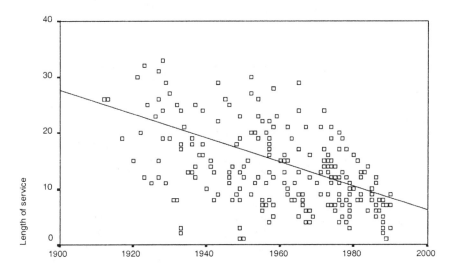

Year of appointment

Note: R^2 0.277; Standard error 6.5772; β-coefficient –0.526; Sig. 0.000; N = 305

Figure 2.1 Year of appointment and length of service of top civil servants.
Sources: See Table 2.1.

secretaries the β-coefficient is −0.49 with an R^2 of 0.24 when length of service is regressed against appointment year. For agency heads the corresponding coefficients are −0.526 for the β-coefficient with an R^2 of 0.277, a reflection of the fact that the variation in their length of service is slightly smaller than for permanent secretaries.

With the shorter service, the Danish civil service has changed dramatically. The political executive has demonstrated that a top civil servant's position is not for life: that top civil servants must expect to have to leave their posts after less than 10 years in office. Several incidents have further demonstrated that the career at the very top of the civil service can end at any time, thus aligning the incentives for both incumbents and prospective candidates who compete for a post at the top.[11] The question is whether party politics is a factor that explains the change. Even though top civil servants do not leave their posts when a new minister takes over, it might be hypothesized that ministers want to replace their permanent secretary as well as some of the agency heads with a person who is closer to their own party or policies. However, according to the hypothesis, this only happens after a time lag during which ministers form an impression of the operation of their ministry and especially of their closest advisors and confidants. To test this hypothesis, the party affiliations of both appointing and dismissing ministers have been brought in as control variables. Table 2.3 summarizes the results.

Party affiliation generally contributes little to explaining the shorter length of service for top civil servants over time. This is most clearly seen

Table 2.3 Length of service of top civil servants after control for ministers' party affiliation*

Appointing minister	Dismissing minister	R^2	Standard error	β-coefficient	Significance	Number**
Permanent secretaries						
Center-left	Center-left	0.245	5.8219	−0.495	0.016	23
Center-left	Center-right	0.015	4.0095	−0.123	0.719	11
Center-right	Center-right	0.258	4.8408	−0.508	0.063	14
Center-right	Center-left	0.002	3.2267	0.041	0.882	16
Agency heads						
Center-left	Center-left	0.019	4.7267	0.138	0.452	32
Center-left	Center-right	0.065	6.1362	−0.256	0.250	22
Center-right	Center-right	0.732	2.7255	−0.855	0.000	15
Center-right	Center-left	0.408	4.5245	−0.639	0.000	31

Notes

* Party affiliation is dichotomized in the following way. Ministers representing the Social Democratic Party and the Radical Liberals are coded as center-left. Ministers representing the Liberal Party and the Conservative Party as well as other parties (all center parties) are coded as center-right.

** This includes only civil servants who left their position before the age of 65 and who had not died before that age.

when symmetric cases where appointing and dismissing ministers have the same party affiliation are compared with asymmetric cases where their party affiliations differ. So the big changes in length of service for top civil servants took place when a center-left minister both appointed and dismissed a top civil servant, and especially when a center-right minister both appointed and dismissed a top civil servant. But the same trend toward shorter periods of service continued after 1993 when a center-left government replaced a center-right government. Negatively, these results are interpreted as a rejection of the party politicization hypothesis. In positive terms, they support the conclusion that the Liberal-Conservative government during the 1980s brought a dramatic change to the Danish civil service. This renewal of the merit system has been continued by the center-left government during the 1990s. The new policy has not affected the merit character of the Danish civil service, but has brought a radical change to the conditions under which top civil servants operate. The result is a top civil service that is similar, in important respects, to the German pattern (Derlien, 1999). But instead of moving into *Ruhestand* (enforced temporary leave of absence) from where they can be called upon to serve a new minister, Danish top civil servants in principle keep their position unless a new minister transfers them to a more or less empty advisory position.

The transformation of the top civil service has another noteworthy aspect. Even if there are strict limits to the politicization of the civil service in the Danish parliamentary system, ministers use the civil service system in a way that maximizes their chances of having as their right hands persons who combine proper professional qualifications with personal qualities that the minister in question values. This means that modern top civil servants can no longer expect to stay in office over several ministerial periods. On the contrary, they have the chance of being promoted to another and perhaps more prestigious top position in the civil service and run the risk of being removed after a few years at the top. When the latter risk materializes, there is no legal protection of their interests as ministers have the authority to sack civil servants on a discretionary basis. In economic terms, however, their level of protection is high, particularly as central government has seen an increase in the number of well-paid but sometimes sinecure positions to which former top civil servants who have fallen into ministerial disgrace may be catapulted.

Do civil servants behave?

Above it is argued that the changes in the Danish civil service since about 1980 have radically altered the incentives of top civil servants to show more responsiveness toward the political executive. The logical next question is whether this has worked. Has it made civil servants behave? And if so, has it made them behave differently from before, thus meeting the new and presumably more stringent needs of ministers?

Empirically, the issue is difficult to tackle in a cross-time analysis that tries to map and account for changes taking place over half a century. Still, it is noteworthy that Danish ministers, irrespective of their party affiliation, at one and the same time have become more explicit about their expectations of their civil servants, while acknowledging the skills and professionalism of their departmental staff. This is the consistent result when former ministers are asked to evaluate their civil servants' performance. This was also the general message when in 1997–98 the Ministry of Finance task force investigating minister–civil service relations conducted a series of interviews with former and serving ministers. These ministers and ex-ministers focused any criticism on the advice and service provided by their department in connection with the media and other public relations (Betænkning 1354, 111–113).

Another approach is to look at changes to the duties of civil servants in areas that from a conventional politics–administration dichotomy would be considered beyond the scope of a neutral civil service (see Figure 2.2).

Ministers tasks	Political executive				Party leader		
	Managerial and executive decision-making	Parliament	International	Interest organizations	Public relations	Constituency and campaigning	Party related offices
Scope of advisory role							
Policy analysis and advice	+/++	+/++	+/++	+/++	+/++	+−/+−	−/−
Political strategy and tactics	+/++	+−/+	+/++	+−/++	+/++	−/−	−/−

Figure 2.2 Changes in the scope of civil service assistance to ministers since the 1960s.

Note
+ or − denotes that civil servants provided/did not provide ministers with advice and assistance in the particular respect. The + or − before the slash contains an estimate for the situation in the 1970s, after the slash for the situation in the late 1990s. + or − denotes strong variation between departments, while ++ denotes an increased intensity of the particular service. The data covering the change from the 1960s to the late 1970s were collected by the author through interviews with all permanent secretaries in 1978–79 (Christensen, 1980, 98–112). The data covering the situation in the 1990s were collected through an inquiry, conducted by the Ministry of Finance task force investigating minister–civil servant relations in 1997–98. The questionnaire used in the inquiry asked the same questions that were asked 20 years previously (Betænkning 1354, 1998, 109–120).

It can be questioned whether this normative standard has ever been implemented. Still, there are indications both that top civil servants set limits to the type of services they would provide to the minister, and that ministers define spheres of activity where they would neither accept interference by nor ask for assistance from the civil service. To capture changes in this respect, Figure 2.2 introduces a distinction between two aspects of Danish ministers' tasks. One dimension distinguishes between the ministers' tasks as political executive and their tasks as party political leader. In the former capacity, ministers provide the linkage between the political and the bureaucratic worlds. As such, ministers are involved in intra-ministerial management issues as well as close interactions with parliament, international organizations, interest organizations and the media/the public. However, in a prominent position as members of the cabinet, ministers also entertain responsibilities toward their party and its organization. The other dimension distinguishes between civil servants' advice and assistance on substantive policy issues and on issues concerning political strategy and tactics.

In the late 1970s, all permanent secretaries were interviewed, among other things, on their role as ministerial advisors. The estimates that resulted from these interviews are reported before the slash in Figure 2.2. The general impression was that, despite some interdepartmental variation, Danish ministers received extensive advice from or through their permanent secretaries; also that permanent secretaries were moving toward giving more intensive advice on issues that had earlier been deemed too "political" for civil servants to engage in. But limits were placed on giving ministers advice of a strategic and tactical nature, and particularly on assisting them in activities and tasks that were seen as purely party and campaign matters. If ministers held offices within the party, there was no question of their being provided assistance and advice on those matters (Christensen, 1980, 98–112). In 1997, the Ministry of Finance task force repeated this analysis, this time through a written questionnaire to all ministers. The resulting estimates are reported after the slash in Figure 2.2 (Betænkning, 1354, 1998, 109–120; see also Jensen, 1999, for similar conclusions).

Allowing for the fragile evidence on which this analysis must be based, in a behavioral perspective Danish top civil servants have never practiced a very restrictive or dogmatic interpretation of the politics–administration dichotomy. Rather, they have gradually adapted to meeting the increasing demands of their political masters. The conclusion is also that this process continued through the 1980s and into the 1990s. Yet civil servants are still reluctant to touch ministers' campaigning and party-related activities, a field where the opposition is on the lookout for ministers' abuse of government capacity for party political purposes. Finally, there are fields where ministers keep an eye on civil servants' activities, e.g. participation in meetings and hearings in parliamentary standing committees and with Members of Parliament.

With similar reservations, the analysis also provides a basis for drawing conclusions on changes over a period of several decades. Another limit is that it focuses mainly on the minister's policy-making and public relations tasks, while neglecting the executive side of the job. Therefore it is difficult to reach any conclusions as to the responsiveness of civil servants when it comes to policy implementation, especially rule application and resource management. However, ministers were and are strongly involved in these tasks, even though they are delegated to civil servants in ministerial departments or agencies.[12] This problem is even more difficult to subject to empirical analysis, although there are also some empirical indications on how ministers behave.

Since the 1980s, several politico-administrative scandals have been subject to special investigations by the National Auditors and *ad hoc* courts of investigation. The bases for the investigations are partly ministerial files, partly public hearings of the civil servants and ministers involved. Afterwards, voluminous reports that document and analyze the case have been published.[13] Although these cases probably represent a highly biased sample, they shed some light on three important issues.

First, when ministers receive cases of a critical and potentially explosive nature, whether legal, financial, or political, can they expect advice and assistance from their civil servants? The answer to this question, judged from the disclosures published in the investigations, is that civil servants have actively engaged in ministerial advice in these cases. Further, they have gone a long way to anticipate the predilections of the incumbent minister or government.

Second, to what extent have civil servants, advising ministers on these cases, made a clear distinction between their obligation to demonstrate due loyalty to the incumbent minister and their parallel duty to make clear to the minister the legal constraints on his or her executive authority? Here the conclusion is not unequivocal. Top civil servants seem aware of the distinction and its relevance to their advisory and executive role, but in practice they demonstrate considerable pragmatism in applying it. In none of the cases subjected to investigation do civil servants seem to have clearly indicated when a minister approached the blurred border between a 'gray' decision that might be legal but couldn't survive public scrutiny, and a clearly illegal decision.

Third, were civil servants of the 1980s and the 1990s more amenable to political pressure than their predecessors? The basis for shedding light on this question is even less satisfying. Most of the cases referred to above originate since about 1980. However, two cases from the 1950s indicate that also at that time civil servants showed no difficulty putting themselves in the place of their ministers and advising them accordingly (Jens Peter Christensen, 1997, 135–154; Dansk Udenrigspolitisk Institut, 1997).

Conclusions

The analysis leads to three conclusions on the character of the Danish civil service and its specificities compared with the civil service in other Western countries. First, the Danish civil service has kept the traits of a merit civil service. None of the criteria indicate a general politicization. To the extent that ministers set up advisory bodies, recruitment is intra-departmental and purely merit based. Similarly, top civil servants are recruited from within the civil service on merit criteria. In the few instances where agency heads were recruited from the political world, the circumstances indicate that the appointments were both exceptional and different in nature from appointments in a politicized bureaucracy. However, the civil service has changed in a rather dramatic way. Until 1970, top civil servants could expect life-long tenure in their position, but in the 1980s and the 1990s could on average only expect to serve in that position for less than 10 years. As the age of appointment has been constant since the 1920s, the implication is that Danish top civil servants leave their positions before the age of 60. Unlike their German colleagues, they do not leave the civil service to "tend their dahlias" (Peters and Pierre, Chapter 1 above), but move to positions mostly stripped of hierarchical authority. There are no indications that party political considerations are behind these dismissals or resignations. Rather, they demonstrate how the government has used its strong formal authority to reinstate ministers' and the cabinet's responsibility for hiring and firing top civil servants.

With these changes in personnel policy, Danish incumbent and prospective top civil servants face a changed set of incentives to accommodate ministers' demand for advice and assistance and their preference for solutions that are politically expedient. The basis for concluding whether or not this has made top civil servants more pliable to ministerial demands is weak. On the one hand, their advisory role has always been conceived in pragmatic terms, implying that little was foreign to them if political contingencies pointed in that direction. On the other hand, it seems that they gradually go further in providing their political masters with assistance, even if this implies a break with traditional conceptions of a politics–administration dichotomy. This flexibility and adaptability comes close to the pattern found in other merit-based systems (Lægreid and Olsen, 1979; Barker and Wilson, 1997).

The changes identified here raise the question of the nature of the Danish civil service. In a recent paper, Christopher Hood introduced the notion of a "*public service bargain*" (Hood, 1999). There are three aspects to this conceptualization. First, it is a way of distinguishing between different civil service traditions and systems. Second, it posits that the character of a particular system is the result of a bargain between politicians and civil servants. Third, it introduces a dynamic dimension into the analysis as it is possible that a new bargain changes the character of the civil service. Applied to the Danish civil service, the implication is a move from a *schafferian* to a *hybrid* bargain. In the schafferian bargain, politicians win civil servants' loyalty to and competent service of the government of the day. In return, they provide permanent tenure, trust and avoidance of public blame for policy. In the hybrid bargain, politicians expect competent service with party or personal loyalty. In return, they guarantee civil servants trust and limited public blame for policy. With the reservation that party is of little relevance in the Danish context, this rather precisely describes what has happened since about 1980 in the Danish senior civil service.

First, the personal aspect of the minister–bureaucrat relationship comes with the short length of service observable since the 1980s. Even if Danish parliamentarianism has not allowed a politicization in the strict sense defined by Peters and Pierre (Chapter 1 above), through successive adaptations of the top civil service ministers have managed to secure themselves the services of dedicated mandarins. The incentives of prospective and incumbent permanent secretaries and agency heads to show responsiveness to their political principals, whoever they might be, have been strongly increased. Simultaneously, the combined effect of the selection and dismissal procedures is to ensure ministers as their right hands persons whom they find congenial. Second, civil servants are no longer protected from public blame. In the scandals mentioned above, both the center-right government of the 1980s and the center-left government of the 1990s showed little restraint when it came to passing the buck to civil servants. This applies equally to civil servants who advised ministers and those who made the formal decision on behalf of the minister. Often they seem to have been removed from their position as a result of a pre-emptive ministerial strategy to divert political attention from their own part in the affair.

There are two puzzling perspectives in this development. First, the legal regulation of the accountability of civil servants is comparatively clear (Jens Peter Christensen, 1998). Nevertheless, legal considerations had little effect in practice. Second, the move from a schafferian to a hybrid bargain might be seen as detrimental to the systematic effort to strengthen the incentives for political responsiveness. Here, however, the career motive and intra-civil service competition for promotions seem so strong that the risk of ending up as scapegoats for ministers has been of little effect.

Appendix: Data

The analysis is based on biographical data for all permanent secretaries and all agency heads in 1935, 1950, 1960, 1970, 1980, 1990, and 1999. Members of both groups were identified on the basis of *Hof-og Statskalenderen* years listed. The government website www.danmark.dk was used as a subsidiary source for 1999.

As well as permanent secretaries, directors general and the director of the Ministry of Foreign Affairs were coded as belonging to that category. Civil servants with managerial authority were coded as agency heads if they met the criteria listed below:

1   They headed a central administrative organization that reported directly to either a minister or a department.
2   This body had regulatory authority or authority to coordinate the management of at least two other central government organizations.
3   Their position was placed in grade 38 or a higher grade, or at least grade 28 in 1950 and 1960. For 1935 the equivalent grade was A7.
4   The Central Bank, the National Auditing Authority and the National Agency of Statistics are coded as agencies.

The primary source for biographical data has been *Kraks Blå Bog* ('The Danish Who's Who'). Due to the rather restrictive criteria listed above, most members of the two groups may be found there. However, a few supplementary sources have been used where the information was not found in *Kraks Blå Bog*, i.e. *Juridisk og Økonomisk Stat, Greens Hvem er Hvem i Den Offentlige Sektor.*

Acknowledgment

I am grateful to research assistance from Lotte Bøgh Andersen who collected the data and set up the file for analysis.

Notes

1   See Bjerregaard *et al.* (1994). Characteristically, this contribution to the debate was, like several others, the output of a joint group of former ministers and incumbent top and senior civil servants. See also Nielson (1987).
2   In the early 1990s, a Liberal tax minister installed a secretariat of tax policy analysts in his department. The staff were handpicked by the minister from within the department. When he moved to the Ministry of Economic Affairs, he took the group with him. However, in 1993, the Social Democratic tax minister reinstalled the body with the same staff as his Liberal predecessor.
3   This incident is fully analyzed in Christensen (1980, 110–112).
4   These recent developments are more fully analyzed in Christensen (2001).
5   The open conflict between the government and the opposition on this issue may be seen as an instance of the importance of the size of the core as defined by the distance between the government's preferred policy and the position taken by opposition parties whose consent the government needs to make a decision. It further illustrates how such situations give opportunities for the administration to act autonomously, in this case to openly resist politicization. Here, it is not of much use to the government that it can legally act unilaterally without prior consent from parliament (Hammond, 1996, 140–144). Another noteworthy trait in this conflict was that the civil service managed to have the issue moved to an arena where they dominate, and where the government was not represented (Christensen, 1997).

6 After the civil service reform of 1958, a distinction between civil service and employee status was introduced. Since then, only, but in no way all, government officials belonging to this category, civil servants holding managerial positions, enjoy civil service status (Betænkning 483, 1969; Betænkning 1354, 1998).

7 Starting at this level, civil servants receive royal appointment, a relic from two centuries of absolutist rule that seems important to many bureaucrats in a bureaucracy otherwise stripped of formalities.

8 Information supplied by top civil servants who commented on an earlier version of this chapter.

9 Information provided by Anders Eldrup, permanent secretary in the Ministry of Finance; other permanent secretaries commenting on an earlier version of this chapter deny knowledge of this understanding.

10 According to the Civil Servants Act, tenured civil servants must retire no later than in the month of their 70th birthday; for many years 67 was seen as the correct retirement age for civil servants. In this analysis people who leave their position after their 65th birthday have been coded as retired because of age.

11 Christensen (2001) provides an extensive analysis of this problem.

12 Two inquiries, in 1977 and 1997, were conducted into ministers' allocation of time to different tasks. In both years, ministers spent around 40 percent of their long hours (about 70 per week) on intra-ministerial management (Christensen *et al.*, 1979, 22–31; Betænkning 1354, 1998, 104–107).

13 Jens Peter Christensen (1997) presents an extensive legal analysis of 14 of these investigations. Other reports have since been added.

References

Act 173 (1971) Lov om kongelig udnævnelse og åremålsansættelse af visse tjenestemænd. [Act on royal appointment of certain civil servants for fixed terms.] *Lovtidende* 1971.

Act 680 (1998) Bekendtgørelse af lov om åremålsansættelse af tjenestemænd og ansatte på tjenestemandslignende vilkår. [Announcement of law on appointment of civil servants for fixed terms.]

Barker, Anthony and Graham K. Wilson (1997) "Whitehall's Disobedient Servants? Senior Officials' Potential Resistance to Ministers in British Government Departments." *British Journal of Political Science*, 27, 223–246.

Betænkning 483 (1969) *Betænkning afgivet af tjenestemandskommissionen af 1965. 1. del. Tjenestemandsloven.* Copenhagen: Statens Trykningskontor.

Betænkning 1354 (1998) *Forholdet mellem minister og embedsmænd. Betænkning fra udvalget om forholdet mellem minister og embedsmænd.* Copenhagen: Statens Information.

Bjerregaard, Ritt *et al.* (1994) *Ministeren. Vilkår for politisk ledelse.* Copenhagen: Spektrum.

Boston, Jonathan (1999) "Departmental Secretaries: The New Zealand Experience." Draft chapter for R. A. W. Rhodes and P. Weller (eds) *Mandarins or Valets? The Changing World of Top Officials.* Buckingham: Open University Press (forthcoming).

Christensen, Jens Peter (1997) *Ministeransvar.* Copenhagen: Jurist- og Økonomforbundets Forlag.

Christensen, Jens Peter (1998) *Offentligt ansatte chefers ansvar – en udredning af visse forhold af betydning for offentligt ansatte chefers retsstilling.* Copenhagen: Finansministeriet/Schultz Information.

Christensen, Jørgen Grønnegård (1980) *Centraladministrationen: Organisation og politisk placering.* Copenhagen: Samfundsvidenskabeligt Forlag.

Christensen, Jørgen Grønnegård (1985) "In Search of Unity: Cabinet Committees in Denmark." In Thomas T. Mackie and Brian W. Hogwood (eds) *Unlocking the Cabinet. Cabinet Structures in Comparative Perspective.* London: Sage Publications, 114–137.

Christensen, Jørgen Grønnegård (1997) "Interpreting Administrative Change: Bureaucratic Self-Interest and Institutional Inheritance in Government." *Governance,* 10, 143–174.

Christensen, Jørgen Grønnegård (2001) "Parlamentarismens ministre og deres embedsmænd." In Gorm Toftegaard Nielsen (ed.) *Parlamentarismen. Hvem tog magten?* Aarhus: Aarhus Universitetsforlag.

Christensen, Jørgen Grønnegård *et al.* (1979) *Politiske ledelsesforhold i centraladministrationen.* Copenhagen: Samfundsvidenskabeligt Forlag.

Dansk Udenrigspolitisk Institut (1997) *Grønland under den kolde krig.* Copenhagen: DUPI/Gyldendal.

Derlien, Hans-Ulrich (1999) "The German Public Service." Paper presented at the Comparative Public Service meeting, Sandbjerg Slot, 9–12 September, 1999.

Dunn, Delmer D. (1997) *Politics and Administration at the Top. Lessons from Down Under.* Pittsburgh: University of Pittsburgh Press.

Finance Committee (1993) "Aktstykke No. 144 af 26.2. 1993 til Folketingets finansudvalg." Parliamentary Year 1992–93.

Hammond, Thomas H. (1996) "Formal Theory and the Institutions of Governance." *Governance,* 9, 107–185.

Hood, Christopher (1998) "Individualized Contracts for Top Civil Servants: Copying Business, Path-Dependent Political Re-engineering – or Trobriand Cricket?" *Governance,* 11, 443–462.

Hood, Christopher (1999) "Public Service Bargains and Public Service Reform." Paper presented at ECPR Joint Meetings, Mannheim, 26–31 March, 1999.

Horn, Murray J. (1995) *The Political Economy of Public Administration. Institutional Choice in the Public Sector.* New York: Cambridge University Press.

Ingraham, Patricia Wallace (1995) *The Foundation of Merit. Public Service in American Democracy.* Baltimore: The Johns Hopkins University Press.

Jensen, Lotte (1999) "Departmental Secretaries in Denmark 1970–98." Draft chapter for R. A. W. Rhodes and P. Weller (eds) *Mandarins or Valets? The Changing World of Top Officials.* Buckingham: Open University Press (forthcoming).

Johnson, Ronald N. and Gary D. Libecap (1994) *The Federal Civil Service System and the Problem of Bureaucracy. The Politics and Economics of Institutional Change.* Chicago: The University of Chicago Press.

Knudsen, Tim (1995) *Dansk statsbygning.* Copenhagen: Jurist- og Økonomforbundets Forlag.

Lægreid, Per and Johan P. Olsen (1979) *Byråkrati og beslutninger.* Oslo: Universitetsforlaget.

Nielson, Poul (1987) *Politikere og embedsmænd.* Copenhagen: Danmarks Forvaltningshøjskole.

Olesen, Kjeld (1975) "Regeringen må have overskud til at tænke tanker." *Ny Politik.*

Prime Minister's Office (1998) "Oversigt over regeringsudvalg." Copenhagen: Statsministeriet, 22 September 1998.

Weber, Max (1918/1988) "Parlament und Regierung im neugeordneten Deutschland," in *Gesammelte Politische Schriften*. Tübingen: J. C. B. Mohr.

Weber, Max (1921/1980) *Wirtschaft und Gesellschaft*. Tübingen: J. C. B. Mohr.

3 Politicization of the Swedish civil service

A necessary evil – or just evil?

Jon Pierre

The degree to which the Swedish civil service is politicized has for long been a debated issue. To some extent this is because such politicization has a somewhat special appearence in Sweden, as will be demonstrated in this chapter. Even more controversial is the issue about the extent to which the civil service should be operating under close political control. Meanwhile, the institutional arrangements of the Swedish state are exceptionally well geared to maintaining a separation of politics and administration, as we will see later in this chapter. Indeed, in a comparative perspective the Swedish case provides an almost ideal setting for ensuring that the civil service does not become politicized. Similarly, the number of political appointees in the Swedish public sector is probably much lower than in most other countries.

Sweden displays an intriguing case where it is almost a *faux pas* to mention politicization in the heart of a state's political and administrative spheres; interviewees frequently deny the political dimension of their work. Politicization has a distinctly pejorative connotation in these respects in Sweden. Almost any institutional reform which can be accused of politicizing the civil service is not very likely to be fully implemented. This becomes all the more ironic as the Swedish civil service in a comparative perspective belongs among the least politicized. The Swedish institutional arrangement has several safeguards against detailed political control over the bureaucracy, as we will see in this chapter. So why is it, in this political and institutional milieu characterized by a strict division between policy-making and administration and between political appointments and career appointments, that the notion of politicization has become so controversial? And, given the controversial and sensitive nature of this issue, how do the political elite ensure some degree of responsiveness among the public servants and in the administrative institutions?

The Swedish civil service has historically speaking been influenced by two different, and potentially conflicting, systems of norms and rules as regards its modus operandi and relationship to the political echelons of government. On the one hand, Sweden has a strong *Rechtsstaat* tradition, emphasizing legality, equal treatment, predictability, due process, and a distinct separation between the political and administrative spheres of the state. This tradition portrays the public employee as a loyal servant of the government of the day; indeed, Kaufman's (1956) notion of "neutral competence" is an apt image of the civil servant in this administrative tradition.

On the other hand, the Swedish public sector was the key administrative vehicle in implementing a large number of comprehensive programs under the umbrella of the welfare state. The emerging phase of the welfare state witnessed some degree of administrative hesitancy toward such programs; it is fair to say that the "neutral competence" heralded by the *Rechtsstaat* tradition may work indirectly against large-scale political projects, signaling a new political course with a new role for the state in society (Pierre, 1995a; Rothstein, 1996). However, as the Social Democrats remained in office for more than 40 years and have been a party of government for much of the remainder of the twentieth century (1932–76, 1982–91 and 1998 to the present), some degree of Social Democratic sympathy is to be expected also among non-political appointees in the civil service.

The joint outcome of these two clusters of norms and expectations on the Swedish civil service and the long tenure of the Social Democrats has been a rather odd model of politico-bureaucratic relationships. While much of the post-war period saw little change in the political control of the civil service at a systemic level, there developed an indirect type of politicization through the appointment of civil servants with an overt political affiliation to senior posts in the public bureaucracy. The consequences of this incremental development became obvious in 1976 as Sweden elected the first non-socialist government in more than 40 years. The incoming government soon learned that Social Democrats controlled a large number of senior, tenured, meritocratic positions in the civil service (Levin, 1983; Ahrland, 1983). Four decades earlier, in 1932, the Social Democrats had come into office with an extensive reform agenda, only to find that the cadre of career senior civil servants were difficult to mobilize for the new type of policies. In both cases, nominally non-political civil servants slowed the execution of policies because they were not convinced about the validity of these new ideas (see Pierre, 1995a).

Thus, the issue of the politicization of the civil service in Sweden is embedded in the historical trajectory of the state and, ultimately, the role of the state in the transformation and governance of society. A civil service which becomes overtly politicized runs the risk of being viewed as merely the administrative instrument of the government of the day with limited legality and integrity, something which may lead to a decreasing legitimacy in the public eye. A public sector governed strictly by legal and regulatory frameworks, on the other hand, may indirectly become an obstacle to political change as promoted by the political elite, in which case the civil service will become perceived as rigid, self-serving, bureaucratic, and elitist. Thus, the debate on politicization in Sweden has to a considerable extent been a matter of striking a delicate balance between these two different aspects of the civil service and the public sector more generally.

Institutional arrangements and the issue of politicization

In Chapter 1 above, the editors define politicization as "the selection, retention, promotion, rewards, and disciplining of members of the public service." The purpose of politicization in the advanced Western democracies is said to be "to control policy and implementation, rather than just supply jobs for party members." This chapter will highlight tendencies toward politicization of the Swedish civil service at two different institutional levels.

The chapter first discusses changes in the central government office staff (*regeringskansliet*). The central government office comprises all the departments and the Prime Minister's Office (*statsrådsberedningen*). In the early 1990s, the departments were merged into one overarching organization, partly in order to strengthen policy coordination and partly in order to encourage staff mobility. Thus, while departments still have their own ministers and staff, they now are technically part of one and the same organization. Here, the border between political and merit-based appointment cuts right through the organization. During the 1990s there has been a debate as to whether the number of political appointees has increased, a development which, if true, has been criticized as politicizing the central government office.

Second, we discuss changes in the degree of politicization at the implementation stage. In this context we will look both at what is believed to be an increasing tendency toward politicized appointments of the directors general of the agencies as well as a tendency toward bureaucratic initiatives on policy matters. This latter point illustrates a point made in Chapter 1 above that sometimes politicization manifests itself in a pattern whereby civil servants *de jure* or *de facto* assume roles and functions which historically have been considered political.

In the tight web of elected officials and senior civil servants which is a defining feature of the Swedish government, the politics of appointing agency heads and the production of policy advice may sometimes make it difficult to maintain a crystal-clear distinction between elected office and senior civil service posts. Again, this problem has become all the more pertinent as a result of the long period of Social Democratic rule when senior civil servants were either hired because they had the formal requirements as well as their political heart in the right place, or when the Social Democrats were convinced that staffing reform bureaucracies with traditional, merit-based employment would not bring about the desired political and social change (Rothstein, 1996).

A proper understanding of these developments must depart from a discussion about the institutional features of the Swedish government and the historical trajectory of political control of the public service. Further-more, during the severe cutbacks in public expenditures during the past decade there has also been a debate on whether Sweden ought to intro-duce a more distinct New Public Management (NPM) model of public service production. This development would place elected officials at arm's length from the public service. While the 1990s saw a clear down-playing of political control over the public service, this development was less an NPM-style reform and more a result of the introduction of a man-agement by objectives-style political guidance of the bureaucracy.

The Swedish politics–administration interface is more distinct in insti-tutional terms than in most other countries; agencies (*ämbetsverk*) have been a feature of the Swedish institutional system for centuries, enjoying considerable autonomy from the departments (*departement*) (Ruin, 1991). Departments formulate policy; they organize Royal Commissions to look into policy problems and present a policy proposal. Historically more than presently, perhaps, Royal Commissions played an important role in gener-ating consensus on these policy proposals among key actors such as polit-ical parties and organized interests.

The debate on the politicization of the civil service in Sweden illustrates to a large extent the dual image of the virtues and perils of politicization related to the tension between *Rechtsstaat* norms on the one hand and political responsiveness on the other. The existing arrangement with autonomous, non-politicized agencies in charge of policy implementation enjoys considerable support among the political and administrative elite (Larsson, 1993).

However, there has been much debate over the past several years about the true nature of the agencies with regard to their degree of politic-ization. Not least, the increasing tendency of the government of the day to appoint directors general sympathetic to its policy to head the agencies has stirred a debate about the extent to which this represents an informal, but probably effective, way of ensuring some degree of political respon-siveness at the agency level (Lindbeck *et al.*, 2000; cf. Jacobsson, 1984). Observers critical of what they see as an increasing politicization of the agencies and a blurred distinction between the spheres of policy and administration emphasize that the Swedish Constitution rests on a theory of a division of powers and that senior civil servants must be hired exclus-ively on the basis of their personal skill and aptitude. Such requirements, they argue, seem to include political affiliation, too, to an increasing extent. As a result, constitutional arrangements ensuring that power and responsibility rest with the same actors have been distorted (Lindbeck *et al.*, 2000: 61–5, 151–3).

Another, related debate takes a normative approach and discusses whether there ought to be an institutional reform allowing the govern-ment to exercise some degree of political control over the agencies. This argument is basically a recognition of the frequent informal contacts between departments and agencies. These contacts, which appear to be crucial for the institutional system to function, appear to be fairly institutionalized and stable over time (Molin *et al.*, 1979; Petersson, 1990; Pierre, 1995a).

An additional reason for changing the system is that the balance between agencies and departments in terms of staff and financial resources has shifted over time to the benefit of the agencies. One of the ideas behind the institutional arrangement in Sweden was that departments should be bigger and better resourced than the agencies. Over time, the departments have remained fairly small institutions while the agencies have expanded quite significantly in terms of both staff and financial resources. Thus, while the departments remained relatively small institutions – in part probably to dismiss any allegations of expanding the political side of the politico-administrative exchange – agencies have been able to capitalize on their discretion in the management of financial resources (Vedung, 1992). As a result, agencies today harbor considerable amounts of expertise and, relatively speaking, financial resources, and are thus well equipped not just to implement policy but also to engage in more long-term policy planning and advice.

Finally, and related to the previous comment, there has been some tendency among the agencies to become increasingly involved in formulating policy, a role which in constitutional terms rests with the departments. However, several agencies are reacting against what they see as an absence of clear policy objectives in their sector and have engaged in a *de facto* policy formulation and the promotion of the political values sustaining their policy area. We have seen the emergence of what has been labeled the "policrat," i.e. a civil servant engaged in the reproduction of political and ideological values and the formulation of policy goals and objectives (Rothstein, 1998).

Thus, as the Swedish case illustrates, we need to be aware of the distinction between politicization in the partisan sense on the one hand and politicization meaning tight control over the civil service by elected officials on the other. This latter meaning of politicization refers more to a particular institutional arrangement in which politicians *tout court* have the means to exercise such control. In Sweden, very few official posts indeed are political in the meaning that civil servants are expected to resign when there is a change in government.

The latter type of politicization is, arguably, more common, but this pattern is largely due to the long Social Democratic tenure in government during which individuals with the qualifications required to become civil servants were also card-carrying Social Democrats. The incoming non-socialist government in 1976 encountered a "forest of red needles" (a badge worn by Social Democrats), i.e. senior civil servants on tenured employment with a clear Social Democratic ideological orientation. More recently, the main topic of conflict concerning politicization has revolved around the government's power to appoint directors general of the agencies, an issue to which we will return later in the chapter.

Politicization of the government's central office

In some ways, the government's central office in Sweden is a hybrid between the public service and the policy-making institutions of government. On the one hand, this institution is the very heart of political power; this is where policy is formulated, government bills are drafted, Royal Commissions are initiated and monitored, and where executive decisions are made. The vast majority of employees in the office are not political appointees but rather employed through a merit-based system. There is a clear border between the political and the non-political insofar as criteria for employment and assignments are concerned. The non-political sphere of the institution emphasizes neutral competence and the provision of policy advice which presents options rather than priorities.

Obviously, these organizational features do not set the Swedish government's office very much apart from its functional equivalents in most other jurisdictions. What is perhaps more unusual is that any increase in the number of political appointees in the government's central office over the past couple of years has been regarded with substantive criticism by the opposition and the media (see Wallin *et al.*, 1999: 285). Table 3.1 presents the total number of employees in the government's central office and the number of political appointees during the 1990s.

To an outside observer, the percentage of political appointees probably seems quite low; the flip-side of the observation that 3–4 percent of the employees are politically appointed is of course that 96–97 percent of them are not. This pattern probably strikes observers as intriguing, given that this is where the key political decisions on public policy are made. Apart from ministers and deputy ministers, this group also comprises departmental staff in charge of public relations and external information.

As Table 3.1 shows, political appointees have never comprised more than about 4 percent of the total number of employees. Given that this figure refers to the key political power center in the country, it is counter-intuitive in some ways that the analysis should focus on any increase, however subtle, in the number of political appointments and not on the extremely low percentage of political appointees. In most international comparisons, the percentage of political appointees in the central government's office would probably come out as extremely low rather than unusually high.

More than anything else, the debate that nevertheless erupts every now and then is proof of the sensitive nature of the issue of politicization in Sweden. Just as one of the standard jokes about Swedes is that they love millionaires as long as they do not know how they became rich, Swedes

Table 3.1 Government's central office: number of employees and political
appointees, 1993–2000

Year	1993	1994	1995	1996	1997	1998	1999	2000
Emp.	3484	3515	3770	3893	4149	4025	4220	4472
Pol.	144	129	135	134	127	111	126	159
%	4.1	3.7	3.6	3.4	3.1	2.8	3.0	3.6

Source: Regeringskansliets Årsbok 2001.

Notes
Emp. stands for the total number of employees in the government's central office.
Pol. represents the number of political appointees.
% indicates political appointees as a percentage of the total number of employees.

probably do not mind that the central government's office makes decisions on policy as long as those decisions are not made by politically appointed people. On a more serious note, political appointment serves many functions which are critical to democratic government such as policy choice and accountability but these positive aspects of political appointments in the central government's office are frequently overshadowed by fears of politicization.

This type of politicization of the civil service is thus not a defining feature of the Swedish government. The organizational culture and the environment's perception of the central government's office seem to emphasize that neutral competence goes a long way in planning and executing public policy, even when this policy has a clear reformist direction and objectives. Also, as Wallin *et al.* (1992) point out, politicization in the narrow sense of the word is not necessarily a prerequisite for ensuring administrative compliance with political decisions; there is a widespread consensus – the typical Swedish word here is *samsyn*, meaning shared visions – among the senior levels of the political and administrative spheres (Wallin *et al.*, 1999: 292). Senior civil servants are more likely than the average citizen to become politically involved, e.g. as members of a political party. Thus, although most senior posts in the civil service are not filled according to political criteria, some degree of *samsyn* will emerge nonetheless. These shared visions of policy objectives and on how the civil service should be managed provide an important glue between politics and administration in the Swedish system.

In order to understand the complexities of ensuring administrative responsiveness vis-à-vis political ideas more generally, we need to place the central government's office in the larger institutional framework of the Swedish system of government. It is interesting to note, as Rothstein (1996) observes, that when the Social Democrats came to power with a distinctly reformist political agenda in the early 1930s, they seemed to be more concerned with ensuring loyalty and compliance at the agency level than at the departmental level, probably because they believed that it was at this level that public policy is effectively designed. Let us therefore turn to the issue of politicization at the level of the agencies.

Politicization of the agencies

Another irony in the politicization debate in Sweden – alongside the conspicuously limited number of political appointees in the central government's office – resides in the question of the politicization of the agencies. In this system of government designed long before the emergence of political democracy, agencies were intended to focus strictly on implementing policy decisions made by the political elite, a concept which for long could be translated into the king and his circle of advisors. It was also assumed that departments and agencies should be of roughly similar size, or that departments should be the stronger institution of the two.

Given the trajectory of political and societal change since this system was first designed, it should not surprise anyone that the current situation differs in many important respects from the original idea. First of all, the pace of organizational change at the agency level has been much higher than at the departmental level. The number of agencies has grown significantly and there has been a large number of institutional mergers, abolitions, and creations (Premfors, 1999). Second, while departments remained rather small organizations, many of the key welfare state agencies such as those in the education, medical care, and social welfare sectors developed into huge structures with extensive knowledge, expertise, and professionalism. Add to this picture the constitutional arrangement according to which departments are not allowed to give detailed instructions to agencies but – by way of the parliament, *Riksdagen* – are rather to steer the bureaucracy through the budget and through defining the legal framework for the agencies.

The joint result of these structural features is a system of government *de facto* tilted toward its executive, non-accountable structures and where departments have no self-evident and undisputed upper hand in terms of resources or expertise. This pattern explains why the issue of agency politicization has become so sensitive; the massive agencies were accepted as long as their capabilities were not employed for politically driven projects. It also explains why at times the political elite has been tempted to find ways of giving the agencies political directives; it is, after all, at the agency level that much of the expertise, networks with subnational government and professional organizations, and other critical resources are located. And, finally, it explains why from time to time the argument has been put forward that agencies should be brought under some form of more direct and politically accountable control (see Pierre, 1995a).

How, then, can departments ensure that agencies carry out policies and programs? The textbook literature on Swedish public administration typically identifies four different types of steering instruments. First, there is steering by allocating budgetary resources to specifically targeted programs which the agencies will implement. Second, departments and the Riksdag define the legal framework for the civil service. Third, the cabinet appoints the director general of the agency. It is this latter type of steering which speaks to the current discussion about the politicization of the Swedish civil service. Finally, the government exercise influence over the agencies through audits and other means of controlling their activities.

Recent studies of the extent to which the incumbent government actually uses its right to appoint directors general of agencies to impose candidates who are sympathetic to its policy suggest that roughly one in every four directors general appointed during the 1990s has a political background, usually within the party in power (*Statstjänstemannen*, 1999). In some ways, the debate on these issues is not too different from the philosophical argument about whether the proverbial glass is half full or half empty; is one out of every four a high or a low figure? For some observers, like the trade union press (*Statstjänstemannen*, 1999) the ratio causes no concern; after all, some 75 percent of agency heads are clearly hired on merit grounds. Others, however, are more alarmed by 25 percent of agency heads having a political background (Lindbeck *et al.*, 2000). What is at stake, these critics argue, is not so much whether appointing directors general on political grounds is a means for the government to ensure bureaucratic loyalty for its policies but more that the tendency toward politicizing these appointments undercuts professionalism, efficiency, merit-based career systems, and in the longer term the apolitical nature of the civil service. The agencies, in this perspective, become loyal to the government of the day but with no institutional integrity and with a weakened trust among actors in its external environment.

The problem we seem to be faced with presents a choice between two politico-administrative models of exchange, neither of which is very attractive. On the one hand, there is the autonomous agency which over time has developed into a sizeable institution. The agency implements programs but it also initiates and executes its own programs by virtue of its relatively autonomous control over budgetary resources. Political institutions have very limited instruments to correct the course taken by the agency whose key decisions are taken by a group of senior civil servants and a director general appointed exclusively on merit grounds. The other scenario presents an agency operating under closer political control. Senior appointments are made with primary consideration to political affiliation. The agency's programs shift direction whenever a new political party takes over government. Since senior posts are politically appointed, there are few and weak incentives for civil servants to strengthen their merits in order to ascend to these levels of the agency.

Fortunately, the real world presents a third standpoint between these two options. Arguably, this middle way incorporates some of the positive features of both models. In the current system of government, agencies nominally operate with significant autonomy vis-à-vis the political echelons of government. However, informal contacts between departments and agencies are extremely frequent, primarily at the middle and lower institutional levels. The rationale for these contacts is that both parties have strong incentives for entering a dialogue. Departmental staff need to consult agency officials on an informal level for policy advice and also to try to influence the agency on how policies are to be implemented. Similarly, from the point of view of the agencies, informal contacts with departments represent an important avenue for pre-policy input, i.e. an opportunity to shape the policies they are later to implement. We have already mentioned the stability of these networks over time; it is fair to speak of some degree of institutionalization of informal exchange between departments and agencies. These contacts probably have systemic value; it is difficult to conceive of any increase in efficiency in this system of government without these networks.

The return of the political expert?

Politicization in this volume refers both to political penetration of the civil service and to bureaucratic encroachment of the political sphere of government. This latter aspect of politicization manifests itself in civil servants assuming political or policy-formulating roles. It seems clear that during the past decade we have witnessed an increasing number of instances where agencies and their employees have taken a political profile which transcends their original assignment.

To some degree, this development reflects institutional inertia. During the time of expansion of the public sector, agencies were created to implement core welfare state programs and policies. This was the heyday of proactive, interventionist policies in Sweden. From the early 1990s, however, this policy style has gradually been replaced by one which is more typical of an enabling state than of a steering and intervening state. In terms of policies, this change has meant that agencies are given a less active role.

The industrial policy sector is a case in point. The key agency in this sector, NUTEK, was created as a merger of three agencies in the early 1990s. These three agencies – the industrial policy agency (SIND), the energy agency and the board for technical development (STU) – had long experience of implementing rather detailed government policies. In the early 1990s, however, their assignment was redefined to focus on identifying and removing obstacles to economic growth, many of which were government regulations of private businesses. At the same time, industrial policy was notably downplayed. Over time, NUTEK and its staff became frustrated by what they believed to be a "void" of policy in their sector. In their opinion, a distinct and coherent industrial policy no longer existed and the agency therefore formulated an industrial policy and tried to generate support for it in the Ministry of Industry and Trade.

First of all, this is a case of institutional politicization rather than politicization at the level of individual civil servants. The politicization can be explained by agencies' frustration at what they see as a rolling back of policy which leaves them without clear objectives and without political support. One might be tempted to argue that this politicization is also a reflection of bureaucratic struggle to survive by devising a clear task for the agency. This could well be the case but it is probably more accurate to suggest that the assertive strategy of several agencies – NUTEK is but one of several examples – is proof more of a genuine concern about the lack of policy objectives in their respective areas than merely of organizational survival. The legacy of proactive policies remains strong in many of the Swedish agencies.

To sum up this section, the politicization that can be seen at the agency level has several different causes and drivers. One important driver of politicization is simply a need for the government to ensure some degree of administrative compliance with policy, something which is difficult in the institutional order in Sweden with its autonomous agencies.

Conclusions

The picture painted in this chapter of the politicization of the Swedish civil service presents a dual image. We have seen that there is some degree of politicization in terms of political appointments of agency heads and, albeit to a lesser extent, of senior staff in the government's central office. Also, there is some tendency for public servants to assume political roles, a pattern which is – slightly ironic, perhaps – the outcome of a remarkably low number of political employees in the government's office and also as a result of some agencies taking on a policy formulating role during the 1990s. What seems to explain the Swedish pattern of politicization is an organizational culture which emphasizes ensuring shared values and objectives more than formalized political appointments. Party membership is a way of indicating such political alignment, although obviously such membership can never be a requirement for a non-partisan type of employment; that would be a clear violation of the Constitution which emphasizes skill and aptitude as the sole criteria for civil service employment. The key issue is rather that of fostering *samsyn* – a shared vision – between politicians and senior civil servants.

Seen from the point of view of the political elite, hiring people with the merit requirements but who also are sympathetic to your political project is a way of ensuring responsiveness in the senior civil service without increasing the number of political appointees. As we have shown in this chapter, the number of card-carrying individuals among the groups of directors general in the agencies or at the senior level of the departmental staff has increased during the past decade or so. These are individuals who belong to the middle class and who obviously see politics and public employment as an attractive career path.

That said, it also appears that this type of subtle politicization is somewhat of a systemic necessity for achieving policy coordination in the machinery of government in a system which in constitutional and formal terms has a very low level of politicization of the public service. When people are appointed who have the merits necessary to uphold a particular position in the public service but who *at the same time* are members of the incumbent party, it becomes impossible to tell which of these qualifications played the main role in the hiring decision. It is thus a strategy which fends off any accusation of politicizing the public service but at the same time helps ensure responsiveness in an institutional arrangement where such responsiveness is difficult to attain.

The question raised in the title of this chapter is whether some degree of politicization of the civil service is a necessary evil or just an evil. A plea for necessity would have to depart from the standpoint of bureaucratic responsiveness and compliance vis-à-vis elected politicians. The architecture of the Swedish government is deliberately designed to prevent detailed political steering of the civil service. The reasons for this are to a large extent historical, and any initiative to change the system of government toward some degree of clearer political control has been countered with arguments that echo the debate on these issues during the long Social Democratic tenure. However, most observers would probably agree that the main reason why the system works as well as it does is the informal but institutionalized contacts between department and agencies. Thus, an argument in favor of a somewhat increased politicization would be that a reform in that direction would help make politico-bureaucratic interaction more visible and ultimately more accountable.

This said, the arguments against politicization still seem to have the upper hand in the debate. First and foremost, politicization undermines merit-based systems of employment and promotion in the civil service. Second, politicization is believed to jeopardize bureaucratic integrity and, further down that road, the legalistic nature of the civil service and its decision-making processes. What is at stake here, ultimately, are values such as administrative credibility and legal security. These are values that sit deep in the Swedish administrative tradition. Politicization, in this perspective, transforms the civil service from an autonomous center of power to a body which is subordinate to the government of the day.

These are ultimately matters of a normative and constitutional character. As this chapter has shown, there is a subtle tendency toward increasing politicization of the civil service in Sweden. Part of this politicization manifests itself in an increasing ideological congruence among the political elite and the senior levels of the agencies. This congruence is to some extent the result of the selection of candidates for the posts of director general where merit and experience remain important but shared political views also seem to play a growing part. Furthermore, some agencies are taking a higher political profile and putting forward policy proposals.

This development can to a large extent be explained by "voids" in public policy; today, governments of all ideological persuasions devise policy which is less interventionist and less regulating and more oriented toward supporting an enabling role for the state. This creates policy "voids" which leave the agencies searching for a role and also for objectives. Thus, politicization, to reiterate an observation made in Chapter 1 above, must not necessarily be seen as driven by politicians; it frequently takes the form of civil servants assuming political roles.

References

Ahrland, K. (1983), "Nej, Fru Statsråd!" [No, Minister!], *Statsvetenskaplig Tidskrift* 65: 145–52.

Jacobsson, B. (1984), *Hur Styrs Förvaltningen? Myt och Verklighet Kring Departmentens Styrning av Cambetsverken* (Lund: Studentlitteratur).

Kaufman, H. A. (1956), "Emerging Conflicts in the Doctrine of Public Administration," *American Political Science Review* 50: 1059–73.

Larsson, T. (1993), *Det Svenska Statsskicket* [The Swedish Government] (Lund: Studentlitteratur).

Levin, B. (1983), "En Skog av Röda Nålar: Om Politiseringen av Department och Förvaltning" [A Forest of Red Needles: On the Politicization of Departments and Agencies], in B. Rydén (ed.), *Makt och Vanmakt* [Power and Powerlessness] (Stockholm: SNS Förlag), 91–100.

Lindbeck, A., P. Molander, T. Persson, O. Petersson and B. Swedenborg (2000), *Politisk Makt med Oklart Ansvar* [Political Power with Ambiguous Responsibility] (Stockholm: SNS Förlag).

Molin, B., L. Månsson and L. Strömberg (1979), *Offentlig Förvaltning* [Public Administration] (Stockholm: BonnierFakta).

Petersson, O. (1990), *Maktens Nätverk* [The Networks of Power] (Stockholm: Carlssons).

Pierre, J. (1995a), "Governing the Welfare State: Public Administration, the State, and Society in Sweden," in J. Pierre (ed.), *Bureaucracy in the Modern State: An Introduction to Comparative Public Administration* (Aldershot: Edward Elgar), 140–60.

Pierre, J. (1995b), "La réforme administrative en Suède: Vers un déclin du contrôle politique de l'administration?," *Revue Française d'Administration Publique* 75 (July–September): 367–76.

Pierre, J. (1996), "The Policy–Operation Divide in Sweden: A Report from Utopia," in B. G. Peters (ed.), *Policy and Operations* (Ottawa: Canadian Centre for Management Development), 50–3.

Pierre, J. (1998), "Dépolitisée, repolitisée ou simplement politique?: La bureaucratie suédoise," *Revue Française d'Administration Publique* 86 (April–June): 301–10.

Premfors, R. (1999), "Organisationsförändringar och förvaltningspolitik – Sverige" [Organizational change and the politics of public administration in Sweden], in P. Laegreid and O. K. Pedersen (eds), *Fra opbygning til ombygning i staten* [From construction to reconstruction of the state] (Copenhagen: Jurist – og Økonomforbundets Forlag), 145–68.

Rothstein, B. (1996), *The Social Democratic State: The Swedish Model and the Bureaucratic Problem of Social Reforms* (Pittsburgh, Pa.: University of Pittsburgh Press).

Rothstein, B. (1998), *Just Institutions Matter: The Moral and Political Logic of the Universal Welfare State* (Cambridge, MA: Cambridge University Press).

Ruin, O. (1991), "The Duality of the Swedish Central Administration: Ministries and Agencies," in A. Farazmand (ed.), *Handbook of Comparative and Development Public Administration* (New York and Basel: Marcel Dekker), 67–80.

Statstjänstemannen (1999), "Politikerna i minoritet" [Politicians in Minority], 8: 16–19.

Vedung, E. (1992), "Five Observations on Evaluation in Sweden," in J. Mayne, M.-L. Bemelmans-Vedec, J. Hudson, and R. Conner (eds), *Advancing Public Policy Evaluation: Learning from International Experiences* (Amsterdam: Elsevier Publishers), 71–84.

Wallin, G., P. Ehn, M. Isberg, and C. Lindhe (1999), *Makthavare i Fokus: Attityder och Verklighetsuppfattningar hos Toppskikten inom Politik och Förvaltning* [Focus on Powerful Actors: Attitudes and Perceptions at the Senior Levels of Politics and Administration] (Stockholm: SNS Förlag).

4 The politicization of the German civil service

A three-dimensional portrait of the ministerial bureaucracy

Eckhard Schröter

Introduction

This chapter sets out to provide an empirical overview of the current state of politicization in the German ministerial administration (for earlier full accounts see in particular Mayntz and Derlien 1989; a more recent account of the German senior civil service is Goetz 1997, 1999). In doing so, its focus is mainly on the federal level of government; however, in view of the significant role that *Länder* administrations play in the decentralized German political system, where appropriate available information from ministerial departments of the federal states will be included, too. In order to identify how the situation has developed over time, the analysis seeks – as a rough guide – to cover a time span from the early 1970s to the recent turn of the century. In view of the scope of this chapter, however, the survey of the literature aims at the 'larger picture', so that the above-mentioned portrait will be sketched only in a broad-brush manner.

Conceptually, the following draws on a well-established distinction between various meanings of the term 'politicization' (see, for example, Derlien 1985, 1987, 1996, and Peters and Pierre, Chapter 1 above). To start with, politicization can be understood in terms of the involvement of administrators in genuinely political (however, not necessarily party political) activities. Here, the institutional role of the ministerial bureaucracy in the wider politico-administrative system is at stake. In this sense, 'functional' or 'institutional' politicization is to be seen as a corollary of the closely intertwined spheres of the 'political' and 'administrative' realms at the ministerial level. More on a micro-sociological level, the understandings of roles, work-related attitudes and political values of senior bureaucrats have been highlighted as crucial factors in shaping administrative behaviour (Aberbach *et al.* 1981), so that cultural dispositions or 'attitudinal' politicization deserve our attention, too. Finally, the extent to which party political patronage encroaches on the supposedly 'neutral' or 'impartial' role of public bureaucrats and jeopardizes their professional expertise has been a recurrent theme and source of concern in comparative public administration. Seen from this angle of 'party political politicization', the individual civil servant appears to be the target of partisan mechanisms to control the professional bureaucracy.

The inbuilt tension between the pull towards politicization in all its variants on the one hand and the 'tried and tested' principles of the professional career civil service on the other hand will be the thread running through the following discussion. It will be argued that the political environment of federal ministries forces political roles onto top career civil servants, who require both well-developed 'political craftsmanship' (Goetz 1997, 1999) and corresponding role understandings. Seen from this vantage point, 'functional politicization' may live in harmony with civil service professionalism. The government change of 1998 illustrates that the institutionalized mechanism of political control over ministerial staffing matters through the 'temporary retirement' of higher civil servants continues to offer a relatively mild form of partisan politicization, thus balancing the need for political loyalty and the need for professional expertise. As will be shown below, the German case serves to illustrate the general increase in politicization of the civil service, particularly on the 'functional' dimension, during the last quarter of the twentieth century. However, there is virtually no indication that the – overall, moderate – changes are associated with the international 'New Public Management' reform agenda.

The institutional setting of the federal ministerial bureaucracy

Organizational structure and civil service rules

The core ministerial bureaucracy – currently organized into 15 government departments (including the Federal Chancellery) – is a predominantly policy-making institution of – comparatively – rather modest size (for a more detailed analysis, see Mayntz and Scharpf 1975, Mayntz 1984, Goetz 1999, Schnapp 2000). In total, the 2001 Federal Budget provided funding for 12,426 ministerial officials. Focusing on members of the 'higher administrative class' (i.e. the highest of four career categories) brings this number down to roughly 5,100 civil servants (ranging from pay grade A13 for university graduates at the start of their professional careers to the rank of *Staatssekretar* or pay grade B11 at the pinnacle of the grading system; see Table 4.1). From this reservoir of higher ministerial posts, the four top ranks in the departmental hierarchy are commonly singled out as elite positions. According to this definition, the size of the 'administrative elite' boils down to some 1,800 leading officials, including – moving upwards in the hierarchy – the heads of sections (*Referate*, pay grade A16/B3), sub-divisions (*Unterabteilungen*, pay grade B6) and divisions (*Abteilungen*, pay grade B9), plus, of course, the state secretaries (*Staatssekretare*, pay grade B11), as the highest-ranking professional civil servants in each government department. The rather smallish sections *(Referate)* – as highly specialized centres of administrative-technical expertise – are the basic operating units of the ministerial organization, whereas the divisional management level is the decisive transfer point in the departmental communication and information channel, thus selectively amplifying or filtering policy proposals on their way up or down the ministerial hierarchy.

The structural lay-out of the ministerial bureaucracy and the set of regulations governing the senior civil service provide important factors in framing processes of politicization. In this context, the German case shows an interesting degree of ambivalence. On the one hand, the principles of a merit-based professional and tenured career civil service are not only – in keeping with the strong 'state tradition' – well enshrined in (constitutional) law, but also underpinned by deeply rooted cultural aspects (such as the prevailing legalist approach towards public administration) and safeguarded by additional institutional barriers to infringements of the traditional principles of an impartial civil service meritocracy. In particular, the law-clad system of personnel management based upon comparatively rigid and detailed civil service regulations acts as an institutional constraint against overt patronage at the expense of professional qualifications (e.g. promotion decisions – as 'administrative acts' – can be challenged and taken before administrative courts). By the same token, the shared background of senior administrators in the legal profession (roughly two-thirds of them hold law degrees; see Derlien 1990a, 1990b,

Table 4.1 Senior civil servants in government departments (2001)

Department	B11	B9	B6	B3	A16	A15	A14	A13
Chancellery	1	6	15	31	22	45	25	3
Foreign Office	2	12	22	62	38	190	111	36
Interior	2	12	17	82	52	173	87	24
Justice	1	6	14	45	17	101	38	2
Finance	3	10	31	122	47	260	132	33
Economics and Technology	2	8	22	90	41	175	100	12
Consumer Affairs	2	6	16	54	30	131	64	13
Labour	2	8	16	59	38	104	62	31
Transport	2	7	25	84	34	229	112	34
Defence	2	7	22	104	35	219	112	5
Health	1	4	7	30	19	54	30	11
Environment	1	6	13	43	22	98	45	26
Development	1	3	8	31	24	73	35	14
Education and Research	1	7	15	47	33	125	60	27
Family	1	4	8	24	22	38	23	2
Total	24	106	251	908	474	2015	1036	273

Source: Federal Budget Plan 2002.

1996) supposedly fosters this legalist notion of public management. Also, the (independent, but ultimately government-controlled) Federal Personnel Commission (*Bundespersonalausschuss*) acts as a watch-dog to make sure that those civil service standards are in principle also applied in cases of 'outside' recruitment. Only candidates for the apex of the bureaucratic hierarchy, state secretaries, are exempt from this scrutiny. On the other hand, the system allows for a number of loopholes for patronage and generally accepts party politicization more widely than we would expect in the light of the Weberian legacy. As a case in point, the federal ministerial bureaucracy lacks a central recruitment and personnel management agency; rather, the strong drift towards departmentalism in the federal machinery of government has left its mark on the highly decentralized personnel policies. Consequently, there are no uniform recruitment and promotion procedures and, in fact, there are very few formalized ways of selecting the group of top bureaucrats. More fundamentally, members of the higher civil service are not treated as party political eunuchs and the party political groups normally organized by the two major political parties in each ministry are part and parcel of the 'administrative culture' (see Dyson 1977, Goetz 1999). In a similar vein, it is widely acknowledged and accepted that political executives have influence over job placement and promotion decisions in their ministries. This is especially true of the posts of state secretary and division head (*Ministerialdirektoren*), as well as the political support staff (see below).

The only significant exception to the constitutionally enshrined principles of the professional civil service, however, is the institution of the 'political civil servant', which applies to the top two ranks of the bureaucratic hierarchy and allows ministers to send their top advisers into temporary retirement without any justification. This 'political retirement' tradition (which dates back to the early days of parliamentarization in Prussia after the revolution of 1848; see Kugele 1978) recognizes the right of ministers to dismiss leading staff members if there is any doubt about their basic congeniality with their political masters. Rather than inserting an extra layer of political appointees on top of existing civil service machinery, this model rests on the assumption that the incumbents of the two top-ranking posts are in principle still career civil servants. At any given time, this group of 'political civil servants' comprises some 125 top bureaucrats (Derlien 1988). In view of the institutional design and moderate size of this special status group, the German system appears to keep an equal distance from the two more extreme versions of balancing 'professional expertise' and 'party political loyalty' which are typically associated with the Washington, DC, and Whitehall models (see for a cross-national and historical comparison Derlien 1996).

This classic structural design – combined with the overarching framework of civil service regulations – has proved to be relatively impervious to reform pressures inspired by the new public management movement

(Schröter 2001). Recent amendments to the Federal Civil Service Framework Law (Civil Service Reform Law 1997), aimed at modestly increased flexibility in appointments to top administrative positions by instituting a two-year probationary period for senior positions, are scarcely implemented: only one federal civil servant (out of a total of 109 cases) had to return to his or her previous rank after (unsuccessfully) completing a probationary period (BMI 2001).[1] The latest move towards greater flexibility in managing the administrative budget, an increased emphasis on cost-accounting and controlling techniques, as well as the use of written performance agreements, mainly focuses on 'subordinated' federal agencies, and although this is likely to add a superficial gloss to the job profile of increasing numbers of senior civil servants, a general departure from the established mix of political and bureaucratic steering does not seem to be on the agenda (for a government report on the reform measures, see BMI 2002). In fact, it appears that every effort has been made to keep organizational change as compatible as possible with the existing machinery of government. In particular, this finding holds true for the relationships between politicians and civil servants.

The political habitat of the ministerial bureaucrats

Contrary to what the rather traditional, Weberian grid of the ministerial organization in which they operate suggests, federal higher civil servants occupy a much politicized habitat. In view of the blurred boundaries between 'politics' and 'administration', this appears to be a rather trivial observation. In view of the political environment of federal ministries, however, senior civil servants face a particularly challenging range of politico-administrative tasks and functions which require highly developed political skills (for a similar account, see Goetz 1997, 1999). It can be argued that a number of gradual changes – related to the roles of political parties and interest groups, the legislature and the federal states in the policy-making process – have resulted in an increasingly politicized job profile for the administrative elite.

The role of political parties and political leadership

For its executive model, the Federal Republic has a long tradition of coalition government. This political setting adds an extra challenge to the job of senior civil servants who not only have to read the mind of their own minister and that of the Chancellor, but must also factor in the vaguely defined and delicate variable of coalition politics. On top of that, the federal bureaucrats cannot leave the parliamentary opposition parties out of the equation. While forming the opposition in the Bundestag, those parties may well have gained the upper hand in the Federal Council (Bundesrat): this makes early policy negotiations necessary (see below). In view of a – comparatively speaking – consensus-oriented political culture and well-entrenched rights of the parliamentary minority (as opposed to the 'winner takes it all' principle in the Anglo-Saxon tradition), opposition parties may in important instances also take advantage of the tendency to 'co-government' between the government parliamentary groups and the national opposition. In this working environment, the ability of civil servants to act strategically and sensitively in regard to party politics will certainly be an important asset.

The role of organized interests

The German ministerial bureaucracy can justifiably claim to serve as *the* major focal point for lobby work. In fact, representatives of organized interests accord even more political weight to their (formal and informal) contacts with senior government officials than to their working relations with parliamentary institutions, and put federal ministries clearly at the top of the list if asked to rank political actors in order of their significance for lobbyists (Sebaldt 2000). Since these close working contacts tend also to serve the interests of the ministerial bureaucracy, which relies on first-hand information and seeks support for its own policy proposals, a certain 'comradeship' may evolve between senior civil servants and lobbyists which comes close to the capture of individual sections or divisions (see also Benzler 1989).[2] While this preferred pattern of interaction has a distinctive neo-corporatist flavour (given its emphasis on institutionalized contacts with peak associations) and a truly pluralist interest group regime with a great variety of interests and while free access even for promotional groups is still fairly rare, it has also been observed that since the 1980s the system of neo-corporatism has eroded considerably and given way to a more pluralistic mode of interest mediation. So, the formalized contacts – most notably the mandatory hearings organized by the federal ministries – now 'take place in a much more pluralized political environment than 20 years ago' (Sebaldt 2000: 197). It flows from this that interactions with organized interests tend to become less 'cosy' and require even more 'outward-oriented' and politically astute officials.

The role of the legislature

From an American perspective, the Bundestag has been labelled the 'most powerful legislature in Europe' (Aberbach *et al.* 1981), and the relatively strong parliamentary impact on federal policy-making has also been highlighted in recent accounts of legislative politics in Germany (von Beyme 1997, 2000). Most notably, the sophisticated structure of standing legislative committees – seconded by a highly developed professional support service – left its mark on many enacted pieces of legislation. Closely shadowing the portfolios of the government departments, these parliamentary committees are crucial decision-making bodies and also serve as interfaces between the legislative and executive branches of government. In addition, the assertive role of the majority parties in parliament gives a much more proactive spin to the traditional role of parliamentary scrutiny of government legislative proposals (Goetz 1997, Schreckenberger 1994, von Beyme 1997). In fact, parliamentary leaders of the government coalition partners have proved to be prime actors on the policy-making stage, backed by the parliamentary parties' own infrastructure and personal resources that help to translate their political ambitions into concrete policy proposals. Against this background, well-established channels of communication and information with legislative actors are in the vital interest of ministerial bureaucrats.

The role of the federal states

In regard to the legislative process at the federal level, the federal states seem to be determined to compensate for the steady decline of their individual law-making powers by using their collective competences in the Federal Council (Bundesrat) to the full. Effectively acting as a second chamber, the Bundesrat – the members of which are routinely senior officials representing the *Länder* executives – may, as a rule, influence any piece of federal legislation affecting the *Länder*, that is almost 60 per cent of bills. Increasingly, this constitutive element of regional representation in a federal system has been strategically used for party political purposes, especially when the federal governing coalition parties do not command of a safe majority in the Federal Council. This said, however, it still holds true that many amendment proposals by the *Länder* articulate genuine interests of the federal states, so that the federal cabinet cannot even be confident that a government bill will be carried by the *Länder* governed by parties of their own political camp. This situation is further complicated by the startling variety of coalition models which has developed in the *Länder* since unification, making it much more difficult to predict majorities in the Federal Council. Even more time has now to be spent by federal ministerial bureaucrats on preparing 'package deals' and hammering out agreements with potentially dissenting *Länder* executives in order to win political support for their own policy initiatives.

Functional politicization: political hotbeds of the administrative elite

While the factors discussed above have a bearing on shaping the job profiles of senior civil servants generally, in certain positions ministerial bureaucrats are particularly exposed to 'political heat' and need to place greater emphasis on political skills as opposed to technical expertise. It has been shown that those categories of jobs tend also to be crucial phases in the career of a civil servant who aspires to the upper reaches of the ministerial bureaucracy. In his investigation of the workings of the higher civil service, Goetz (1997) identified the following 'training grounds for acquiring political craft'.

Secondment to the Federal Chancellery

Despite the inherently conflicting organizing rationales of the 'chancellor principle' and the 'departmental principle', there is good reason to call Germany's executive government 'chancellor government' (Niclauss 2000: 69). Arguably, the relative strength of the Chancellery stands and falls with the Chancellor's capacity to provide leadership to the cabinet, to control his own party and to mobilize support from the majority parties in parliament. After earlier fruitless attempts, the Chancellery – under the strong leadership of Helmut Kohl during the second half of his chancellorship and apparently under Gerhard Schröder – now occupies a much more pivotal role in coordinating the activities of individual ministries and preparing the government's guidelines (Goetz 1997, Busse 1994, Berry 1989). It has been continually expanding since the 1950s and today employs a staff of about 450 (see also Muller-Rommel 1994). The policy units of the Chancellery are either 'mirror sections' (*Spiegelreferate*), which shadow the policy fields of individual ministries, or 'cross-sectional sections' (*Querschnittsreferate*), the responsibilities of which deliberately cut across several ministries, e.g. the unit dealing with relations between the federation and the *Länder*.

Whereas regular careers in the ministerial bureaucracy are typically confined to just one government department, the Federal Chancellery relies heavily on transferees from the ministries, thus offering the only institutionalized system of personnel rotation (see Table 4.2). In doing so, the Chancellery provides an invaluable opportunity for aspiring high-flyers, who are often just on the verge of being promoted to section head, to put their specialized expertise in wider perspective. Of course, this holds especially true for staff of cross-cutting policy sections. What distinguishes the new job profile of the transferees from their previous work, however, is that they now have to 'read between the lines' to evaluate the political ramifications of departmental policy initiatives and assess possible inconsistencies with other policy measures. In their new role as members of *the* 'central' staff organization of the federal government, the seconded civil servants also have to develop a great range of micro-political skills and informal contact networks in order to extract as much information as possible from the line departments they shadow, to effectively act as the Chancellor's 'early-warning' system and to persuade line departments to bring their policy stance closer to the Chancellor's guidelines. What also elevates these staff members over their departmental counterparts of similar rank is that their contact networks tend to include a much greater share of political actors or state secretaries.

Table 4.2 Secondment to the Chancellery

Seconding department	2001	1996
Foreign Office	12	17
Interior	9	2
Finance	17	4
Justice	2	3
Economics and Technology	13	11
Consumer Affairs	2	2
Labour	5	6
Transport	6	5
Defence	3	8
Health	2	2
Environment	3	4
Development	1	1
Education and Research	3	5
Family	1	5
Total	85	80

Rank	2001	1996
B11 – State secretary	0	0
B9 – Division head	2	2
B6 – Sub-division head	5	5
B3 – Section head	16	16
A16 – Section head	18	11
A15 – Section staff	26	30
A14 – Section staff	7	7
A13 – Section staff	11	9
Total	85	80

Sources: Goetz (1997); Federal Budget Plan 2001; author's calculations.

Political support units

When confronted with the permanent bureaucracy, German political executives may suffer from the 'loneliness of the short-distance runner'. Cabinet ministers however, are given an ostensibly free hand to pick and choose their immediate support staff (see Goetz 1997). As a rule, this political support team consists of a personal assistant, the Minister's Office, the Office for Cabinet and Parliamentary Affairs and the Press and Information Office (for a general overview of support staff see Schimanke 1982, Wagner and Rueckwardt 1982, Mester-Gruner 1987). Despite their critical role in assisting the minister to run the department and, in particular, in connecting him or her with other cabinet members, parliamentarians or political parties, these political support units – even if integrated in a so-called *Leitungsstab* – still differ considerably in size and function from French- or Belgian-style *cabinets*. They have not grown into a 'counter-bureaucracy' which provides specific expertise and engages in interest mediation and policy development; nor do they serve as training grounds for young politicians *in spe* or as a hidden (government-financed) machinery of a political party (see for the Belgian and French cases, for example, Brans and Hondeghem 1999 and Rouban 1999). While it has been argued that the German ministerial organization has witnessed a 'pronounced trend towards larger and more powerful political support units', so that 'line officials have to learn to live with more assertive support staff' (Goetz 1999: 149), it still seems fairly safe to assume – more in line with the conventional interpretation of the functional division of labour with federal ministries – that political support units generally take a more outward-looking perspective rather than overseeing internal departmental workings.[3]

In view of the relaxed selection procedures for support unit staff and the political nature of these recruitment decisions, the support units have proved to be major points of entry for outsiders (professional journalists in the case of press officers, but mainly staff from the political parties and their parliamentary groups) into the top administrative ranks. While not all of them may stand up to the scrutiny of the Federal Personnel Commission, they can still be offered job contracts as public employees, thus bypassing the stricter civil service regulations. In spite of this loophole for lateral entry, the ministerial ranks still provide the largest recruitment pool for political support staff. For many of the personal assistants or heads of support units, this career stage will serve as an important stepping stone, if not catapult, on their way towards the most senior positions, as closer investigations into the administrative elite have shown: roughly one-third of the division heads usually served in those functions earlier in their careers (Goetz 1997, Otremba 1999; for senior civil service careers in detail see Derlien 1990a, 1990b). Rather than being caged in the narrowly defined confines of a departmental section, the job profile of support staff so close to the 'political heat' exposes these officials to a broad variety of issues and relates them to a contact network well beyond the departmental boundaries, in fact reaching out to senior representatives of both 'chambers' of the legislature, political parties and federal states. It is just this external orientation that gives those leading staff members an objective advantage over their fellow competitors for higher posts, although, to be sure, their – more often than not – swift career advancement may in some cases also be interpreted as a reward for loyal service to the leading (party) political executive.

Service for parliamentary parties

One of the most outstanding features of the prevailing career patterns of the German administrative elite is that they also frequently include work for one of the parliamentary parties (for the staff of parliamentary parties more generally, see Jekewitz 1995). Probably no other 'path to the top' better illustrates both the extent to which the upper reaches of the ministerial bureaucracy are functionally enmeshed in the workings of the parliamentary system of government and the wide gulf between recruitment and selection practices in what used to be the traditional 'Anglo-Saxon' systems and the German model. Rather than placing a special premium on temporary outside experience in the business world or directly hiring private sector management experts to civil service ranks or adviser posts, German political executives apparently scorn the New Public Management creed and value proximity to political decision-making arenas. But one should be quick to recognize, of course, that generally politicians may be attracted to either side of the coin. On the one hand, civil servants who opt for this career move declare publicly their party political allegiance, thus setting their names on an unwritten 'transfer list' for a time when 'loyal' staff are needed. On the other hand, the high degree of 'political craftsmanship' (Goetz 1997) acquired from first-hand experience of work with leading policy experts and functionaries of parliamentary party groups, as well as the personal network of contacts with MPs, party leaders and lobbyists, has a strong professional appeal to executive politicians.

There are probably about 70 or 80 higher civil servants on unpaid leave from ministerial departments serving as support staff for parliamentary parties in the Bundestag at any given time (see Table 4.3). The majority of them are probably well-established officials in their mid-career stage (probably heading a section) who will not return to their departments before they have completed a two- to four-year stint. As our comparison over time shows, the overall pattern of distribution among parliamentary parties, seconding departments and ranks in the bureaucratic hierarchy remains generally stable. So the Foreign, Interior, Finance and Economics ministries continue to provide the largest supply for those positions. A notable difference between the data gathered before and after the 1998 government change relates to the number of civil servants opting for the Social Democratic Party in the Bundestag, both in absolute terms and in comparison to the parliamentary party group of the Christian Democratic Union (CDU) and its Bavarian sister party, the Christian Social Union (CSU). Apparently, the ministerial career prospects for outspoken followers of the Social Democratic Party improved while the parliamentary party still provided an attractive option for disappointed or frustrated top administrators with a conservative leaning who saw their wings clipped under the new political leadership. As this example indicates, the practice of granting leave for service with parliamentary parties not only offers an invaluable training ground for political 'on-the-job-learning' but also provides additional access to the ministerial bureaucracy for opposition parties.

Table 4.3 Serving for parliamentary parties in the Bundestag

Seconding department	2001	1996
Foreign Office	8	8
Interior	12	11
Finance	12	10
Justice	1	2
Economics and Technology	15	14
Consumer Affairs	3	2
Labour	3	4
Transport	2	3
Defence	2	5
Health	4	1
Environment	0	0
Development	1	1
Education and Research	3	4
Family	1	3
Total	67	82

Rank	2001	1996
B11 – State secretary	0	0
B9 – Division head	0	0
B6 – Sub-division head	3	0
B3 – Section head	10	20
A16 – Section head	25	34
A15 – Section staff	19	19
A14 – Section staff	5	6
A13 – Section staff	5	3
Total	67	82

Parliamentary party	2001	1996
Social Democratic Party	15	26
Alliance '90/The Greens	2	0
Christian Democrats	41	45
Party of Dem. Socialism	0	0
Total	67	82

Sources: Goetz (1997); Federal Budget Plan 2001; author's calculations.

Cultural patterns: role understandings and attitudes

Given this considerable functional politicization of civil servants' roles, the question arises of whether top officials in ministerial bureaucracies are adequately equipped for their politicized job profiles. In this context, we are less concerned with the formal qualifications and expert knowledge higher civil servants may (or may not) bring with them; rather it is the prevailing pattern of cultural dispositions that deserves our attention. For our purpose, 'administrative culture' is understood as a set of dominant beliefs, attitudes and understandings of their role among civil servants (Schröter 1992, 1995, Schröter and Röber 1997). These orientations are seen as major factors in shaping administrative behaviour. Also, it has become part and parcel of the conventional wisdom of sociologically oriented organizational research that an adequate administrative culture – congruent with functional requirements – is an important precondition for the effective operation of a given system. The by now well-established strand of (often comparative) research on cultural dispositions of senior civil servants has produced a rich body of empirical evidence on which the following discussion relies heavily (see most importantly Putnam 1973, Aberbach *et al.* 1981, Derlien 1988, Aberbach *et al.* 1990, Derlien 1994).

Conceptually, most of the research findings revolve around the seminal – empirically derived – typology introduced by Aberbach *et al.* (1981) in their path-breaking work on administrative elites. The authors started from the assumption that the degree of a bureaucracy's responsiveness to its social and political environment depends largely on the beliefs and understandings of the bureaucrats themselves. Briefly summarized, their model identifies the ideal types of the 'classical bureaucrat' and the 'political bureaucrat', which constitute the polar ends of a wide-ranging continuum. Whereas the 'classical bureaucrat' can be characterized as rule- or procedure-oriented, the 'political bureaucrat' directs his or her activities according to political and social problems or programmes. While the former operates within a monistic conception of the public interest, the latter has a much more pluralistic outlook, recognizing the need to take account of political influences on policy-making and accepting the role of institutions such as parties and pressure groups. More importantly, political bureaucrats do not restrict themselves to a purely executive role but take on an active role in policy-making, for example by initiating, formulating and coordinating policy proposals and by building political support for them or by brokering conflicting interests. Classical or technocratic bureaucrats, on the other hand, are inclined to rank technical criteria higher than political criteria in decision-making and view politicians at best as intruders in the administrative sphere.

Contrary to what the still cultivated (and in the light of the 'lawyers' monopoly', understandably so) heritage of the law-abiding civil servant of the Weberian mould may suggest, the prevailing cultural patterns among the federal (and *Länder*) administrative elites lend convincing support to the hypothesis that the stereotypical top administrator in the Bonn or Berlin ministries has chosen a moderate version of the 'political bureaucrat' as a role model.

Whether the upper crust of the ministerial administration is to be classified as a group of predominantly reactive or proactive bureaucrats depends crucially on their individual contributions to the policy-making process and on their evaluation of the political environment in which they operate. The question of whether senior ministerial bureaucrats themselves accept the political side of their job typically serves as a litmus test in this regard. As the available data illustrate, the vast majority of respondents from federal and *Länder* ministerial departments not only accept this component as an integral part of their profession but seem to hold it in particularly high esteem (Derlien 1988, 1994, Schröter and Röber 1997). In fact, more than three-quarters of the surveyed elite officials liked this aspect of their job profile without qualification (and broadly comparable studies in the early and mid-1990s rendered similar results for Bonn and *Länder* officials). Interestingly, this unqualified support for the 'political grey area' has gone up from the already high level of 45 per cent revealed by the 1970 survey (Derlien 1994). Additional hints implying that German senior civil servants have a politically open-minded understanding of their role come from responses to questions concerning their job satisfaction and notion of the policy-making process. The vast mjority of interviewees treasure the sphere of political bargaining and compromise since it contributes significantly to their career satisfaction. Furthermore, they are inclined to see a legitimate role for themselves in this grey area, and regard government policies as a joint product of elected politicians and appointed bureaucrats.

Concerning the principal motives of leading government officials for taking on and maintaining a public service career, it is evident that 'being interested in matters of policy and politics', 'having an impact on shaping society', and 'exerting influence in the state apparatus' are among the most salient motivations (Derlien 1994; see also Schröter and Röber 1997). In line with the findings discussed above, the major thrust of civil servants' job motivations appears to have shifted over time from more inward-looking organizational aspects of the job to explicitly power- and policy-oriented role components. More fundamentally, the investigations into the bureaucrats' thinking about their functions provide another clue that chimes nicely with the general tenor of the evidence so far. So the overwhelming majority of the elite stratum accept for themselves a bro-kering and mediating role in their administrative capacities. In particular, they stress the need to transmit political directives into the lower echelons of the bureaucratic apparatus or to bridge the gap between public administration and the outside world by maintaining effective links with other societal and economic actors. Against this background, it does not come as a surprise to see that only a small minority – barely more than 10 per cent according to the datasets – of top bureaucrats endorse a strictly legalistic interpretation of the administrative process by agreeing to the questionnaire item that 'a senior official should limit his (or her) activity to the precise application of the law' (Derlien 1988, 1994, Schröter and Röber 1997). On the contrary, there seems to be a comprehensive consensus among the administrative elite that 'it is at least as important for a public manager to have a talent for politics as it is to have any special management or technical subject skills': some 86 per cent of the sample members agreed (Mayntz and Derlien 1989, Derlien 1994).

In more general terms, the political attitudes and values of the surveyed federal and *Länder* administrators show only very few traces of technocratic or apolitical understandings of the political process as measured by the prevalent response patterns to questions concerning the role of party influences on political and societal conflicts or their assessment of the proper role of technical considerations versus political factors in policymaking. In comparative perspective (see Aberbach *et al.* 1990), the 'tolerance of politics' shown by (West) German sample members[4] surprisingly even surpasses that of the traditionally politically open-minded American federal bureaucrats (perhaps reflecting the relatively calm political seas surrounding the German ministries if compared to the rough waters of the more adversarial policy style in Washington, DC).

Putting together the various pieces of the mosaic laid out above, we arrive at a portrait that shows the archetypical top administrator as a political bureaucrat or 'policy facilitator', who manages decision-making and implementation processes alike and who keeps open the lines of communication between various segments of the policy arena, whereas the contours of the reactive classical bureaucrat who retreats to his or her technocratic expert role in public administration have largely faded away. But one should quickly point out that this attitudinal politicization falls short of an amalgamation of bureaucratic and political roles in the German higher ministerial bureaucracy (Mayntz and Derlien 1989, Derlien 1994). Rather, senior officials clearly contrast their self-images with those of politicians and still tend to subscribe almost unanimously to the role models of 'executor' and 'expert', whereas the role model of 'party politician' is greeted with resentment (see also Schröter and Röber 1997). Admittedly, none of the reviewed survey studies were particularly geared to shed light on explicitly managerial role understandings and work-related attitudes. Also, we lack more recent interview data which capture the slow but steady advent of New Public Management-oriented reform measures since the mid- and late 1990s. In this context, however, the available data show, if anything, even a diminished role of managerial thinking in civil servants' job understandings since the planning and budget reform-oriented phase of the early 1970s.

The party political dimension of politicization

Party membership in the higher civil service

From what the available survey data tell us, the number of party members in the higher echelons of the (West) German civil service has been increasing constantly (from a British perspective, however, the German administration appeared to be run by party members as early as the mid-1970s; see Dyson 1977). While there is only patchy evidence available for the period before 1970, the findings suggest that party membership started in the formative years of the Federal Republic from a relatively low base. In fact, even among the group of highest-ranking officials (permanent state secretaries) between 1949 and 1969 the percentage of declared party members was as low as 18 per cent (von Beyme 1971: 103; see Derlien 1985). After the first change of the major governing party in 1969, party politicization apparently sharply increased at the federal government level (for the following data see Mayntz and Derlien 1989, Derlien 1994). However, responses from a sample of civil servants (including division, sub-division and section heads) in 1970 showed that only comparatively few were party members (28 per cent). In 1972, a different sample design (which tilted the balance more in favour of the more senior positions by including state secretaries and excluding section heads) gave 37 per cent party membership in federal ministerial departments. When a comparable sample group were interviewed in 1981, the percentage of party members increased significantly to some 52 per cent. Finally, in 1987, an even more comprehensive survey (including office-holders from the top four ranks of the departmental hierarchy) showed that the number of non-members had dwindled further: no less than 57 per cent of the respondents declared themselves official party members. This high level of party affiliation among top bureaucrats – with percentages hitting the 60 per cent mark – was confirmed in a more recent survey of the national elite (Bürklin *et al.* 1999).[5]

It comes as no surprise to recognize a clear rank effect in the datasets: the closer to the centre of political gravity, the higher the proportion of party members among office-holders. At the pinnacle of the bureaucratic hierarchy, some 70 per cent of the state secretaries declared their party membership in the 1987 survey; among the division heads almost 65 per cent were avowed party members; further down the departmental pecking order, one in two sub-division and section heads had a (formal) party political affiliation (Derlien 1994).

As we would expect, the distribution of membership along the party political spectrum tends – at least broadly and allowing for a certain time lag – to reflect the electoral success of the political parties. Consequently, members of the ruling coalition parties by far outnumber those of their defeated opponents (in 1981, under Chancellor Helmut Schmidt (SPD), roughly 60 per cent of declared party members identified themselves as SPD members, while during the chancellorship of Helmut Kohl (CDU) in 1987, 64 per cent of the party affiliates declared CDU membership). In view of the above time series, however, it is worth noting that at any point in time, members of opposition parties continued to serve the government of the day in senior administrative positions, including the rank of division head (Derlien 1994).

By and large, the contours of the general picture presented so far seem to overlap with the patterns of party politicization emerging from studies of the *Land* administrations. In fact, in ministerial departments at the federal state level there appears to have been a similar, if not even more pronounced, increase in party membership among leading civil servants. According to survey data collected between 1989 and 1995, some 40 per cent of senior administrators in *Länder* bureaucracies are on the membership lists of political parties (Herbert 1989, Schröter 1992, Damskis and Möller 1997: 83–4). As a closer look at the findings for individual hierarchical levels reveals, party membership among division heads – who, in contrast to the federal level, are not considered 'political civil servants' – is (at least) equal to that at the federal government level (ranging between 55 and 65 per cent; see Steinkemper 1974, Damskis and Möller 1997). In view of strong regional party dominance, the governing parties seem to have an even tighter grip on the administrative elite in the *Länder*, as the available data illustrate (e.g. in the federal state of Saxony 81 per cent of party members belong to the governing CDU, whereas in Brandenburg 74 per cent have an SPD membership card; see Damskis and Möller 1997: 87).[6]

Changes in government and party political patronage

Over the first 50 years of the Federal Republic, federal governments have enjoyed remarkable stability: (West) Germany's post-war history is divided between a first era of Christian Democratic chancellors (from 1949 to 1969), followed by 13 years under a Social Democratic leadership, before a centre-right coalition led by Chancellor Helmut Kohl regained political control in 1982. It was not until the 1998 general elections that the political pendulum swung back in favour of the left and brought the Social Democratic and Green Party coalition (also known as the Red–Green coalition) under Chancellor Gerhard Schröder into office. How did this government change impact on the composition of the federal administrative elite (for a comprehensive treatment of this question in 1969 and 1982 see Derlien 1984, 1988)?[7]

The incoming government had a total of 136 senior administrative posts designated for 'political civil servants' (24 state secretaries and 112 division heads) in order to bring the upper ranks of the ministerial bureaucracy closer in line with the new political mood (for the following data, see particularly Otremba 1999). In particular, the new cabinet had to decide how to deal with the incumbent officials (22 state secretaries and 103 division heads – the remaining positions were vacant). In roughly 57 per cent of the cases, the office-holders (16 secretaries of state and 55 division heads) were dismissed and sent into temporary retirement soon after the Schröder government took office. While this can hardly be called a full-scale 'purge' – after all, 54 senior administrators (including six state secretaries) remained in office – the Red–Green coalition opted to clean its house more thoroughly than its predecessors on comparable occasions (see Otremba 1999 and Derlien 1988; also Christensen, Chapter 2 above). The party political shake-out following the 1969 government change was of relatively modest scale: roughly 29 per cent of the total positions were reallocated (40 per cent of state secretaries and 25 per cent of division heads). The return of the Christian Democrats to power in 1982 brought a temporary halt to the career of 38 per cent of political civil servants (i.e. one in every two state secretaries and one in every three division heads). By way of contrast, in the changes following October 1998, more than 70 per cent of the state secretaries and more than 50 per cent of division heads were temporarily retired (see Table 4.4).

In interpreting this increasing use of 'political' retirement, one has to bear in mind that the government changes of 1969 and 1982 contained an element of continuity in political control: the first centre-left cabinet of 1969 was preceded by three years of grand coalition government, with the Social Democratic Party controlling six ministries; and after 1982 the Free Democrats remained on the government benches as junior coalition partner. However, the election results of 1998 paved the way for a completely new start of the Red–Green coalition at the cabinet table.

The risk of being temporarily retired – if 'risk' is not a misnomer in view of the comfortable financial cushions provided for the top bureaucrats in question – is rather unevenly distributed among 'political civil servants'. Apart from the already clearly recognizable rank effect, the feature that distinguishes the dismissed officials from the 'survivors' is their perceived closeness to the former political masters. Picking up on an earlier point of our analysis, serving in a political support unit (e.g. a press office or minister's office) or on the staff of the majority parliamentary parties or being initially recruited from the relevant party organizations (including party political foundations and 'think tanks') labels civil servants as trusted followers of individual political executives or parties as a whole. As a matter of fact, almost 70 per cent of the 'politically' retired top bureaucrats in 1998 could be categorized in this way and became obvious targets for the incoming government. In purging this group from the two top civil service ranks, the new Red–Green cabinet ended particularly successful

Table 4.4 Government changes and temporary retirement of political civil servants

	1969–70		1982–83		1998–99	
	N	%	N	%	N	%
State secretary	11	41	13	54	16	73
Division head	27	25	35	34	55	53
Total	33	29	48	38	71	57

Sources: Derlien (1988); Otremba (1999); author's calculations.

administrative careers: typically, these were high-flyers who had joined the ranks of the federal bureaucracy comparatively late in their professional careers (average entry age: 35), had rapidly reached a top position (on average after 15 years of service) and had (theoretically) still 10 years of service until regular retirement when they were dismissed from their positions (Otremba 1999).

'High-risk' and 'low-risk' positions can be distinguished in the following manner. While *Ministerialdirektoren*, in charge of more specialized line divisions, have a better chance of 'surviving' a change in government, the odds tend to be against the heads of divisions for 'planning and general policy development' (*Grundsatzabteilungen*), whose work requires a particularly close relationship with the political executive: only one out of nine of those division heads retained their position after the Red–Green coalition took over political control of the federal bureaucracy. By the same token, higher civil servants with responsibility for the politically sensitive 'general management divisions' (*Zentralabteilungen*), who have a tight grip on staffing, budgeting and reorganization, tend to be trusted confidants of the minister of the day. Consequently, no more than two out of the 16 division heads remained in their positions.

As for individual government departments (including the Federal Chancellery), turnover rates in the aftermath of the 1998 change of government show the greatest possible variation, ranging from zero in the Foreign Office to 100 per cent in the Chancellery. Given its centrality in the federal machinery of executive government, the Federal Chancellery (*Bundeskanzleramt*) has always undergone a complete change of 'political civil servants' when the colour of the Chancellor's party has changed from conservative 'black' to Social Democratic 'red' or vice versa (Derlien 1988). Additional information suggests, however, the long arm of personnel policy reaches further down the bureaucratic hierarchy. Following the inauguration of Gerhard Schröder, new appointments were made for two-thirds of the Chancellery's sub-division heads; roughly 50 per cent of the sections have come under new leadership (see BT-Drucksache 2001). In interpreting those data, one has to bear in mind that the extent of party politically motivated personnel change is partly obscured by the routine of personnel rotation between the Chancellery and the ministries (see above).

A mix of political and organizational factors can account at least partly for the apparent discrepancies between ministerial turnover rates. Most conspicuously, Foreign Minister Joseph Fischer (Alliance '90/The Greens) made a point of retaining most of the leading staff inherited from his predecessor, one of the world's longest-serving foreign ministers, Hans-Dietrich Genscher (Free Democratic Party), in order to send out the signal that professional diplomatic standards were being maintained, together with a high degree of policy stability. In a similar vein, the Ministry of Economics – which had also long been considered a stronghold of the Liberals and now shows relative continuity in staffing – has not only lost a lot of its former political clout, but is currently headed by a political executive who has no formal affiliation to any of the governing coalition parties. In terms of organizational micro-politics, the size of a government department may have a role, inasmuch as smaller ministries offer less room for organizational reshuffles and horizontal movements of leading personnel.

Even more important than removing potentially recalcitrant top administrators who seem not to be sufficiently aligned with the new minister's political persuasions, policy preferences or personal style in office is the task of selecting more congenial staff. How did the Red–Green government coalition fill those vacancies? In relation to the former changes of the Chancellor's party, a rather conventional strategy seems to have governed this recruitment process. As a rule, great care has been taken to avoid extreme career jumps or upsetting the established professional civil service by introducing a flood of outsiders. Intriguingly, the incoming government – in line with the prevalent recruitment patterns in 1969 and 1982 – used the federal ministerial bureaucracy as the largest recruitment pool and avoided dramatically increasing the number of outsiders beyond the customarily accepted standard. As on earlier comparable occasions, no more than 20 per cent of the new incumbents have a background in party organizations, trade unions or even legislatures (compare Otremba 1999 and Derlien 1988). Instead of giving in to the temptation to fill the loopholes with overtly party political advisers, the new cabinet called upon the federal 'administrative elite in waiting'. This stratum of the bureaucratic hierarchy typically comprises a cohort who entered the federal bureaucracy in the early 1970s, advanced under Social Democratic chancellors to the middle-management levels of section or sub-division heads and saw their further career prospects effectively hampered during the long years of the subsequent centre-right era.

Incoming governing coalition parties, however, which have served several consecutive legislative terms on the opposition benches (or, as in the case of Alliance '90/The Greens, have never formed a federal government before), have at their disposal only a limited pool of civil servants from the ministerial ranks who promise to be politically sympathetic and loyal policy advisers and who also have a senior administrative standing and highly developed professional capacity. In Germany's federal system, the *Länder* administrations (many of which have either a well-entrenched Social Democratic or a Christian Democratic party political dominance) provide the necessary training ground for the federal elite and the valued recruitment reservoir which facilitates the transitions after federal government changes without jeopardizing the professional standards of the career civil service (see also Derlien 1988). In fact, the transition period after the 1998 government change is notable for its heavy reliance on the 'brain drain' from the federal states to the federal ministerial bureaucracy

– no less than one-third of the newly recruited elite members had previously worked for (Social Democratic-led) *Länder* governments.

In one crucial respect, the group of new top administrators closely resembles the group of those dismissed: while the party political affiliations have most likely changed, the resilience of certain stepping stones in administrative careers, which expose civil servants to the 'political heat' in political support units or parliamentary parties, has not. Again, roughly 70 per cent of the new incumbents have gone through politically oriented 'socialization agencies' during their professional careers (Otremba 1999). This finding lends support to the suggestion that it is probably not only party membership that appeals to the new political masters; but that it is – in functional terms – the 'political craft' (Goetz 1997) acquired what they find indispensable.

Conclusion

Pulling the various threads of evidence together shows that it is relatively safe to suggest that the German senior civil service is a highly politicized institution. Most significantly, this finding holds true for the ministerial bureaucracy, an institution which puts bureaucrats in situations where they perform *de facto* political roles. In terms of this 'functional politicization', top federal administrators may – confronted with assertive (parliamentary) political parties and growing influence from the federal states – have now less control over agenda-setting and initial policy formulation than they had in the 1970s or early 1980s, but the increasingly heavy emphasis that is being placed on policy coordination and interest mediation is intensifying the involvement of senior career officials in political activities and making civil servants' capacities to 'facilitate' the policy process ever more valuable for political executives. In this regard, the horizontal and vertical fragmentation of the German politico-administrative system is a recurrent theme in pointing to the essential need for politically astute top officials who are trained in the art of policy management. This political side of the job appears to be an integral part of the prevailing role understandings of higher civil servants and is well supported by their political and work-related attitudes – again, more so than during the early 1970s. The party political facet of the 'politicization portrait' also seems to be painted in much brighter colours than formerly, as the growing percentages of party members and the (moderately) increased proportion of 'politically retired' leading officials indicate.

In this sense of individual politicization, however, the German case stops well short of a hybrid model in which individual civil servants are so closely associated with political parties that the institution becomes essentially a political body. That said, this 'politicized' ministerial bureaucracy seems to coexist peacefully and relatively harmoniously, if not symbiotically, with the still highly valued and enforced principles of a merit-based career civil service. Despite the more assertive role of ministerial staff units (or – on a much larger scale – of the Federal Chancellery), political executives are not yet cocooned (by their own counter-bureaucracy or external political advisers) against line administrators; nor has this trend led to a new breed of 'conviction civil servants'. Rather, the dominant roles of (political) bureaucrats and ministers are kept separate, and there is little indication that new 'politico-administrative hybrids' fight for each other's turf. Most importantly, the repercussions of government changes do not appear to disrupt the 'functional village life' of the career civil service by either moving towards a US-style 'government of strangers' or provoking (cultural and professional) clashes between political advisers and 'Whitehall mandarins' as in Britain.

The German case shows an evolutionary development towards increased politicization on all three dimensions during the last quarter of the twentieth century – already starting from a high level, to be sure. In this context, the increase in 'institutional' or 'functional' politicization over the last decade appears to be most pronounced. The gradual shifts portrayed above are 'variations on a theme' rather than abrupt changes or drastic departures from hitherto established practices. In explaining developments over time, long-term changes in political (as regards the assertive role of parliamentarians and (party-)politicized intergovernmental relations) and societal structures (in view of the composition of the interest group universe), as well as the ever more pervasive role of political parties as the most important link between these groups of actors, seem to be more appropriate than recent measures of administrative reform. Most intriguingly, the international wave of New Public Management reform has had very little, if any, impact on the political functions and role understandings of Germany's senior civil servants or on the use of party patronage in the higher ranks of ministerial departments. As there was virtually no change in the modes of administrative and political management, there was little reason for the 'political empire' – as in more managerially inclined systems – to 'strike back' and reassert its hold on key administrative positions.

Notes

1 This pattern also holds true for the federal states: only 10 out of 760 civil servants failed the probationary period. The *Länder* administrations, however, are allowed to introduce more far-reaching models of fixed-term contracts for top officials. In these instances, temporary executive duties are limited to two terms of office of no more than 10 years in total. In the meantime, nine federal states have ventured to introduce these measures. In a recent report (Bundesministerium des Innern (2001), *Erfahsungsbericht zur Dienstrechtsreform 1997*, Berlin: Bundesministerium des Innern) assessing the recent practical experience with the reform law, the more restrictive federal rules were identified as a 'deficiency'. This highlights the need for the introduction of (renewable) fixed-term contracts for top federal civil servants, too.

2 The particularly close relationships between employers' associations and the Ministry of Economics, the established ties between trade unions and the Ministry of Labour and Social Affairs, and the strong bonds between the former Ministry of Agriculture and the relevant interest groups can serve to illustrate this point. As Peters and Pierre explained in Chapter 1 above, this form of interest-based politicization may well override partisan considerations. Thus Chancellor Kohl utilized for most of his chancellorship the expertise and networking capacity of an SPD member who served as sub-division head in the Chancellery (see BT-Drucksache 14/37, 18 November, 1998).

3 Even the smaller of the Belgian ministerial *cabinets* (with some 50 staff members) employ on average more than twice as many officials as average-sized support units in German ministries. In some cases, leading members of political support units are even integrated in the line hierarchy, thus heading a smallish division. More generally, important '*cabinet*' functions such as general policy planning are taken care of by 'general policy development' divisions (*Grundsatzabteilungen*) which count as particularly politically sensitive units (see below for data on personnel fluctuations after changes in government).

4 It should be noted in passing that after German unification research into the cultural dispositions of higher civil servants socialized in East Germany has shown that they maintained a greater distance from politics and were inclined to adopt a more reactive understanding of their role.

5 However, it is also true that most civil servants limit their party activity to paying membership dues. Only a small minority of some 10 per cent of the surveyed sample members hold party political office or act as a local or regional official.

6 Since these data reflect the situation in two of the 'new' *Länder*, it could also be argued that the unprecedented challenge to rebuild *Länder* administrations virtually from scratch in what used to be the German Democratic Republic led necessarily to relaxed recruitment procedures and standards which eventually engendered the by-product of increased party politicization. The general finding of a high level of party politicization at the *Länder* level, however, also holds true for Western federal states, such as North Rhine–Westphalia (SPD) and Bavaria (CSU). Interestingly, these two *Länder* provided personnel and administrative aid to Brandenburg and Saxony respectively during the transition period.

7 The fact that the practice of temporary retirement of 'political civil servants' is not confined to transitional periods after government changes must be borne in mind. For example, 34 *Ministerialdirigenten* (division heads) were dismissed between 1985 and 1997; 21 of those top bureaucrats had been promoted to this rank after the 'right of centre'-coalition took office in 1982 (see BT-Drucksache 1997).

References

Aberbach, J. D., Putnam, R. D. and Rockman, B. A. (1981), *Bureaucrats and Politicians in Western Democracies*, Cambridge, MA: Harvard University Press.

Aberbach, J. D., Derlien, H.-D., Maytnz, R. and Rockman, B. A. (1990), 'American and West German Federal Executives – Technocratic and Political Attitudes', *International Social Science Journal* (123), pp. 3–18.

Benzler, B. (1989), *Ministerialburokratie und Interessenverbande*, Baden-Baden: Nomos Verlagsgesellschaft.

Berry, P. (1989), 'The Organization and Influence of the Chancellery during the Schmidt and the Kohl Chancellorships', *Governance* (2), pp. 339–55.

78   *Eckhard Schröter*

Beyme, K. von (1971), *Die politische Elit in der Bundesrepublick Deutschland*, Munich: Piper-Verlag.

Beyme, K. von (1997), *Der Gesetzgeber*, Opladen: Westdeutscher Verlag.

Beyme, K. von (2000), 'The Bundestag – Still the Centre of Decision-Making?', in L. Helms (ed.), *Institutions and Institutional Change in the Federal Republic of Germany*, London: Macmillan, pp. 32–48.

BMI (2001), *Erfahrungsbericht zur Dienstrechtsreform 1997*, Berlin: Bundesministerium des Innern.

BMI (2002), *Bilanz 2002: Moderner Staat – moderne Verwaltung*, Berlin: Bundesministerium des Innern.

Brans, M. and Hondeghem, A. (1999), 'The Senior Civil Service in Belgium', in E. C. Page and V. Wright (eds), *Bureaucratic Elites in Western Democracies*, Oxford: Oxford University Press, pp. 121–46.

BT-Drucksache (1997), Antwort der Bundesregierung auf die Kleine Anfrage der Fraktion Bundnis 90/Die Grunen: 'Politische Beamte im einstweiligen Ruhestand seit 1982', 12 September 1997, Bundestags-Drucksache 13/8518.

BT-Drucksache (2001), Antwort der Bundesregierung auf die Kleine Anfrage der CDU/CSU-Fraktion zu 'Personalveranderungen im Bundeskanzleramt', 7 March 2001, Bundestags-Drucksache 14/5480.

Bürklin, W. *et al.* (1997), *Eliten in Deutschland: Rekrutierung und Integration*, Opladen: Leske & Budrich.

Busse, V. (1994), *Bundeskanzleramt und Bundesregierung*, Heidelberg: Huthig.

Damskis, H. and Möller, B. (1997), *Verwaltungskultur in den neuen Bundeslandern*, Frankfurt/Main: Peter Lang.

Derlien, H.-D. (1984), 'Einstweiliger Ruhestand politische Beamte des Bundes 1949 Gis 1983', *Die Öflentliche Verwaltang* (37, 17), pp. 689–99.

Derlien, H.-D. (1985), 'Politicization of the Civil Service in the Federal Republic of Germany: Facts and Fables', in F. Meyers (ed.), *The Politicization of Public Administration*, Brussels: International Institute of Administrative Science, pp. 3–38.

Derlien, H.-D. (1987), 'Public Management and Politics', in K. Eliassen and J. Kooiman (eds), *Managing Public Organizations*, London: Sage, pp. 129–41.

Derlien, H.-D. (1988), 'Repercussions of Government Change on the Career Civil Service in West Germany: The Cases of 1969 and 1982', *Governance* (1), pp. 50–78.

Derlien, H.-D. (1990a), 'Continuity and Change in the West German Federal Executive Elite 1949–1984', *European Journal of Political Research* (18), pp. 349–72.

Derlien, H.-D. (1990b), 'Wer macht in Bonn Karriere? Spitzenbeamte und ihr beruflicher Werdegang', *Die öffentliche Verwaltung* (43), pp. 311–19.

Derlien, H.-D. (1994), 'Karrieren, Tatigkeitsprofil und Rollenverstandnis der Spitzenbeamten des Bundes – Konstanz und Wandel', *Verwaltung und Fortbildung* (22), pp. 255–72.

Derlien, H.-D. (1995), 'Public Administration in Germany: Political and Societal Relations', in Jon Pierre (ed.), *Bureaucracy in the Modern State*, Aldershot: Edward Elgar, pp. 64–91.

Derlien, H.-D. (1996), 'The Politicization of Bureaucracies in Historical and Comparative Perspective', in B. G. Peters and B. A. Rockman (eds), *Agenda for Excellence 2. Administering the State*, Chatham, NJ: Chatham House Publishers, pp. 149–62.

Dyson, K. (1977), *Party, State, and Bureaucracy in Western Germany*, Beverly Hills, CA: Sage.

Goetz, K. H. (1997), 'Acquiring Political Craft: Training Grounds for Top Officials in the German Core Executive', *Public Administration* (75), pp. 753–75.

Goetz, K. H. (1999), 'Senior Officials in the German Federal Administration: Institutional Change and Positional Differentiation', in E. C. Page and V. Wright (eds), *Bureaucratic Elites in Western European States – A Comparative Analysis of Top Officials*, pp. 147–77.

Herbert, W. (1989), *Burgernahe Verwaltung als Leitbild öffentlichen Handelns*, Speyer: Forschungsinstitut für offentliche Verwaltung.

Jekewitz, J. (1995), 'Das Personal der Parlamentsfraktionen: Funktion und Status zwischen Politik und Verwaltung', *Zeitschrift für Parlamentsfragen* (26), pp. 395–423.

Kugele, D. (1978), *Der politische Beamte: Entwicklung, Bewahrung und Reform einer politisch-administrativen Institution*, Munich: Tuduv.

Mayntz, R. (1984), 'German Federal Bureaucrats: A Functional Elite between Politics and Administration', in E. N. Suleiman (ed.), *Bureaucrats and Policy-Making: A Comparative Perspective*, New York: Holmes and Meier, pp. 174–205.

Mayntz, R. and Derlien, H.-D. (1989), 'Party Patronage and Politicization of the West German Administrative Elite 1970–1987: Towards Hybridization?', *Governance* (2), pp. 384–404.

Mayntz, R. and Scharpf, F. W. (1975), *Policy-Making in the German Federal Bureaucracy*, Amsterdam: Elsevier.

Mester-Gruner, M. (1987), 'Ministergehilfen als Filter am Flaschenhals der Regierungspartei. Zur Transparenz politischer Assistenz', *Zeitschrift für Parlamentsfragen* (18), pp. 361–8.

Muller-Rommel, F. (1994), 'The Chancellor and his Staff', in S. Padgett (ed.), *Adenauer to Kohl: The Development of German Chancellorship*, London: Hurst, pp. 106–26.

Niclauss, K. (2000), 'The Federal Government: Variations of Chancellor Dominance', in L. Helms (ed.), *Institutions and Institutional Change in the Federal Republic of Germany*, London: Macmillan, pp. 84–105.

Otremba, W. (1999), 'Der Personalaustausch bei den politischen Beamten nach dem Regierungswechsel im Oktober 1998 – eine Analyse', *Der Offentliche Dienst* (52), pp. 265–71.

Putnam, R. D. (1973), 'The Political Attitudes of Senior Civil Servants in Western Europe: A Preliminary Research Report', *British Journal of Political Science* (3), pp. 253–90.

Rouban, L. (1999), 'The Senior Civil Service in France', in E. C. Page and V. Wright (eds), *Bureaucratic Elites in Western European States*, Oxford: Oxford University Press, pp. 65–89.

Schimanke, D. (1982), 'Assistenzeinheiten der politischen Leitung in Ministerien', *Verwaltungsarchiv* (73), pp. 216–29.

Schnapp, K.-U. (2000), *Ministerial Bureaucracies as Stand-In Agenda Setters? A Comparative Description*, Discussion Paper FS III 00–204, Berlin: Wissenschaftszentrum Berlin für Sozialforschung.

Schreckenberger, W. (1994), 'Informelle Verfahren der Entscheidungsvorbereitung zwischen Bundesregierung und den Mehrheitsfraktionen: Koalitionsgesprache und Koalitionsrunden', *Zeitschrift für Parlamentsfragen* (25), pp. 329–46.

Schröter, E. (1992), *Verwaltungs rungskrafte aus Ost und West Datenreport Berlin*, Occasional Papers No. 27, Berlin: Fachochschule Verwaltung und Rechtspflege.

Schröter, E. (1995), *Verwaltungskultur in Ost und West*, Berlin: Freie Universität Berlin.

Schröter, E. and Röber, M. (1997), 'Regime Change and Administrative Culture', *American Review of Public Administration* (27), pp. 107–32.

Schröter, E. (2001), 'A Solid Rock in Rough Seas? Institutional Change and Continuity in the German Federal Bureaucracy', in B. G. Peters and J. Pierre (eds), *Politicians, Bureaucrats and Administrative Reform*, London: Routledge, pp. 61–72.

Sebaldt, M. (2000), 'Interest Groups: Continuity and Change of German Lobbyism since 1974', in L. Helms (ed.), *Institutions and Institutional Change in the Federal Republic of Germany*, London: Macmillan, pp. 188–205.

Steinkemper, B. (1974), *Klassische und politische Burokraten in der Ministerialverwaltung der Bundesrepublik Deutschland*, Cologne: Carl Heymanns Verlag.

Wagener, F. and Rückwardt, B. (1982), *Führungshilfskrafte in Ministerien: Stellenbesetzung und spätere Verwendung von Personlichen Referenten und Leitern von Ministerburos in Bundesministerien*, Baden-Baden: Nomos Verlagsgesellschaft.

5   Politicization of the civil service in France

From structural to strategic politicization

Luc Rouban

Since the beginning of the Fifth Republic, interaction between politics and public administration in France has been an ever-growing but changing process. A brief methodological introduction is required before analysing the pace and meaning of this process.

Any discussion about the 'politicization' of the civil service has to take into account some basic considerations. First of all, a couple of naive and/or traditional academic arguments should be abandoned. The classical Weberian view of a dichotomy between politics and bureaucracy is at the heart of the French political system, as it is in all Western democracies. Legal or informal rules – especially the corporative structure of the civil service – prevent politicians from bypassing the merit system, and civil servants from denying equal treatment for all public service users on the basis of political considerations. Similarly, careers and professional rationales are not dominated by the same values, nor do they enjoy the same social status. But, as Peters and Pierre (Chapter 1 above) put it, there is at the same time a permanent interaction between the two worlds which may explain, to some extent, why the civil service is 'naturally' and 'functionally' politicized.

Additionally, this co-operative process between elected leaders and higher civil servants may be expressed through 'pragmatic', i.e informal, arrangements in order to safeguard common interests and to protect the elites from any serious popular reactions. Given the informality that characterizes the relationship between public administration and politics, at least at the senior levels, it becomes extremely difficult to provide a seminal analysis of these exchanges. This is a major challenge for any researcher because the intricacy of strategies, and of collective or personal interests, is not easily demonstrated empirically. This is especially true in France where senior civil servants, as representatives of the State in its *Reschsstaat* meaning, regard themselves as the only people who can understand the rules of the game.

In order to explain how and why the interaction between politics and public administration has changed, it is necessary to use longitudinal data, paying due attention to the various political and social structures that have characterized the French political system since 1958. History has taught us that periods of politicization may alternate with periods of 'neutralization', when professionalism is praised and regarded by citizens as a sign of democratic progress (Dreyfus, 2000). But the meaning of 'politicization' or 'professionalization' may differ as expectations and common knowledge about what should be the essence of 'public administration' or 'political neutrality' may vary from one period to another and from one country to the next, especially in Europe where one cannot observe any convergent pattern (*Revue Française d'Administration Publique*, 1998). In France, the high frequency of political changes since 1981 has been combined with a new set of political values giving more weight both to individualistic consumerism and to collective action, demanding a new policy style.

A third basic point is related to the necessity of making some assessment of this changing relationship. Traditional public administration studies use concepts which sound rather 'academic' for those professional civil servants who are the actors or the witnesses, sometimes even the victims, of this political evolution. Politicization is not just a game between two teams, *the first* of which claims 'We have been elected, you have to be responsive', while the other counters 'We have to manage, please don't interfere'. Civil servants are themselves part of the electorate and any French government must appreciate their political weight, as they represent up to one-sixth of the electorate. Moreover, 'public management values' are not so clear that they can be evoked readily (Bouckaert and Pollitt, 2000). Public policies are more easily defined in academic circles than in real bureaucratic life where a public manager has to handle many programmes simultaneously. Also, implementation does not always follow conceptualization, nor does it necessarily precede any systematic evaluation on given lines.

In brief, data or analytical frameworks cannot give the whole picture of what is really perceived and understood by both politicians and bureaucrats in their mutual relations. For instance, a few political appointments may initiate a revolt among professional civil servants because the symbolic and political meaning of this change is more important than its quantitative weight. It is then perceived as a direct threat against what is regarded as a satisfactory balance between professional interests and political considerations or as an example of a new model of interaction which could be extended to other parts of the public administration. This kind of reaction could be observed, for instance, during the first Mitterrand years when senior civil servants of the Foreign Office felt threatened by the appointment of three new ambassadors who were close friends of the President. The 'real' effect of politicization was significantly amplified by the collective reaction of the Quai d'Orsay civil servants who tried to ally with other *grands corps* (see below). Thus, any assessment of the politicization process has to include the individual or collective reactions of civil servants.

A fourth point is that, whatever the difficulties one may encounter in a global evaluation of the administration–politics relationship, there are criteria that may be used to evaluate the degree of politicization. These criteria may be found throughout the life stories of individual civil servants; the number of political positions occupied during an average career may shed some light on the necessity for civil servants to obey the politicization rules. The fact that a growing percentage of senior civil servants are actually involved in politics (at the local level, as party members, etc.) may suggest that the frontiers between professional life and political activity are vanishing. The turnover in higher positions imposed by each new government, as well as the proportion of non-professionals entering the public administration ranks through politicized positions, may also indicate the nature of the change. Surveys may also reveal senior civil servants' reactions to this change. Finally, some kind of objective measurement of the real impact of politicization on careers may be found in an analysis of promotions. It is especially the case with ministerial cabinets; what is the professional fate of a former member of a cabinet? It can be assumed that if a 'politicized' position does not allow any further promotion, this kind of professional experience will soon be abandoned.

In order to understand the trend of politicization in France, it is thus preferable to assess the evolution over the 42 years of the Fifth Republic. France is a good example of a transformation occurring in the politics–*bureaucracy* relationship, as this relationship was of a structural character up to the 1980s and, then, began to change, giving way to a strategic politicization, which could be defined as a mixture of party politicization and policy loyalty.

The classic model of interpenetration of politics and administration under the Fifth Republic: structural politicization

The classic relationship between public administration and politics under the Fifth Republic can be described as a model of 'structural politicization'. This model rests on the elite structure and the technocratic rationale of the new regime. The Fifth Republic political programme is a clear rejection of 'partisan politics' which was the main explanation, from the Gaullist perspective, of the Fourth Republic's failure. The institutional architecture of the Fifth Republic is based on a systematic interaction between politics and public administration, supposedly giving the executive pre-eminence over Parliament, at least as long as the President can count on a huge majority.

Thus, since 1958, the overall nature of the relationship between the senior civil service and elected officials has been as follows. A first element is related to the fact that civil servants are at the heart of political life and outnumber other actors. There are about 5 million public servants in

France, i.e. approximatively 22 per cent of the active population, who have had direct control for many years over public monopolies such as electricity and public transport. Thus, it is important to acknowledge that the public administration is a political force. Despite their different ideological orientations, both Prime Minister Juppé in 1995 and Prime Minister Jospin in 2000 experienced the weight of public service strikes and demonstrations. Even if unions are not hugely powerful (only 13 per cent of civil servants are members of a union), any government has to avoid direct confrontation as public opinion generally supports the public service. This basic dimension of political life in France has not changed since the end of the Second World War.

Second, a career in the civil service is a necessary first step in any political career at the national level. Every President of the Republic (with the notable exception of François Mitterrand), every Prime Minister and most ministers were recruited from the ranks of the civil service; since 1958, the proportion of ministers coming from the public service has varied between 44 and 69 per cent, with an average of 52 per cent. Similarly, the proportion of former civil servants within the ranks of Members of Parliament has increased over time from 19.5 per cent in 1958 to 46 per cent in 1997 (De Baecque and Quermonne, 1981; Rouban, 1998). These data have always been interpreted as describing a mechanism of social and functional cohesion between the political and administrative worlds.

Most scholars have underlined the homogeneity of professional profiles. Politicians as well as higher civil servants are likely to come from the same professional schools, notably the Ecole Nationale d'Administration (ENA), an institution which has supplied a government elite to political and administrative positions (Suleiman, 1978). On closer inspection, the apparent homogeneity of professional career paths is called into question by subtle mechanisms of social discrimination or exclusion. Members of the *grands corps*[1] occupy most upper-ranking positions within ministerial cabinets and within the Prime Minister's staff offices in the Matignon. Since 1962, between 10 and 14 per cent of all Members of Parliament have been members of the *grands corps*. The *grands corps* play a central role in this structural politicization. Organized along the lines of a powerful professional corporatism, they influence the model considerably in three different directions.

1   Real political appointments, i.e. appointments explicitly referred to party membership, are very few. This politicization may be regarded as 'structural' because the participation of members of the *grands corps* in the political decision-making process does not prevent them from protecting their professional autonomy. Members of the *grands corps* do not have to submit to political power; they participate in the exercise of that power. They are partners, not subordinates. The fact that

most politicians come from their ranks suggests that both groups understand the rules of the game and the role of each other. The participation of senior civil servants in the political decision-making process is legitimized therefore in the name of a neutral, technocratic, expertise. They like to underline the fact that they are serving the State, not a specific government whose authority is based upon a casual electoral equilibrium. One of the side-effects of this system is that some major policies of the 1960s were designed and set up more in accordance with the professional interests of some *corps* (this is noticeably the case of the nuclear programme or the transport programmes, connected with the overhelming power of engineers) than from the perspective of a democratic debate based on a pluralistic evaluation of the various stakeholders.

2   Members of the *grands corps* behave as brokers between the political and the administrative power centres. Their strong presence within ministerial cabinets and strategic staff positions allows them to fulfil a 'go-between' function. They are eager to express the needs of the whole administrative apparatus (or, at least, as they are expressed and conceived by the *grands corps*) inside political circles. They also advise politicians about the best way to use or to reform the administrative machinery. In the 1990s, major State reform committees such as the Picq Committee in 1993 were in the hands of *grands corps* members. The ministerial cabinet system allows institutionalization of policy advice, giving ministers the right to appoint and dismiss members on the basis of political or personal considerations without jeopardizing the merit system. It is an institutionalized twilight zone operating as a buffer between the government and the bureaucracy, as there are no permanent secretaries in French ministries.[2] Furthermore, functions within the cabinets are clearly distinguished as there is a cabinet director managing up to about 30 advisers with sectoral policy responsibilities and a cabinet chief acting as the minister's personal secretary in charge of political questions affecting the constituency or the political parties.

3   Appointments to the higher administrative positions (especially department heads) are made within the inner world of the senior civil service. Political recruitment of ministerial cabinet staff as well as of ministerial department heads or task forces is not open to the private sector managers or to professions outside the realm of the public sector (with the possible exception of specialized legal expertise). Only very few members of ministerial cabinets are not civil servants; indeed, from 1958 until 1972, the proportion of civil servants in *ministerial* cabinets never fell below 90 per cent. This system proved satisfactory until 1975–80 because it corresponded nicely with the political and institutional management of the welfare state (Rouban, 1994b; Hayward, 1982).

The transformation of the politicization pattern between 1981 and 2000

The traditional balance between public administration and politics began to change at the end of the 1970s, during the presidency of Valéry Giscard d'Estaing. Senior civil servants were still at the heart of most decision centres but the presidency demanded from them a clearer commitment in favour of the presidential programme. The senior civil servants came to be considered less as neutral experts and more as experts dedicated to apply a political programme defined and controlled by the Elysée.

This loss of professional autonomy was rooted in a new practice and new conception of the politics–bureaucracy interaction. Civil servants were no longer asked to find new solutions but to apply those that had been described and promised during the electoral campaign by the victorious presidential candidate. Policy loyalty is required but this loyalty can hardly be distinguished from partisanship, as each government tries to define a new set of policies as 'solutions' to societal problems. What is new is the fact that these policies, in content as well as in institutional inception, are elaborated by think tanks or partisan spheres before and during political campaigns, when it appears that the traditional strength of the Gaullist majority is fading. The 1974 presidential campaign was the first real confrontation between the Right and the Left since 1958. President Giscard d'Estaing was elected by a very thin margin, having received 50.6 per cent of votes compared with 49.3 per cent for the Socialist candidate, François Mitterrand. For the first time, Giscard d'Estaing could build his own 'presidential style', developing a fashionable image in the media and relying more on his staff than on his own personal background. More importantly, he was now also in a position to launch a 'reform programme'.

When the Left candidate won the presidential election in 1981, this process was accelerated. The Socialists sought a radical break with their political predecessors as well as with the Fifth Republic rules concerning the roles of politicians and senior civil servants. The Socialist victory could be regarded as a middle-class reaction to a State whose central structures were monopolized by upper-class civil servants. New policies require new men and the border between policy loyalty and partisanship was erased, seemingly permanently. The political will of the new government was to give room to social forces at large. This called for a renewal of the elite population in ministerial cabinets and networks.

To some commentators, the electoral victory of the Left favoured a heavy politicization of the higher civil service, not very different from the American-style spoils system (Birnbaum, 1994; Peters, Chapter 7 below). This is certainly true for the years 1981–83 and for the conservative (neo-Gaullist) reaction of 1986. However, one cannot analyse the evolution of interactions between public administration and politics for the last 20 years without assessing the influence of successive political changes in 1988, 1993, 1995 and, finally, 1997. It is also necessary to consider that the programme of the Left was distinctly modified in 1984 when Laurent Fabius became Prime Minister and the Socialist Party acknowledged the existence and constraints of the market economy, thereby marginalizing the Communist Party and adopting a more mainstream European social democratic political stance. The transformation of the relationship between public administration and politics is real but can be explained to a greater extent by the evolution of welfare social structures than by the political will of the government.

The institutional practice of the various governments since 1981, whether of the Right or Left, has only accelerated a long-term process already at work: a progressive politicization of every social debate as civil society takes a greater part in policy design as well as in the policy implementation process. Additionally, partisanship has remained confined by the legacy of the strong structures inherited from the early years of the Fifth Republic, i.e. the priority of the public service over private business or public interest groups. This is a typical case of 'path dependency'; partisanship has become more important but it is still balanced by structural politicization.

What have been the main characteristics of senior civil servants' appointments since the early 1980s? Most senior civil servants' appointments in 1981–82 were clearly partisan. A new era begins of high turnover rates within the higher administrative positions. Important changes, quantitatively and qualitatively, have been decided in sectors regarded as symbolically or strategically important. This is particularly true of the National Education Ministry, the Interior Ministry and the Culture Ministry. About half of the ministerial department heads were replaced within one year of the electoral victory of the Left. In 1983, two-thirds of the department heads had been replaced by officials sharing the views of the government (Lochak, 1986). When the conservative government of Jacques Chirac took power in 1986 this practice was repeated; between 1986 and 1988, two-thirds of the department heads were once again removed (Rouban, 1996).

Another example is the tremendous displacement of prefects in 1981. During the first three months of the Mauroy government, 55 prefects were moved in 95 territorial *départements* (excluding the overseas territories). Between April and June 1986, there were only 23 cases of *replacements* as the nominations had to be negotiated between Jacques Chirac and François Mitterrand who rarely agreed on *these* matters. By way of comparison, only 10 prefects were moved between January and March 1959, when the first government of the Fifth Republic was established (Rouban, 1999b).

However, a basic feature of this partisan politicization is that it does not follow a clear line and has frequently proved to be quite irregular. During some periods, such as 1981–83 and 1986–88, civil servants came under strong political pressure. On the other hand, the *cohabitation* (the fact that the President and the Prime Minister do not share the same political colour, a situation which calls for compromises and diplomatic arrangements) reduced the pace of the politicization process, as happened in 1993–95 and 1997–2002. This is illustrated by the proportion of prefects appointed on political criteria, i.e. prefects who do not come from the ranks of the *corps préfectoral* but from various positions, including ministerial cabinets or line administration (see Table 5.1). Political change has a real impact on the politicization rate as well as on the social profile of senior civil servants. This influence is obviously not mechanical and there has always been some latitude for professional considerations. For instance, some prefects are security professionals and hence likely to be appointed more frequently when fighting terrorism is high on the political agenda. It is also necessary to take into account the legal constraints which define the exact proportion of political appointments allowed or the social profile of each *corps* which can determine the careers of its members.

That said, it seems clear that *politics matters* even if its influence may vary significantly. The social background of ministerial department heads varies only slightly; 45 per cent of the department heads appointed by the Mauroy government in 1982 and 1983 belonged to the upper classes, compared with 52 per cent of those appointed by the Chirac government in 1986 and 1987. This minor difference is due to the professional requirements for ministerial top positions; candidates should be both 'red and expert'. However, a quick look at the ministerial cabinets tells quite another story. The ministerial cabinet members appointed by the Left government between 1984 and 1996 came from the working and middle class in large proportions: 37.5 per cent, compared with 18 per cent of those appointed by Right governments.

Thus, there is a linkage between party politicization and class but this linkage works both ways. Politics offers opportunities to those who lack the social resources to compete with the traditional members of the *grands corps*. This is clearly the case in ministerial cabinets; 43 per cent of secondary school teachers and 54 per cent of members of the private sector are actively involved in politics (as militants or holders of elected party offices), compared with 14 per cent of administrative *grands corps* representatives and 3 per cent of technical *grands corps* representatives. On the other hand, there is sometimes a cumulative process; because you are a top civil servant, you are elected at the local level; because you have strong family connections in the business world, you gain access to the Prime Minister's cabinet. Thus, 53 per cent of ministerial department heads come from the upper classes but this proportion rises to 67 per cent for those who are also local elected leaders (generally mayors of small towns) and 73 per cent for those who have been members of the Prime Minister's cabinet.

Table 5.1 Politicization and social background of prefects by major political period (%)

	Political appointments	Social Background		
		Upper class	Middle class	Working class
De Gaulle 1958	15	50	25	26
Pompidou 1969	3	55	24	20
Giscard d'Estaing 1974	7.5	53	25	22
Mitterrand 1981	26	41	28	31
Chirac 1986	15	71	15	15
Mitterrand 1988	27	53	29	18
Balladur 1993	21	54	19	28
Chirac 1995	8.5	60	19	22

Of course, this implies 'structural' politicization, rather than party politicization.

A second characteristic of this new form of politicization is that it is regulated by a political learning process; both the President and the Prime Minister, who share the constitutional power of appointment of senior civil servants, know that quick and drastic changes may raise strong protests within the senior civil service. Also, public opinion is against 'head hunting', as it is inconsistent with the ideals of a neutral public service. The 1997 Socialist government delayed such appointments in order not to expose itself to this criticism.

A third point is that whatever their number, appointments are still dominated by former civil servants. Representatives of the rest of society are always a minority compared to former civil servants. Despite the dramatic changes during the 1980s, it is difficult to see a genuine spoils system *emerging* in France.

This can be illustrated by the development of the ministerial cabinets. Between 1958 and 1972, only 6 per cent (as an average) of the cabinet members came from civil society (associations, liberal professions, political parties, private business, etc). Between 1984 and 1996, this average proportion climbed to 20 per cent and has not varied with the successive governments (Rouban, 1997). Meanwhile, the proportion of *grands corps* members within the ministerial cabinets declined dramatically from 34 per cent between 1958 and 1972, to 16 per cent between 1984 and 1996. However, 98 percent of the most prestigious positions within the cabinets, especially that of director, were still held by civil servants between 1984 and 1996. ENA graduates still make up 21 per cent of directors.

Another example is related to the career ladder of the ministerial department heads, legally appointed by ministers on a discretionary basis. Although government control over the appointments has been tightened since 1981, most of the department heads still come from the civil service. Between 1984 and 1994, only 20 per cent of them came not from the central administration but from private or public enterprises, quangos or the Paris municipality – that is, were not civil servants. As shown in Table 5.2, a huge proportion of department heads originates from within the same ministry or other ministries.

All these data indicate a social change. Generally speaking, the background of civil servants occupying political positions has changed under the various Left governments. They come more frequently from middle-class categories, especially school teachers or academia. If the number of ministers coming from the civil service remains high, the proportion of those coming from the senior civil service has fallen: to nine out of 23 under the Mauroy government of 1981 compared with 14 out of 19 during the Barre government of 1976. A few years later, things became more balanced. Left governments are still middle-class oriented but the proportion of ministers coming from the ENA, for instance, may vary considerably within the same political sphere. On the Left, only 10 per cent of ministers under the Fabius government in 1984 had an ENA background, compared with 21 per cent under the Rocard government in 1988 and 31 per cent under the Jospin government in 1997. On the Right, too, there are differences between different governments; for example, 25 per cent of ministers were from the ENA in the Chirac government of 1986, compared with 15 per cent in the Juppé government of 1995. Elite networks may differ from one government to the next, even if they share the same

Table 5.2 Origin of ministerial department heads before appointment, 1984–94 (%)

	1984–85	1986–87	1988–89	1992	1993–94	Average of the total
Same ministry, at a lower level	26	19	21	12	22	19
Same ministry, as department head	6	3	1	10	2	4
Another ministry, as department head	8	3	5	12	5	8
Ministerial cabinet	32	16	28	17	12	23
Another ministry, at a lower level	4	12	13	5	14	10
General Inspectorate	0	1	1	0	6	2
Grand corps member	3	8	5	12	9	7
Public company or quango	3	13	9	17	14	11
Private business	6	9	5	0	6	5
Paris municipality	0	8	0	0	6	2
Foreign service	12	10	9	15	5	9

Source: Rouban (1996).

political beliefs and the composition of each government is a political message informing to what extent the Right governments are more or less business oriented and the Left governments are more or less elitist.

A look at Parliament show that civil servants are still very much present within the ranks of MPs: 39 per cent in 1978, 50 per cent in 1981 and 46 per cent in 1997. Nevertheless, the sociological composition has changed because the number of teachers is considerable (36 per cent in 1981 and 25 per cent in 1997 as compared to 20.5 per cent in 1978 and 9 per cent in 1958). Thus, political life is generally still dominated by civil servants.

Towards a new pattern of relationship between public administration and politics: strategic politicization

In the 1981–88 period, the traditional pattern of relationship between senior civil servants and the political system was transformed. Two aspects of this change should be underlined.

First, the *changes* were institutionalized as subsequent governments used the same kind of mix, albeit in various proportions, between structural politicization, interconnecting networks of ENA graduates or members of intellectual clubs, and open partisanship calling for a clear linkage with political party leaders, national or local. The tendencies observed after 1981 have since been largely confirmed: a retrenchment of the administrative *grands corps*, which have become increasingly reluctant to send their members to ministerial cabinets, an increasing number of political appointments, greater vulnerability of civil servants to political change, and an expansion of quangos as well as of publicly-funded associations offering positions to political allies.

Second, this change should not be interpreted as an 'Americanization' of the Fifth Republic. In fact, it constitutes a dramatic evolution by which politicization has become more profound; that is, civil servants are more subordinate to political power. One crucial aspect of the politicization process is the creation of political networks within the public administration, controlling bureaucratic life and, sometimes, amounting to a parallel decision-making process. Such a change cannot be easily quantified as it rests on an institutional policy aiming at reinforcing political staff. A good illustration is the growing weight of ministerial cabinets. They comprised 224 members in 1975 under the Chirac government, 391 in 1982 under the Mauroy government and 332 in 1993 under the Balladur government (Quermonne, 1991; Rouban, 1997). Various proposals were introduced in order to reverse this trend. However, they did not prove successful until the Juppé government in 1995, when a reduction was introduced as a major element of a more comprehensive government reform. There were, however, still 286 cabinet members in the Juppé government. Furthermore, the Jospin government appointed more than 300 people to ministerial cabinets.

This is not, of course, the whole story. Ideally, official data should be supplemented with facts about the unknown number of unofficial cabinet members, of whom there are approximately as many as there are official members (for instance, some of these serve as shadow advisers without leaving their professional position). Moreover, staffs have multiplied; each department head in the major ministries has created his or her own cabinet. Also, *ad hoc* groups and task forces have been used systematically to support government policy. In most cases, political and policy networks can hardly be distinguished because they both rest on specific local or corporate interests and are monitored by cabinet members.

Sometimes, the two types of networks come into conflict. This happened notably in the negotiation networks set up for the EU integration process which needed expertise and technical advice as well as interbureaucratic arrangements controlled by middle-level managers, not senior civil servants. This can be illustrated by the new networks dealing with environmental protection and consumer health. Members of the cabinet or department heads have no real room for manoeuvre as they are not involved in the technical debates on new regulations. Their only function is to serve as 'gatekeepers' for the co-ordination of national and European networks. For instance, ministerial experts must obtain clearance from senior officials before they approach representatives of the European general directorates outside their jurisdiction. This situation creates a new dichotomy within the State services between those who are in charge of the day-to-day European tasks and those who serve as political controllers.

As a consequence, civil servants have lost their traditional independence and they worry about it. A survey of 500 senior-level managers substantiates the fact that a sense of growing politicization pervaded the 1990s (Rouban, 1994a). When asked the question 'Do you think that the civil service is more politicized, equally politicized or less politicized than a few years ago?', 47.5 per cent responded that it was more politicized while 45 per cent thought it was equally politicized (that does not mean of course that this politicization was not apparent a few years ago) and only 6 per cent thought that politicization had decreased. 'No answers' constituted 2 per cent.

As shown in Table 5.3, the perception of politicization of the civil service is particularly significant among members of the administrative

Table 5.3 Perception of civil service politicization by administrative professional group (%)

	Grands corps	Ministries	Field offices
More politicized	59.7	54.7	41.7
Equally politicized	38.7	40.3	48.3
Less politicized	1.6	3.6	7.3
No answer	0	1.4	2.7

Source: Rouban (1994a).

grands corps while there are, relatively speaking, more field office managers who think politicization has not changed or has even decreased.

The fact that a large number of *grands corps* members believe that the civil service is more politicized is particularly significant. The closer civil servants are to the centre of political power, the better they are placed to assess the degree of politicization. Senior civil servants who used to participate in the political decision-making process on a regular basis today feel subordinate to the political echelons of government. They also believe that they are facing a transformation of their professional role that they cannot control. Other data confirm this interpretation; senior civil servants who graduated from scientific schools are less aware of this politicization. Their scientific or technical expertise might protect them from political subordination, unlike their colleagues who received a purely administrative management training (Table 5.4).

What are the main factors behind this politicization? Answers given by the higher-ranking civil servants show that they amount to a global social trend connected with the decision-making process more than a development driven by political conflict or personal preferences (Rouban, 1994a). There are no indications of a lesser sense of State or public service (items obtaining respectively 7 per cent and 6.4 per cent; multiple responses were possible). Purely political explanations are relatively unusual. They include responses underlining the effects of the centralization or decentralization process (less than 1 per cent of the responses), the role of ministerial cabinets (2.2 per cent), the effects of political change-over at regular intervals (2.8 per cent), pressure to find good jobs for political friends (3.4 per cent); and political radicalization and a lesser sense of the State among elected leaders (4.4 per cent). Senior civil servants, by contrast, explain politicization by a transformation of the whole decision-making process. The responses are distributed between three major items:

1   'a will to implement the government programme more thoroughly' (22.4 per cent);

Table 5.4 Politicization by professional school (%)

	None	Administrative school	ENA	Scientific school	Ecole des Ponts-et-Chaussées	Poly-technique
More politicized	40.2	52.5	66.7	40	50	26.7
Equally politicized	51.6	42.6	28.7	46.7	45.5	53.3
Less politicized	6.4	3.3	2.8	8.3	4.5	20
No answer	1.8	1.6	1.9	5	0	0

Source: Based upon Rouban (1994a), new calculations.

2   'the will of elected leaders to control administrative work more strictly' (27.3 per cent);
3   'a general evolution of French society leading to the growing politicization of every debate' (37 per cent).

Thus, a majority of senior civil servants do not think that politicization can be explained only by the direct effect that political change may have on the *steering* of the public administration. Instead, taken together, the responses above to item 1 (policy implementation) and item 3 (social evolution) show that politicization is seen as the result of a new type of public action, i.e. reaction to the growing number of political controversies over politically debated issues. Civil servants have to use their professional know-how to defend or promote a government decision. They are now involved in policy advocacy, calling for both party loyalty and technical input into government programmes. A completely new element is that they have also to sell the decisions to public opinion and to public or private interest groups. This is especially the case for prefects who have to convince citizens that State interests and policies have to balance policy choices by local authorities. Ministerial managers and cabinets have to develop arguments in the media in order to get the consent of stakeholders, whether professionals, public service users or taxpayers in general.

For most members of the administrative *grands corps*, this politicization is essentially connected with a general politicization of French society. Nevertheless, a minority identify the behaviour of civil servants (their purported *neglect* of their traditional duty to the State or the public service) or of politicians (who are said to have radicalized government or to have neglected the interests of the State) as sources of politicization. By contrast, the alternative response, 'The enforcement of government decisions', is selected particularly frequently by managers working in central ministries or in field offices. Managers from the three groups underline in equal proportions the will of elected leaders to control the administrative operations, as shown in Table 5.5.

The fact that the most frequent response is 'The global politicization of debates' indicates clearly that the days when senior civil servants were expected to provide neutral expertise within a consensual political project are over. This explanation is especially frequent among members of the *grands corps* who do not think that they are involved in the policy implementation process. To them, politicization means that it is now impossible to work outside political controversy. They also point out 'political radicalization' as a negative reaction to the change they have observed during the past 10 years. For ministerial senior civil servants, politicization is mainly explained by the emergence of governmental circles in which politicians and civil servants work together in *ad hoc* project networks. The perception of politicization obviously depends on the strategic role of each professional group and its location in the State apparatus. Signific-

Table 5.5 Politicization factors by administrative professional group (%)

	Grands corps	*Central ministries*	*Field offices*
A lesser sense of the State	8.0	4.3	8.0
A lesser sense of the public service	6.5	3.0	8.0
The enforcement of government decisions	8.0	27.3	23.0
The will of elected leaders to control administrative operations	25.8	29.5	26.7
The global politicization of debates	45.0	32.4	37.7
The need to appoint political friends	3.0	7.2	1.7
A political radicalization	9.7	6.5	2.3
No answer	14.5	21.6	32.0

Source: Rouban (1994a).

antly, about a third of the field office managers in the survey decline to answer the question *about* the sources of politicization, as they are relatively remote from the political decision-making process.

The meaning of politicization has changed; it does not imply partisan politicization linked to the appointment of political friends or 'strangers' from outside, nor does it refer to the former structural politicization implying co-decision-making between politicians and 'neutral' senior civil servants who do not declare any political allegiances even if they support the global strategy of the government. Today, politicization implies active participation in policy implementation – requiring an explicit political commitment and not merely diffuse support – and administrative subordination to the senior political levels of the political decision-making process. There is now a new process of differentiation between administration and politics. This politicization can be considered as 'strategic', as senior civil servants are asked to defend political choices within specialized networks.

These networks can be identified very precisely. They connect senior ministerial cabinets and central administration department heads. The number of ministerial department heads coming directly from ministerial cabinets reached significant proportions during the various governments of the Left: 22 per cent between 1981 and 1983; 29 per cent between 1984 and 1985 under the Fabius government; 27 per cent between 1988 and 1989 under the Rocard government; and 22 per cent between 1990 and 1992 under the Edith Cresson and Pierre Bérégovoy governments (Rouban, 1996).

Senior civil servants who work within a well-identified and stable decision-making network are more likely than their colleagues who do not work within such networks to think that politicization of the public service can be explained by the politicization of social controversies. In contrast, senior managers working as 'outsiders' and not included in any networks display the classical bureaucratic reaction; they are more likely to argue that politicization is best explained by the will of elected leaders to control the work of civil servants more closely (see Table 5.6).

The strengthening of the political function at the expense of the administrative function does not mean a weakening of the professional corporatism of senior civil servants. When asked the question, 'Does membership in a prestigious *corps* favour a successful career?', respondents give a positive answer – up to 46 per cent for those senior civil servants who are not members of a political party as compared with 49 per cent for those who are. Furthermore, for senior civil servants who are members of a political club, positive responses climb to 52 per cent as compared to 40 per cent for those who are not. This means that politicization is not perceived as a threat to professional structures. Instead, it interweaves with personal career paths and offers opportunities to junior civil servants looking for professional success.

The growing weight of 'individualistic' values, be they translated into demands for more professional autonomy or more personalized rewards, is key to understanding the politicization process. There is an implicit 'demand' for (or expectation from) politicization coming from those civil servants who try to advance their career when prospects are poor due to budget cuts or the low position of their unit within the public administration social hierarchy. The politicization process would be stopped rapidly if it did not offer some rewards. For instance, a position in a ministerial cabinet usually entails opportunities for promotion, especially when civil servants are just contractual agents or belong to a low-level unit. Data show the positive effect on career prospects of service in a ministerial cabinet: of the line managers (*chefs de bureau*) who leave a cabinet, only 23 per cent get a similar job; 29 per cent get another position within or outside the public service (generally in quangos, with higher status) and 48 per cent are promoted to higher administrative positions that would be

Table 5.6 Politicization factors and participation within networks (%)

	Senior civil servants working within a network	Senior civil servants not working within a network
The enforcement of government decisions	22.3	18.3
The will of elected leaders to control administrative operations	24.2	33.3
A global politicization of debates	41.2	35.0

Source: based upon Rouban (1994a), new calculations.

unattainable in the merit system alone, as 9 per cent of these line managers enter a *grand corps* (Rouban, 1997).

The fact that the 'structural politicization' pattern has now given way to the 'strategic politicization' pattern may be further explained by two other interrelated factors. The first is the emergence of new and specialized problems on the political agenda (environment, health protection, support for the elderly or the disabled, professional training, etc.). Controversies have multiplied, the number of actors on the political arena has considerably increased while the economic dimension of public intervention (its cost and its evaluation) has become a sensitive matter. Senior civil servants remain indispensable for their social and technical expertise but they are no longer referees of the social game.

A second factor is the combined effect of institutional reforms introduced during the 1981–95 period. Decentralization and European integration have considerably modified the professional role of senior civil servants. On the one hand, decentralization has changed the strategic balance of the local political scene. Field office senior managers have henceforth to work in partnership not only with local politicians but also with local administrations whose expertise and institutional power are growing in significance. On the other hand, European integration has transformed the role of ministries. As a European decision-making process is on the way, national ministries emphasize the technical dimension of administrative activity. European integration is especially benefiting those civil servants with specialized scientific or legal skills.

Members of the *grands corps* are facing a new challenge, as they have based their social power on their ability to exert high professional mobility throughout (and outside) the State structures in the name of their generalist vocation. As the European integration process asks for more specialists, generalists are feeling displaced. They are looking for a new legitimacy, trying to give up the 'generalist' argument and promoting the 'expert' argument. Meanwhile, State Council members underline their role in the legal process, especially in the transposition of EU rules into national rules; Court of Accounts members are looking for a revival of the policy evaluation process that could give them more weight vis-à-vis Parliament as well as the government, trying to participate more actively in the managerial reform; prefects are eager to demonstrate that they are involved in local economic development as they channel EU regional funds and negotiate contractual arrangements with local authorities.

Whatever the driving force, the decentralization process and European integration require senior civil servants to work more frequently within specialized networks, in co-operation with private or public interest groups. While politicization was at odds with professional values before the Second World War, politicization and technical specialization are now linked together. In this new environment, politicization has a functional dimension as it allows the government to reduce the costs of public action. With political followers appointed to key positions, it is not necessary to modify the civil service culture, which would be a very long and risky process (if possible at all), or to spend precious time in never-ending negotiations with stakeholders. The benefits of politicization are important, as it allows the government to trust the information it receives from the grass roots, reducing uncertainty in a complex environment. Similarly, higher-ranking civil servants may use ready-to-think arguments when they are confronted with public interest groups, other European interests or their own colleagues, and they know that they will have the support of a friendly network.

These 'positive' aspects are balanced by negative outcomes that are generally underestimated because they are not mentioned officially by civil servants, even if most of them suffer as a result of politicization. These side-effects, it could be argued, include a growing climate of suspicion, as people do not easily trust each other when they do not participate in the same network; not all civil servants, even ambitious ones, can win the political game as it is not easy to synchronize with the political cycle, so some of them may be sidelined for many years. Furthermore, good professionals are ignored because they have served in politicized positions in the recent past. Similarly, politicization causes many intermediate-level managers to avoid conflict with their hierarchy and to rely on routine because they are afraid of retaliation. Of course, not all these points can be quantified but they are often raised by senior managers during interviews. On the whole, politicization is one of the consequences of the social change that has occurred since 1981 when a growing proportion of civil servants from the middle class were appointed to senior positions. This 'democratization' has undermined the cultural rules of a *bureaucratic* world dominated by corporatism as well as individual performance, not in a managerial sense but in the tradition which distinguishes the French senior civil service from that in other European countries (Schmidt, 1996).

Conclusion

Since the early 1980s, the pattern of interaction between administration and politics in France has changed. As the original pattern featuring shared power between politicians and senior civil servants has vanished, a new one has emerged, featuring a 'strategic politicization' that implies a new differentiation of political and administrative functions. This 'strategic politicization' pattern is not a step towards some kind of a spoils system. The senior public service's corporatism is still very strong. The professional culture has not been overthrown. Instead, politicization, for senior civil servants, means, first of all, a more active commitment in policy advocacy, particularly for central office managers, where State representatives have to work as partners and sometimes compete with other centres of power, and, second, a reinforcement of the political decision-making circles, notably of ministerial cabinets, leading to a measure of functional subordination for senior civil servants. This subordination is all the more sensitive as it is connected with the proliferation of management tools allowing for more precise information about the individual and institutional performances of civil servants. The frontier between administration and politics has been eroded. In the early 1980s, this frontier separated the *grands corps* associated with politicians from those administrative services involved in policy implementation. In the early twenty-first century, it separates those who participate actively in policy definition, follow-up and implementation within politicized networks from civil servants confronted with day-to-day management, users' requests and budget restrictions. This tension between the two groups is a major factor in the recurrent sectoral social conflicts within the public service in France as this dichotomization opposes bureaucratic worlds which do not understand each other. Increased politicization as a tool for co-ordination may result. On the whole, politicization is the combined outcome of both individual strategies and institutional structures. It represents a new type of public action reflecting changes in welfare theory and practice as well as uncertainty about the nature of contemporary governance.

Notes

1 *Grands corps* are specific professional groups of top civil servants, bringing together the best and brightest students from the administrative and scientific schools (Ecole Nationale d'Administration and Ecole Polytechnique). The administrative *grands corps* are: Conseil d'Etat (State Council), Cordes Comptes (Court of Accounts), Inspection Générale des Finances (General Inspectorate of Finance), Corps Diplomatique (Diplomatic Corps), and to a lesser extent the Corps Préfectoral (Prefect Corps); the technical *grands corps* are: Ponts-et-Chaussées (Infrastructure Corps), Corps des Mines (Mine Corps), Corps des Ingénieurs Télécom (Telecom Engineers Corps). For a discussion of their evolution, see Rouban (1999a).
2 Except for the Ministry of Foreign Affairs and, since 2000, the Finance Ministry, due to its complexity after its merger with the former Industry Ministry.

References

Birnbaum, Pierre (1994), *Les Sommets de l'Etat*, Paris, Seuil, 2nd edn.
Bouckaert, Geert and Pollitt, Christopher (2000), *Public Management Reform: A Comparative Analysis*, Oxford, Oxford University Press.
De Baecque, Francis and Quermonne, Jean-Louis (eds) (1981), *Administration et politique sous la Cinquième République*, Paris, Presses de Sciences Po.
Dreyfus, Françoise, (2000), *L'Invention de la bureaucratie*, Paris, La Découverte.
Hayward, Jack (1982), 'Mobilizing Private Interests in the Service of Public Ambitions: The Salient Element in the Dual French Policy Style?', in Jeremy Richardson, *Policy Style in Western Europe*, London, George Allen & Unwin, pp. 111–40.
Lochak, Danièle (1986), 'La haute administration française à l'épreuve de l'alternance. Les directeurs d'administration centrale en 1981', in *La Haute Administration et la politique*, Paris, CURAPP and PUF.

Quermonne, Jean-Louis (1991), *L'Appareil administratif de l'Etat*, Paris, Seuil.

Revue Française d'Administration Publique (1998), 'Les fonctionnaires et la politique dans les pays de l'Union européenne', 86, special issue.

Rouban, Luc (1994a), *Les Cadres supérieurs de la fonction publique et la politique de modernisation administrative*, Paris, La Documentation Française.

Rouban, Luc (1994b), 'Public Administration at the Crossroads: the End of the French Specificity?', in Jon Pierre (ed.), *Bureaucracy in the Modern State*, London, Edward Elgar, pp. 39–64.

Rouban, Luc (1996), 'Les directeurs d'administration centrale 1984–1994', *La Revue Administrative*, 289, pp. 18–31.

Rouban, Luc (1997), 'Les cabinets ministériels 1984–1996', *La Revue Administrative*, 297, pp. 253–67, 298, pp. 373–88, 299, pp. 499–509.

Rouban, Luc (1998), 'La politisation des fonctionnaires en France: Obstacle ou nécessité?', *Revue Française d'Administration Publique*, 86, pp. 167–82.

Rouban, Luc (1999a), 'The Senior Civil Service in France', in Edward C. Page and Vincent Wright (eds), *Bureaucratic Elites in Western European States*, Oxford, Oxford University Press, pp. 65–89.

Rouban, Luc (1999b), *Les Préfets de la République 1870–1997*, Cahiers du Cevipof, 26, Paris, CEVIPOF.

Schmidt, Vivien A. (1996), *From State to Market? The Transformation of French Business and Government*, Cambridge, Cambridge University Press.

Suleiman, Ezra (1978), *Elites in French Society: The Politics of Survival*, Princeton, NJ, Princeton University Press.

6 The British civil service
Examining the question of politicisation

Charlotte Sausman and Rachel Locke

This chapter examines the question of politicisation in relation to the British case. We begin by defining what politicisation means in the UK context, which might differ from its comparators. Second, we investigate how politicisation has manifested itself in the UK by applying Peters and Pierre's framework (see Chapter 1 above). In the process, a number of themes are used to describe the changes taking place in the British case in relation to people, structures, attitudes and culture, behaviour and decision-making arenas. Finally some kind of assessment of recent changes is made, which focuses on the managerial capacity of the British executive, and the constitutional implications of new roles for and new expectations of civil servants. The British civil service is undoubtedly undergoing significant current change under the Blair government, as it has since the early 1980s. However, the British case illustrates that care is required in discussing politicisation in a comparative context – much of the British system remains intact and evidence of politicisation, where it exists, is located in certain specific spheres of the state often outside the traditional civil service itself. The chapter concludes that the British picture is a complex one, best characterised as a state responding to increasingly demanding politicians while attempting to adapt to a changing social and political environment which includes a consumerist electorate and scrutinising media, at the same time as preserving the highly regarded features of intelligence, impartiality, probity, selection and promotion on merit and public duty that characterise the British civil service.

Defining politicisation and its application to the British case

We agree with Clifford and Wright (1997) that the term politicisation is taken to mean too many different things – that is, it is a convenient 'umbrella term' for many different effects, for example changing relationships, changing behaviours, changing structures. It relies on assumptions about what happened 'traditionally' or 'in the past', as if this were a single period in history and as if the traditional machinery of government were both transparent and easily understood. Descriptions of the traditional British civil service as 'impartial', 'neutral', 'apolitical' or 'objective' illustrate the difference between descriptions used in theory or statute, and observing the actual practice of what goes on in government.

Clifford and Wright (1997) define politicisation in two ways: first, that an increase in political activity is undertaken by civil servants and second, that there is increased control exerted by government over bureaucrats. Peters and Pierre in the framework for this comparative exercise (Chapter 1 above) categorise the first as 'bottom-up' politicisation and the second as 'top-down'. The usual description of the British politicisation case – although we share the problems of identification and verification – would be 'top-down'; that is, politicians attempting to assert their control over the civil service.

In terms of the former definition, there has been no increase in political activity undertaken by British civil servants. As Clifford and Wright (1997) point out, there are no criticisms of civil servants on the grounds of their party political allegiances or activities during recent decades. In a comparative analysis of politicisation it is important to state the clear and sustained difference between administration and party politics in the British case, in contrast to other Western states. Civil servants in management grades are forbidden to be paid-up members of a political party. There are occasions when civil servants become elected officials later in their careers, although they are the exception. As was pointed out in a House of Lords debate, not all retired civil servants who sit in the House of Lords do so on the Cross Benches (House of Lords Hansard Debates, Baroness Symons, 19 December 1996, column 1638). And it should be said that post-war Labour governments viewed the senior civil service as part of the 'establishment' although Thatcher as a Conservative Prime Minister also drew a distinction between her own views and those of the senior civil service establishment.

The British case is also not one in which the civil service has been replaced by a patronage system. No ministerial cabinets have been put in place and Clifford and Wright (1997) state that there was no 'purge' of the civil service under the Thatcher government, although Rhodes (1997: 90) notes the number of permanent secretaries who left the civil service in the early 1980s. There has been no significant change of senior civil service personnel since the Blair government took office. (We refer to the case of Government Information Officers and special advisers in due course.) The head of the home civil service and Cabinet Secretary has since been replaced but he was due for retirement, and stayed for a significant hand-over period after May 1997.

Much of the story of alleged politicisation in the British civil service is about increasing political control of the bureaucracy, more assertive ministers, the opportunities that a lengthy period in office will allow in terms of influencing the culture and ethos of the civil service, and power shifts between civil servants and ministers. The evidence comes in the form of patronage; supplanting the traditional mechanisms of recruitment and promotion in the civil service; a 'blurring' of tasks that should be undertaken by the civil service and those that are 'party political'; and an unwillingness to listen to the advice and counter-arguments of the civil service. It is also important in the British case to look outside the traditional civil service and outside Whitehall since structural change is important in terms of the creation of executive agencies and the huge array of 'quangos' or non-departmental public bodies that now carry out government work.

For Britain the most significant period of politicisation is alleged to have taken place since the early 1980s – during the Conservative administrations of Thatcher and Major, from 1979–97 and under the Labour government of Tony Blair, elected to its second term in 2001. The period therefore covers those civil servants still serving or in retirement. At the same time both the Conservatives and Labour are parties that have been and will be in power for a significant amount of time. This current period is an extremely interesting one because while commentators worried about the ability of officials to deal with a new Labour administration in office in 1997 after 18 years of Conservative control, there are repeated, if not increased, concerns about politicisation with changes instigated by the Blair government. This does allow us to put the case for sustained pressures on the civil service rather than focusing on the particular characteristics of the recent Conservative governments as a 'special case'.

Appointing key officials: increasing the scope for political and personal appointments

A mechanism for gaining control of the civil service is to appoint those who are faithful or sympathetic to one's cause to positions that influence or control policy. Mrs Thatcher participated proactively in the appointment procedures of senior civil servants. Richards (1997: chapter 6) attempts to assess a 'Thatcher effect' on the senior civil service in the 1980s and 1990s, using evidence from ministerial memoirs and interviews with serving and former members of the government. One of the developments he identifies is a 'personalisation' of the appointment procedures for senior civil service posts.

Various examples are given in the literature of outside appointments made to top posts in the civil service by Mrs Thatcher, including a monetarist economist from the London Business School appointed as Chief Economic Adviser, a management consultant to the post of head of the Government Accountancy Service, and the head of Joint United Scientific Holdings to the post of head of the Defence Procurement Executive (Clifford and Wright 1997: 11). What is important about these appointments is that they were made for personal or political reasons. There were also early departures, including for example two most senior civil servants who headed up the civil service when Thatcher came to power. In John Major's government, a senior official who was a member of the Efficiency Unit in Thatcher's government was removed from his post and 'retired' at the behest of the then Minister of Public Service and Science, William Waldegrave, in 1992. There was also a significant increase in the numbers of special advisers appointed.

The trends discussed here during the Thatcher and Major governments have expanded significantly with the Blair government, which has appointed special advisers to the ministries as well as party sympathisers to key posts. The Blair government has currently around 70 Whitehall special advisers, at an annual salary cost of over £4 million, more than any previous government (House of Commons Select Committee on Public Administration Fourth Report 2001: para. 6). They have been appointed at various levels in government; some for general roles, others to advise on specific policies. Table 6.1 shows the current total number of special advisers and the departments in which they work. The table shows how special advisers are concentrated around the Prime Minister, with the majority operating in either Number 10 or the Cabinet Office.

Many of the special advisers in Number 10 and the Cabinet Office occupy senior roles and it is this move by the Blair government that has prompted interest from the House of Commons Select Committee on Public Administration. Senior advisers to Blair have provoked considerable controversy since their appointment, with allegations of bullying of

Table 6.1 Number of special advisers in the Blair government

Cabinet Office and 10 Downing Street	30
HM Treasury	8
DfEE (Department for Education and Employment)	5
DETR (Department for Environment, Transport and the Regions)	5
Department of Health	2
Ministry of Defence	2
MAFF (Ministry of Agriculture, Fisheries and Food)	2
DCMS (Department for Culture, Media and Sport)	2
FCO (Foreign and Commonwealth Office)	2
Home Office	2
DSS (Department of Social Security)	2
DTI (Department for Trade and Industry)	2
Scotland Office	2
Leader of the House of Lords	2
Government Chief Whip	2
Leader of the House	2
Wales Office	2
DfID (Department for International Development)	1
Lord Chancellor's Department	1
Total	76

Source: House of Commons Select Committee Public Administration Fourth Report (2001).

other civil servants, inflated salaries, and the politicisation of advice to the government. Recently their pay structure has been reviewed, at the request of the Prime Minister, in order to bring them in line with permanent civil servants (*Public Service Magazine* 1998: 10). At the top of the pay scale are the head of the Policy Unit and two advisers to the Chancellor Gordon Brown, an economic adviser (who has since taken up the permanent secretary position of Chief Economic Adviser) and press secretary. However, three special advisers receive salaries outside these scales, two of them being advisers to Tony Blair, his chief of staff and his press secretary.

The role of Alastair Campbell, Blair's former press secretary, was significant both in terms of the enhanced role he had, facilitated by the special adviser status he held despite managing civil servants, and also because of his personal status within government. He was the Prime Minister's spokesperson but it was his own view on events and personalities within government that carried significant weight. For example he was a key player in the most significant political issue Blair has faced, that of Northern Ireland Secretary Peter Mandelson's second resignation early in 2001 regarding passport applications for two Indian brothers, the Hindujas. The press secretary was always reported as being present at and contributing to the most delicate political negotiations involving the Prime Minister and it was his press briefing which conflicted with Mandelson's account of events that led to the latter's resignation. Since Blair came to office, Campbell had provoked headlines regarding his actions and status and his is an important case to be cited in alleged politicisation of the civil service. One such incident occurred before the 2001 election was called when he made derisory comments about Conservative economic policy and was reprimanded by the Cabinet Secretary (*The Times* 3 February 2001). He stepped down as press secretary when the election was called in 2001 but after the election he resumed his post.

A government department pays special advisers as it pays the civil service, they work in a government department, and they report to a secretary of state. Unlike civil servants, special advisers are not permanent employees, they are appointed personally by the secretary of state, they may not be anonymous, and they serve their minister and the party, not the crown. Special advisers have been appointed for a variety of purposes, and from a variety of backgrounds, but their primary role is as policy adviser to their minister. With their special status, they are able to interact with ministers in a way in which civil servants are not. Their role is overtly political, communicating policy and 'politics' on a personal level with the minister, civil servants, with Number 10 and with the political party. They are involved in both the formation of policy and its communication and advocacy with other constituencies. In the former role they act as 'guardians of the political agenda which the minister came into office with'. According to a former adviser they are the minister's 'praetorian guard' (Hennessy 1997: 11–13). It is the relationship between advisers and permanent civil servants that has caused concern in the British case. For the first time, two of Tony Blair's senior advisers have managerial responsibility for civil servants. With concern increasing over the role of special advisers through Blair's first term of office, following the election in June 2001 a new Ministerial Code and code of conduct for special advisers were produced, which sets a limit of two advisers for each cabinet minister. However, Blair has extended rather than reduced the majority of special advisers who operate around the Prime Minister.

The case of special advisers is interesting because it reflects the changing demands of politicians. For example, advisers form a vital function in interacting with the media, something in which the civil service has often lacked in expertise yet which is increasingly expected of government. To this end, special advisers provide useful – and complementary – skills to civil servants and, it may be argued, protect the civil service from engaging in activities which threaten their impartial and anonymous status. It might be argued that around 70 special advisers still represent a small amount of support for the government and it is surprising that a stronger network around ministers and the Prime Minister has not developed. Perhaps what is of concern is that the function of such advisers is not clear and open, as in the case of the civil service, and yet they are public employees. There are controls on their numbers and their pay, but it is their interaction with permanent officials, especially when they occupy senior and influential positions, as many do around the Prime Minister, that is key to the question of politicisation.

Civil servants in senior positions have themselves become less anonymous during the 1980s and 1990s due to the opening up of appointments. A significant number of senior posts are advertised externally and more outsiders have been recruited in. This has been an explicit policy to encourage individuals with wider, often managerial experience to enter the civil service. Open competition is a reflection of modern managerial practise and in the early 1990s one-third of appointments were open to external candidates. External appointments have often been made to senior 'managerial' rather than policy advisory posts such as head of the Prison Service and other executive agencies. This reflected a belief among the Conservative government that the private sector was better at managing than the public sector – a belief shared by the Blair government. Blair has also sought external appointments to policy roles in specific areas such as drugs and homelessness. While positions such as Permanent Secretary, the most senior civil servant in a department, have remained insulated from these developments, there are implications such as when a high-profile chief executive reporting to a Permanent Secretary is on a higher salary. Chief executives may bypass the Permanent Secretary and report directly to the minister. The case of the Department of Health has proved interesting in this regard. In 2000 the Blair government combined the posts of chief executive of the National Health Service (NHS) with that of Permanent Secretary at the Department of Health with the appointment of a new chief executive, which meant the incumbent Permanent Secretary was removed and an NHS manager appointed to the new, combined post.

Such changes reflect the need for improved managerial capacity in government and chief executives have clear responsibilities for delivering on government targets. However, an important role of the senior civil service is to advise on policy and here the case of combining the post of senior policy adviser and executive head of the health service means impartial advice from the Permanent Secretary may be compromised.

Structural change: strengthening the core

As well as through key appointments, recent UK governments have also sought to increase their control over the bureaucracy through the manipulation of traditional structures and the creation of new ones. Underlying the changes are a desire on the part of government to ensure that bureaucracy delivers, and delivers on what the government wants. To that end we have seen consecutive Conservative and Labour governments use the creation of new organisations to try to overcome bureaucracy and 'red tape', as well as strengthening the machinery that operates around the Prime Minister. With the Thatcher government we saw deprivileging of the civil service with the alteration of structures relating to appointments and terms and conditions as well as a drastic reduction in civil service numbers. This reflected a personal mistrust of the civil service on the part of Thatcher. The Labour government under Tony Blair was elected on a platform of saving public services but the civil service has been used in key speeches to explain the Prime Minister's frustration at not achieving the change the electorate requires.

Both Thatcher and Blair have sought to increase central control of the bureaucracy. Under Thatcher the Civil Service Department was abolished in 1981. Thatcher did not consider this department of civil servants best placed to carry out her intended change of the management and efficiency of civil service functions. Also abolished was the Central Policy Review Staff. This body was set up to undertake strategic thinking but Mrs Thatcher felt this small group of civil servants produced advice that was too far removed from her government's philosophy. Instead, Thatcher looked to the advice of right-wing think tanks for policy ideas. She also created the Efficiency Unit, under the direction of the head of a leading retail chain, to undertake internal 'scrutinies' of the civil service – costings of the work it carried out.

In terms of structural changes to the centre, it is Blair, however, who has made the most significant reforms to central administration since coming into office. He has significantly increased the size and functions of Private Office, the Number 10 Policy Unit and the Cabinet Office, and brought them closer to the Prime Minister. Commentators have described Blair as centralising and 'presidential' in this regard. Certain projects are regarded as personally linked to Blair such as those on drugs and social exclusion, which warrant direct contact with him. With a second term in office Blair has further concentrated the officials and advisers working directly to the Prime Minister. Private Office and the Policy Unit have been merged to form a 'policy directorate' headed by the Prime Minister's Principal Private Secretary, with a special adviser who is head of policy. The Cabinet Office now has a 'delivery unit' headed by a former special adviser from the Department of Education and Employment, a 'forward strategy unit' headed by a former special adviser and an Office of Public Services Reform.

The use of cabinet apparatus is important for this discussion on structures because there has been a tendency to use this mechanism less in policy making. This in consequence means an increased role for the Prime Minister and key ministers and a reduced role for senior civil servants. Compared to some of her predecessors, Mrs Thatcher made less use of the cabinet structures with only one meeting of the cabinet a week and reduced numbers of cabinet committees. Hennessy (1990: 311) commented that 'without doubt Mrs Thatcher is running the slimmest cabinet machine since before the Second World War'. Under John Major the use of the cabinet was restored, Major being a more conciliatory figure himself. He sought to use the cabinet and standing committees as a means of building 'consensus through full discussion and shared policy making' (Hennessy 1998:10).

The same apparatus is now bypassed again by Blair. Once again the Number 10 Unit plays an important role in policy making and is for instance present at any comprehensive policy review. All public speeches by ministers have to be cleared by the Number 10 Unit, as also do any new policy initiatives: this attacks the autonomy of ministers (Hennessy 1998: 18). Hennessy (1998) observes the part the 'Big Four' played in government policy making in Blair's first term of office, the four being the Prime Minister, the Chancellor, the Foreign Secretary and the Deputy Prime Minister. Decisions were made by this group, which met every Monday morning, rather than by the full cabinet. This group knew about the decision to move interest rate setting to the Bank of England before the cabinet, a historic policy move taken immediately after the Blair government came to power. By way of contrast, full cabinet meetings happen less frequently, they do not often last more than an hour, there is no formal agenda and the headings that are there are not necessarily followed by Blair (Hennessy 1998: 11). An insider has commented on the current position: 'This is not a collective government. We have to accept that the old model of Cabinet government is as dead as a doornail' (quoted in Hennessy 1998: 12).

It is interesting that the balance of power has shifted with the second

Blair government. Much has been made of the power of the Chancellor and the Treasury throughout Blair's term of office, and the reorganisation of the cabinet following the election in 2001 was said to restore the balance in favour of ministers loyal to Blair.

Like Thatcher and Major, Blair has shown a preference for external policy advice, using left-wing think tanks, members of which have been brought into the government at various points since 1997. The implications of these changes for the quality of policy making have been addressed in the British literature. The fact that ministers now act more as policy initiators has contributed to what Foster and Plowden (1996) diagnose as the 'state under stress'. They argue that consultation over policy proposals has diminished and the cabinet committee system during which ministers and civil servants brokered the main differences they had over policy on its way to legislation has broken down. Policy is now decided by ministers at informal meetings to which civil servants are not invited. When policy is made in this way proper records are not taken and conflicting accounts may be given by different ministers reporting how decisions were reached. There is also no one asking awkward questions or putting alternative perspectives to ministers before their mind is made up. For Foster and Plowden, fundamentally, it has altered the long-standing relationship between ministers and civil servants: 'it further threatens the older relationship between ministers and civil servants which relied so much on trust and partnership between them, and on which the integrity and efficiency of public service so much depends' (1996: 215). These authors emphasise the importance of restoring the role of the senior civil service in policy making and reviving the older official cabinet committees in parallel with those of ministers. Otherwise there continue to be serious implications for the quality of government:

> The ministerial role in policy-making is vital and should be decisive but needs to feed upon a richer manure than the product of an introverted political process, which itself is excessively interested in presentation rather than substance, and a sensation-seeking relationship with the media. There is the danger that as ministers rely less on the civil service in the initiation and formulation of legislation that legislation will become less disinterested and more motivated by 'political' considerations.
>
> (Foster and Plowden 1996: 215)

Since 1997 these criticisms have been heightened and they are discussed further in relation to the changing attitudes and behaviour of the civil service.

Attitudes and culture: an increasingly diverse civil service

Politicisation refers to changing the attitudes and culture of the occupants of positions within the public sector and the appointment of officials on a partisan basis. For the civil service the methods of recruitment and promotion have not changed. However, it is important to talk about changes in attitudes and culture among civil servants and to look outside the civil service to the appointments procedures in the wider public sector.

There has been considerable discussion in the British case of changes to the attitudes and culture of senior civil servants in accordance with political direction. In addition to the 'one of us' criterion attributed to Thatcher for describing people who thought like her and supported her programmes, there is support for the argument that there was an impact in increasing the ratio of 'can do' civil servants. This reflects a change in role of civil servants as identified by S. Richards (1996), Barberis (1994, 1996) and D. Richards (1997) from policy adviser to policy executor through the 1980s and 1990s. Those 'wait a minute mandarins', those civil servants who were too keen to give reasons why new ideas would not work, are now said to be bypassed. The emphasis on civil servants' ability to make policies work rather than to review and analyse their feasibility has continued with the Blair government, which in two terms has set itself an extremely broad policy agenda and, as under Thatcher, there is much talk of 'driving through' policies.

Some concern was expressed in 1997 as to whether the civil service would be able to serve a new government after almost two decades of Conservative rule. The evidence from an unofficial survey of 10,000 civil servants supported this concern (Clifford and Wright 1997: 10). The results showed that 73 per cent of the sample believed that Conservative ideology had become part of the civil service culture in the previous seventeen years. As to providing politically impartial advice, some 54 per cent thought that the service could no longer fulfil this function and 71 per cent believed that senior Labour politicians were justified in warning of the 'politicisation' of the service.

Concerns were expressed by the opposition during the Thatcher years of politicisation of the higher civil service. Robin Cook, for example, said

> after a decade and a half in power, the Conservatives have surrounded themselves with senior officials who are incapable of distinguishing between their loyalty to the political ambitions of their Minister and their duty to the nation to provide a civil service about party politics.
>
> (*Tribune*, 21 January 1994, quoted in Theakston 1998: 16)

The White Paper, *Taking Forward Continuity and Change* (Cm 2748 1995), asserted that there had been no politicisation. It maintains that there is 'little doubt that civil servants would be able to demonstrate the same level of commitment to any incoming Government' and asserts its belief that 'the commitment of the overwhelming majority of civil servants to the principle and practice of a politically impartial civil service is undiminished'.

Hennessy (1999) notes in 1999 the zealousness with which the Labour government pursued the implementation of New Labour policies, the drive coming very much from the top – described as the 'Tony (Blair) wants' angle. This is based on Hennessy's (1998) perception of the Blair government as operating on the prime ministerial model (rather than cabinet model), what he terms a 'napoleonic style'. It is the role of bureaucrats to operationalise governmental policy and advise ministers in the formation of government policy. Politicians want civil servants who will implement their policies enthusiastically rather than spend more time debating their relative merits. Hennessy (1999: 5) cites the importance placed on age and getting younger civil servants to the top and also a continuation (from Conservative government) of advertising top posts externally. External candidates are regarded as having proved themselves in the 'real' world of business and commerce and of having the benefits of an outsiders' perspective when dealing with enduring managerial problems such as the relationship with powerful unions.

In addition to influencing the attitudes and culture of civil servants, there has been a new emphasis on 'management' within the civil service, a function traditionally played down in favour of policy advice. Power, responsibility and authority are delegated to agency chief executives, particularly in the case of the largest agencies: the Benefits Agency, the Employment Service, and the Prison Service. Such agencies now undertake the bulk of civil service operations and employ three-quarters of the civil service population. Chief executives appear before select committees, and deal directly with questions from MPs. Chief executives of the larger agencies speak directly to ministers about agency matters and are much higher profile when compared with the traditional anonymous civil servant. For example, an agency chief executive may speak to the media regarding the performance of his or her agency whereas traditional civil servants are rarely heard in public. When things go wrong it is now the chief executive who takes responsibility rather than the elected minister, as the case of prison outbreaks during John Major's government showed.

Finally, it is important to talk about the role of 'quangos' and other non-departmental bodies within the UK public sector since the early 1980s. Quangos or public bodies undertake a range of activities such as in health, the environment or education, and operate at the national, regional and local level. The significance of the development of quangos for the present discussion is that the government is able to control board appointments to these organisations. Weir and Hall (1994) identify 5,521 quangos to which ministers make some 70,000 appointments and which are responsible for functions previously carried out by civil servants or elected local authorities (for example, the Fundraising Agency for Schools). It was a criticism of the Thatcher and Major governments that these board appointments were made on party political grounds. The Blair government promised a reversal of this trend, but commentators point to the increase in the number of new bodies being established, particularly 'task forces', and the continuation of political appointments (Belton 1997; Daniel 1997).

The current Commissioner for Public Appointments, whose remit covers over 12,000 public sector positions, reported on the UK health service in 2000, an area of the British public sector that has been accused of politicisation ever since the creation of NHS independent hospital trusts in the early 1990s. Each trust is responsible for providing health care to NHS patients and has a board comprising five non-executive directors and a non-executive chairman (in addition to five executive directors including the chief executive); all these non-executives are appointed by the Secretary of State for Health. The same corporate structure applies to around 100 local health authorities. In 2000 there were 472 chairs and 2,373 non-executive directors on the boards of NHS trusts and health authorities and they were responsible for an overall expenditure of approximately £31 billion (Commissioner for Public Appointments 2000).

The report by the Commissioner, Dame Rennie Fritchie, found evidence of politicisation in the NHS appointments system, which threatened the selection of candidates on merit. Candidates who declared political activity in favour of the Labour Party were more successful, predominantly due to their nomination by MPs, and one in seven appointments went to local councillors, the majority from the Labour Party (Commissioner for Public Appointments 2000).

Since the report was published the government has announced that an Appointments Commission will take over non-executive NHS appointments from the secretary of state. This change has been welcomed, although it is too early to assess the independence of the new commission.

Behaviour: advocacy and accepting managerial responsibility for government policy

Changing the behaviour of civil servants is an extremely difficult process to document. We do not have clear, substantial evidence in the British case that civil servants undertake different tasks today from in the past or that civil servants are not offering impartial advice to ministers. Once again, however, there are examples of changing practice that are relevant, such as the emphasis on managerial responsibility among senior civil servants mentioned above, which has implications for their role. We must also pick up on the rare, but relevant cases where civil servants have spoken out about pressure from the government to undertake inappropriate tasks, or to compromise their position as civil servants, of which there are examples from both the Conservative and Labour governments since 1980. It is also relevant to talk about the changing policy process, the changing range of actors involved in policy making in government, and the implications of these changes for the contribution that civil servants can make to the process.

There are a number of cases where senior civil servants have been seen to cross or be led to cross the dividing line between work that is party political and policy advice (Clifford and Wright 1997: 13). In the 1980s the then head of the civil service was thought to have acted in an overtly political way during the miners' strike. His involvement in the 'Spycatcher case' led him to lie on behalf of the government. Mrs Thatcher's press secretary and her private secretary, both civil servants, were associated with the Conservative Party's approach and when Mrs Thatcher left office they followed. At a House of Lords debate on the civil service in the winter of 1996 several allegations of politicisation were lodged against the government. They included the misuse of civil servants' time in the following activities: drawing up a press release that exonerated the government after the Scott Inquiry; an NHS White Paper, *A Service with Ambitions*, which contained no legislative proposals and was argued to be no more than a 'campaigning document'; a report that assessed the proposed Labour spending plans if it was elected to office; and a proposed panel of 'cheerleaders' for government policy drawn up by the Deputy Prime Minister, which also suggested prison governors could be included in the panel, themselves career civil servants (House of Lords Hansard Debates 1996: column 1625). Before the 1997 election the head of the civil service stepped in to prevent civil servants undertaking party political tasks for the Deputy Prime Minister.

However, there have been similar allegations against the Blair government, notably in the preparation – at taxpayers' expense – of an annual report on its performance, which is partisan in language and selective in its reporting of achievements. In the election campaign of 2001 there were similar accusations of government using civil servants to undertake party political tasks when a large group of Labour MPs asked the same parliamentary question to the major spending departments, requesting details of the departments' actions in the MPs' particular constituencies. The questions (137 of them) resulted in responses detailing funding for schools, hospitals and other projects (*The Times* 20 March 2001). So there is a case for sustained pressure on the civil service in undertaking tasks for the government of the day.

We refer here to one important recent case where the lines have been blurred. The Government Information and Communication Service was the subject of an inquiry by the House of Commons Select Committee on Public Administration (1998) after a total of 25 heads of information or deputy heads of information were replaced between 1 May 1997 and 1 June 1998 – a rate of turnover described by the committee report as 'unusual' (para. 33). Traditionally staffed by civil servants from the Government Information Service, senior posts are increasingly filled by outsiders to the service, including policy officials. The Select Committee's report recognised the 'tensions between press officers and special advisers since the election', with special advisers seeking the most effective presentation of government policy while press officers – as civil servants – are unable to present government policy 'in a party context' (para. 31). Evidence to the committee heard that some press officers left because of a desire on the part of ministers for information officers to be 'less neutral' than their civil service terms allowed.

A greater role for ministers in appointing information officers was considered by a review that preceded the committee report, although the First Civil Service Commissioner pointed out the dangers of a more 'personalised' system of appointments, most particularly because of the implications for the permanent officer if a minister then moved posts. The committee made a series of recommendations, mostly requiring future monitoring by senior civil servants, including the head of the civil service. It asked the government to describe how the Strategic Communications Unit (headed by the Prime Minister's Chief Press Secretary, Alastair Campbell) 'distinguishes between legitimate activity on behalf of the Government and activity which could unduly advantage the party of government' (para. 23).

Civil servants have occasionally been involved in the political arena, with several highly publicised cases of 'leaking' or 'whistle blowing'. One famous case in the mid-1980s involved an Assistant Secretary at the Ministry of Defence who leaked information to a Member of Parliament about proposed ministerial replies to inquiries in Parliament. The government claimed that the Argentine warship, the *General Belgrano*, was on the attack when it was bombed by British troops. In fact it had been travelling away from the Falkland Islands at the time. The civil servant informed an opposition Member of Parliament that his minister was going to tell a lie and in August 1984 he was charged under the Official Secrets Act. His defence was that he was acting 'in the interests of the state' which was the equivalent to acting in the public interest. Although the judge directed the jury that 'in the interests of the state' actually required civil servants to act in accordance with government policies, the jury found the civil servant not guilty. In doing so, they were making clear that they considered the duties and loyalties of a civil servant to be different from the duties and political loyalties expected by the Thatcher government.

There are also important changes in the overall roles that civil servants now perform. Traditionally, the civil service was responsible for administering services and advising ministers on policy matters but senior civil servants are now required to act like managers. They are now more directly accountable in terms of financial and performance objectives and are more likely to be required to explain and perhaps defend government policies which they are carrying out. The influence of chief executives within the senior civil service is mentioned earlier. During a Royal Institute of Public Administration investigation into appointments and promotions in the senior civil service, fears were noted about civil servants not giving all the arguments to ministers and the 'can do' attitude: 'I sometimes think I see advice going to ministers which is suppressing arguments because it is well known that ministers will not want them, and that for me is the great betrayal of the civil service' (RIPA 1987: 46).[1]

One of the problems here is that advice to ministers may conflict with the role of the civil service to carry out the policy of the government of the day. Senior civil servants have managerial as well as policy advice functions, and it is in the former that the civil service has been criticised for a lack of competence and will. In Chapter 1 above, Peters and Pierre identify some positive responses to politicisation in respect of civil servants delivering the priorities of the government of the day. However, there are some countervailing arguments here. On the one hand, there are positive changes to the managerial capacity of civil servants; they now have a greater understanding of managing and delivering services, of government priorities, and of delivering the policy objectives of the government. On the other, there is a fine line between executing policy and actually playing an advocate role on behalf of government, which should not be the job of the civil service. Change is subtle and complex. For example, senior civil servants have become more visible. It is much harder for them to distinguish between defending their record as managers and deliverers of policy and actually being partisan supporters of the policy itself. It is difficult for the outsider to distinguish between changes of style and substance. To illustrate the changes, the following is an extract from a speech by the current head of the civil service, Sir Richard Wilson, in May 1999. The speech, entitled 'The civil service in the new millennium', highlights the shift:

> Policy making – and I will come back to this issue – was and still is important. But we now require people in public service to be good managers and good leaders of their organisations and to know how to achieve results through the people who are working for them and through the application of project management skills. They also need to have good presentational skills: to be prepared to appear in public, on television, before select committees – indeed, before yourselves – and to be prepared to give interviews to the media and to understand the needs of modern news management.
>
> (Wilson 1999)

Hennessy (1999) highlights several 'areas of concern' regarding the Blair government: 'personalisation' in terms of loyalty to Tony Blair rather than to other authorities – cabinet, or government, for example; a greater stress on age (pledge to have gifted youngsters in the civil service move 'up the ladder more quickly', quoted in the Blair government's civil service paper *Modernising Government* (Cm 4310 1999: Executive Summary); and the 'Tony wants' factor, which subverts professional detachment on the part of career civil servants and downgrades their skills and contribution.

Arenas: moving decision making out of traditional hands

The arenas in which decisions are made has altered as the locus of decision has moved outward to semi-autonomous agencies and quangos in the UK state since the early 1980s. Concern is raised in several areas: over appointments to head up such bodies, in particular the appointment of non-executive directors; over the relationships between the organisations and the centre and among the organisations themselves; over how they are held to account; and the implications for local and regional governance, when many such bodies have appointed rather than elected members and do not interact with traditional democratic arrangements.

Next Steps agencies, to whom government departments have devolved many operational functions and who operate with autonomy from these government departments, and are separately accountable, now account for more than two-thirds of civil servants. Undoubtedly, the creation of these agencies has hived off many functions that were previously the responsibility of the senior civil service in the core departments. Permanent secretaries, as heads of department, previously assumed operational responsibility for all activities within the department, in traditional lines of accountability straight to the secretary of state. Now, responsibility for most operational functions lies with the chief executives of the various agencies, or that function has been privatised. Agencification suggests a weakening of core departments in terms of size, function and influence. Indeed, the Fraser Report which reviewed the relationship between central departments ('headquarters') and Next Steps agencies recommended that once 'the Department has defined its role in relation to Agencies, the functions and staffing of its headquarters should be reduced' (Efficiency Unit, 1991, cited in Pyper 1995: 89).

In addition to departmental agencies, the government recognises 'Non-Departmental Public Bodies' (NDPBs) which may be executive or advisory bodies. When the Blair government came into office in May 1997, there were 305 executive NDPBs and 610 advisory NDPBs, making 915 in all. In April 2000, the total figure was 833, of which 297 were executive bodies and 536 were advisory. The government made a commitment to reduce the number of NDPBs but the figures show that the most important category, those executive bodies serving government departments, had fallen by only two and there are some important new bodies such as the Electoral Commission and the Learning and Skills Council which now exist and are not included in this number. The combined expenditure of the 297 executive bodies in 1999–2000 was just under £24 billion (House of Commons Select Committee on Public Administration Fifth Report 2001).

Task forces also form part of the state apparatus. They are described by the government as temporary advice-giving bodies and, because of their temporary nature, are not included in the annual lists of advisory NDPBs. They are not subject to the scrutiny of the Committee on Standards in Public Life or the Commissioner for Public Appointments. However, they are involved in public policy formulation. The Blair government has shown a particular enthusiasm for task forces and there are currently about 300 in operation. They were largely accepted because the new government was coming into power and required considerable policy support. There is now concern that many of the task forces have continued in operation beyond a proposed time-span of two years, and that if so, they should be redefined as NDPBs and be subject to the same monitoring and review. The House of Commons recently identified 52 task forces that had been in existence for more than two years, of which nine were more than three years old. They cover the range of central government departments and the devolved administrations. Twenty task forces over two years old were in the Scottish Executive (House of Commons Select Committee on Public Administration Fifth Report 2001).

In addition to the quangos operating at departmental level, there are a whole range of quangos representing the local, regional and national geographical make-up of the UK state. Various boards operate in Wales, Scotland and Northern Ireland which have been transferred from the Welsh, Scottish and Northern Ireland offices to the devolved parliament and assemblies. Such bodies are welcomed in the devolved states because of the democratic accountability that operates there. However, for the regional tier in England there are no additional checks. There have therefore been calls for a reassessment of the need for elected regional bodies in the English regions (House of Commons Select Committee on Public Administration Fifth Report 2001).

Finally, there are numerous local bodies which form part of the 'quango state' and which also fall outside many government definitions of such bodies. In health, NHS trusts and health authorities were mentioned earlier. Now the Blair government has established Primary Care Trusts, set to take over the majority of the commissioning role in the NHS. The total number of such bodies, including their counterparts in Wales, Scotland and Northern Ireland is already over 200 and there are currently over 400 Primary Care Groups in England and Wales that are set to form into Primary Care Trusts. Table 6.2 sets out the range of local bodies which may be defined as 'quangos'. They number over 5,000 and cover higher and further education, housing associations, police authorities and registered social landlords in the housing sector. The considerable number of partnerships, zones and other arrangements at local authority level have

Table 6.2 Local public bodies or 'quangos' in 2000

Higher education institutions	166
Further education institutions	511
Foundation schools	877
City technology colleges	15
Training and enterprise councils (England)	72
Local enterprise councils (Scotland)	22
Career service companies (Scotland)	17
Registered social landlords (England)	2,074
Registered social landlords (Wales)	92
Registered housing associations (Scotland)	255
Registered housing associations (Northern Ireland)	40
Housing action trusts	4
Police authorities (England and Wales)	41
Joint police boards/unitary police authorities (Scotland)	8
Health authorities (England and Wales)	99
NHS trusts (England and Wales)	373
Primary care groups (England and Wales)	434
Primary care trusts (England and Wales)	40
Health boards (Scotland)	15
Special health boards (Scotland)	8
Acute NHS trusts (Scotland)	14
Primary care trusts (Scotland)	13
Integrated acute and primary care trust (Scotland)	1
Health and social services trusts (Northern Ireland)	19
Health and social services councils (Northern Ireland)	4
Health and personal social services boards (Northern Ireland)	4
Advisory committees on JPs (UK)	119
Dartmoor Steering Group (Ministry of Defence)	1
Total	5,338

Source: House of Commons Select Committee on Public Administration Fifth Report (2001: Table 6).

yet to be scrutinised by committees. For example, there are 'Action Zones' in the areas of employment, health and education that distribute funds from central government, and are made up of local partners from various organisations.

At the local level the House of Commons report into quangos was critical of local and regional bodies in terms of accountability, consultation and openness, citing failure to undertake measures such as publishing annual reports, allowing agendas and meetings to be available and open to the public, and consulting the general public. The report found poor links remained between local bodies and elected local authorities and was worried about the lack of co-ordination and accountability within such a 'quango state' where each body pursues its own interests and agenda:

> This [damage to local democracy] is an issue which troubled the
> Committee at the time of its last Report and we remain concerned

that, despite welcome moves by government to create links between new local bodies and local authorities, there are dangerous gaps in accountability at the level of local governance. We return to our earlier recommendation of 'a regional structure of accountability' to provide monitoring and oversight of many quangos at regional and local level. ... The regional dimension of the quango state is expanding fast and new responsibilities are already being piled on the new regional development agencies. But these developments are not bedded down in democratic arrangements.

(House of Commons Select Committee on Public Administration
Fifth Report 2001)

So the development of quangos and other such bodies cause concern in that they are increasingly responsible for significant areas of government spending and yet there is no clear mapping of them, along with their responsibilities and accountabilities, which would aid co-ordination. The direct concern over politicisation of the public sector is that such bodies have appointed or self-appointed leaders. The spread of such bodies at the local and regional level creates gaps in accountability at the level of local governance, which promotes the case for elected regional assemblies in England, to match the democratic structures in Wales, Scotland and Northern Ireland.

Discussion: evaluating politicisation in the British case

In this section, we examine the implications of the politicisation debate in the British case. The difficulties of identifying politicisation have already been raised in this chapter. These difficulties endure when the consequences of politicisation are considered: how can we be measured in our statements about its consequences?

In the British case there are a range of organisations and regulations that have either an explicit or an implicit remit to monitor politicisation. They include: codes of conduct such as the Ministerial Code, a code of practise for ministers, and the Civil Service Code; parliamentary select committees such as Public Accounts Committee and Public Administration Committee; the Committee on Standards in Public Life set up in 1994 under Lord Nolan to examine concerns about standards of conduct in public office; an independent Commissioner for Public Appointments set up in 1995 who is responsible for monitoring the process of ministerial appointments to the boards of public bodies such as health bodies and the nationalised industries; the Audit Commission and the National Audit Office; the Office for Civil Service Commissioners; and the parliamentary ombudsmen. The last four organisations do not have an explicit remit to capture politicisation but are part of the internal regulation and monitoring of British government.

In the British case politicisation has been addressed by successive parliamentary committees. The Treasury and Civil Service Committee began an inquiry into the role of the civil service in 1992. Its first report in 1993 highlighted several concerns about the civil service:

> (i) Concern about whether the management changes in the civil service in recent years, most notably the Next Steps initiative, have had fundamental implications which were not anticipated at the time the reforms were initiated; (ii) concern about the impact on the civil service of the market testing initiative and the possible privatisation of some civil service functions; (iii) concern about whether the formation of a higher civil service is suitable both for its management tasks and for the provision of good policy advice to ministers; (iv) concern about an alleged deterioration in standards of conduct in the civil service; (v) concern about the implications for the civil service of a fourth successive election victory by the same political party.
>
> (cited in Drewry 1994: 592)

The committee produced several reports during the 1990s, culminating in a recommendation and draft of a new civil service code, which has since been put into practice. The Public Service Committee and the Select Committee on Public Administration have both reported on the civil service, the former on ministerial accountability and responsibility (1996) and the latter on events concerning the Government Information and Communication Service (1998).

A House of Lords Select Committee produced a wide-ranging report on the public service at the beginning of 1998. It had been asked to consider the impact of 'recent and continuing changes and their impact on standards of conduct and service in the public interest' (House of Lords Select Committee on Public Service 1998: para. 1). The topic of politicisation was not addressed by the report, but its general conclusion was that the civil service, having been through a profound and sustained set of structural changes, needed an assessment of its current position, including evaluation of the impact of those changes. The report was specifically prompted by the privatisation of the Recruitment and Assessment Service in 1996. Of particular relevance to the politicisation debate, the report considered the impact of political advisers to ministers and the effect of outside appointments to the civil service. On political advisers the report did not identify negative evidence, but warned against the 'blurring' of areas of activity between political advisers and civil servants, which it thought would be damaging to the neutrality and independence of the civil service.

The House of Commons Select Committee on Public Administration Fourth Report (2001) investigated special advisers and recommended greater clarity and transparency in their recruitment and the funding of posts as well as limits on the extent to which senior advisers exercise exec-utive authority (currently three have this authority). However, the com-mittee also recognised in its evidence the contribution that special advisers make. Concern was raised about the creation of an alternative network within the civil service – where advisers talk to other advisers rather than to civil servants – and the implications of this network for the role of private offices for ministers, but the committee did not recom-mend changes to the working of special advisers other than to endorse the Neill Committee (on Standards in Public Life) recommendation of a Code of Conduct for Special Advisers.

So there is a range of bodies which undertake to monitor politicisation in the British case. It is interesting that taken on their own, many of the developments that are included in the case for politicisation are wel-comed. The civil service needed to improve its record of managing so as to keep pace with the demands of the electorate in relation to public ser-vices. In its investigation into special advisers the Public Administration Committee acknowledged, as did its expert witnesses, the contribution that special advisers make to government. However, the concern in the British case is that changes to the civil service, and to the wider state, should not impact negatively on systems of accountability, impartiality and, more recently, openness in the executive. Perhaps one of the reasons for the negative view of politicisation in the British case is that change has not been overt; it is what Peter Hennessy (1999: 5) describes nicely as 'creeping politicisation'. The subtle and implicit changes in the nature and function of the British civil service – particularly the senior civil service – are what commentators and wider members of the government and the executive fear.

Politicisation is viewed negatively because it attacks in discrete ways the values and traditions of the civil service. The traditions of the British civil service – in particular, the ability to 'speak truth to power' – are interpreted as important constitutional elements. Commentators associate a period of alleged politicisation with a decline in policy, giving examples of 'policy dis-asters' which took place because senior bureaucrats were not able to speak truth to power (see Dunleavy 1995). The poll tax, the arms to Iraq affair (which led to the Scott Inquiry) and BSE are important episodes in govern-ment that are cited in this context. In the Blair government the recent San-dline case involving the Foreign Office may also be included.

While there is acceptance of some negative qualities of the senior civil service, which include resistance to change and poor managerial capacity, their wealth of experience in the policy process is viewed as a considerable asset, and an important counterbalance to the enthusiasm and also naivety of the elected politician. In the case of policy failures, it is argued that senior civil servants are not listened to, or feel unable to give advice which goes against government plans, and therefore policy ends up being insuffi-ciently examined and tested, particularly for possible negative outcomes.

There are those who argue that the consequences of politicisation are, in fact, deeper than style and managerial capacity. Change threatens the civil service itself, its constitutional role and the traditional separation between party, government, state and parliament in the British political system. The difference between 'politics' and 'government', 'party' and 'government', 'parliament', 'state' and 'crown', and 'party of government' in terms of loyalties of the civil service were the subject of a constitutional debate in the House of Lords prior to the 1997 general election:

> My definition of the Crown – the British state – is Queen in parliament, which is to say that a civil servant's loyalty is not just to the government of the day but to Her Majesty's Government as represented by the state continuing and all Members of Parliament. Part of what has gone wrong in the past 10 to 20 years has been Ministers attempting to use civil servants to deceive Parliament, to disguise from Parliament and to withhold information from Parliament. We cannot get the structure of our Civil Service right unless we also tackle the reform of Parliament.
>
> (House of Lords Hansard Debates 1996: column 1655)

Hennessy (1999), along with many others, including members of the present House of Lords, calls for a Civil Service Act to avoid politicisation in the future and to preserve the 'Gladstonian' traditions of the civil service. Hennessy notes the current 'blurring' of the separation between Prime Minister, government, party, crown and parliament:

> a piece of primary legislation embodying the Northcote-Trevelyan/ Gladstone principles of an impartial, permanent Civil Service (with the detailed Code attached as a schedule that can be updated) would serve as an important defence against any future attempt to politicise the British Civil Service. Primary legislation can only be overridden by another piece of primary legislation.
>
> (Hennessy 1999: 5)

Calls for a Civil Service Act reflect the fact that alleged politicisation and blurring of constitutional lines has all happened implicitly. So Britain needs more explicit measures to set down, and therefore protect, the rights and duties of civil servants, particularly in relation to ministers. However, much of the history of the civil service has been the development of accepted norms and practices, and although a Civil Service Code has been put in place, a Civil Service Act would go against those traditions. Another view is that if politicisation has indeed been 'creeping' and concerns day-to-day practices within government, a Civil Service Act in parliament may not provide much protection against subtle changes in style, ethos and working practices.

Conclusion

The beginning of the second term of the Blair government is an interesting time to examine the question of politicisation. Debate about politicisation was raised during the sustained Conservative period in office from 1979 to 1997 during which considerable reform of the civil service took place. However, during the relatively short period that the Blair government has been in office, concerns about politicisation have been as acute as they were prior to 1997. We can find evidence for politicisation in the areas of: increasing scope for political and personal appointments around the Prime Minister and in the wider state; a strengthening of the core, particularly in Number 10; a civil service opening up to outside appointments; the acceptance of responsibility for government policy; and changes in the location of decision making in the British state. For some commentators, such changes represent a constitutional threat. It is important to note that politicisation continues to be examined by select committees and to be subject to parliamentary debate. We conclude that the British case is a complex one. There is evidence of a state responding to increasingly demanding politicians while attempting to adapt to a changing social and political environment made up of an electorate with rising expectations of public services and a scrutinising media. At the same time there is universal support for preserving the highly regarded features of intelligence, impartiality, probity, selection and promotion on merit and public duty that characterise the British civil service.

Note

1 Quotation by a civil servant taken from an earlier RIPA report, *Is the civil service becoming more politicised?*, of 1985.

References

Belton, T. (1997) 'Beyond quangocracy' *New Statesman* 18 July 1997.

Barberis, P. (1994) 'Permanent secretaries and policy-making in the 1980s' *Public Policy and Administration* 9, 1, 35–48.

Barberis, P. (1996) *The Elite of the Elite: Permanent Secretaries in the British Higher Civil Service* (Aldershot, Dartmouth).

Clifford, C. and Wright, V. (1997) 'The politicisation of the British Civil Service: ambitions, limits and conceptual problems' (Unpublished paper, Nuffield College, Oxford). (French translation appeared in special issue of *Revue Française d'Administration Publique* 86, April/June 1998.)

Cm 2748 (1995) *The Civil Service: Taking Forward Continuity and Change* (London, HMSO).

Cm 4310 (1999) *Modernising Government* (London: The Stationery Office).

Commissioner for Public Appointments (Dame Rennie Fritchie) (2000) *Public Appointments to NHS Trusts and Health Authorities* (London, The Stationery Office).

Daniel, C. (1997) 'May the taskforce be with you' *New Statesman* 1 August 1997.

Drewry, G. (1994) 'The civil service: from the 1940s to 'Next Steps' and beyond' *Parliamentary Affairs* 47, 4, 583–97.

Dunleavy, P. (1995) 'Policy disasters: explaining the UK's record' *Public Policy and Administration* 10, 2.

Foster, C. D. and Plowden, F. J. (1996) *The State Under Stress: Can the Hollow State Be Good Government?* (Buckingham: Open University Press).

Hennessy, P. (1990) *Whitehall* (London: Fontana Press).

Hennessy, P. (1997) *The Prime Minister* (London: Penguin).

Hennessy, P. (1998) 'The Blair style of government: an historical perspective and an interim audit' *Government and Opposition* 33, 1, 3–20.

Hennessy, P. (1999) 'The British civil service: the constitution of Mr Gladstone's legacy as the century turns' *The Stakeholder* 3, 3 (July/August), Supplement.

House of Commons Select Committee on Public Administration (1998) *Sixth Report, The Government Information and Communication Service, 1997–98* (London: The Stationery Office).

House of Commons Select Committee on Public Administration Fifth Report (2001) *Mapping the Quango State* (London, The Stationery Office).

House of Commons Select Committee on Public Administration Fourth Report (2001) *Special Advisers: Boon or Bane?* (London, The Stationery Office).

House of Lords Hansard Debates (1996) 19 December 1996 Columns 1622–68.

House of Lords Select Committee on Public Service (1998) *Public Service Report*, HL 55, 1997–98 (London: The Stationery Office).

Public Service Magazine (1998) 'Cunningham reveals aides' pay' 1, 9, 10.

Pyper, R. (1995) *The British Civil Service* (Hemel Hempstead, Harvester Wheatsheaf).

Rhodes, R. A. W. (1997) *Understanding Governance* (Buckingham, Open University Press).

Richards, D. (1997) *The Civil Service under the Conservatives, 1979–1997: Whitehall's Political Poodles?* (Brighton, Sussex Academic Press).

Richards, S. (1996) 'New Labour – new civil service?' *Political Quarterly* 67, 4, 311–20.

RIPA (Royal Institute of Public Administration) (1987) *Top Jobs in Whitehall: Appointments and Promotions in the Senior Civil Service* (London, RIPA).

Theakston, K. (1998) 'New Labour, New Whitehall?' *Public Policy and Administration* 13, 1, 13–34.

The Times (2001) 'Campbell faces new calls to resign' 3 February 2001.

The Times (2001) 'Labour "using Civil Service for electioneering"' 20 March 2001.

Weir, S. and Hall, W. (eds) (1994) *Ego-trip: Extra Governmental Organisations in the UK and their Accountability* (London, Democratic Audit and Charter 88).

Wilson, R. (1999) 'The civil service in the new millennium' (Speech given to senior civil servants, May 1999). Accessed via Cabinet Office website at: www.cabinet-office.gov.uk/1999/senior/rw_speech.htm, 5 October 1999.

7 Politicization in the United States

B. Guy Peters

The history of the civil service in the United States has been a battle against political domination over the selection of public employees. By the time of Andrew Jackson's presidency (1828–36) the "spoils system" was well institutionalized and virtually all positions in the federal government were in the gift of politicians (White, 1965). From cabinet officers to the lowest clerk, federal employees were beholden to a politician for their job, and much the same was true for state and local government. The populist sentiment that motivated the spoils system was strong, and to some extent remains strong, in the United States and turnover in public offices along with changes of presidents was justified as a means of keeping government responsive and close to the people. The spoils system also, of course, con-tributed to the capacity of politicians to build personal and party support among the public.

As well as limiting efficiency and continuity in the delivery of govern-ment programs, the spoils system often created favoritism in the way in which the clients of government were treated. Again, however, the distrib-ution of benefits was justified as a means of building political careers and political parties (Johnson and Libecap, 1994). The spoils system also created a number of disappointed office-seekers, one of whom assassi-nated President James A. Garfield in 1881.[1] The assassination of President Garfield was followed closely by the passage of the Pendleton Act in 1883. This piece of legislation put forth the guiding principles of the merit system and has been the foundation of a career civil service for the federal government (Ingraham, 1995).

Although the merit system began with the adoption of the Pendleton Act, that system initially was applied to only about 10 percent of federal employees, basically those in the lowest-level positions and in large organizations. The more remunerative positions, and especially positions with a role in making public policy, remained in the gift of political leaders. Over the decades the coverage of the merit system was extended, often through an out-going administration's "blanketing in" their appointments to prevent their being replaced by the incoming adminis-tration. By the end of World War II the large majority of federal employment was covered by some form of merit selection and management.[2] This development of the civil service occurred at the same time as the institutionalized presidency was developing and more opportunities for political appointments were becoming available within the White House itself (Karl, 1979).

The result of the development of the administrative system in the United States is an almost paradoxical mixture of overt political selection and control and extreme commitment to merit and depoliticization. On the one hand, almost all the top positions in government – at present over 4000 positions – are held by political appointees. On the other hand, the remaining public employees are selected by a rigorously enforced merit system and are subjected to numerous restrictions on their political involvement and activities, most notably the Hatch Act (see below). The Office of Personnel Management and the Merit System Protection Board are charged with maintaining the integrity of the merit system, with other institutions in place to pursue any significant violations of the concept of political neutrality.

The American public sector therefore is an attempt to balance the virtues of neutral competence and responsive competence (Aberbach and Rockman, 1994). On the one hand the system has been designed to ensure that most positions in government are not affected by political considerations. On the other hand there are a substantial, and growing, number of positions that can be handed out for political reasons, with the intention of ensuring that the administrative system will follow the direction of the leadership in government. The above two versions of public employment have existed side by side successfully for some years, but political changes since the 1980s have placed pressure on that peaceful coexistence.

Given the overtly political nature of appointments at the top of the pyramid in public organizations, the meaning of politicization in the United States is somewhat problematic (see Chapter 1). The issues that animates the discussion of politicization in other democratic political systems are to a great extent settled in the United States. It is clear, and generally accepted by the players within the system, that those several thousand positions at the top of government will be open to political appointment. In many ways the openness about having numerous political appointments depoliticizes politicization. That is, both major political parties accept the notion that incumbent leaders will have the opportunity to select their own people and be able to place them at the top of federal organizations. This "government of strangers" (Heclo, 1974) is justified in terms of the responsiveness of the political system to changes in party control, as well as the desire to keep government more closely linked with civil society. This openness is very different from the European debates in which politicians may use various subtle techniques to gain control over the senior civil service appointments.

On the other hand, politicians have continued to debate expanding or contracting the number of political appointments at the margin. Both academics and practitioners have expressed concerns about attempts to expand the number of political appointments, and to create political positions that could be used primarily to exercise generalized political control over civil servants. These are in contrast to line positions involved directly with the work of the agencies to which they are appointed. Further, there are a number of concerns about attempts by the George W. Bush administration to remove civil service protections from federal employees, and to utilize performance management systems to enforce, or at least to encourage strongly, political conformity (see below). Further, some critics of the emerging public management system in the federal government have argued that the continuing emphasis on contracting out public services may be a means of using public funds to create a more politically compliant work force. Of course, the employees performing contracted services are not formally in the public sector but they will continue to perform functions that are public, that had been performed by government, and that are paid for by public expenditures. These emerging forms of politicization are subtle, but they still threaten to alter the rather delicate balance of power toward political control of many aspects of the public administrative system that have been meant to be depoliticized.

The other aspect of politicization of the civil service in the United States that differs from most other industrialized democracies is that the US civil service has two political masters – Congress as well as the President. In the other industrialized democracies the debate over politicization is largely around the capacity of a prime minister and his/her associates to use political appointments to undermine the neutrality of the civil service. In the United States the quest for a responsive bureaucracy centers on the executive branch, but the legislative branch certainly has something to say about the management of the public bureaucracy. One role for Congress in managing the civil service has been to limit the capacity of the executive to make patronage appointments, and to institutionalize more fully the merit system in the face of attempts to create a more "administrative presidency." Micro-management is the other Congressional response to increased attempts by the executive to control federal employment, organizations, and policy. Lacking the capacity to place their own people in positions with those organizations, legislators can mandate reporting and oversight, and write detailed procedural regulations to achieve the same level of control (Rourke, 1993; Gilmour and Haley, 1994).

This chapter will examine the political recruitment of top public officials in the United States and also examine the continuing pressures toward even more political appointments of public officials. Presidents coming into office often promise to make fewer political appointments and to reduce the size of the Executive Office of the President, and especially the personal staff of the President. Once in office, however, they find that the pressures and opportunities for appointments are too great to resist. In addition to political appointment at the top of government, we will discuss the desires on the part of some political leaders to eliminate or reduce the protections available to public employees through the civil service system. The proposed changes in employment practices are not justified or discussed in terms of increasing political control of the bureaucracy, but the consequences of the change may well be to expand the use of political criteria in the selection, and especially in the management, of public employees.

The impermanent executive: political appointment at the top of government

Even after the merit system was extended to its current level of coverage, there was still a much larger number of political appointments than would be found in other democratic systems. When President George W. Bush assumed office in 2000 he and his cabinet officers were able to appoint approximately 4500 people to positions in government. Many of these employees would be in positions that would be occupied by career public servants in other democracies. In particular, political appointments extend down several levels into the management of departments and agencies, and perform managerial as much as policy advice functions. Therefore, the President and his administration are assumed to be capable of gaining substantial control over the machinery of implementation, as well as over the machinery of policy formulation. The President also has a substantial personal staff in the Executive Office of the President (Hart, 1995) and these officials can be used as a "counter-bureaucracy" to control the permanent bureaucracies.[3]

Several scholars have pointed to the increasing level of politicization in the federal government. Paul Light (1995) has pointed to the "thickening" of government, as a number of new positions have been created that are being filled by political appointment. Likewise, Patricia Ingraham et al. (1995) found that at least under Reagan and to some extent under Clinton, the administration created a number of new political positions. These positions were being created differentially in agencies that are the most politically sensitive, e.g. the Environmental Protection Agency and some parts of the Department of Health and Human Services. The apparent logic in the selective use of appointees is that if the President and his administration are to be held accountable for the outcomes in these sensitive policy areas they want to be certain that they have sufficient control to produce the types of outcomes that they set out to when elected (see also Light, 1995, 88–92).

It would be easy to overplay the importance of partisanship in presidential appointments. Those appointments made by the President and his associates certainly do involve political criteria, but there are often also other criteria involved in the selection of individuals. First, the issue is now generally not expertise *or* political reliability, but rather expertise *and* political affinity with the administration. As Hugh Heclo (1978) first noted over twenty years ago, the executive branch is now surrounded by issue networks composed of experts who are interested in influencing policy and/or serving in government. There may be Democratic or Republican ways of doing the policy, but both parties require expertise.

When there is a change of government the individuals who have been in the administration tend not to disappear from the policy scene but to remain involved in their policy area. They may take positions in think tanks in and around Washington, in the consulting firms that surround Washington (the "Beltway Bandits"), in universities, or in lobbying organizations. At one point in history the majority of political appointees may have been purely political hacks who would return home after a stint in Washington, but making and implementing public policy is now more professionalized and more expert. Some experts will move in and out of government several times in the course of their career, developing both greater expertise and more political contacts.

Second, there had been some tradition of appointing at least a handful of individuals with links to the "out party" to posts in the administration. In some cases – *mirabile dictu* – this was done simply because they were the best people for the job. In other cases the selection may be more strategic, being a means of maintaining good relationships with the other party, especially on issues such as foreign and defense policy that until recently have been conducted in a relatively bipartisan manner. That tradition has been in decline with the increased partisanship of American government, so that the past several administrations have had virtually no appointees from outside their own party, and even have favored certain wings within their party.

The thickening of government described by Light appears to involve some movement back toward more strictly political officials being placed in positions of control over organizations in the federal government. Part of the thickening has been simply "jobs for the boys (and girls)." Also, as American government has become more ideological and party loyalty has become more important, administrations have felt the need to impose more direct command over government. The offices that are being created tend to have little direct line authority over policy or programs but rather are in a position to monitor policy activities and to attempt to insure compliance with the administration's programs.

Oddly enough, the addition of a number of new appointive posts in the federal bureaucracy may actually dilute rather than enhance the capacity of the President to exercise control over the bureaucracy. As the number of layers between the president and line operatives in government increases, the number of stages required to get the President's programs across to the lower echelons also increases. Therefore the proliferation of

political appointments may permit cabinet secretaries and lower-level officers to run more of their own show, and to insulate themselves to some
extent from presidential control. That assumes, of course, that these
appointees want that autonomy and are not just good foot soldiers for the
President.[4]

Although there is a high level of political appointment in the federal
executive branch there is also a strong belief in a depoliticized, merit
system for the vast majority of federal employees. There is a substantial
legal and institutional apparatus to defend the merit system, and to some
extent that apparatus has been strengthened. The reforms implemented
during the Carter administration (Ingraham and Ban, 1984) separated
the implementation aspects of the merit system – testing, hiring, etc. –
from the adjudication of claims against unfair treatment in an attempt to
strengthen the system. Even with reforms of testing and of implementing
the ideas of merit, that concept has remained cenral to personnel management in the federal government.

In addition to the basic principles of the merit system, the Hatch Act
was adopted to prevent career civil servants from being involved in partisan political activity. This piece of legislation prohibited almost all political activities by civil servants other than voting. The idea behind that
legislation was to remove the civil service almost entirely from the political
process, and therefore prevent their political "masters" from placing pressure on them for political involvement and campaigning. Over the past
several decades legislation has been adopted to permit civil servants to
engage in political activities so long as they do not run for office or use
their positions to advance partisan political causes.

Increasing politicization

As noted, there have been increasing pressures, and increasing opportunities, for politicization of the public service in the United States. The most
important pressure for increasing political control has been the increasingly ideological nature of American politics. There is no clear date for
marking that change but it could be identified rather clearly in the Nixon
administration, the Reagan administration, and then again after the
Republicans won the House of Representatives in the 1994 election and
began to press their "Contract with America." In all these cases a more
ideological group of politicians came to Washington with agendas for
transforming the prevailing policy regime, and saw the bureaucracy as a
major barrier to that transformation. It is not surprising that all three
cases involved the Republican Party, given that part of the belief system of
that party has been that the area within the Beltway is dominated by liberals and Democrats.

The Nixon administration set out to create what has been called "the
administrative presidency" (Nathan, 1984). The strategy that evolved was

to use administrative means to overcome opposition from Congress to the policy ideas of the administration and to use the Executive Office of the President, and later loyalists appointed to positions within the bureaucracy, to overcome opposition from the career bureaucracy. The belief that opposition would be coming from the bureaucracy was deeply entrenched in the Nixon administration, and the evidence was at that time that the bureaucracy was indeed heavily Democratic in its policy preferences and its voting behavior (Aberbach and Rockman, 2000, 108).

During the Reagan administration there was also a clear sense among the political appointees that the bureaucracy they inherited was not overtly political but was tacitly committed to the policy agenda of the Democratic Party (Aberbach and Rockman, 1994). Therefore, that administration attempted to impose control over the bureaucracy and to impose its own policy agenda through the bureaucracy (Savoie, 1994). The number of political appointees was increased and the administration attempted to use a variety of monitoring and management devices to ensure that the bureaucracy did what the political level in their organizations wanted. In addition, the administration applied an "ideological litmus test" to its appointees to an extent that was not evident in previous administrations.

The Civil Service Reform Act of 1978 – "Carter's Gift to Reagan" – facilitated the administration's attempts to politicize the civil service. The Act created a Senior Executive Service (SES) from what had been the "supergrades" of the civil service. In exchange for the opportunities for bonuses and for additional responsibilities, the Act removed some civil service protection. In addition, the President became able to appoint 10 percent of the general SES.[5] Most of the individuals appointed to these positions were already members of the civil service, but they had to be willing to accept a political appointment and were to be chosen for political reliability. In addition, the President and cabinet officers were given more capacity to move senior civil servants around within government and could in the process use appointments to gain control of programs or to punish and reward individual SES members. Finally, this legislation created a merit pay system of bonuses that can be used to reward outstanding performance by members of the SES. The fear raised then, as well as subsequently, is that "outstanding performance" could be taken to mean close conformity with the political ideas of the superior.

The manner in which members of the Senior Executive Service are selected also provides an important mechanism of control for the President and his appointees. The members of the SES are selected by executive resources boards composed largely of non-career officials. These boards have the opportunity to shape the senior public service in determining not only the quality of the career officials but also their political leanings. The evidence is that this power was used rather effectively in the Reagan administration to attempt to reorient the Senior Executive Service to be more amenable to Republican policies (Aberbach and Rockman, 2000, 20).

Reform and the potential for politicization

Although the manifest attempts at politicization were evident in the Nixon and Reagan administrations, the reforms introduced during the Clinton administration opened the door for some enhanced political control over public employees. The National Performance Review made a number of specific suggestions, but its fundamental goal was to debureaucratize and reform what was considered a stultifying system of rules and controls. Given that fundamental premise about the problems of the public sector, a logical response was to begin to deregulate the internal management of the civil service (DiIulio, 1994; Peters, 2000, Chapter 5). In particular, the formal set of rules governing the hiring, firing, and disciplining of career employees were weakened, with agencies being given the ability to develop less formalized and uniform means for personnel management, provided the basic concept of merit was honored.

The second Bush administration

As did the Reagan administration, the second Bush administration came to office assuming that the civil service was in essence Democratic. After eight years of a Democratic administration Republicans assumed that the putative general disposition of the bureaucracy toward an activist government would have been reinforced by the Clinton administration. All administrations appear to have some need to influence the bureaucracy but those needs are exaggerated after the opposing party has had a long run in control of the presidency. Further, Republicans have tended to assume that the career bureaucracy was more receptive to the policy paradigm of the Democratic Party than to that of the Republicans. The evidence is that the senior bureaucracy has become at least as partial to the Republican program as to the Democratic (Aberbach and Rockman, 2000, 57), but the belief about Democratic dominance persists. Therefore, the Republican administrations perceive a much greater need to impose direct controls over the bureaucracy than would be the case in Democratic administrations.

This administration proceeded rapidly to fill all the positions that were available to it, and to apply its own versions of ideological litmus tests to candidates for positions. The evidence is that the second President Bush, unlike his father, has been concerned with putting true believers into the available positions, rather than using the positions for more clearly patronage purposes (see Ingraham *et al.*, 1995). The ideology that has been applied by the Bush administration has been to some extent different from that employed during the Reagan administration, with the focus being more on the social policy agenda than on economics as under Reagan.

The Clinton administration discontinued performance bonuses for political appointees, believing that it was inappropriate to reward political officials who would be in government for only a short period of time in the same way that career public servants were rewarded. The Bush administration is reinstating bonuses for some appointees – notably the non-career SES members – using executive orders rather than legislation to implement the change. Critics fear that this plan will place more pressures for political conformity on the appointees and on the civil servants with whom they work. Performance may well come to be defined by acceptance of the political goals and means of the administration rather than more public interest or efficiency criteria.

The emphasis on performance management that is at the heart of President Bush's management agenda (Office of Management and Budget, 2002; Sanger, 2001; *The Economist*, 2002) is therefore a potential backdoor opportunity for the politicization of the federal work force, or at least increased political influence over the actions of career employees of the federal government. Performance in public sector organizations is to some extent quantifiable, but it is also to some extent subjective (Bouckaert, 1984). Therefore, the managers who are permitted to determine the extent to which individuals or organizations have performed well are able to shape the meaning of "performance" (de Bruijn, 2002). The General Accounting Office as a part of the negotiations surrounding the Government Performance and Results Act to some extent defines the standards of performance for federal government organizations but the standards for individual contributions to the organization remain more subjective.

Another policy initiative from the Bush administration may also utilize apparent competition among public employees as the means of enhancing political control over the career civil service. The President has proposed making approximately 850,000 federal jobs subject to competition from private sector providers in order to (in his statement) enhance efficiency and reduce costs (Stevenson, 2002). These positions would remain in essence public jobs but the selection of the employees and administration of the reward system would be managed outside the civil service system by contractors (Krugman, 2002).[6] A similar plan has already been approved for most of the employees of the newly-created Department of Homeland Security (Parks and Cochran, 2002), with almost 100,000 employees losing their civil service protections when they were moved into the new department. The justification for this change in the status of employees in Homeland Security is that the sensitive nature of their positions, and the requisite commitment to national security goals, make them inappropriate for civil service or union membership. Interestingly, however, most career employees of the Department of Defense are still managed under the civil service system, and the Central Intelligence Agency has its own merit system analogous to the civil service.[7]

The reforms being implemented by the second Bush administration are to some extent simply a continuation of the administrative reforms instituted during the Clinton administration, when the rigidity of the civil service system was attacked as a central component of the National Performance Review – the Gore Commission (Kettl and DiIulio, 1995). That said, the proposed changes emanating from the Bush administration are substantially more extensive than those introduced through the Gore Commission. The figure of 850,000 employees moving into partially privatized employment is apparently a real target for the second Bush administration, and would amount to moving approximately half of total federal employment out of formal civil service employment. The argument being made by the Bush administration on behalf of this change is that these employees are working in programs, or in positions, that have clear analogues in the private sector, and hence could be managed better by utilizing private sector principles. In this view the goal of efficiency trumps all other goals in the management of public programs and the personnel within them.[8]

Politicization and advisory committees

The politics of the United States have often been described as non-ideological, and that characterization has probably been correct for most of recent history. However, as ideological fervor has tended to decline in much of Europe, it has increased in the United States (Stonecash *et al.*, 2003). There has been a pronounced economic component within the ideology that has become more operative in American politics, as the economic policies of Ronald Reagan and George W. Bush have indicated clearly. The dominant element of contemporary ideology, however, has been concerned with social issues such as abortion rights, the treatment of homosexuals, and the role of religion in public life (Peters, 2003, Chapter 11). Given the centrality of that dimension of ideology, politicization of government has come to mean not only putting Democrats or Republicans into public positions but also putting ideologues committed to certain social policy agendas into the offices that are most likely to influence social policies.

The importance of conflicts over social policy, or "culture wars," has been evident in American politics since the early 1990s. For example, during the Clinton administration there was a controversy over Dr. Jocelyn Elders' appointment as Surgeon General of the United States, given her strongly pro-choice stances and her overt advocacy of birth control.[9] The importance of commitments by nominees to certain positions on social issues has become more evident in the second Bush administration as a number of appointments to advisory committees of the Food and Drug Administration and the National Institutes of Health have gone to religious conservatives who appear to be using their positions to advance their agendas (Weiss, 2003). The most egregious case has been Dr. W. David Hager's appointment to an advisory committee on women's health. He is a qualified gynecologist but has made his negative views on all forms of artificial contraception widely known, as well as writing about the power of prayer to cure all manner of health problems (*Washington Post*, 2002). In short, the critics of the administration have been arguing that appointments to these positions are being made for ideological, political, or even religious reasons rather than for professional reasons.[10]

Although the source of the ideology in operation is perhaps less clearly defined, analogous forms of politicization have been noted in appointments in defense and intelligence programs. Again, the style of politicization is less overt partisan control of appointments and more the selection of personnel who are likely to support a particular view of policy. In particular there has been an attempt to create intelligence and defense policy analysis that might be more "hawkish" on issues of terrorism and the Iraqi threat than are many employees within the Department of Defense or the various intelligence agencies. Rather than shaping policy *per se*, politicization through encouraging ideological agreement on these positions may be more important as an attempt to influence public opinion to support the administration in its foreign policy initiatives. Appointments to advisory committees and other public boards are one of the least visible aspects of the federal government structure, and the individuals appointed to these positions are by no means full-time public employees. Despite their apparently insignificant role, these appointees can be important in shaping public policies. The Food and Drug Administration (FDA), for example, relies on professional committees for advice on a number of important policy issues, and given the specialized nature of the decisions that must be made by this organization the expert panels are likely to have a significant impact on the final decisions made by the FDA. Virtually all federal departments and agencies utilize advisory committees for some aspects of their role in making policy, but the ones associated with organizations such as the Department of Health and Human Services (including the FDA) have been the most popular targets for the attentions of, and politicization by, the social conservatives in the Bush administration.

Conclusion

Politicization in the United States must be understood in a rather different context than politicization in the other countries surveryed in this volume. First, there is a historical legacy of the spoils system and the populist belief that public sector jobs should be widely available, rather than controlled by a career elite. In practice the socio-economic characteristics of appointees of both parties would make them members of the elite, but they are not a single permanent group dominating government. Second, and more importantly in the twenty-first century, the political appointment of several thousand individuals at the top of the pyramids of the federal agencies is widely accepted by almost all participants in government. Finally, there are strong political pressures coming from the second President Bush to privatize, or at least partially privatize, as many federal jobs as possible. This proposal would seriously undermine the civil service system and potentially open the door to subtle forms of politicization.

In addition to the above pressures toward greater politicization, the demands for greater performance management in federal organizations are now functioning as a mechanism for enforcing a political agenda throughout the career civil service. The people who are in positions to define the criteria of adequate or excellent performance in carrying out duties in the civil service are able to influence the behavior of the individuals who will be rewarded or punished on performance grounds. This use of performance management will not make the career civil servants political appointees but it will enable political officials to enforce political criteria and also potentially to influence the behavior of civil servants in office to be more responsive than responsible. The conduct of politicization in American government is different, but the general question of how political leaders can control civil servants is the same.

Notes

1 Abraham Lincoln said that every time he gave out a job he created ninety-nine enemies and one ingrate.
2 The white-collar civil service is covered by the General Schedule system and blue-collar employees by the Wage System. There are also separate personnel systems for the Post Office, the Tennessee Valley Authority, the CIA, and several other smaller agencies.
3 For example, the National Security Council in the Executive Office of the President shadows the Departments of State and Defense and gives the President a better chance of countering the programmatic preferences of those organizations. As noted, much of the expansion of the presidency began with Franklin D. Roosevelt during the Great Depression and World War II.
4 The CEO management style of George W. Bush appears to depend upon substantial delegation, but within the context of personal loyalty and agreement on basic political principles.
5 Most members of the SES were in the general part of the service; approximately 8 percent are in the technical component.
6 This shift would be analogous to the "compulsory competitive tendering" that was put into place by the Conservatives in the United Kingdom, although this program applied primarily to local governments.
7 The cynic might argue that the President was simply using the uproar over terrorism and domestic security as a convenient justification to achieve other goals for management within the federal government.
8 For a critique of this approach see Stein (2000).

9 George W. Bush's nominee for Surgeon General, Richard H. Carmona, was criticized for having little or no public health experience and as being selected primarily for his reliability on issues such as abortion (Stolberg, 2002).

10 While appointments to these committees might be thought to be an opportunity for patronage there appears to have been some attempt to create balance historically (Kerwin, 2000). In part, the Federal Advisory Committee Act mandates inclusiveness on these committees, especially when they are directly involved in rule-making.

References

Aberbach, J. D. and B. A. Rockman (1976) "Clashing Beliefs Within the Executive Branch: The Nixon Administration Bureaucracy," *American Political Science Review* 70, 456–68.

Aberbach, J. D. and B. A. Rockman (1994) "Civil Servants and Policymakers: Neutral or Responsive Competence?," *Governance* 7, 461–9.

Aberbach, J. D. and B. A. Rockman (2000) *In the Web of Politics* (Washington, DC: The Brookings Institution).

Barr, S. (2002) "Agencies Chipping Away at Civil Service Monolith," *Washington Post*, December 22.

de Bruijn, H. (2002) *Managing Performance in the Public Sector* (London: Routledge).

DiIulio, J. (1994) *Deregulating Government* (Washington, DC: The Brookings Institution).

The Economist (2002) "The CEO Presidency," June 15, p. 34.

Gilmour, R. S. and A. Haley (1994) *Who Makes Public Policy?* (Chatham, NJ: Chatham House).

Hart, J. (1995) *The Presidential Branch*, 2nd edn (New York, NY: Chatham House).

Heclo, H. (1974) *A Government of Strangers* (Washington, DC: The Brookings Institution).

Heclo, H. (1978) "Issue Networks and the Executive Establishment," in A. King, ed., *The New American Political System* (Washington, DC: The American Enterprise Institute).

Ingraham, P. W. (1995) *The Foundation of Merit: Public Service in American Democracy* (Baltimore, MD: Johns Hopkins University Press).

Ingraham, P. W. and C. Ban (1984) *Legislating Bureaucratic Change: The Civil Service Reform Act of 1978* (Albany, NY: State University of New York Press).

Ingraham, P. W., J. R. Thompson and E. F. Eisenberg (1995) "Political Management Strategies and Political/Career Relationships: Where Are We Now in the Federal Government," *Public Administration Review* 55, 263–72.

Johnson, R. N. and G. D. Libecap (1994) *The Federal Civil Service and the Problem of Bureaucracy* (Chicago, IL: University of Chicago Press).

Karl, B. (1979) *Executive Reform and Reorganization in the New Deal* (Chicago, IL: University of Chicago Press).

Kernell, S. and M. P. McDonald (1999) "Congress and America's Political Development: The Transformation of the Post Office from Patronage to Service," *American Journal of Political Science* 43, 792–811.

Kerwin, C. (2000) *Rule-Making*, 2nd edn (Washington, DC: CQ Press).

Kettl, D. F. (1996) *Civil Service Reform: Building a Government That Works* (Washington, DC: The Brookings Institution).

Kettl, D. F. and J. DiIulio (1995) *Inside the Reinvention Machine* (Washington, DC: The Brookings Institution).

Krugman, P. (2002) "The Payoffs from Privatization," *The New York Times*, November 18.

Light, P. C. (1995) *Thickening Government* (Washington, DC: The Brookings Institution).

Nathan, R. (1984) *The Administrative Presidency* (New York, NY: Wiley)

Office of Management and Budget (2002) *The President's Management Agenda* (Washing, DC: O M B).

Parks, D. J. and J. Cochran (2002) "OMB Burns Midnight Oil Trying to Plan for Homeland Security Department," *CQ Weekly* 60 (October 12), p. 2636.

Peters, B. G. (2000) *The Future of Governing*, 2nd edn (Lawrence, KS: University Press of Kansas).

Peters, B. G. (2003) *American Public Policy: Promise and Performance*, 6th edn (New York, NY: Chatham House).

Rourke, F. E. (1993) "Whose Bureaucracy Is This Anyway? Congress, the President and Public Administration," *PS: Political Science and Politics* 26, 687–92.

Sanger, D. E. (2001) "Trying to Run a Country Like a Corporation," *New York Times*, July 8.

Savoie, D. J. (1994) *Reagan, Thatcher, Mulroney: In Search of a New Bureaucracy* (Pittsburgh, PA: University of Pittsburgh Press).

Stein, J. G. (2000) *The Cult of Efficiency* (Toronto: Anansi Press).

Stevenson, R. W. (2002) "Government Plan May Make Private Up to 850,000 Jobs," *New York Times*, November 15.

Stolberg, S. G. (2002) "Senators Ask Bush Nominee About Record and Ability," *New York Times*, July 10.

Stonecash, J. M., M. D. Brewer, and M. D. Mariani (2003) *Diverging Parties: Social Change, Realignment and Party Polarization* (Boulder, CO: Westview Press).

Washington Post (2002) "Abortion Opponent Appointed to Panel on Women's Health," December 31.

Weiss, R. (2003) "New HHS Panel Makeup Draws Ire of Patient Advocates," *Washington Post*, January 5.

White, L. D. (1965) *The Jacksonians: A Study in Administrative History* (New York, NY: Macmillan).

8   The search for a responsive bureaucracy in Canada

Donald J. Savoie

Canada may not be a one-party state, but it is not far from it. The Liberal party has been described as Canada's natural government party and well it might be.[1] The party has held power for fifty of the years since 1935 and it is poised to stay in office for the foreseeable future. To be sure, the Liberal domination of the national government has forged a special relationship between politicians and career officials. This chapter reviews the relationship between politicians and career officials in the Canadian government, documents recent developments and seeks to determine to what extent the public service has been politicized.

Liberal domination has not prevented ministers, however, from both parties that have held power from searching for ways to make the public service more responsive to their wishes. This was particularly true when the Progressive Conservative party held power under Brian Mulroney between 1984 and 1993. But it has also been true for the Liberal party during the Trudeau (*c.*1968–84) and Chrétien (*c.*1993–2004) eras. The search has taken various forms but the goal has been the same – ensuring that the government's policy objectives are pursued with enthusiasm. This is all the more remarkable given that both the Liberal and Progressive Conservative parties occupy the centre of the political spectrum and hold similar policy objectives. The objective, it seems, is more one of avoiding being captured by the bureaucracy than ensuring that the bureaucracy pursues the party's policy goals and implements its party platform.

This chapter looks at the efforts of Canadian politicians to secure a more responsive public service. It deals with issues raised by B. Guy Peters and Jon Pierre in Chapter 1 above. Accordingly, it assesses the degree of politicization in the Canadian public service, the application of the merit principle and the extent to which career officials are required to perform tasks that might be better performed by political aides.

Looking back

Although Canadian political institutions have their roots in British tradition, the administrative practices found in the Canadian public service reveal both British and American influences. In the case of the merit system, for instance, the influences have been predominantly American.[2] The Canadian battle to rid government of the political spoils system took place at about the same time as the British and American ones. By the early 1900s, it had become clear that Canada's national government needed people with the skills to carry out more complex tasks, and reformers pointed to developments in Great Britain and the United States for inspiration. Moreover, the call for dealing with political patronage began to fall on attentive ears among the general public, which started to comprehend the great value of 'efficient administration' and appreciate the wasteful results of patronage.[3]

The Canadian reformers finally won the day in 1918 when nearly the entire civil service and virtually all appointments were placed under the Civil Service Commission. The mandate of the commission was strengthened and a new system of classification and pay was introduced. On this front, Canada would look to the American system for inspiration. It did not, for example, recognize a distinct administrative class to which young university graduates would be recruited. It sought to classify positions 'minutely', according to specific duties and tasks.[4] Thus, a strong central agency was born, one which would hold partisan political patronage in check and which would create a distinct administrative space for career officials to provide policy advice to their political masters and to administer government programmes.

The Canadian public service did witness a golden era. Indeed, there was a time, not long ago, when Canada's civil service was regarded as one of the best in the world. In *The Ottawa Men*, J.L. Granatstein documents the kind of civil service that served the Canadian government between 1935 and 1957. One can make the case that the golden era extended to the early 1970s, albeit with some difficult moments during the Diefenbaker years (1957–63). The era was characterized by a relatively small, not well-paid civil service that shared a profound belief that public service was a civic virtue, a vocation.

The mandarins of that era clearly understood that they only possessed a 'power of a sort'. Here, Granatstein explains: 'The Ottawa Men lacked the ultimate power that comes from the ballot box: the power to move men. All the mandarins had, essentially, was influence on politicians.'[5] Career officials knew this intuitively, as did ministers. Granatstein argues that this explains why senior public servants such as Jack Pickersgill, Lester Pearson, C.M. Drury and Mitchell Sharp eventually left the civil service for partisan politics. They appreciated that partisan politics and the civil service occupied different territory. In short, career officials who wanted to be politicians and make policy decisions left the public service and ran for Parliament. Those civil servants who stayed were driven by one objective, to serve 'their minister well'.[6]

On the public policy front, Canadians emerged from the Second World

War determined never to permit another depression of the kind witnessed in the 1930s. By war's end, the public's belief in the ability of government to intervene and to manage the economy was high. Large latent demand and rapid population increase, combined with the realization that the government management of the war effort had been successful, gave them *carte blanche* to expand. Canadians had learned during the war that governments were able, in moments of crisis, and when moved by an all-consuming goal, to lead the country to high levels of economic activity and employment. Not only had the allies won the war but unemployment had fallen to zero, and yet prices had been held down. Growth of productivity and real GNP had accelerated, inequalities among social groups diminished, civilian consumption actually increased, there were no balance of payment crises, and foreign exchange rates remained stable. When the war ended, everyone was prepared for measures to avoid a return of the depression years. But the expected severe economic downturn did not materialize and the measures proved unnecessary. Still, governments (in particular, the federal government) were now convinced that they possessed a new arsenal of economic policies to achieve high employment and generally to manage the economy.[7]

Canadians also believed that they had in place the required machinery of government to deliver the right mix of public policies. Politicians knew that they were in charge and welcomed the advice of the senior mandarins. Again, politicians and senior civil servants knew each other well and were comfortable with one another. Mitchell Sharp, a deputy minister who later became a senior cabinet minister, reveals that there existed a particularly strong relationship between the minister and his deputy minister. He explained that policy was prepared by the deputy minister and his associates, while the minister decided what was politically saleable and what was not.[8]

The process worked well in large part because it was simple and straightforward. Politicians and bureaucrats ran their distinct worlds as closed shops, keeping important information off limits to outsiders. In any case, Canadians had little interest in getting inside information. Trust in the ability of government to do the right thing was high. There were precious few voices calling for access to information legislation. Nor did politicians and bureaucrats have to concern themselves with affirmative action programmes, or official languages legislation. It was a world akin to a small village where everyone knew everyone else, knew their own space in the general scheme of things and how to get things done without fuss.

In brief, the village that provided a home for civil servants and politicians was small, accessible, comfortable for them and, in its day, an effective mechanism for governing. The doctrine of ministerial responsibility worked well and politicians and civil servants had, for the most part, a strong working relationship. Ministers did not complain that career officials had too much influence, and they saw little need to change things.

But things did start to change in the environment of politics, in the nature of political leaders and in government operations.

The role governments played in society fell out of favour in many western countries during the early 1970s, and a slowdown in economic growth coupled with rising inflation gave birth to a new and dreaded word, *stagflation*. One concern was related to the apparent inability of governments to deal simultaneously with the issues of unemployment, inflation, balance of payments and debt. Another concern extended to the apparatus of government itself – specifically, the bureaucracy, which by now was regarded as a barrier against, rather than a vehicle for, progressive change. Those few who still argued against tampering with the existing machinery of government and its 'armies' of entrenched officials were dismissed by both political left and right. Even people who had supported the ideas and social welfare programmes of leaders such as Franklin Roosevelt, Clement Attlee, Hugh Gaitskell, T.C. Douglas and Adlai Stevenson were now calling for changes to the apparatus of government.[9]

Canadian politicians from both the right and the left had become critical of bureaucracy by the 1970s. The right-of-centre Progressive Conservative party had long been suspicious of the public service, and their suspicions turned to public criticism after the Joe Clark government lost a confidence motion in Parliament in 1979 after only a few months in power. They lost the subsequent election, and Flora MacDonald, minister of External Affairs in the short-lived government, went on the lecture circuit to denounce senior public servants, claiming that they employed clever ruses to push their own agendas and to circumvent cabinet and ministerial direction. She itemized what she termed the officials' entrapment devices for ministers, which included bogus options and delayed recommendations. Joe Clark himself became critical of the public service and spoke of misguided programmes 'concocted by a small group of theorists' within the public service.[10]

That members of the Progressive Conservative party would be critical of the public service surprised few people. It was, however, a different story to find leading members of the Liberal party also doing so. The Liberal party, which held office for forty-six of the fifty years between 1930 and 1979, had struck a particularly close working relationship with the public service. They had built Canada's welfare state together, and by the 1970s some were even arguing that an incestuous relationship had developed between the ruling Liberals and the senior civil servants. It therefore surprised more than a few people when the deputy prime minister, Allan MacEachen, reported that if Liberals had learned anything during their brief stay in opposition it was that his party would no longer rely as much as it had on the advice of senior public servants. Other senior Liberals joined in and publicly criticized the policy advisory and management capacities of public servants.[11]

Ministers in the Trudeau government began to voice concern that they were no longer in charge. One minister in the Trudeau era spoke of his experience when he was first appointed to the cabinet:

> It's like I was suddenly landed on the top deck of an ocean liner and told that the ship was my responsibility. When I turned to the captain (i.e., deputy minister) I was told that he was appointed there by someone else and any decision to remove him would be made elsewhere ... When I asked for a change in the ship's course, the ship just kept on going on the same course.[12]

Another minister in the Trudeau government revealed that:

> I found it very difficult to communicate, to seek out advice, when I needed it. I felt that the ritual of the paper work – the chain of command – made it virtually impossible to get the kind of information I needed when I needed it and I felt very helpless.[13]

Ministers were also making the point that their role in the policy process was much too limited. They argued that their role was essentially limited to saying yes or no to what their departments wanted. They insisted that saying no was a negative power and consequently they were hesitant to exercise it. They wanted to be present when policy options were being considered and not be relegated to a policy role after the fact, or when the die had already been cast. These observations were all the more relevant because they were made by Liberal cabinet ministers, of the party which, as already noted, held power for much of the twentieth century and which had become quite comfortable with bureaucratic influence.

Looking for responsive policy advice

Political leaders in Canada, as in other Anglo-American democracies, came to the conclusion that the civil service lacked the ability or the willingness to provide sound and unbiased policy advice, that it had its own agenda, and that they could never secure the kind of advice they wanted to ensure that the public sector could or would actually change course.[14]

They began to insist on responsive competence or at least on a proper blend of neutral and responsive competence. Career officials, meanwhile, were left to square this development with the basic values of their institutions as derived from the traditional tenets of Whitehall: an anonymous, neutral and merit-based career service designed to promote detached, non-partisan and objective policy advice. For some, these values would die hard, if die at all. Indeed, a federal government task force on values and ethics, chaired by a former deputy minister of Justice, and inspired by the work of Aaron Wildavsky, stressed as recently as 1996 the importance for career officials to 'speak truth to power'.[15]

At about the same time that politicians were seeking to make policy advice more responsive to their views and their policy agenda, policy making became more complex. New organizational sites or space in the form of think tanks and research institutes were born which broke the monopoly career officials had on the provision of advice. Modern technology served to make information on virtually any public policy issue more accessible. Think tanks, lobbyists, consultants and interest groups are now all able to access information quickly and many are able to analyse it as well as anyone in government. As Patrick Weller argues, 'policy advice, once an effective monopoly of public servants, is now contestable and contested.'[16] Career officials were also being challenged on other fronts: the shift towards a more collective policy-making process and the growing dominance of the prime minister and his office in that process; the pervasiveness of public opinion polling to provide policy answers; the need to make policy on the run to accommodate 'news breaks' from more aggressive media; and policy overload and the interconnected nature of public policies.

A new model would emerge in Canada which is probably not much different from developments in other western democracies – a model that would force career officials to look outside their departments to shape new policy measures. By choice or not, politicians would henceforth look to several sources for policy advice, not just to their senior departmental officials. Career officials would no longer be allowed to occupy the policy advisory space by themselves. If nothing else, this allowed ministers to turn to a variety of sources to test the policy advice of their career officials.

Mulroney

On coming to power in 1984, Prime Minister Brian Mulroney decided to introduce a chief of staff position in all ministerial offices. Mulroney's decision had one purpose – to check the permanent officials' influence on policy. The position was established at the assistant-deputy-minister level and government press releases described the position as an 'official in the American style'.[17] Although both senior government officials and outside observers argued that the move was incompatible with Canada's machinery of government, Mulroney pressed ahead with his decision.[18]

Mulroney was concerned that the machinery of government he had inherited would be resistant to change and in particular to his conservative policy proposals. Officials, one senior Mulroney adviser explained, 'should get back to their real job – to implement decisions and see to it that government operations run smoothly and leave policy to us'.[19] There is no doubt that many of Mulroney's key ministers and advisers were pushing him to go even further on this front. It is worth quoting at length a senior minister in the Mulroney government on this matter:

Something is basically wrong with our system of government. We are
the only ones elected to make decisions. But we do like the British.
We move into government offices with no support. Everything in
these offices belongs to the permanent government. We are only vis-
itors, barely trusted enough not to break the furniture. I prefer the
American way. Politicians there move in with their own furniture
[their own partisan advisers] and run the show for however long they
are elected to office. Then they move out with their furniture to let
the next crowd in. I have discussed this with the Prime Minister and so
have many of my colleagues. But, you know, this kind of thinking so
upsets the bureaucrats that he feels he cannot go much further than
he has. Appointing chiefs of staff was seen in many quarters in the
bureaucracy as a revolutionary act – no, an act of high treason.[20]

All ministers had a chief of staff within days of Mulroney's coming to
power. His transition team had put together a list of potential candidates
for ministers to pick from as they were appointed. The chiefs of staff,
however, had a mixed reception, often dependent on the quality of the
incumbent. They introduced a new level between ministers and permanent officials, which gave rise to a number of misunderstandings and
complications. In some instances, the chief of staff acted as a mediator
between the minister and permanent officials, screening advice going up
to the minister and issuing policy directives going down to officials,
much to the dismay and objections of deputy ministers. Many chiefs of
staff took a dim view of the competence of permanent officials, while
senior officials took an equally dim view of chiefs of staff. The arrangement, one official said, 'has on the whole hardly been a happy or a
successful one'.[21]

A former Prime Minister's Office staff member explains why the position was created. She writes that it 'was in large measure created to act as a
check on bureaucratic power, to enable the government to do what it was
elected to do'.[22] She makes it clear that chief of staffs could 'offer policy
advice over and above that provided by the department [and that] he or
she could achieve this in part by soliciting opinions different from those
held by the departmental advisors'. If the chief of staff had little expertise
in the department's policy field, then the minister was encouraged to hire
one or more additional 'senior policy advisor'. She adds that the chief of
staff 'provided an interesting challenge to the deputy minister and the
department in terms of policy development and control'. Though the
verdict on the experiment was mixed, it did have an important impact on
the policy process. One student of government explains:

While data gathering and basic analysis was still being done within
most departments, in general those involved in policy work were
much more cautious in how they cast their findings or how their

findings were utilized within their departments. Alternatively, they simply called what they were doing something other than policy analysis.[23]

Mulroney, like Margaret Thatcher, also expanded the scope for appointing outsiders to senior positions.[24] Though he was never able to attract as many outsiders as he had initially hoped to serve as deputy ministers, he did bring in a number of high-profile individuals, notably Stanley Hart as deputy minister at the Department of Finance. In addition, within twenty-four months of assuming power, Mulroney made certain that all deputy ministers who had survived the change of government or remained in government had new positions.

Mulroney was not the first prime minister to turn to appointments to make the civil service more responsive. When Trudeau appointed Michael Pitfield as clerk of the Privy Council and secretary to the cabinet, he sent out a clear signal that he valued responsive competence more than neutral competence and that he had difficulty in accepting the notion that the civil service was a self-governing body. Until the Pitfield appointment, there was strong support among the community of deputy ministers for the one among them chosen to become clerk and secretary to the cabinet. This was true for Arnold Heeney, Norman Robertson, Bob Bryce and Gordon Robertson. They stood above their colleagues in qualifications and experience. In addition, Heeney and most of his successors up to Gordon Robertson (who held the appointment from 1963 to 1975) saw the focus of their role and functions more properly tied to the cabinet than to the prime minister.

Pitfield, as clerk-secretary in 1975, would change the role for ever. Trudeau and Pitfield had, for many years, maintained a close friendship. Trudeau appointed Pitfield at the age of thirty-seven and, in so doing, overlooked more senior public servants who had served for many years as deputy ministers both in line departments and in a central agency. Pitfield's experience in government, meanwhile, had largely been acquired in the Privy Council Office (PCO). The contention is that Pitfield turned things upside down, and instead of seeing the clerk of the Privy Council as representing the public service to the prime minister and cabinet, he represented the prime minister to the public service. The argument also is that no clerk since Pitfield has been able to revert to the old understanding of the role. If Arnold Heeney successfully resisted Mackenzie King's desire to make the secretary to the cabinet 'a kind of deputy minister to the Prime Minister', or 'the personal staff officer to the Prime Minister', secretaries to the prime minister from Pitfield to today have not been as willing to resist the desire of the prime minister to make the position 'a kind of deputy minister to the Prime Minister'.[25]

When Joe Clark came to power in 1979, he fired Pitfield as being 'too partisan'. Colin Campbell writes that 'when Trudeau restored [Pitfield] to clerk-secretary after his return to power [in 1980], he confirmed definitively the politicization of Canada's top bureaucratic job.' Campbell adds that the fall and rise of Pitfield 'tipped the scales toward the conclusion that the Trudeau–Pitfield friendship has short-circuited the distance that previously existed between the prime minister and a clerk-secretary'.[26]

In his memoirs Gordon Robertson reports that when reviewing the list of possible successors, he wrote next to Pitfield's name 'too soon. Michael has not yet established the necessary credit and respect in the public service generally.' Robertson adds with obvious regret that Pitfield's appointment had become a contentious issue in the House of Commons and in the media. Joe Clark, then opposition leader, asked the prime minister to make a statement 'outlining the principles to be followed in appointments to the senior public service . . . and show whether the elevation of Michael Pitfield indicates a replacement of the merit system by the buddy system'.[27] The media also raised concerns over the politization of the public service at the highest levels.[28]

Mulroney also moved important parts of the machinery of government outside the sphere of influence of career officials. Although during the election campaign he was careful not to commit his party to privatizing any crown corporations, there was a flurry of activity on this front within weeks of his coming to power. He established a ministerial task force on privatization and later an Office of Privatization and Regulatory Affairs to manage the various activities associated with privatization and deregulations more effectively. The minister of Industry declared after less than two months in office that the government would sell all assets of the Canada Development Investment Company within a year. The assets included large concerns, including de Havilland, Canadair, Teleglobe and Eldorado Nuclear. Addressing the issue of privatizing crown corporations, the minister of Finance declared in his first budget that 'Crown Corporations with a commercial value but no ongoing public policy purpose will be sold.' The government also moved quickly to put other corporations up for sale and to dissolve a handful that were either not active or in direct competition with other levels of government.[29]

Chrétien

Chrétien, on coming to power in 1993, abolished the post of 'chief of staff' for ministerial offices, though he was careful not to do so when it came to his own office. In abolishing the chief of staff position in ministerial offices, he made the case that his government would value the work of public servants more than the previous government. However, he continually sent out mixed signals on this issue. For example, in reference to the work of the Canadian military in Afghanistan, he explained: 'They have to do their jobs. It's not a bunch of bureaucrats, these soldiers. They have to do their job. And after that, they report.'[30] In any event, the chief of staff post introduced a new dynamism to Ottawa that still lingers today. Executive assistants to ministers in the Chrétien government did not enjoy the same salary levels that chief of staffs to ministers in the Mulroney government did. But much as during the Mulroney years, some executive assistants did not hesitate to challenge the views of career officials on policy. Consultations with career officials in Ottawa suggest that relations between ministerial exempt staff and career officials changed after Chrétien came to power but only at the margins. Some executive assistants, much like some chiefs of staff, worked well with career officials while others did not. Most tried to influence policy and some were successful while others were not.

Loretta J. O'Connor, in 1991, outlined the major tasks and functions of a chief of staff. There is precious little in her description that did not apply to the role of executive assistant in the Chrétien government. Executive assistants, like chiefs of staff, are the senior political advisers to the minister, act as director of operations and controller for a minister's office, and ensure that ministerial directives are carried out within the department to increase ministerial control and accountability.[31] It is also important to recall that ministers under the Trudeau government had started to expand the role and size of their offices long before the Mulroney government came to office.[32] For example, Lloyd Axeworthy, as minister of Transport in the early 1980s, had 'a staff of about seventy-five', we are told, 'to bend the operations of his department to his political will'. The seventy-five staff members amounted to 'two or three times' the usual staff complement for a cabinet minister. The breakdown included '31 seconded from government, 12 term civil service staff and 16 exempt staff'.[33] Lastly, recent consultations with senior officials with the Public Service Commission reveal that ministerial executive assistants in the Chrétien government were ranked for staffing purposes at the Executive Category (EX) 2 or 3 level. This level is considerably higher than was the case in the Trudeau years or before the chief of staff concept was implemented.

The Chrétien government, if anything, increased the government's willingness and capacity to look outside government departments and agencies for policy advice rather than rely on career officials. Paul Martin, for example, took great comfort and pride, as minister of Finance, in making use of private sector figures instead of relying exclusively on his officials to forecast budgetary revenues. In his December 2001 budget speech, he declared:

> as in the past, we have consulted some 19 private sector forecasters to obtain their best estimates of the economic outlook. Based on that survey, we then consulted with the chief economists of Canada's major chartered banks and then leading forecasting firms to discuss the most recent numbers and their implications for this budget's economic and fiscal projections.[34]

Martin decided to turn to outside forecasters shortly after being appointed minister of Finance. The huge discrepancy between the projections in the last budget of the Mulroney government in April 1993 and the actual numbers in November had astounded him. Martin concluded that 'either the department had known the numbers to be wrong or it had got them wrong' and he resolved never to let that happen to him. When he decided to go outside the department to audit its figures, Finance officials 'swallowed hard'. They told Martin's exempt staff that 'a public flogging would undermine the department's credibility both publicly and within the federal bureaucracy', but 'Martin didn't relent'.[35] Martin's decision served notice that career officials could no longer be trusted and that he would go elsewhere to get more reliable advice and not suffer the humiliation of previous Finance ministers like Michael Wilson and Don Mazankowski. He also made the point that Finance officials would no longer be allowed to occupy the forecasting and budgetary advisory space by themselves.

The Chrétien government has also gone outside government for the review of major policy areas such as health care, the environment, fisheries, the knowledge economy, and here too the list goes on. Such developments prompted two students of public policy to conclude that 'consultation has become an expected feature of the public policy process in Canada in the 1990s'.[36] Until the early 1980s, such policy advice would have been largely generated by career officials operating inside government.

The Chrétien era also introduced a plethora of new think tanks and research centres or strengthened a number of existing ones. Some of these groups are known to be particularly responsive to the government of the day or have as their goal the promotion of 'networking' between the private and public sectors. The Public Policy Forum is an Ottawa-based organization funded at least in part by the federal government and seeks to act as a 'trusted facilitator'. The Forum maintains that its purpose is not to 'sit in judgement of what government does, but [to look] at how public policy is developed....'[37] Still, David Zussman, head of the Forum, has close ties to the prime minister and the Liberal party and the organization has been particularly useful to the Chrétien government in reviewing certain sensitive policy issues.[38]

The Chrétien government was the key player in the establishment of the Canadian Policy Research Networks (CPRN). It is Ottawa-based and employs about twenty-five full-time people. CPRN reports that during 1999 it received 'a long-term unrestricted grant of $9,000,000 from the Government of Canada'.[39] It also revealed in the same report that it received project funding from seventeen federal government departments and agencies. CPRN's web page reports that 'funding has been contributed by 61 departments or organizations, and 59 researchers from 16 universities have completed research contracts. This is what networking is all about.'[40] If nothing else, CPRN encourages government departments to look outside their own organizations for new ideas or research findings, and academics to look to government departments to tailor or shape their research interests. In brief, it has received funding for taking networking in the public policy process to new heights. Judith Maxwell founded CPRN. She was a participant and presented a paper at the Aylmer conference which Jean Chrétien organized when in opposition to plan his platform for the 1993 election.

Chrétien, like Mulroney, has had a favourite pollster at court. Pollsters, in Canada as elsewhere, have become modern-day witch doctors, advising ministers on the national mood, on hot button issues, on national priorities, on policy prescriptions, on timing, and on the popularity of government policies and programmes. Ministers have come to rely heavily on pollsters to point the way to getting elected and, once elected, to remaining in power. Career officials may wish to speak policy truth to power, but pollsters are there to offer a different kind of truth, one that resonates better with the electorate.

Consultant firms have grown substantially in numbers and size in Ottawa over the past forty years. The yellow pages in the Ottawa telephone directory now contain hundreds of consulting firms in economics, programme evaluation, and various aspects of public policy. Many of these employ former federal career officials and perform tasks once performed by career officials. We are informed that a number of government departments now turn to consultant firms even to prepare documents for cabinet and Treasury Board submissions. This would have been unthinkable forty years ago. This is not to suggest that these consultants are invariably unfaithful to the facts. Still, they do not have to live with the requirements of the traditional bargain in their relations with politicians. In addition, consultants do not enjoy security of tenure and they have an economic interest to promote. The next contract may well depend on how they deliver on the current one, and for this reason they may well want to deliver what they think the client wants to hear. They speak 'truth to power' at their peril and at a potential economic cost. One can ask whether consultants, given their need to secure new contracts, are prepared to be nay-sayers to power. One former senior official explained the importance of this role for career officials. He writes:

> No one enjoys being a nay-sayer constantly pointing out difficulties. But when the difficulties are real, and important, you have no choice; to express unwarranted optimism, or to just keep quiet and let your minister discover the hard way that a pet idea won't work, is an abdication of what you're paid to do.[41]

Consultants do not have 'a minister'; they have clients, while career officials not only have ministers, they must live with the consequences of their policy advice.

There is another breed of consultant which, according to Jeffrey Simpson, has grown 'like Topsy in the last two decades' in Ottawa. They are lobbyists or, if one wants a more dignified term, 'government relations experts'.[42] From a dead start in 1965 there are now forty-two lobbying firms listed in the Ottawa directory. This number does not include law firms which have 'hired guns' to look after lobbying on behalf of their clients. By one count, there are now 1,500 lobbyists in Ottawa. A number of these lobbyists are highly paid and politically partisan, and could not easily survive a change of political power in Ottawa. However, because they are politically partisan, they have access to ministers and they are always at the ready to offer advice. They are hired to promote the interests of their corporate clients and paid to sell truth to politicians about government policy, as their clients see it.

Career officials in Ottawa insist that the arrival of lobbyists has made an important difference to their work. If nothing else, politicians can now turn to any number of paid lobbyists to get a second opinion on a policy issue. There are lobbyists available to argue any side of a public policy issue. One is reminded of the answer a Tennessee school teacher gave at a job interview to the question: 'Is the world round or flat?' 'I can teach it either way.' If a politician is looking for arguments to support a position, then he or she can always find a lobbyist to do just that. There is even a pro-tobacco lobby in Ottawa. There is evidence that the work of lobbyists is having an impact there. We know, for example, that a lobbyist was instrumental in having the prime minister overturn the advice of career officials in the purchase of new corporate jets.[43]

Though selling access to ministers is an important part of the Ottawa lobby industry, it is much more than that. It has created a substantial number of post-career employment opportunities for public servants which in itself is a major development in the values of the public service and the operations of government. We know that since the late 1980s, a large body of senior civil servants, including former deputy ministers and assistant deputy ministers, have joined lobby firms, bringing with them an intimate knowledge of how government works and who the key decision makers are. They also bring with them an insider's knowledge of how to present a case and how to influence government policies and operations. They also know where to pitch a message to have maximum impact. On this point, Jeffrey Simpson goes to the heart of the matter. He writes:

> When surveyed, lobbyists and interest groups consistently placed members of Parliament at or near the bottom of their lists ... lobbyists press the clients' case, if possible, to the Prime Minister's Office, then to senior ministers and top bureaucrats. They may make the rounds with MPs, but more as a courtesy or an insurance policy, because they understand that MPs have no power and only scattered influence.[44]

Whatever their actual impact on policy, research institutes, think tanks, consultants and lobbyists have made the government policy-making process much more porous and more responsive to the wishes of ministers.

Canadian politicians, at least those who are in power for any length of time, have yet another means at their disposal to make the public service responsive to their wishes. Specifically, section 39 of Canada's Public Service Employment Act provides for the priority appointment of a partisan political assistant after three years of service in a permanent public service position. No such provision exists in Australia or Britain. Ministerial assistants can (and many have over the years) been appointed to a position without competition, providing they meet established requirements for it.

One senior official with the Public Service Commission reports that the practice began in earnest during the Trudeau years. Nor did it change when ministerial assistants began to occupy more senior positions during the Mulroney years (e.g. chiefs of staff were ranked at the assistant deputy minister level). Today, executive assistants in ministerial offices are classified at the senior executive 2 or 3 levels (just below the assistant deputy minister level) for the purpose of priority appointments to the Public Service Commission.

This is significant in the sense that someone appointed on a priority basis at a junior level will be exposed to public service values before he or she occupies an executive position. However, it is a different story for someone who was hired originally in part for his or her ties to the party in power and who sits in a minister's office one day, looking after the partisan interests of the minister, but the next day occupies a senior position in the public service, expected to have lost all partisan interests overnight. Pierre Tremblay, a former executive assistant to the then Public Works minister, Alfonso Gagliano, was accused by the auditor general of having an 'appalling disregard' for rules and regulations in approving government advertising contracts in his director general position with the department of Public Works.[45]

It is difficult to imagine that a senior partisan adviser who has served as chief of staff or executive assistant to a minister for three years, and has established strong ties with other ministers and their staff, can, overnight, rid himself or herself of partisan political interests and embrace fully the professional and non-partisan values of the public service. One can assume that Alfonso Gagliano felt confident that his party's political interests would be better served if his former executive assistant was sitting in the chair of the director general responsible for government advertising contracts than if this were a career public servant who had come up through the ranks. One questions whether Pierre Tremblay and other former executive assistants to ministers can enter the public service and the next day, or the next year, declare, as a former senior career official once said, 'It is a matter of perfect indifference to me which [political party] is in power.'

The application of the merit principle in Canada has also been sufficiently flexible to enable the government to introduce change through the back door. For one thing, the merit principle has never been defined in law in Canada. It is a concept which may suggest 'truth', but its application has been sufficiently flexible to accommodate new objectives or new truths whenever the need arose. We know, for example, that the merit principle has not prevented the government from promoting gender equality, linguistic requirements, the hiring of persons with disabilities, Aboriginals and visible minorities. The objective, in terms of hiring the most competent individual, has on many occasions taken a back seat. The Employment Equity Act does not set quotas. However, it does refer to 'numerical goals' to be achieved through 'reasonable progress'. Aboriginals, for instance, are given priority status for positions which directly concern them. Accordingly, appointing the most competent individual from an open competition is less important than other objectives.

The civil service has also lost more of its earlier characteristics. The organizational space of the federal government is in a muddle which has also enabled it to introduce change through the back door. We have traditional line departments, operating agencies within these departments, large departments recently transformed into agencies, and new arm's-length foundations or organizations. There is also now a much greater tendency to contract out for services and to hire consultants to undertake policy work.

There are models that do enjoy greater autonomy and operate differently from traditional departments. The Canada Customs and Revenue Agency, Parks Canada, and the Canadian Food Inspection Agency are separate federal entities with their own chief executive officers reporting to a minister and enjoying more autonomy than a traditional line department. They do not have to live with the same centrally prescribed administrative, financial and human resources rules as do traditional departments. For example, the agencies enjoy separate employer status. This means that the work of the Public Service Commission, in particular its preoccupation with the application of the merit principle, applies to traditional departments but not to agencies. Are we to believe then that the federal government has created a two-tier public service, one of which is more pure than the other, and less subject to political pressure to make partisan political appointments, and one which attaches less importance to the merit principle? Have we created two distinct types of career officials and by ricochet two different organizational spaces – one that has to play by the rules of the Public Service Commission whereas the other does not?

There are also new organizations to which the government has delegated full discretionary authority for planning, programme design management, and service delivery. The authority is delegated to a corporate board of directors that operates within a very broad strategic framework. Examples include the Canada Foundation for Innovation ($3.15 billion), the Canada Millennium Scholarship Foundation ($2.5 billion) and Genome Canada ($300 million).[46] These foundations promote activities that properly belong to the public sector and spend public money but play by completely different rules from traditional departments and agencies. Finally, the federal government has entered into special collaborative arrangements with the provinces, the private and the voluntary sectors where both programme authority and risk are shared. In the fiscal year 2000–01, for example, the government reported the existence of one mixed enterprise, three joint enterprises, eighteen international organizations and 133 shared governance corporations.[47]

The impact

The above changes have had a profound impact on the civil service. The institutional self-confidence so evident under the traditional bargain up to the 1970s has been severely battered. Morale has plummeted. A former secretary to the Treasury Board and a highly respected career official, J.L. Manion, wrote that senior civil servants were openly talking about a civil service 'in trouble, demoralized, losing confidence in its leaders and themselves, unsure of their roles and futures, overburdened with work, and chafing under perceived unfair criticism'.[48] Surveys comparing morale in the federal public service and the private sector concluded that 'almost without exception, the private sector managers had a more positive view of the management practices in their organization than did their public sector counterparts, working at similar levels in their organization.' They also found that 'as one moves down the bureaucratic hierarchy, managers are less satisfied and less positive about managerial practices in their organization.'[49] Surveys at the departmental level were even more worrisome. A 1990 study on the department of External Affairs reported that 'External Affairs' advice is ignored and its staff made subject to public scorn, rebuke and ridicule. Motivation has plunged and morale is abysmal. The department is under siege from the outside and consumed by ferment from within.'[50] By the early 1990s, every large department could produce similar studies revealing serious morale problems. This situation has not changed, despite substantial increases in salary in the late 1990s. 'The problem', one senior Treasury Board official observed, 'has nothing to do with pay; it has everything to do with a lack of respect for career government officials.'[51]

Career officials became uncertain about their policy work. The provision of fearless advice became difficult to sustain once a high degree of responsiveness was demanded. One could discern a tendency on the part of officials to recommend safe policy options and what 'politicians would wear'. They insist that no 'challenging' policy work is being carried out on 'big ticket programs' and that there is an unwillingness to 'say "*No Minister*" or even "*Be Careful Minister*"'.[52] There is a reluctance to explain why things must be so, to provide objective, non-partisan advice, and to explain what kind of tradeoffs are required if a certain decision is taken, and so on. One former deputy minister wrote that 'loyalty itself is being redefined as obsequiousness and fawning. The honest public servant is in danger of being superseded by the courtier.'[53]

Career officials reveal that politicians want to see position papers that support their 'prejudices and ... they do not have a favourable view of neutrality – or neutral competence – as they used to'. One official remarked at a seminar in Ottawa in the 1990s that 'I see advice going to ministers which is suppressing arguments because it is known that ministers will not want them, and that for me is the betrayal of the civil service.' This atmosphere is reflected in the philosophy: 'Don't tell me why I shouldn't do it, but how I can do it.'[54] One can get a sense of how the policy world inside government has shifted by contrasting the views of two deputy ministers, one writing in 1961, the other in 1996. Al Johnson, in 1961, insisted that 'frank talk' is paramount even if it may endanger a happy union between him (career official) and his political chief. He quoted Sir Warren Fisher that 'the preservation of integrity, fearlessness, and independent thought and utterance in their private communion with ministers of the experienced officials selected to fill up posts in the service is an essential principle of enlightened government.'[55] Contrast this with what George Anderson, a deputy minister in Intergovernmental Affairs in the Privy Council Office, wrote in 1996: 'Overbearing advisers have a way of being cut down to size. The officials with most influence are those who are best attuned to the views and needs of ministers.'[56]

If one were to take the message of politicians at face value then one would assume that today's politicians were not concerned with the above. They may want career officials to become competent managers like those in the private sector and government operations to run more efficiently. Politicians and their partisan advisers, we are told, want to look after policy issues but they need strong managers to operate government programmes and deliver services. To be sure, cabinet ministers in Canada now have in place a multitude of sources from which to draw policy advice and support. Ministers may have at their disposal a much more responsive machinery of government. They may well have, however, lost a thing or two in the exchange – a source from which to draw fearless advice and a career public service certain of its role and contributions.

This chapter suggests that Canadian politicians, much like politicians elsewhere, as reported in this book, have pursued measures to secure a more responsive public service. This is true despite the fact that Canada is close to being a one-party state without actually being one. B. Guy Peters and Jon Pierre have identified in Chapter 1 above several conceptions of politicization of the public service, and Canada has embraced all of them in one fashion or another. In brief, Canadian politicians have altered the traditional bargain between them and career officials.

Notes

1 Reginald Whitaker, *The Government Party: Organizing and Financing the Liberal Party of Canada, 1930–58* (Toronto: University of Toronto Press, 1977).
2 J.A. Corry and J.E. Hodgetts, *Democratic Government and Politics* (Toronto: University of Toronto Press, 1946), p. 501.
3 R. MacGregor Dawson, *The Government of Canada* (Toronto: University of Toronto Press, 1973), p. 252.
4 O.D. Skelton, *Life and Letters of Sir Wilfred Laurier* (Toronto: University of Toronto Press, 1921), p. 270.
5 J.L. Granatstein, *The Ottawa Men: The Civil Service Mandarins, 1935–37* (Toronto: University of Toronto Press, 1982), p. 281.
6 Christina Newman, 'The Establishment that Governs Us', *Saturday Night* (Toronto), May 1968, p. 24.
7 A.W. Johnson, *Social Policy in Canada: The Past as It Conditions the Present* (Halifax: Institute for Research on Public Policy, 1987), p. 1.
8 For a discussion on how the process worked, see Donald J. Savoie, *Governing from the Centre: The Concentration of Power in Canadian Politics* (Toronto: University of Toronto Press, 1999), chapter 2.
9 An excellent example here is John K. Galbraith. See *Dimension*, Winter 1986, p. 13.
10 Flora MacDonald, 'The Minister and the Mandarins', in *Policy Options*, vol. 1, no. 3, September–October 1980, pp. 29–31; Jeffrey Simpson, *Discipline of Power* (Toronto: Personal Library Publishers, 1980), pp. 119–20.
11 See, for example, Donald J. Savoie, *The Politics of Public Spending in Canada* (Toronto: University of Toronto Press, 1990), chapter 9.
12 Quoted in Donald J. Savoie, 'The Minister's Staff: The Need for Reform', *Canadian Public Administration*, vol. 26, no. 4, 1983, p. 523.
13 Quoted in Thomas A. Hockin, *Government in Canada* (London: Weidenfeld and Nicolson, 1975), p. 136.
14 B. Guy Peters and Donald J. Savoie, 'Civil Service Reform: Misdiagnosing the Patient', *Public Administration Review*, vol. 54, no. 5, September–October 1994, p. 418.
15 Canada, *Discussion Paper on Values and Ethics in the Public Service* (Ottawa: Privy Council Office, December 1996).
16 Patrick Weller, 'Introduction: The Institutions of Governance', in Michael Keating, John Wanna and Patrick Weller, *Institutions on the Edge?* (St Leonards, Australia: Allen and Unwin, 2000), p. 4.
17 See Peter Aucoin, 'Politicians, Public Servants and Public Management: Getting Government Right', in B. G. Peters and D. Savoie, eds, *Governance in a Changing Environment* (Montreal: McGill-Queen's University Press, 1995), p. 121.
18 See Donald J. Savoie, *Thatcher, Reagan, Mulroney: In Search of a New Bureaucracy* (Pittsburgh: University of Pittsburgh Press, 1995), p. 224.
19 Ibid., p. 226.
20 Ibid.
21 Ibid.
22 Loretta J. O'Connor, 'Chief of Staff', *Policy Options*, April 1991, pp. 23–5.
23 Herman Bakvis, 'Building Policy Capacity in an Era of Virtual Government',

paper presented at the conference 'Public Policy and Administration at the Turn of the Century', Lady Margaret Hall, Oxford, 10–11 July 1998, p. 11.

24 See Jacques Bourgault and Stéphane Dion, 'Governments Come and Go, But What of Senior Civil Servants? Canadian Deputy Ministers and Transition in Power (1867–1967)', *Governance*, vol. 2, no. 2, 1992, pp. 124–51.

25 Quoted in Savoie, *Governing from the Centre*, p. 188.

26 Colin Campbell, *Governments Under Stress: Political Executives and Key Bureaucrats in Washington, London, and Ottawa* (Toronto: University of Toronto Press, 1983), p. 83.

27 Gordon Robertson, *Memoirs of a Very Civil Servant* (Toronto: University of Toronto Press, 2000), pp. 308–9.

28 *Journal* (Ottawa), 9 October 1974, and Robertson, *Memoirs*, p. 309.

29 See Canada, Department of Finance, *Securing Economic Renewal: Budget Papers*, 23 May 1985, pp. 26–7. Dissolved corporations included Loto Canada, Canagrex and Canadian Sports Pool Corporation.

30 See quote of the week, *Globe and Mail* (Toronto), 23 March 2002, p. A9.

31 O'Connor, 'Chief of Staff', p. 24.

32 See, among others, Savoie, *The Politics of Public Spending in Canada*.

33 'The Axeworthy Empire', and 'Transport Ministry Staff Ballooned under Liberals', *The Globe and Mail*, 4 December 1984, pp. A1, A4.

34 Hon. Paul Martin, *The Budget Speech 2001: Securing Progress in an Uncertain World*, Ottawa, Department of Finance, 10 December 2001, p. 4.

35 Edward Greenspon and Anthony Wilson-Smith, *Double Vision: The Inside Story of the Liberals in Power* (Toronto: Doubleday, 1996), p. 67.

36 This is not to suggest, however, that the two authors think that the federal government has been successful in its consultation efforts. See Mark C. Baetz and Brian Tanguay, 'Damned If You Do, Damned If You Don't': Government and the Conundrum of Consultation in the Environmental Sector', *Canadian Public Administration*, vol. 41, no. 3, Fall 1998, p. 396.

37 See www.ppforum.com about history.

38 One example is the government's handling of a request for financial support of Canada's hockey teams in the National Hockey League.

39 *Annual Review, 1999–2000* (Ottawa: Canadian Policy Research Networks, 2001), p. 29.

40 www.cprn.com.

41 Arthur Kroeger, 'Reflections on Being a Deputy Minister', Speech to the Canadian Club, Ottawa, 25 January 1991, p. 6.

42 Jeffrey Simpson, *The Friendly Dictatorship* (Toronto: McClelland and Stewart, 2001), p. 174.

43 See 'Lobbyists Had Role in Purchase of MPs' New Jets', *National Post*, 23 September 2002, p. A7.

44 Simpson, *The Friendly Dictatorship*, p. 175.

45 See, among others, 'Auditor General Asks RCMP to Probe Federal Contracts', *National Post* (Toronto), 9 May 2002, p. A1.

46 Others include Aboriginal Healing Foundation, Canadian Foundation for Climate and Atmospheric Sciences, Green Municipal Enabling Fund, Green Municipal Investments Fund, Canada Foundation for Sustainable Development Technology and Canada Health Infoway. See, among others, Canada, *Matters of Special Importance – 2001*, Report of the Auditor General, 4 December 2001, p. 13.

47 Canada, Royal Commission on Financial Management and Accountability, *Final Report* (Ottawa: Minister of Supply and Services Canada, 1979), p. 364.

48 J.L. Manion, *Dalhousie Conference on Career Public Service* (Ottawa: Canadian Centre for Management Development, 1990), pp. 10–11.

49 David Zussman and Jack Jabes, *The Vertical Solitudes* (Montreal: IRPP, 1989), p. 196.
50 Daryl Copeland, *Foreign Service in the Nineties: Problems and Prospects* (Ottawa: Professional Association of Foreign Service Officials, 1990), p. 27.
51 Consultations with a senior Treasury Board Secretariat official, Ottawa, December 2001.
52 See Savoie, *Thatcher, Reagan, Mulroney*, p. 341.
53 B. Ostry, 'Making Deals: The Public Official as Politician', in John W. Langford, ed., *Fear and Ferment: Public Sector Management Today* (Toronto: The Institute of Public Administration of Canada, 1987), p. 171.
54 The observation was made by a senior line department official at a CCMD-sponsored seminar held in 1996 to review papers produced for the book edited by B. Guy Peters and Donald J. Savoie, *Taking Stock: Assessing Public Sector Reforms* (Montreal: McGill-Queen's University Press, 1998).
55 A.W. Johnson, 'The Role of Deputy Ministers: III', *Canadian Public Administration*, vol. IV, no. 4, December 1961, p. 373.
56 George Anderson, 'The New Focus on the Policy Capacity of the Federal Government: I', *Canadian Public Administration*, vol. 39, no. 4, Winter 1996, p. 471.

9 Dire expectations but subtle transformations?
Politicisation and the New Zealand Public Service

Robert Gregory

Introduction

New Zealand is a country of about 3.8 million people, with a unitary state, a unicameral Parliament, and a largely unwritten constitution. The governmental system has been strongly centralised since the abolition of provincial government in 1876, and the processes of policy advice and implementation are heavily concentrated in the bureaucratic apparatus located in the capital city of Wellington.

Traditionally the doctrine of ministerial responsibility legitimated portfolio ministers of the crown as the formal heads of their respective departments, though the practical realities of governance, together with statutory prescription, located responsibility for the day-to-day administration of the agencies squarely in the hands of their topmost executive, the departmental permanent head. While in New Zealand, as elsewhere, the fabricated character of a clear policy–administration split was fully understood, nevertheless a set of practical conventions underpinned the relationship between ministers and their permanent heads, conventions which embodied territorial distinctions between what properly constituted political activity and what constituted efficient agency management. For about seven and a half decades the New Zealand system of central governmental administration, modelled on the lines of Westminster parliamentary democracy, had embodied a unified state services career structure. This was centrally administered in a way that separated the political executive from the day-to-day management of personnel policy for the state services as a whole, including the Public Service.

The fourth Labour government, under Prime Minister David Lange, swept into office in 1984, having earlier promised while in opposition 'the most radical shake out of the whole [Public Service] system since the demise of provincial government'. Thus, from the mid-1980s to the early 1990s New Zealand's state services, including the Public Service,[1] were subjected to massive reforms, driven by new institutional economic theory and the tenets of what has since become known as New Public Management (NPM) (see Treasury, 1987; Boston *et al.*, 1996). One central rationale for this package of changes, though not necessarily the most strongly advocated one, was the need to render departmental officials much more 'responsive' to the political executive, the Cabinet. National Party governments had held office for 29 of the 35 years between 1949 and 1984, and the incoming Labour government was suspicious of the willingness or ability of incumbent departmental permanent heads to faithfully toe new policy lines.[2]

On the other hand, the reforms also sought to enhance the operating autonomy of public executives, particularly those in so-called 'crown entities' (essentially parastatal 'quangos'), which are not part of the Public Service, but which are single-purpose agencies administering a wide range of regulatory, quasi-judicial, service delivery and commercial functions. Many of these functions were previously administered within Public Service departments, so their 'hiving off' to crown entities whose governing boards are appointed by the political executive has widened the potential scope for what many might see as 'politicisation' in New Zealand governmental administration.[3]

The specific means by which the responsiveness of the bureaucracy to the political executive would be enhanced became apparent during the Lange government's second term of office, when the introduction of the State Sector Act 1988 abolished the unified career service, replaced permanent heads with chief executives appointed on fixed-term contracts, gave the political executive more effective and transparent control over the appointment of chief executives, provided the basis for a new and complex accountability regime for chief executives, and devolved to individual chief executives the authority to appoint their own organisational employees.

Critics of these aspects of the reforms argued that the viability of the doctrine of ministerial responsibility, which had ensured the accountability of permanent heads to their ministers and of ministers to Parliament, would be threatened by 'politicisation' of the Public Service.

But what was meant by 'politicisation'? The term carries a number of differently nuanced interpretations, usually combining descriptive and pejorative meanings. In New Zealand the State Sector Act undoubtedly opened the way for politicisation in an essentially descriptive sense, that is, the capacity for the political executive to exercise authority directly in the appointment of top governmental officials. As Mulgan (1998: 6) points out, 'the right of governments to appoint their own people to senior public service positions' constitutes 'the key feature of a politicised public service'. However, pejorative 'politicisation' is what Peters and Pierre in Chapter 1 above describe as 'the substitution of political criteria for *merit-based criteria* in the selection, retention, promotion, rewards and disciplining of members of the public service' (emphasis added). As they say, this form of politicisation in the industrialised democracies is not primarily about political patronage in bureaucratic appointments, but about 'attempts to control policy and implementation, rather than just supply jobs for party members'.

Some New Zealand critics feared that the new legislation would see a return to the sort of political patronage that had characterised the appointment of public servants in the decades leading up to the establishment of a merit-based unified career service with the introduction of the Public Service Act 1912. Then, hundreds of Public Service employees had been appointed – often on a 'temporary' basis for many years – in return for their political support of the incumbent government. Many of them were unqualified for the work they had to carry out; some were illiterate. One premier's (prime minister's) response to opposition criticism of the practice of providing public service jobs to his party's friends was simply the retort, 'Do they expect us to give them to our enemies?'

However, there was little danger that the reforms of the latter part of the century would see any regression to discredited practices prevalent during the early part. The entrenchment of norms and values of technical competence, of merit-based public service recruitment and promotion, together with the increasing complexities of public policy-making and administration, had foreclosed any such possibility. The political costs of any personnel practices that promoted manifest political cronyism over technical competence would quickly become unsustainable. What constitutional expert K. Scott had observed in 1962 remained just as relevant in the 1990s: 'The central constitutional facts about government employment in New Zealand are the absence of political patronage and the correlative political neutrality of the public service' (Scott, 1962: 137).

Rather, New Zealand's Public Service reforms raised questions about more subtle forms of 'politicisation', whereby officials are appointed by the political executive not necessarily on the grounds of their party political affiliation, but because of their ideological orientation, and/or their association with particular policy commitments. In such circumstances 'politicisation' in a strongly pejorative sense occurs if such appointments clearly compromise merit principles. In other words, appointments which are influenced by the appointee's ideological orientation or policy commitment but which involve no obvious trade-off of general merit and competence are likely to be viewed as less 'politicised' than those in which merit and technical competence are clearly compromised by the appointment. Clearly, any such 'politicisation' in this pejorative sense can often be a matter of judgement, and often the degree of 'politicisation' involved will, like beauty, lie in the eye of the beholder. Therefore, judgements about these types of 'politicisation' – as distinct from the actual capacity of the political executive to involve itself in the appointments of officials – are inherently political, and modern governments are likely to try to avoid any appearance that merit and technical competence are being lost in favour of other values, notwithstanding the demise of old-fashioned political patronage.

Throughout the 1990s the centre-right National Party was the single or dominant governing party, until the advent late in 1999 of the centre-left minority coalition government of Labour and the Alliance, led by Prime Minister Helen Clark. Hence, the advent of Clark's government has provided the first opportunity to gauge the type and scope of politicisation in circumstances where there has been a clear shift in the ideological orientation of the political executive.

What has occurred? In terms of the usual interpretations of politicisation, not a lot. The main fears expressed by some have proved unwarranted. But there is evidence that the public sector reforms in New Zealand have 'politicised' the Public Service in new and perhaps more subtle ways.

Appointing New Zealand's top public servants

In many dimensions of governmental activity there are often important distinctions to be made between *de jure* and *de facto* relationships, and this is certainly so in regard to top Public Service appointments in New Zealand. Unlike the situation prevailing in some other 'Westminster' governmental systems such as Australia, Canada and Britain, before the introduction of the State Sector Act 1988 New Zealand's departmental permanent heads were appointed by the central personnel agency, the State Services Commission (SSC), and not by the political executive. This was the *de jure* position, as embodied in the former State Services Act 1962, but informal consultation over appointments between the Commission and the political executive was common practice, to help ensure that prospective top advisers would have the confidence of and be compatible with their ministers.

Permanent heads in the past might have been quietly moved sideways, on occasion discreetly encouraged to take early retirement, or (on one notable occasion in the mid-1960s when a departmental head was advised that he did 'not enjoy the confidence of the business community or the Government to the measure desired of the Permanent Head of your Department') manoeuvred out of their job by the rules being bent.[4] However, such actions have seldom been publicly perceived as a cloak for cronyism or party patronage.

A Royal Commission of Inquiry into the State Services had recommended in 1962 that the prime minister of the day should have effective veto power over the appointment of any permanent head recommended by the SSC. This would render transparent the sort of informal influence that cabinet members had been able to exercise over some appointments in the past: power and responsibility would thus be better matched. However, the government of the day rejected this recommendation, which was not embodied in the subsequent State Services Act 1962.

It was not until 1988 that such *de facto* influence by the political executive was afforded *de jure* status, with the passage of the State Sector Act. This legislation established a process for the appointment of departmental chief executives (no longer called permanent heads, since they were now appointed on fixed-term renewable contracts) whereby cabinet had an effective veto over any appointee proposed by the SSC.[5] The former system of appointments, which concentrated power in the hands of the SSC and those appointed by it – a group known as the 'College of Cardinals' – was widely seen to have been self-protective, promoting a privileged oligarchy of people to the top departmental positions, a group that has been described as 'almost exclusively white, middle-aged, male and, by disposition, cautious and conservative' (Boston, 2001). The new system of contractualised appointments was also intended to open up lateral entry (which had previously been almost non-existent) into the upper reaches of the Public Service, and so to attract top executives from the private sector.

The *de jure* provision of the power for the political executive to effectively control the appointment of departmental chief executives can be understood as Mulgan's 'key feature of a politicised public service', but this conceptualisation is obviously inadequate. It is only the *de facto* use that is made of such formal authority that enables judgements to be made about the type and extent of 'politicisation' that results from it.

By the end of the 1990s the statutory provision for the government to reject a prospective chief executive proposed by the SSC, *and to make its own appointment,* had never been used, though in one controversial case in 1990 the incumbent Labour government rejected a nominee but accepted a second person named by the SSC. It is unsurprising that this case was an exception, since the SSC could reasonably be expected to nominate only those people who it knows, through both formal and informal means, will have the confidence of the government. Very little of this can be said to comprise 'politicisation' in any pejorative sense. On the contrary, a central tenet of the reforms, ostensibly facilitated by the right of the political executive to have a say in the appointment, reappointment or non-reappointment, of departmental chief executives, was the perceived need to enhance the responsiveness of chief executives to the will of their political superiors.

'Politicisation' and state sector reform in New Zealand

As Peters and Pierre observe in Chapter 1 above, political criteria in appointments may be more important in safeguarding democratic values in governing than are conventional merit values. They note that the 'responsive competence' of public servants is especially important for political systems attempting to implement basic changes within the administrative system. So-called 'neutral competence' does not mean, of course, that the work carried out by public servants is or should be value-neutral. All political engagement is value-laden, from policy formulation right through to implementation and evaluation, and in this sense the politicians involved in the governing process may be divided into two groups: those who are elected and those who are appointed. 'Neutrality' in this context is actually a paradoxical virtue – as a defining feature of the professionalism of public servants it refers to their ability to serve faithfully, conscientiously and with full commitment whichever government is properly elected to office. But as Peters and Pierre ask, should governments really be content with civil servants who have few commitments to policy, or even to the government? (The moral dimensions of this argument can be set aside here.)

While in New Zealand since the state sector reforms there has been no evidence of party partisan – or patronage – appointments to Public Service positions, the evidence regarding two other types of pejorative politicisation is more relevant to the present discussion. These are what Mulgan (1998: 7) calls *policy-related politicisation* and *managerial politicisation*. The former occurs when people are appointed who have 'well-known commitments to particular policy directions that may render them unacceptable to a future alternative government', while the latter involves 'the replacement of incumbent public servants, particularly on a change of government, when there is no good reason to question their competence and loyalty but simply in order to facilitate imposition of the government's authority'. As Peters and Pierre argue, something very similar to policy-related politicisation characterised the Thatcher years in Britain, when appointments were shaped by allegiance less to the Conservative Party *per se* than to the programme of radical reform of the public sector. During the mid to late 1980s when the radical reform of the New Zealand state sector was proceeding apace there is little doubt that the appointment of several top bureaucrats was strongly influenced by their personal commitment to the government's policy changes. Perhaps most notably, one of the architects of the reforms, the Deputy Governor of the Reserve Bank, was appointed to take the place of the retiring State Services Commissioner (who had expressed some strong reservations about the nature of the reforms).

The more overt forms of pejorative politicisation will carry substantial political costs, especially if it is widely perceived that partisan concerns are undermining a hitherto strongly entrenched ethos of public service professionalism. Governments may seek to avoid the costs of pejorative politicisation by adopting different means to secure responsive competence in the domains of both policy advice and policy implementation. Two principal ways, both of which have been used in New Zealand, are the increased use of ministerial staff for policy advice, and the establishment of 'arm's-length' crown entities (quango-type organisations) which are controlled by boards of directors appointed by the government.

Regarding the former, before the 1980s the offices of ministers of the crown were comprised almost entirely of secretarial staff, and ministers depended on their departmental officials for policy advice. But especially since the advent of the Lange government it has become normal practice for ministers to recruit their own policy advisers to supplement (and sometimes challenge?) the advice tendered through the traditional public service channels. There has also been a huge increase in the number of press secretaries, or 'spin doctors', as they are colloquially called, employed in ministerial offices. And the Prime Minister's Office – separate from the Department of the Prime Minister and Cabinet – has also grown in size and in political and policy significance.

As already noted, a raft of crown entities were established to provide single-mission management of many of the functions formerly administered within departmental conglomerates. This strategy has helped to institutionalise the values of a more technocratic approach to governance in New Zealand, in that managerial imperatives have tended to supersede those of democratic accountability. Yet given that technocratisation entails the disguise of political power rather than its displacement, in times of controversy the political executive is still required to try to match with effective power its perceived responsibility for the activities of crown entities. The establishment of increasing numbers of crown entities, with the government empowered to appoint their board members, arguably enhances rather than diminishes the opportunity for politicisation in the wider – parastatal – sector, albeit by more indirect means.[6]

The New Zealand experience is entirely consistent with the Weberian proposition that rationalistic norms and values inexorably transform the character of modern political systems. The entrenchment of such rationalistic norms, inextricably linked to the higher standards of education demanded of governmental officials, has precluded any possibility of a return to the older and cruder forms of political patronage that were prevalent before the introduction of a professionalised, merit-based, public service. The spoils system of those times will remain a thing of the past. Today, the perceived virtues of a meritocracy hold firm sway. Those who head the governmental bureaucracies are not only younger on average than they were before the state sector reforms, they are much more highly educated. According to one observer,

> While it would be wrong to suggest that there is now a standard or normal route to the top, undoubtedly a post-graduate degree in economics and a substantial assignment in the Treasury constitute major advantages for those seeking to lead a department.
>
> (Boston, 2001)

Departmental heads, too, are much less likely to have spent most of their working lives in only one agency, and more likely to have had private sector working experience (although only a handful have been appointed directly from the private sector). Now, too, more of them are women. Moreover, whereas the average length of service for those appointed before 1970 was about nine years, for those appointed in the mid to late 1980s it was about six years.

Arguably, what has emerged in New Zealand since the state sector reforms has not been (using Mulgan's terms) *partisan politicisation* but rather *policy-related politicisation*, similar to that which has occurred in Britain (Clifford and Wright, 1997). But as in Britain, so too in New Zealand, policy-related politicisation has tended to reflect partisan preferences. One survey has shown that the great majority of departmental heads, at least in the mid-1990s, expressed an electoral preference for the National Party, and were 'significantly to the right of most other "opinion leaders" and the community as a whole' (Boston, 2001). Such evidence suggests that partisan politicisation can result from apparently non-partisan processes of appointment, of the kind that were originally engineered to prevent its cruder forms in decades past.

The pool of available talent from which suitable public service chief executives can be appointed is quite limited in New Zealand, given the country's size. This problem is exacerbated by the fact that even since the state sector reforms (which saw a large decrease in the numbers of Public Service in-house employees) there have continued to be around forty departments in existence (several fewer by 2001). Moreover, since 1997 the SSC has abandoned its policy of trying to keep chief executives' remuneration in line with that paid in the private sector, where salary packages during the 1990s ran far ahead of those applying in the Public Service. This has meant that although the abolition of the unified career service, and the introduction of fixed-term contractual appointments, facilitated lateral entry into the upper reaches of the public service, there have been very few appointments made from outside the public sector. In New Zealand, therefore, top public servants continue to be people who have developed their careers within the public sector. Hardly any departmental chief executives are recruited from the private sector, but some top public servants on leaving their positions have found employment in the corporate world, usually as directors on company boards. And only rarely in New Zealand have top public servants sought election to Parliament.

Thus, the policy-oriented politicisation that seems to have occurred in New Zealand might be worsening the impact of these constraints on the overall quality of the country's departmental chief executives. This may be particularly so because in New Zealand, unlike in other Western democracies, the economic and social changes introduced through the late 1980s and early 1990s were notable for their market-liberal ideological coherence rather than for the sort of politically pragmatic approach that had characterised policy-making in the decades after the Second World War. Especially between 1984 and 1987 there was a dramatic sea change in the dominant public policy-making paradigm, a general rejection of neo-Keynesian ideas and assumptions in favour of those of the neo-classical school of economics, at the heart of which were strong political beliefs in the efficacy of 'economic rationalism' (see Bertram, 1997). There is no doubt that a major factor in the appointment of most departmental chief executives was their willingness and ability to embrace the new policy paradigm.

Politicisation and the impact of top contractual appointments

Probably the most pertinent question to be raised about the New Zealand developments relates to the effect of contractual appointments on the convention that departmental chief executives offer their ministers 'free and frank' advice, deemed to be advice that is 'honest, comprehensive, independent, forthright, informed and politically-disinterested' (State Services Commission, 1995). In 1988 the then Prime Minister David Lange wrote to all departmental chief executives reassuring them that they would not be penalised for offering advice contrary to the government's policy preferences, and the requirement has been written into performance agreements, with ministers and the guidelines specifying the expected behaviour of departmental heads.

It has to be remembered that departmental heads are appointed by the SSC, which is also responsible for assessing their performance, and not by the political executive (even though the views of portfolio ministers are taken into account during the performance assessment process conducted by the Commission). Nevertheless, the question remains: to what extent, and under what circumstances, does 'responsive competence' become pejorative politicisation that weakens the norms and values of a professional public service?

In New Zealand there is considerable scope for research into this question. One such project has produced mixed evidence. Voyce (1996) found that while the convention remained in a generally healthy state, perhaps because of its strong tradition in New Zealand, it was widely recognised that some departments seemed more committed to it than others.[7] Treasury, in particular, continues to be robust in its willingness to challenge the views of the political executive, while other departments are thought to be more inclined to tailor their advice to ministerial expectations. Voyce also found that some ministers preferred to have chief executives who were managers rather than policy advisers, while others were concerned that their officials were not bold enough in the advice they offered.

What needs to be assessed is the relationship between such factors as the political security of individual agencies, the status and personalities of the various departmental heads, and the robustness or attenuation of the convention of 'free and frank' advice. For example, while the Treasury has traditionally been a powerful and secure central agency in New Zealand, it is also true that in the early 1990s moves were made to beef up the policy advice capacity of the Prime Minister's Office to act as a counterweight to the Treasury, and there has also been talk from time to time of hiving off a separate ministry of finance from it. What about agencies that are less secure in their status and mission? How do the chief executives of these organisations respond? And how do changing political circumstances affect the convention, when, for example, chief executives themselves become the focus of political controversy in their own right? Definitive answers to questions like these await more empirical investigation.

On the last of these questions, the New Zealand experience has thrown up contradictory pressures on top public servants. On the one hand, the managerialist imperatives behind the state sector reforms have accentuated the management role of chief executives *vis-à-vis* the policy advisory one. It is almost certainly true now that fewer top departmental officials have the scope, desire or capacity to be policy entrepreneurs than had a significant number of their permanent head predecessors. On the other hand, the 'decoupling' of policy-making from operational management – particularly in the statutory distinction drawn between policy 'outputs' and 'outcomes' – and the impact of the Official Information Act (which preceded the reforms) have all combined to make top public servants more visible participants in the political process. In this sense the topmost levels of the public service can be said to have become more 'politicised' since the late 1980s.

These conflicting pressures on top public servants arguably make life at the top of the public service more stressful and demanding than in earlier times. This is compounded by the fact that parliamentary select committees in New Zealand are now providing a much more effective public forum for the scrutiny of departmental operations than has been the case in the past. It is also exacerbated by the 1996 shift from an FPP (first-past-the-post) electoral system to the Mixed Member Proportional system based on the German model. Although this change has not seriously threatened the strong conventions of Public Service professionalism, as some had feared it might, it has rendered the political dimensions of policy-making and implementation more complex and fluid than under the former system. In short, therefore, the life of the top public servant has been simultaneously managerialised and politicised. This constitutes a recipe for considerable work stress, probably much greater than that experienced by top officials under the former system.

For reasons such as these, together with remuneration rates that are greatly inferior to those paid in the private sector, high-quality departmental chief executives have incentives to do the best they can to ensure that the contractual arrangements under which they are appointed provide optimal compensation. In New Zealand since the early 1990s the remuneration packages paid to top public servants under contract, even though much lower than those paid to top business executives, have risen markedly relative to those formerly paid to permanent heads, and in relation both to the lower-level employees in their organisations, and in comparison with the average wage of the country's workforce. (There was, however, no direct compensatory move such as that in Australia in 1994 when incumbent permanent heads were given a 20 per cent remuneration increase in return for their formal loss of tenure.) Moreover, while they are no longer tenured as were former permanent heads, nevertheless the terms of their contracts with the SSC have almost ensured *de facto* permanent tenure in the overwhelming majority of cases. By the end of the 1990s no departmental heads had had their contract terminated before its expiry for inadequate performance. Only one contract was not renewed when it expired, and only a few have been renewed for shorter terms than the incumbents would have wished. In New Zealand there has been virtually no evidence of the 'boiling in oil' contractual regime that Lane (2000: 189) regards as necessary to avoid the possibility of chief executives shirking.

The move to contractual appointments, while it has not reopened the door to the more pejorative forms of politicisation in the New Zealand state services, like partisan appointments, has nevertheless politicised the appointments process in another significant way. First, in the late 1990s there have been a number of political controversies surrounding allegedly exorbitant remuneration paid to top officials in some state-owned enterprises and other crown entities. There were also several well-publicised instances of large 'golden handshakes' being paid to top appointees in some of these agencies, apparently as the only means of terminating their contracts prematurely. Such instances have been much less apparent in respect of the Public Service as such, although there have been on-going news media campaigns critical of such remuneration components as performance pay and bonuses payable to state sector employees, including public servants.

There has, however, been a major ground-breaking controversy over the chief executive of New Zealand's largest government department, the Department of Work and Income (the DWI, with about 5,500 staff). In the months leading up to the 1999 general election she had been subjected to vociferous criticism by the opposition parties. A Labour Member of Parliament who was to become her new minister after the election had called more than once for her to be sacked. It was therefore widely expected that her contract would be terminated soon after the new government came to office.[8] But this did not occur, since it would have required the government to buy her out of the contract, a move considered to be too expensive, both financially and politically. Instead, the State Services Commissioner determined that her contract, due to expire in July 2001, would not be renewed, a decision that was made public. After earlier having made public statements about why she thought she should be reappointed, the chief executive announced in April 2001 that she was suing the State Services Commission for $NZ818,000, claiming that the political executive had 'interfered' illegally in the Commissioner's decision not to reappoint her, and that an announced move to amalgamate the DWI and the much smaller Ministry of Social Policy (with about 200 staff) was contrived to restructure her job out of existence. Both allegations were denied by the government, whose decision not to reappoint her was subsequently upheld by the Employment Court.[9]

Regardless of the outcome, this particular case has shown that the appointment of top public servants on fixed contracts can itself become a highly public and politicised process. This was also possible under the former system of appointments, as attested by the case mentioned in Note 4. But the contractualist regime introduced by the state sector reforms may have enhanced the potential for, if not the incidence of, a politicised game in which the political executive, the State Services Commission, opposition parties and actual or prospective chief executives are leading players. Such controversies do little to alleviate the growing mistrust of public institutions that has been experienced in New Zealand, as in many other Western democracies.[10] The New Zealand experience suggests that under such a contractualist regime top government officials could have stronger incentives to engage in opportunistic remuneration-shaping behaviour. In a worst-case scenario it could signify the emergence of a new type of 'spoils' system within an ostensibly merit-based regime. Time will tell.

In short, such actual and possible behaviour constitutes a politically negative outcome a reverse effect – of the move to abolish permanent tenure with its trade-off between lower remuneration and greater security, especially when the attenuation of the doctrine of ministerial responsibility has meant that top public servants can no longer depend, virtually as of right, on the political protection that was usually afforded them by their ministers' accountability to Parliament and the public. They have become much more publicly visible, in many cases, and much more exposed to critical public scrutiny, by no means all of it politically sympathetic.

Politicisation and biculturalism

In New Zealand the idea of politicisation also needs to be understood in the context of bicultural politics. The numbers of Maori, the indigenous people of New Zealand (Aotearoa), have been growing at a faster rate than the non-Maori population since the 1940s, and by 1999 had reached about 15 per cent of the population. Maori are expected to comprise 19 per cent of the total population within the first three decades of the twenty-first century. The Treaty of Waitangi, signed by the crown and many Maori tribal leaders in 1840 – but thereafter largely ignored by successive New Zealand governments – had by the 1980s become a central component in New Zealand's constitutional framework, after Maori grievances against European colonisation, especially in regard to land matters, became an increasingly pressing dimension to political life. For governmental purposes Maori, as the *tangata whenua* (indigenous people), are officially in a *bicultural* partnership with the crown.

All government departments are required to pursue Equal Employment Opportunity (EEO) personnel policies, which are monitored by the SSC. While only about 7 per cent of the positions in the upper reaches of the Public Service are filled by persons who identify as Maori – that is, less than half of the percentage of Maori in the population as a whole – this is more than double the number in these positions before the state sector reforms. Moreover, through the 1990s the number of Maori employed in the Public Service at all levels has increased steadily to about 13.5 per cent, compared with about 8 per cent of the total employed labour force.

The political debates that have occurred in some other countries about the proclaimed negative effects of affirmative action programmes on traditionally defined 'merit' criteria have not been mirrored in New Zealand governmental experience. There has been little, if any, suggestion that politicisation in a pejorative sense, whereby technical merit is seen to have been displaced by ethnicity criteria, has occurred. Nevertheless, as ethnicity-based political issues become increasingly pressing in New Zealand it is perfectly conceivable that arguments, well-founded or otherwise, about this particular dimension of politicisation might become increasingly likely.

From centre-right to centre-left: the first major test

The real test of arguments about the politicisation of the Public Service comes with changes of government. That is when it becomes possible for a new government, meaning one of a different political and ideological persuasion from the out-going one, to replace able and well-performing incumbent public servants with others who it considers will be better attuned to its policy initiatives and preferences – what Mulgan calls *managerial politicisation.*

As mentioned earlier, in New Zealand the abolition of the centrally administered public service career system has meant that departmental chief executives are responsible for staff appointments within their respective agencies. The political executive has no statutory right to seek to intervene in the appointment of staff other than chief executives, a fact that on one occasion gave rise to a highly publicised confrontation between a minister and his departmental head.[11] This arrangement can enhance the potential for policy-related politicisation, since chief executives might be expected to appoint senior executives who they considered to be of the right policy orientation. Therefore changing the chief executive could be seen as a key to changing the policy orientation, if not organisational culture, of any government department.

When in 1990 a National government led by Prime Minister Jim Bolger replaced the Labour government there were no changes made among departmental chief executives, which could have reflected the fact that the State Sector Act of 1988 had by then had little impact on the strong culture of permanent headship and a professional public service. The first real opportunity to test the possibility of managerial politicisation arose with the 1999 election of a centre-left coalition government, led by Prime Minister Helen Clark, to replace the centre-right governments that had held office during the preceding nine years.

This change was seen to have important implications for the state sector, including the Public Service. In opposition both the Labour Party and the Alliance had been critical of what they saw as a loss of public service ethos from governmental agencies reformed, under the tenets of NPM, in the image of the private sector. Many of their public comments had suggested that opposition politicians sympathised with the sort of sentiment expressed by Peters and Pierre, that NPM changes make public servants 'responsive to a different set of internal motivations and values, but still largely self-directed rather than responding to their political masters'. The new Prime Minister had indicated dissatisfaction with what she saw as an unacceptable level of *policy-related politicisation* in the Public Service, especially in the Treasury. Several months before the 1999 election she expressed concern about the ideological leanings of the Ministry of Education and the Ministry of Commerce. The former, she said, had a 'decidedly market tinge', while she did not believe the latter had 'the capacity or the will' to administer the Labour Party's industry policy.[12] However, shortly after her government came to power, the new Minister of State Services, in reaffirming that it was 'a test of public servants to implement the policy of a new government', pointed out that if 'state chiefs are able to implement the new government's policies, there will be no difficulties with ministers', and there were no chief executives Labour was not prepared to work with.[13]

Early in its term the new government did engineer the removal of the Commissioner of Police (partly because of an alleged personal indiscretion but largely as a result of a costly failure to successfully implement a new police computer system), and it effectively forced the retirement of the chairperson of the state-owned enterprise, Television New Zealand, amidst public controversy over the exorbitant financial costs of a botched contractual arrangement with a television newsreader. But the government has made no wholesale and immediate efforts to replace parastatal board members with persons of its own choosing, apparently preferring instead to 'let nature take its course', with its own new appointees replacing those chosen by the previous government on the expiry of individual terms. It is also worth noting that the Clark government did not recall either former centre-right Prime Minister Jim Bolger from his posting by the previous government as New Zealand's ambassador to the United States, nor a former attorney-general in the Bolger administration from his post as High Commissioner to Britain. It would not have been setting any precedent had it done so.

Nor has there been much, if any, evidence of overt managerial politicisation, in the sense depicted by Mulgan, or of what Peters and Pierre describe as the selection or deselection of civil servants on the basis of 'personal, almost clientelistic, loyalties as well as partisan allegiance'. The figures in Table 9.1 show little significant change in the pattern of appointments, reappointments and departures of Public Service chief executives in 2000–01 from that of previous years. Certainly in the nine-month period till March 2001 more appointments were made of new chief executives than in preceding years, but this is a largely circumstantial increase and is not accompanied by any significant change in the numbers of reappointments or (perhaps more significantly) departures. Most notably, despite news media speculation to the contrary, departmental chief executives of the main central agencies such as the Treasury, the Department of the Prime Minister and Cabinet, and the State Services Commission, who were inherited by the incoming Clark government, have remained in their jobs.

In fact, the statutory provisions governing the appointment and contractual retention of departmental chief executives would have rendered it very difficult for the government to try to engage in any wholesale changing of the top Public Service guard even if it wanted to do so, unless it was prepared to spend huge sums of taxpayers' money on buying them

Table 9.1 Movement of Public Service chief executives

Year ended 30 June	Appointed	Reappointed	Departed[a]
1996	7	6	8 (3)
1997	5	1	6 (2)
1998	9	2	4 (2)
1999	3	2	3 (2)
2000	1	5	5 (2)
2001 (at 31 March)	10	6	4 (2)

Source: State Services Commission.

Note
a The number who resigned is shown in parentheses.

out of their contracts. The government would have been fully conscious of this, and of the real political costs of appearing to be pushing what would generally have been seen as pejorative politicisation, against a background of previous public controversy over the payment of large 'golden hand-shakes' to other public sector executives.

The irony in this is that the contractualist and performance pay regime introduced as a central component of the state sector reforms has led to 'politicisation', in the sense of greatly enhanced news media and public scrutiny of the whole process of recruitment and remuneration of top public executives. Consequently, the current centre-left government expressed its desire to reinforce 'public service' rather than managerialist values in government administration, and established an advisory State Sector Standards Board to assist in this endeavour.

It has also moved to redesign contracts to make it easier for it to take action in respect of under-performing chief executives. In general, it can be anticipated that the government will be more patient, exerting its proper influence over chief executive appointments as their contracts come up for renewal. Political chickens may then come home to roost more quietly, in a manner that fosters a form of 'politicisation by anticipated reactions'. In an age of increasing career mobility and opportunism, and in which there is now in New Zealand, as elsewhere, increasing scope for top government executives to move into attractive positions in the private sector, these same officials may feel disinclined to continue working with a new government, or even a new minister, and may anticipate similar sentiments among those politicians. Such responses may be sharpened when individual contracts are nearing their completion date. Whether or not there is emerging a new pattern of informally understood 'rules of the game' could be better tested by interview research with former state sector, particularly departmental, chief executives who resigned or were not reappointed on the termination of their contract.

Conclusion: an unfolding story. . .

Expectations that the state sector reforms that occurred in New Zealand during the late 1980s and early 1990s would lead to a return to the sort of partisan politicisation that had been prevalent before the establishment in the early twentieth century of a professional, unified public service career system have proved unfounded. By and large, the impact of NPM on New Zealand governmental administration has merged well, in this respect at least, with the commitment to the long-standing values of a non-partisan, professional, Public Service. There is, however, evidence that policy-related politicisation became much more prevalent in the years after the reforms, particularly in view of the ideologically focused nature of market liberal economic and social policy directions taken by governments through the 1990s. This contrasted with the more politically pragmatic and eclectic policy-making style of the preceding decades. The advent of a centre-left government at the end of 1999, after ten years of National Party-dominated government, raised the possibility that New Zealanders might see for the first time a turnover of chief executive appointments that would have much more in common with the expectations in other political jurisdictions, like the United States and Germany. This has not proved to be the case. Instead, the impact of the change in electoral fortunes on public service personnel seems likely to be reflected in a more gradual and subtle manner as chief executives' contracts come up for renewal. Whether or not this is deemed by New Zealand citizens to be an acceptable face of 'politicisation' is as yet uncertain.

Notes

1 In New Zealand, the state sector encompasses all agencies, including but not limited to ministerial government departments, that are owned and operated by the state. The Public Service is defined under the State Sector Act 1988 and incorporates 37 departments under direct ministerial control, together with the Audit Office and the Crown Law Office.
2 The Labour Party was in power 1957–60 and 1972–75.
3 By 2000 there were about 170 functional crown entities in existence, in addition to the 2,660-odd boards of trustees of primary and secondary schools, which are also categorised as crown entities.
4 The Secretary of Industries and Commerce (Dr W.B. Sutch) was an active advocate of essentially protectionist industrial development policies, of a kind not favoured by the incumbent government or by some sectors of the business community (see Henderson, 1990; Bollinger, 2001).
5 Under the current legislation the State Services Commissioner makes recommendations to the government on the appointment of any departmental chief executive. If the government rejects the Commissioner's nominee, ministers may either ask for a second recommendation or select someone of their own choice. In the latter event, the decision must be officially published.
6 Early in 2000 the new government forced the resignation of the chairperson of Television New Zealand, a state-owned enterprise, at a time when there was a major public controversy regarding the high remuneration paid to television newsreaders.
7 Many believed that the introduction in 1982 of the Official Information Act had affected the tradition more negatively than had the State Sector Act.
8 Notwithstanding the fact that chief executives are employed by the State Services Commissioner, and not by the political executive.
9 The idea of 'political interference' in this context seems problematical to say the least, given that one of the intentions of the State Sector Act 1988 was to enhance the responsiveness of chief executives to their ministers. This case was also expected to test whether the Employment Relations Act 2000, sponsored by the new government to replace the employer-favoured Employment Contracts Act 1991, effectively undermined the validity of all fixed-term contracts in the public and private sectors, notwithstanding the clear intentions of the State Sector Act 1988.
10 During the past 15 years or so New Zealanders have become increasingly cynical

and distrusting towards politicians and political institutions generally, a situation confirmed late in 1998 by a nation-wide survey of attitudes and values regarding politics and government (Perry and Webster 1999). They found, *inter alia,* that whereas in 1985 about 11 per cent of people were 'not at all' confident of the good intentions of their government, by 1998 this figure had doubled.

11 See Boston (1994).

12 In 1981, when she was a political studies lecturer and a Labour parliamentary candidate, the Prime Minister had written:

> A reform-minded Labour government faces innumerable obstacles in trying to bring about social and economic change. Labour confronts a secure and permanent public service ... The people that Labour claims to represent are a world away from the top public servants who, for the most part, have little conception of the needs and attitudes of Labour's constituency.
>
> (Clark, 1981: 136)

(Ironically, much of the economic reform instituted by the 1984–87 Labour government also seemed, to many, to have little regard for the needs and attitudes of that constituency.)

13 See 'Jittery Mandarins Await New Government', in *The Dominion,* 6 December 1999.

References

Bertram, G. (1997) 'Macroeconomic Debate and Economic Growth in Postwar New Zealand', in C. Rudd and B. Roper (eds) *The Political Economy of New Zealand,* Auckland: Oxford University Press.

Bollinger, T. (2001) 'The Administrative Career of Dr W.B. Sutch, 1958–65: A Study in New Zealand Bureaucratic Politics', unpublished PhD thesis, Department of History, Philosophy, Political Science and International Relations, Wellington: Victoria University of Wellington.

Boston, J. (1994) 'On the Sharp Edge of the State Sector Act: The Resignation of Perry Cameron', *Public Sector,* 17 (4), pp. 2–7.

Boston, J. (2001) 'Departmental Secretaries: The New Zealand Experience', in R.A.W. Rhodes and P. Weller (eds) *The Changing World of Top Officials: Mandarins or Valets?,* Buckingham: Open University Press.

Boston, J., Martin, J., Pallot, J. and Walsh, P. (1996) *Public Management: The New Zealand Model,* Auckland: Oxford University Press.

Clark, H. (1981) 'Government and Decision-Making for Social Change', in P. Davis (ed.) *New Zealand Labour Perspectives,* Auckland: Ross.

Clifford, C. and Wright, V. (1997) 'The Politicisation of the British Civil Service: Ambitions, Limits and Conceptual Problems', unpublished paper, Nuffield College, Oxford.

Henderson, A. (1990) *The Quest for Efficiency: The Origins of the State Services Commission,* Wellington: State Services Commission.

Lane, J.-E. (2000) *New Public Management,* London: Routledge.

Mulgan, R. (1998) 'Politicisation of Senior Appointments in the Australian Public Service', *Australian Journal of Public Administration,* 57 (3), pp. 3–14.

Perry, P. and Webster, A. (1999) *New Zealand Politics at the Turn of the Millennium: Attitudes and Values about Politics and Government,* Auckland: Alpha Publications.

Scott, K. (1962) *The New Zealand Constitution*, Oxford: Clarendon Press.

State Services Commission (1995) *Public Service Principles, Conventions and Practice: The Senior Public Service*, Wellington: State Services Commission.

Treasury (1987) *Government Management: Volumes I and II*, Wellington: Government Printer.

Voyce, E. (1996) *The Provision of Free and Frank Advice to Government*, MPP Research Paper, Graduate School of Business and Government Management, Victoria University of Wellington.

10 Politicization in the Belgian civil service

Guido Dierickx

Introduction

Before the reforms of the 1980s–1990s, the last fundamental overhaul of the Belgian civil service occurred in 1937, when the so-called Camu reform granted a uniform statute to all civil servants in all ministries and stipulated their duties and rights in order to protect them from the whims of their political masters. At the same time it sought to guarantee their functional expertise by making their recruitment subject to educational requirements and an examination organized by a central agency, the Permanent Recruiting Secretariat (PRS). It distinguished four levels in the civil service, access to the highest level (level 1) requiring first a university degree and then a pass in a special competitive examination organized by the PRS.[1] Once admitted to level 1, a new recruit could look forward to a career leading from rank 10 to the senior civil service (SCS) ranks such as director or inspector-general (rank 15), director-general (rank 16), and secretary-general of the ministry (rank 17) (Molitor, 1974).

The Camu reform imposed its strictly bureaucratic organization patterns on the Belgium civil service until the 1990s. While elsewhere reforms, inspired by New Public Management ideas, were being introduced, the Belgian civil service was the object of much complaint but little actual reform. Its prestige as a paragon of bureaucratic rationality could hardly be questioned. Another reason why the civil service was never a 'loud issue' (Aberbach and Rockman, 2000) in the Belgian political arena is that the electoral system of proportional representation ensures that dramatic shifts in power are quite exceptional. The governance system is headed by coalition governments and by a rather strong continuity of government elites. Until 1999 the Christian Democrats remained the linchpin of government power, seeking a coalition partner sometimes from the left (the Socialists), and sometimes from the right (the Liberals). As a consequence the civil service has never been regarded as totally unresponsive (or as totally responsive) to a new coalition government. New governments have never had a strong partisan motive for launching a major attack on the existing civil service system, disguising it as a reform, as has been the case in Britain and in the US. This is not to say that the civil service has not figured as one of the spoils of political war. The Belgian political elites have devised their own ways of dividing these spoils, some of them rather subtle, some quite crude.

First, however, Belgium, that small strip of land of about 11,700 square miles between the Netherlands to the north and France to the south, should be described. This country of about 10.2 million inhabitants is composed of 58 per cent Dutch-speaking Flemish, 32.6 per cent French-speaking Walloons, and 9.4 per cent mostly French-speaking (but with a sizeable Flemish minority) inhabitants of the capital region of Brussels. This situation has been the source of a never-ending constitutional debate. The Flemish have long enjoyed a demographic majority, but this potentially unbalancing feature of the political system has been made harmless by a constitutional provision which protects the Francophone minority both in the (federal) government and in the (federal) parliament. More germane to the recent history of administrative reform is the fact that the once 'poor' Flemish now also form a socio-economic majority. As recently as 1955 Wallonia had a share of 34.2 per cent of the Gross Domestic Product, Brussels a share of 17.3 per cent, and Flanders of 48.5 per cent. The corresponding figures for 1997 are 25 per cent, 14.3 per cent, and 60.7 per cent respectively. Understandably, more Flemish than Walloons tend to advocate the devolution of ever more political, economic, and fiscal power to the regions. Generally the average Belgian citizen does not favour separatism, or indeed confederalism, but at times, as is often said, it looks as if only four things keep the country together: a well-respected monarchy, a strong social security system, the intractability of the problem of splitting up a bilingual capital city, and a huge public debt.

One would be ill advised, however, to focus only on the 'ethnic' opposition in Belgium. The country has a tradition of several, more or less cross-cutting, oppositions. Besides the ethnic one there is the opposition between the socio-economic left and right and between Catholics and non-Catholics. These oppositions have led to the crystallization of subcultures, some of which have been organized in 'pillars' of subculturally loyal associations and interest groups. The 'cautious' distrust between these subcultures and their political parties makes it difficult to keep the civil service immune from the conflicts in the society at large. The Belgian administrative system has had to maintain itself amidst a turbulent political environment and this it was unable to do without paying the price of a more or less regulated politicization. Unfortunately, this was not the only price it had to pay.

This chapter sets out to describe and explain an evolution. The *terminus a quo* is the end of the 1980s, the *terminus ad quem* the year 2002. In between is a period of considerable constitutional change and, partly as a result, of administrative change as well. For data on the *terminus a quo* we can rely on a round of extensive interviews, conducted in 1989 and 1990, with 51 members of the House of Representatives, 28 cabinet* chiefs or deputy chiefs, and 157 SCS of ranks 17, 16, and 15. This study focused mainly on the SCS: 14 secretaries-general (63 per cent of the total) were interviewed, 77 directors-general (58 per cent), and 66 inspectors- or administrators-general (22 per cent). Politicians and ministerial staffers were also represented in the research design[2] to allow us to establish the networking between these major actors in the Belgian governance system and to compare their respective political cultures. Care was taken that civil servants were represented according to the size of their ministry.[3] Developments since then have been tracked through official documents and interviews with a number of privileged witnesses in the governments of the newly federalized Belgian state.

Our *terminus a quo* was a period of political turmoil. It was a time of budgetary retrenchment, a policy to which the successive coalition governments of Christian Democrats and Liberals were committed. Naturally the civil service was one of the most obvious victims of the cutbacks. In 1988 a coalition of Christian Democrats and Socialists took over the reins of government but in administrative matters the agenda remained largely the same. The demands of the public would have to be met with less money, less personnel, and more public management. Simultaneously the process of federalization dragged on with apparently no end in sight. Constitutional reform was high on the agenda of the politicians and crowded out many other concerns. It certainly created much confusion and uncertainty among the SCS of both the national and the embryonic regional administrations. These were not happy times for the SCS and we could have been tempted to view the data in the light of this historical setting. However, we soon discovered that we had to replace the findings about our SCS in a longer time perspective and to view them as the heirs to a long Belgian tradition.

The organization of the Belgian administration had remained more or less the same since the Camu reform of 1937. The Belgian civil service was therefore – and had long been – characterized by a strict division of labour between civil servants and politicians, a strongly hierarchical structure, an equally strong compartmentalization of ministries and services, and by long careers based both on seniority and, paradoxically, on an almost proverbial reliance on partisan patronage. The domination of the politicians, more specifically of the ministers and the government, over the civil servants was accepted by all as both a fact and a principle. Any mention of the very emancipated position of the Dutch SCS was met with a mixture of envy, disbelief, and horror. Have things changed since then? To a certain extent they have.

---

*Throughout this chapter, the term 'cabinet' is used in its Belgian sense, to mean a minister's team of personal staffers.

Cabinet staffers and civil servants

An essential feature of the Belgian governance system up to the time of our study was the pronounced marginalization of the SCS in the policy-making networks. This is in itself a paradox. How can a modern state afford to do without the human resources and expertise of civil servants when designing policies that have to be, by necessity, expertise consuming? The government, parties, and parliament could not do the job on their own. And indeed, they don't. The traditional Belgian answer to the requirements of modern policy-making has been a modest appeal to a limited number of civil servants, a distinct appeal to the think tanks of the major interest groups, and the development of large 'cabinets' of staffers assisting each government minister. These cabinets could (and can) number up to more than 50 staffers who are recruited, for the period of ministerial duty of their master, from the academic world, from interest groups, and, yes, also from the ranks of the civil service. We found that about 50 per cent of the cabinet staffers are high-flyers from the civil service to which they usually return (often in a higher rank) after their tour of duty in the ministerial cabinet. These cabinet staffers are chosen because they are intelligent, energetic, and hard working but even more because they can be counted on to be loyal to their minister. Other motives can of course play a role. They can be recruited to enlist the support of important interest groups or to prove that the minister is willing to exercise personal patronage. The overriding motive, however, is partisan loyalty. It is the party that creates a reservoir of candidates eager to launch their careers by taking a job as a cabinet staffer. Recently fun has been poked at the ministers of smaller parties who were able to get a post in the government but had no pool of candidates to draw their cabinet staffers from. These cabinet staffers have been and still are the foremost rivals of the SCS. They provide the minister with the main line of defence against both the (supposed) party political neutrality of some civil servants and opposing party loyalty of many others.[4]

There can be little doubt that these cabinet staffers formed the hub of the policy-making networks in Belgium. Following the methodology and the reporting proposed by Aberbach *et al.* (1981), we discovered that our SCS have regular contacts mainly with other SCS of their own ministry (93 per cent), with cabinet staffers of their own ministry (86 per cent), and with the secretary-general of their own ministry (73 per cent). Only 41 per cent of them claim to have regular professional contacts with their own minister, 33 per cent with national interest groups, 26 per cent with SCS of other ministries, 20 per cent with cabinet staffers of other ministries, 13 per cent with ministers of other ministries. Regular contacts established with other politicians were (and are) few and far between. When we compare this to similar data in the countries studied by Aberbach *et al.* and to German data obtained in 1987 we have to conclude that the

Belgian SCS were confined to communication networks which rarely reached beyond their own ministry.

Figures 10.1a and 10.1b display the networks that existed between the major political actors in the early 1990s, the former excluding, the latter including, cabinet staffers. The figures are the percentages of respondents (MPs, SCS, staffers) having (fairly) frequent contacts with other participants in the policy-making processes (MPs, SCS, ministers). For instance, among our SCS respondents 41 per cent have (fairly) frequent contacts with ministers, 10 per cent with MPs (Figure 10.1a) and 86 per cent with staffers of their own ministry (Figure 10.1b). It is easy to see that without the staffers the networks would suffer a fatal lack of density. The cabinet staffers simply had to step in to fill the void left by the SCS. They had more regular contacts with about every potential partner in the policy-making process: the premier and premier's cabinet, with the government as such, with their own and other ministers, with cabinet staffers of other ministers, with all kinds of politicians, even with SCS of other ministries.

The crucial question here is whether the SCS have some advantage of their own with which to offset the comparative advantage of the cabinet staffers, for example their own party loyalty. Findings showed that almost all of them did. However, even adding this show of party loyalty to their technocratic loyalty to the state could not prevent them from being marginalized. Our data show that party support among the SCS is more than a parlour game: party labels matter when it comes to networking with politicians. SCS with the same party label as their ministers or, at least, with a label of one of the coalition parties, were able to make contact more successfully with ministers, staffers and MPs of the majority than could

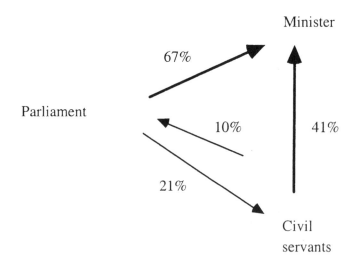

Figure 10.1a Belgian policy-making networks without staffers.

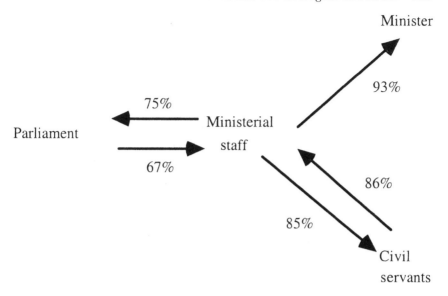

Figure 10.1b Belgian policy-making networks with staffers.

those with the wrong label or with no label. The lack of party reliability of SCS who happened to wear the wrong label was certainly one of the factors leading to their marginalization. Ambitious young civil servants realized this and were intent on picking the right label to promote their careers and avoid being sidetracked in the policy-making process. However, the tactic has never been entirely effective. Civil servants can never appear more loyal than cabinet staffers and, if the wrong minister wields the power in the department, they risk being viewed as totally unreliable. One should point out, however, that partisan unreliability was probably not the only cause of their marginalization. Politicians found it difficult to work with civil servants whose professional culture, marked as it was by technocracy and political neutrality, was alien to their own. East is East and West is West, and never the twain shall meet . . .

Marginalization was a real enough problem for individual civil servants. Was it also a serious problem for the Belgian governance system as a whole? After all, a system based more on cabinet staffers than on civil servants may function quite well. Cabinet staffers are on average younger, more energetic, and able to tap more sources of information in society at large as they can be recruited from all kinds of organizations. On the other hand, cabinet staffers are available only for short-term appointments, cannot build up the same specialized expertise, cannot provide the necessary 'organizational memory', and are surely too few in number to cope with all the complexities of contemporary society.

In brief, in 1991 the Belgian governance system had a hub of about

3,500 cabinet staffers. They were the cause and, to some extent, the result of the marginalization of the civil servants. Many observers were and are highly critical of this 'specifically Belgian' phenomenon. But the fact of the matter is that the system could not and cannot function without them, at least for the time being.

The cabinet staffers derive their functional necessity from the outspoken desire of ministers to be supported by collaborators who are loyal to their party and, if possible, to their person. Getting their job from their minister, and losing it when the minister steps down, is a very strong source of loyalty. Even those staffers who were selected from, and who can return to, the ranks of the civil service are likely to experience the loss of their minister as a personal loss. The system of cabinet staffers is a foremost expression of the will of Belgian politicians to control their administration. Of course civil servants claim to be loyal servants of the state and of whatever minister is put in charge of the ministry. But it is easy to see why ministers would prefer servants who are loyal to them and their cause (*ceteris paribus*) rather than those who claim to be loyal to the state. Indeed, the latter claim is more often than not difficult to prove. As a result most civil servants, especially among the highest ranks, end up having a party label. Party patronage is so ingrained that those who refuse (or try to refuse) such a label are definitely handicapped in the *cursus honorum*. Having no label is almost as bad as having the wrong one.

There were, then, at least two vicious circles at work here. Civil servants were competing with each other to obtain the right political label. If some were induced to play this game, the others had to follow suit. And because many civil servants had the wrong (or an unclear) label, or because ministers tended to think that even a correct label was too weak a guarantee of loyalty, they preferred to work with staffers whose loyalties were beyond doubt. To this many SCS react by emphasizing their technocratic impartiality as 'servants of the state'. However, this tactic failed to make them appear as reliable as the staffers, given that many ministers continued to prefer party loyalists to impartial servants of the state.

The indiscreet charm of politicization

Party loyalty is a strong currency in Belgian political life. The system of governance has long been built (and is still built) on coalitions formed by the political leaders of very distinct and often very opposed subcultures: Francophones and Flemish, economic right and left, Catholics and non-Catholics. These subcultural oppositions have now subsided in the public arena, at least the latter two, but in political circles they are still more alive than many outsiders would like to believe. That is why politicization has not been restricted to the cabinet staffers, who are expected to be political appointees, but has expanded to the career civil service, which officially was supposed to be governed by the bureaucratic rules of the merit system. The political parties in the government coalition have been engaged in a kind of prisoners' dilemma that forced them to appoint and promote as many of 'their own people' as possible among the SCS (and even, to an increaing extent, in the ranks below). Is it not reassuring to know that you have some of your own people in the ministry? They might be useful as advisers or informants to your political party, if not in the short run, then at least in the long run.

We intend to tackle two questions here. How was the tradition of politicization of the civil service, especially of the SCS, maintained? And to what extent does it matter? We begin with the first question, which is also the easier to answer.

Officially many measures have been taken to stop the vicious circle of politicization. The dysfunctions of this tradition are well known. A loss of expertise is to be expected when the recruitment and promotion of civil servants are open to party patronage. Even if it is not in a party's interest to patronize low-quality candidates and if therefore loss of quality should not be exaggerated, the effects on the moral of civil servants are real enough. Even if promotions happen not to be based on party sponsorship, it is hard to convince the losing candidates that such is not the case. Actual or suspected politicization is the ideal breeding ground for much envy and discontent. At the time of our interviews (1989–90) this was a topic about which respondents were willing to talk almost endlessly.

In academic circles some have tried to match the disadvantages of politicization with advantages that would make it more respectable. The noblest concept used here is that of a 'representative bureaucracy'. Among SCS, however, this notion is rarely voiced explicitly, except to point to a lack of equilibrium in the party composition of the senior civil service and to claim that this equilibrium should be restored by promoting more of 'our own people'. Of course, opinions about the correct definition of equilibrium differ. Thus wrangles about appointments and promotions can go on for ever, further poisoning relationships between colleagues. However, this theoretical legitimization is only rarely and timidly used. Most of our respondents heartily deplored the politicization phenomenon, sometimes adding that, fortunately, 'things are not as bad in my own service as elsewhere'. Almost all of them agreed to define the situation as bad and going from bad to worse. It is interesting to note that both politicians and SCS shared this poor opinion of the present situation but more SCS were inclined to see it as getting worse (65 per cent). Clearly, they disliked the game they were forced to play and would have preferred depoliticization as required by the principles of bureaucratic technocracy. Meanwhile, most of them must have thought that it was better to carry on with the game than to lose it.

Those who timidly pointed to some merits of the phenomenon were respondents with leftist bearings. The reason for their tolerance of it is not so much that they are underrepresented among the leading civil servants

– the centre-right Liberals being even less represented – but is probably an ideological one: Socialists tend to have a different perspective on what a civil service should be. We shall return to this topic.

As was mentioned earlier, the Camu reform of 1937 had created a central PRS. This 'Vast Wervingssecretariaat' organized competitive and official examinations as the necessary means of entry to a career at one of the four levels. It served all the ministries of all the governments (federal and also regional since the recent constitutional revisions). This recruit-ment procedure was highly respected. However, it did not succeed in closing all loopholes. The government was still allowed to recruit civil ser-vants at its own discretion when new offices were created for which no duly recruited career civil servants were available. It could proceed to recruit temporary appointees ('contractuals') who would later, under the pressure of the labour unions, be upgraded into the ranks of the regular civil servants. And, last but not least, it was at liberty to recruit civil servants to the very highest ranks of the ministries. A government about to leave office was often eager to reward its faithful cabinet staffers with some senior position in the administration (or in one of the parastatals and state enterprises to which the Camu statute did not apply).

While recruitment could be said to have been largely carried out according to objective, non-partisan criteria, such was not the case with promotions. The Camu reform had imposed an examination at each level of entry. Promotions within level 1 (from rank 10 to rank 17) were to be based on a rating by superiors that rapidly became perfunctory, on the advice of a board of high-ranking civil servants who could propose a shortlist of candidates from among whom the minister could choose, and on 'experience', i.e. length of career. The end result was that it became difficult to reward the good and to sanction the mediocre, that SCS tended to be older men nearing the end of their careers, and that those with the correct labels, whose parties (Christian Democrats and, to a lesser degree, Socialists) had participated in many governments, enjoyed better career prospects. The one criterion for promotion that could have limited the drive towards politicization, i.e. the advice of the board of high-ranking civil servants, did not yield the expected results: it could itself have a specific political colouring; moreover, ministers were not held to the advice unless it was unanimous, and even then they could disregard it, citing a particular reason for promoting another candidate.

For promotions (or appointments) of SCS, political motivations had been allowed by Camu (and the advice of the board of high-ranking civil servants was not required). For the position of secretary-general, and also for other senior civil service positions, the appointment of a relative out-sider such as a former cabinet head (or a high-flying civil servant of lower rank) was considered to be the rule rather than the exception. It must be said that many of these political appointees proved quite successful.

Cabinet heads are rightly seen as the best and the brightest among the Belgian political elites in general.

The politicization spiral threatened to become a nuisance not only for many civil servants but also for the governing coalitions. Coalitions are based on delicately balanced agreements that can be easily upset by disputes about appointments. So in the 1960s the governing parties decided to introduce a procedure they could not and would not abolish. They entrusted political appointments in the central administration to a special committee of representatives of the coalition parties, known by the names of their successive chairmen (Dekens, Mangeleer, and Missant). This move was intended, first of all, to centralize all political appointments in the hands of party representatives, thus avoiding the attempts at patronage by various cliques and interest groups, and second to work out a carefully negotiated settlement between the parties. At one point printed scoring cards were used in which the position of secretary-general was given a value of five points, that of director-general three points, and so on.[5]

It has been asserted that this almost proportional distribution of appointments is a fine example of Belgian consociational democracy at work. It is nothing of the kind. It is rather an example of the art of dividing the spoils of war: only the representatives of the coalition parties participated in the negotiations and only on their own behalf. The net effect of this institutionalization of party-based promotions was clearly non-consociational. The longer and the more often a party had been a member of the governing coalition, the stronger was its overrepresentation among the SCS. Only many years later did the committee agree to reserve a (minor) share of the appointments for the opposition parties and for non-affiliated civil servants, realizing that minority parties should not be provoked into retaliation when they joined a later coalition.

Politicization and administrative culture

Did this politicization of the civil service matter, not only for the careers of the civil servants, for their morale, and for the relationship between them and their political masters, but also for the running of a government? There are plenty of anecdotes about civil servants blocking the implementation of a policy they did not like. On the other hand, in our survey the Belgian SCS proved very willing to go along with a policy they opposed. A large majority said they would bow to the will of the governing politicians, thus proving to be more submissive than their German colleagues would be. So is the party loyalty of the Belgian SCS only superficial, used to obtain political patronage but discarded as soon as this is no longer needed? Many of our respondents readily admitted that they had joined a party. At the same time most of them denied being politically active, except perhaps at the local level, in their village where they happened to be the only expert who could be trusted e.g. with the communal finances.

Again the comparison with Germany is suggestive: more of the Belgian respondents admitted to having a party membership card, but fewer admitted to being political militants. The conventional wisdom that politicization of the (senior) civil service matters greatly for policy-making requires some closer scrutiny, since nominal party membership is not the same as ideological commitment or party activism. A more pertinent question would be whether ideological commitment leads to party activism, without and within the confines of the public administration. Survey data cannot be expected to give a definitive answer to this question. What we can examine is whether these 'politicized' SCS have indeed developed a consistent ideology and whether this ideology has had an influence on their other attitudes and activities.

Since *The American Voter* (Campbell *et al.*, 1960) we know that comparitively few citizens can be termed 'ideologues'. They have not organized their political opinions into a system of sufficient consistency to deserve this epithet. However, political elites, such as members of parliament and SCS, have the motivation and the opportunity to organize their political opinions to a much higher degree. According to this venerable scientific tradition civil servants are expected to have a well-elaborated ideology as private citizens. However, the rules of administrative propriety require them to put this partisan ideology to one side while at work as civil servants and to proceed solely on the basis of the non-partisan political culture of their profession. It might even be the case that the non-partisan professional culture of the civil servants transforms or obliterates their partisan ideology. We thus face a double question. First, if our civil servants indeed have a consistent ideology, does it show the influence of their professional experience? Second, does their ideology influence their professional culture? If so, partisan ideology would really matter: it might not directly impinge on their professional activities (we cannot hope to inquire into this anyway), but it would certainly have an impact on their attitudes towards their professional responsibilities.

Political scientists agree that almost everywhere individuals' political ideologies can be compared on a left–right scale. But what is the precise meaning of left and right, especially in a country like Belgium which is known to have a political arena with a multidimensional ideological space? The ideologies of the major political families (Socialists, Liberals, Christian Democrats, Nationalists, and Ecologists) differ from each other on more or less independent socio-economic, linguistic, cultural, and philosophical-religious dimensions. In what follows we will mainly focus on the (socio-economic) left–right dimension because it is salient and comparable in all countries, not because it is the only or even the most important one in Belgium.

A scale of left–right attitudes was constructed on the basis of six items in the questionnaire of our study of 1989/1990. To gauge the socio-economic flavour of the resulting scale it is useful to reproduce them here.

1   We owe the progress made in our society to social conflicts.
2   Only by taking from the rich is it possible to help the poor.
3   Decreasing inequalities in income has correctly been viewed as a task of the government.
4   Much of the doubt and fear about ever-increasing state intervention in social and economic matters is entirely justified.
5   On a scale representing economic systems ranging from state domination at one extreme to free competition at the other, where would you situate your ideal system?
6   On a scale representing the political spectrum from left to right, where would you situate yourself?

A further examination of the scores on these items, and of the scale that results from them, reveals that the SCS are indeed 'ideologues' as defined above and hardly less so than the MPs we interviewed. In general their political opinions are only slightly less well integrated than those of the politicians and therefore far better than those of the average citizen. Both samples contain a large majority of ideologues and a small minority of non-ideologues. This finding is entirely consistent with the findings in the original study of Aberbach *et al.*

On this left–right index the sample of SCS were somewhat to the right of the MPs. They were also clearly less radical (see Figure 10.2). This ideological centrism of the SCS is easy to explain by referring to the politicization of the promotions. The parties that have been in the government for longer have had longer to patronize their loyalists. Therefore Christian Democrats are overrepresented among the SCS, as we have seen above. Among them the ideology of the socio-economic centre prevails.

However, party patronage is only part of the explanation. When SCS are compared to MPs of the same party they appear less extreme. Socialist SCS are less to the left and Liberal SCS less to the right than, respectively,

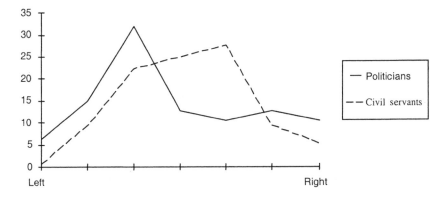

Figure 10.2 Left–right index.

Socialist and Liberal MPs. The centrism of the SCS is not only the consequence of the overrepresentation of the Christian Democrats but also of the moderation of both the Socialists and the Liberals. In sum, there seems to exist a centrist tendency among civil servants in general (or a radical tendency among politicians).

According to Aberbach *et al.* (1981) this bureaucratic centrism would hinge on the job experience of civil servants. They are more directly confronted with the feasibility problems of political projects than are politicians, who mostly debate about principles and long-term objectives. Civil servants are therefore wary of radical proposals coming from either right or left – unless of course they are actually politicians in disguise, as is the case in the US.

Further Belgian data make this 'bureaucratic experience' hypothesis even more plausible. The respondents were asked about the other two major divisions in Belgium. The socio-linguistic division between Flemish and Francophones led to fierce debates among political elites during federalization. At the time of the interviews the first constitutional steps had been taken to divide Belgium into three (or four) regions that were to become member states of what was until then a unitary state. Nationalists advocated further, sometimes radical, devolution of political authority to the regions, unionists pleaded in favour of retaining as much power as possible for the central state. We put this issue to our respondents, asking them to situate themselves on an eleven-point scale ranging from unionism to confederalism (and separatism).

The results are striking. The SCS of each of the parties clearly tend more to unionism than the MPs of their own party. Obviously job experience is, again, the major factor here. For civil servants, most of whom were active in the federal administration, the devolution of power to the regions and the distribution of authority over several levels of governance and different ministries meant a lot of trouble. Complaints about the ensuing confusion were to be heard in the corridors of all the ministries.

A similar eleven-point scale about the opposition between 'Catholics' and 'non-Catholics' yielded the expected results: the Christian Democrats took pro-Catholic and Socialists non-Catholic positions. Here, however, civil servants did not differ significantly from politicians. The reason seems to be that most civil servants hardly ever have to cope with philosophical questions in their professional life. Since this kind of issue has not been part of their job experience, it has not shaped their ideological positions in this domain. Philosophical issues matter to them as private citizens; socio-economic and socio-linguistic issues matter to them both as private citizens and as civil servants. Hence the contrast.

The next question is whether their private ideological commitment matters for their professional culture. As a first indicator of professional culture we use a technocratcy index, composed of the following items:

1   In social and economic matters today technical considerations deserve more attention than political ones.
2   The efficiency and the effectiveness of a government are more important than its programme.
3   In order to rationally assess government policy one should detach oneself from political considerations.
4   Very few people know what is really in their interest in the long run.

On this new index 43 per cent of the SCS get a high score, against only 10 per cent of the politicians and 8 per cent of the cabinet staffers. The average score of the civil servants is also much higher than that of either politicians or staffers. That much we could have guessed. Of more interest are the data in Figure 10.3 displaying the percentage of strong technocrats among politicians and civil servants of the ideological left, centre, and right.[6]

Both among politicians and civil servants those of the right lean more frequently towards technocracy than those of the left. Not a single leftist politician has developed an acute case of technocracy, but 53 per cent of the rightist civil servants have done so. Among the Belgian SCS, however, the correlation is not overwhelming, mainly because the relationship is curvilinear: the highest number of technocrats can be found in the centre. Apparently these Christian Democrats feel that they are the true champions of the general interest and that therefore they always ought to be in search of the single correct solution. Perhaps the metaphysics and the ethics taught in the Catholic subculture have contributed something to their technocratic perspective.

Another striking aspect of political culture in Belgium is political alienation. A first indicator we termed 'Affinity' (with the political process). As one would expect, more civil servants of the right experience their 'political' activities as unappealing (48 per cent) than of the left (26 per cent). The relationship becomes clearer when we turn to another, more sophisticated indicator of political alienation:

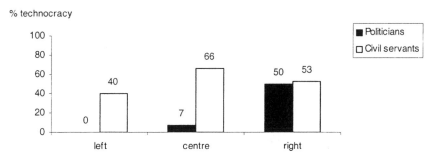

Figure 10.3 Ideology and technocracy.

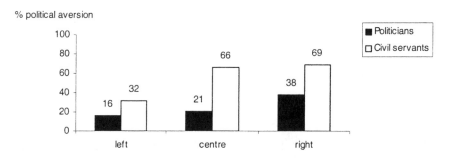

% political aversion

Figure 10.4 Ideology and political aversion.

'Aversion from political actors'. This scale was obtained by aggregating the scores on four closed items that measured the degree of aversion from four political actors: interest groups, parties, parliament, and politicians.[7] The percentages of very 'averse' respondents are shown in Figure 10.4.

The correlation between ideology and political aversion is low (0.09), again because the relationship is not a completely linear one: at least in the subsample of civil servants centrists are almost as often averse from political actors as rightists are. However, the contrast between leftists and rightists amounts to no less than 37 percentage points. The relationship between ideology and this central aspect of Belgian administrative culture is striking.[8]

Politicization and partisan action

Political ideology does have an impact on professional culture, and more than might sometimes be expected. However, the ultimate question is whether it also has an effect on political activism in a public administration where such behaviour is not deemed appropriate. Unfortunately we can only marshall indirect, circumstantial evidence to make the occurrence of such activism plausible. Survey data try to fathom the perceptions and evaluations of respondents, not their activities. The best one can do is to look for perceptions and evaluations that reveal a readiness to engage in partisan activities. We shall discuss four such 'proxy' indicators of partisan activities.

The first of these is an index of political radicalism that estimates the willingness of the respondents to pay the price of conflict to reach their political objectives. This index contrasts a 'hard' with a 'soft' political style. In Belgium such an index has a special significance since many observers want us to believe that the political elites act as pacifiers in a consociational democracy (Lijphart, 1999) and that they therefore are imbued with a (very) soft political style.[9] The four items are the following:

1 In political debates one should avoid extremes because the correct answer usually lies somewhere in the middle.
2 The stability and continuity of public policy are more important for a country than the opportunity to change governments.
3 Members of parliament ought to reconcile the diverging interests of the groups in society.
4 Politics is the art of the possible and therefore the authorities in our country should be preoccupied more with the feasible in the short term than with ideals and grand designs.

Those who favour moderation in political debates, the stability of government, the reconciliation of interests, and feasibility in the short run foster a soft political style. The data show that civil servants of the left tend to be harder than those of the right and certainly than those of the centre: the relationship is curvilinear instead of linear, with a difference of 25 percentage points between leftist and centrist civil servants. This is a suggestive finding. We can plausibly assume that civil servants who foster a hard political style will be more open to partisan-ideological commitments in the policy-making processes. Hence the penetration power of leftist prejudices in a bureaucratic organization should be greater than that of centrist or rightist prejudices. This would correspond well with the conventional wisdom. In their professional life civil servants erect a wall against the political logic of power, conflict, and utopia: they are less radical and less partisan than politicians. But rightist and centrist civil servants erect a higher wall than their leftist colleagues.[10] If this interpretation is correct, more leftists will engage in partisan activities within and most probably also beyond their professional sphere.

Other facts tend to support this hypothesis. Membership of a party is quite unexceptional in the Belgian civil service but it occurs more frequently among leftists (81 per cent) than among centrists (76 per cent) or rightists (69 per cent). We must note, though, that this most conventional of indicators is, in Belgium, not very revelatory of partisan activism. Civil servants join a party for all kinds of considerations, among others to further their career. On the other hand, it is not without significance that rightist respondents seem to be more embarrassed by the notion of party membership than leftists. They are more emphatic in denying any suggestion of party membership and in seeking an excuse (such as a service to the local community) when admitting it.

Anyhow, for our purposes it is safer to fall back on an indicator of subjective partisan sympathies than of objective membership. During the interviews the respondents were asked to give a score, ranging from very positive to very negative, to each of the political parties. This crude general measure worked surprisingly well. Several features of the results may be instructive. First, civil servants tend to differentiate less between the parties than politicians, and rightist civil servants less than leftists. In other words, leftist civil servants find it less difficult to differentiate between good and bad guys. Leftists also feel closer to their most preferred party than either centrists or rightists and more distant from all other parties. Leftists thus like their own party more and other parties less than their colleagues of the right and the centre. In contrast, the rightists tend to keep their distance from all political parties, have only moderate confidence in their most preferred party and differentiate only vaguely between political parties. It is hardly surprising that they feel less inclined to transform their ideology into partisan action.

The general conclusion should be that Belgian SCS have formed an ideology that is hardly less well elaborated than the ideology of Belgian MPs but that has features of its own: it tends to be moderate, because of specific job experience, and somewhat centre-right, because of the politicization of promotions among the SCS. This ideology does matter for their professional culture. Socio-economic leftism tends to foster less technocracy and less political alienation. This ideology also matters for partisan commitment outside and, probably, inside the administration. Leftists tend to become more engaged in party politics.

Administrative reform, at last (?)

In the late 1980s there was a widespread feeling among both SCS and many politicians that politicization had gone too far, that some autonomy should be restored to civil servants, and that their role in the policy-making processes should be upgraded. The opportunity to do something in that direction presented itself with the first wave of the New Public Management reform in the 1990s. Why did the breakthrough of that reform movement finally come about so late? An important factor has been the constitutional reform, initiated in 1980, expanded in 1988, and (provisionally) completed in 1993. This transformed Belgium from a unitary, centralized state into a federal state with several governments and several administrations. The final institutional reform of 1993 laid down the premises of any civil service in Belgium but left it to the federal and the regional governments to fill in the specifics of their own civil service.[11]

Why, then, has the new Flemish government (which is located in Brussels and is responsible for various socio-economic and socio-cultural or 'personalized' matters) taken advantage of this opportunity more promptly and more thoroughly than the federal government and certainly more than the governments of the Walloon region (which is located in Namur and is responsible for a socio-economic agenda), the Francophone community (which is located in Brussels, serving the Francophones of both Wallonia and Brussels, and is responsible for a socio-cultural agenda), and the Brussels region?

From the start the new Flemish government opted for a single ministry composed of six (later seven) departments and structured in a matrix type of organigram: horizontal relationships across departments would be almost as important as the usual vertical relationships within departments. Two of these departments (Co-ordination and Finance) were 'horizontal' departments that would support and co-ordinate the functioning of the other line departments (Education, Health and Welfare, etc.). This organigram focused on co-ordination and departed considerably from the traditional division of the Belgian administration into separate fiefdoms called ministries. This centralization would provide the opportunity to impose a top-down reform, if only the right ministers and the right SCS were put in charge.[12]

This lucky state of affairs came about in the early 1990s when the new Flemish civil service was entrusted to two energetic Socialist ministers, first Tobback and then Van den Bossche, and when the Ministry of Finance was headed by the equally enterprising Christian Democrat Demeester. Since the Flemish government functions more as an integrated body than the federal one, these strong personalities were able to muster the support of their colleagues for their grand design of administrative reform. Equally important was the fact that the new ministry could profit from the appointment of a new set of secretaries-general. Most of them had been 'chief of cabinet' in the former government. As individuals they therefore belonged to the best and brightest of the governing elites. Together they formed a board of strong personalities bent on claiming more responsibilities for themselves and for the SCS in general. They would not be satisfied with the traditional, bureaucratic definition of their post. They wanted to be more than mere executors of policies conceived and decided elsewhere, by ministers and their cabinet staffers. They aspired to become the managers of the civil service and, together with the cabinet staffers if necessary and without them if possible, the designers of public policies.

In the federal government the same conjunction of events did not occur. The administration remained divided among many autonomous ministries. Some ministries were quite interested in administrative reform, others were not. Thus the federal SCS did not launch reform proposals of their own because they were divided among many ministries, because they often guessed correctly that any reform would end up cutting their personnel, and because the technocratic culture and the legalistic overregulation of the civil service did not invite any imaginative reform proposal. Although from the 1980s on there had existed a board of secretaries-general that met regularly, its advice covered administrative matters only. Although, in 1994 a separate Ministère de la Fonction Publique – Ministerie van Ambtenarenzaken was created to promote reform, the service (ABC) charged with this task within that ministry was small and could offer its expertise only at the request of other ministries.[13] In the 1990s more new ideas were being circulated than in the 1980s but on the whole these have not produced many genuine innovations either. In the federal administration reform had to face a tougher uphill fight than in Flanders

(Stenmans, 1999). Optimistic observers were nevertheless confident that some day something would happen. For this optimistic assessment they counted on the new generation of civil servants whose academic training, e.g. in university economics departments, had made them familiar with many of the ideas underpinning the managerial reform movements elsewhere. They would have to wait until the recent Copernicus reform programme to see their dreams come true.

Why have the new Walloon and Francophone administrations generally been even slower in responding to the impetus of the reform movement? Of course resources are scarce in Wallonia and the Walloons tend to refer to (the lack) of reforms in Francophone countries. One puzzled observer ventured another hypothesis. According to him the Walloon mentality does not welcome the reformist ideas floating around because it fears the insecurity, the stress and the job losses they would entail. The cautious, 'humanistic' approach chosen by the Walloon region is closer to this mentality than the carrot-and-stick approach of the Flemish ministry. The slower pace of reform among the Francophones might also be caused by the stronger impact of the Socialist Party in their administrations. The latter has, after all, been dominant in Wallonia and, to some extent at least, also in Brussels, whereas in Flanders Christian Democrats have been prevalent. Whatever the causes, the fact itself cannot be questioned. In Wallonia, and also to some extent in the Francophone community, not only the resources but the aspirations to reform have been weaker among politicians, if not among civil servants. Politicization is still the rule, by allocating to the coalition parties a contingent of political promotions proportional to their electoral strength, by an extensive recruitment of 'contractuals', and by the creation of many new, semi-public agencies 'of public utility', moves which open up opportunities for appointments to which the Camu regulations do not apply.

The fact that reform initiatives were neither equally ambitious nor equally successful in all the governments of the federalized Belgian state should not obscure the fact that the motives were almost always the same, and the same as in other Western countries. The fiscal crisis was particularly pressing for an EU member state that found it unthinkable not to join the European Monetary Union from the start and at all costs but whose annual public deficit ran into double figures for several consecutive years and whose accumulated public debt per capita was the highest of all the member states, even Italy. The call to do more with fewer (but better) personnel rang loud and clear and met with much approval, even among the SCS.

A second motive was inspired by the need to strengthen the performance of the civil service now that economic competition between member states of the EU was being based, at least partly, on the services its administration could offer to the private sector. Accordingly, policy design should no longer be reserved exclusively to the ministers and their cabinet staffers. Indeed, in a complex and turbulent societal environment policy design requires human resources and expertise that cabinet staffers, numerous as they are in Belgium, can no longer provide. It becomes ever more necessary to call on civil servants to contribute to this phase of the policy-making cycle.

Last, but not least, there was the need to bridge the gap between government and citizens that in Belgium had led to a disturbing level of political distrust and alienation. A greater degree of friendliness towards the customers could perhaps contribute to disarming their hostility to the political elites and their inclination to vote for extremist parties.

Political control of the administrative elites

The various measures that emerged in the first wave (in Flanders) and second wave (in the federal government) of New Public Management reforms can be categorized under three headings borrowed from organization sociology that point to the perennial fault lines in any organization: the definition of objectives, the definition of functions, and the co-ordination of functions. Here we will focus mainly on the first of these reform categories: the (political) definition of objectives.

To implement this reform, civil servants must be persuaded, first, to examine closely what they are actually doing and, next, to formulate as precisely as possible what they should be doing. On the basis of this analysis the SCS should negotiate a 'management contract' about the results they have to produce. The SCS are then to be granted a temporary mandate to achieve the promised results. Mandate holders could, in the most radical option, be chosen, without much regard for rank or length of career, from all the civil servants of level 1, or at least from those who belong to an elite corps, having passed a supplementary test of their aptitude to manage. This mandate is a temporary promotion (of about six years in the recent proposals) that does not have to be prolonged, thus giving the minister or the top SCS the possibility to sanction his/her managers for nonperformance. If a second mandate is denied to mandate holders they return to their more modest former position, but can keep certain privileges.

However, mandate systems come in degrees, the earlier versions being more moderate than the most recent. In the ministry of the Francophone community the mandate system was and is a mitigated one. The top civil servants now rely on a 'pool' of collaborators; this means that the SCS are allocated for a period of a few years to a specific post, with the provision that they can later be moved to another post, frequently at the will of politicians. In principle, though, the politicians can only choose a post holder from this pool. Thus it might be preferable to change the 'attributions' or responsibilities of the SCS rather than their rank. This of course leaves open the possibility of exercising the veteran strategy of artful sidetracking. It also remains difficult to create vacancies for new, more proactive policy-makers. In the more radical variety, introduced in the Flemish administration during its first wave of reforms in the 1990s, mandate holders can be selected, without much regard for rank or seniority, from all the civil servants of level 1, with the necessary management capacities. The new SELOR agency, which replaced the old PRS and was intended to focus more on the specific needs of a government service, would guarantee the quality of a shortlist of candidates.

For quite some time the reforms in the Flemish administration were seen, at least by the advocates of the NPM, as the example for the federal administration and Walloon and Francophone administrations to follow, as the reform movement there seemed to have found an equilibrium point. However, in 2000 national and regional elections led to new coalitions led by the Liberals and excluding the Christian Democrats for the first time since 1958. The new federal government launched an ambitious reform proposal (under the name Copernicus) clearly inspired by the New Public Management orthodoxy. More surprisingly, a new overhaul of the administration was proposed in the Flemish administration too. Clearly, the equilibrium reached in the late 1990s had proved to be unstable. Now the emphasis was no longer on the autonomy of the SCS and their horizontal co-operation and co-ordination. It was shifted to more ministerial control over the SCS of the department, avoiding undue interference from other departments and services. The initially much acclaimed matrix structure of the single Flemish ministry with its board of secretaries-general was abandoned and replaced by 13 separate ministries and services whose administrations would be headed by managers directly responsible to the minister. Something similar was envisaged in the federal Copernicus proposal. Aberbach and Rockman (2000) have stressed that the practise of the New Public Management theory is likely to vacillate between autonomy of the civil service and centralization by the politicians. This seems to be illustrated in the successive episodes of administrative reform in Belgium. After having stressed the first objective, the new reformers are now focusing on the second. Clearly, it is difficult to reconcile the two.

The old reform in the Flemish administration granted a rather strong status to the board of secretaries-general. In spite of being political appointees they enjoyed a good deal of autonomy from political and partisan pressure because they had full tenure until retirement age, because they were supposed to be managers in charge of personnel and budgetary policy, and above all, because they could act as a board. As such, policy design was part of their agenda. The chairperson of this board, being also the secretary of the Flemish council of ministers, would be extremely well informed and able to pass on information from there to colleagues.[14]

In the new reform the top SCS will be 'contractuals' who have to individually negotiate and renegotiate management contracts with the minister and his or her cabinet chief. They will be picked from a shortlist of suitable and expert candidates selected by an independent institution (SELOR), but it is the minister who will do the picking.[15] Moreover, the contractual's position will always be precarious, as their mandate is limited to six years. Also actual performance is never fully measurable but always open to hostile questioning, as has recently been shown by the tribulations of the managers of parastatals and public enterprises who got their jobs from earlier governments. If these new reform proposals are carried through, the locus of politicization will shift to the selection and the control of temporary managers with a rather weak position *vis-à-vis* their political masters.

The 'Copernicus project' launched by the first Verhofstadt government (1999–2003) to reform the federal administration, being more novel than the Flemish reform, ran into fierce opposition, first of all because it intended to call not only on civil servants but also on managers from the private sector to fill in the top jobs (close to 450 in total). As the latter would not enjoy the protection of civil service status, their job insecurity would have to be compensated by much higher salaries, to the dismay of the career civil servants. And, more essential for our concerns, these high-ranking 'contractuals' would be overly dependent on the whims of their ministers. Their precarious position would reinforce not the autonomy of the administrative elite, but rather the political control of partisan politicians.

There are other objections to this mandate system as well. Some opponents contend that policy objectives cannot always be defined with the precision needed, that success in reaching the objectives is likely to be assessed on the basis of subjective, even partisan, criteria, and that the politicians can impose the objectives without at the same time providing the resources required to achieve them.[16] In the first year of the second Verhofstadt government, several of the new top mandate holders held a collective and rather unusual press conference at which several of the new top mandate holders complained publicly about the lack of resources, material and juridical, that keeps hampering the implementation of the policies required from them by their contracts with the government.

Doing away with partisan loyalty?

What else can be done to draft the SCS into the policy-making process? Obviously, their marginalization by the cabinet staffers must be stopped. In Wallonia and even in the Francophone community few measures appear to have been taken to tackle this problem. The Flemish government had decided to limit the size of the cabinets to force the ministers to depend more on their civil servants during the phase of policy design. However, the net effect of this and other measures is still in doubt. Some ministers are reputed to have sidestepped the measure by removing the less useful cabinet staffers from their payrolls and keeping on their essential political advisers. The cabinet chiefs more often than not still decide which civil servants will serve as members of committees working on policy design, sometimes without much say from their administrative superiors.

More recent proposals (2000) were intended to reduce the ministerial cabinets to five or so personal assistants. The SCS would certainly be able to strengthen their position if they had to contend with a few part-time, short-term advisers rather than with the present numerous full-time cabinet staffers. This proposal has received much public applause (it has even been submitted to a quasi referendum) but also surprisingly strong political opposition. In the federal government a number of (mainly Francophone and Socialist) ministers have flatly rejected it. The resulting compromise was that some ministers would be allowed to keep their cabinet staffers until the end of the legislature, when they would no longer be needed anyway, and that the others would in principle dismiss theirs by the end of 2001. When Verhofstadt I ended, only two federal ministers actually did so, Van den Bossche himself and the Prime Minister. The idea was that the old cabinets would be replaced with a slimmed-down version with the new title of 'political secretariat', comprising only six senior and eight junior personal assistants under a powerful chief of staff. Each ministry (or 'federal public service') would moreover enjoy the support of a cell of policy designers, to be recruited by the minister from inside or outside the civil service. These two features of the new ministries clearly show why the opposition claims that the number of cabinet staffers will be reduced only by half, if not less. Perhaps this new brand of ministerial staffers will be less politically powerful as they will not necessarily be given full-time jobs. Perhaps appointments will also be less dependent on party and personal loyalty to the minister as they may be screened by SELOR and recruited more for specific expertise. Still, this means that the cabinet staffers will not fade altogether from the political arena and that the change is at least partly cosmetic. This prediction appears to be confirmed by recent developments under Verhofstadt II. It does look as if the political secretariats and the cells of policy designers are going to be installed as planned. But at the same time the voices advocating the retention of a number of cabinet staffers are growing louder. The new minister in charge of the administration is not of the same opinion as Van den Bossche.

Another, more informal but perhaps equally reforming measure would be obligatory concertation between cabinet chiefs and top civil servants. Again this is an idea which has been implemented to different degrees by different administrations. It appears to work rather well in Flanders, but it does not yet amount to much in the federal government.

The psychological effect of these and other measures should not be underestimated. Civil servants are delighted to be allowed to make even a modest contribution to policy-making and in certain situations this contribution can become quite substantial, e.g. when working groups, consisting of a mix of cabinet staffers and expert civil servants, become more or less institutionalized. Such mixed working groups are becoming a new tradition, at least in the Flemish governance system. Even in the best cases, though, the contribution of the SCS, however gratifying, tends to remain modest. Without real think tank capacities civil servants cannot possibly hope to propose complete policies. And many politicians do not really feel the need to provide them with such capacities since they can rely on the services of other think tanks, e.g. on those of their own party and of major 'friendly' interest groups.[17] As a result of this defective intellectual apparatus the contributions of the SCS to policy design will mostly be limited to remarks about problem areas, possible implementation alternatives, feasibility, and the like. And they will hardly ever enjoy the privilege of approaching their minister face to face.

A second condition for empowering the SCS is to enhance their credibility by removing their party labels. The phenomenon of partisan appointments has been limited, at least in Flanders and to a lesser degree in the federal civil service, by granting the SCS more authority to recruit and to promote their subordinates (in some cases these decisions are left to external consultation bureaux). Previously different boards of SCS had the right, indeed the obligation, to give their advice on these matters, but the ministers could quite easily ignore their advice. Now, however, they are placed under the obligation to follow this advice, especially if it is unanimous. Because the SCS are eager to have their best people promoted, they tend to give unanimous advice as often as possible. As a result the special Dekens–Mangeleer–Missant committee which used to stand guard over the balance of partisan appointments, has become superfluous. Only the top appointments, such as secretary-general or director-general, are still the privilege of the government. Critics have made the observation that in this way partisan appointments will not be excluded but only made less visible. The SCS in charge of recruiting and promoting are expected to make deals among themselves. And the appointment of a civil servant to a mandate will depend very much on the 'discretion' of the minister and his/her cabinet. This could result, so some observers fear, in more rather than less politicization of the senior ranks of the civil service.

It is a puzzle for political scientists why depoliticization has never seemed to be a major concern in Wallonia. SCS promotions are still being allocated, on a proportional basis, to the parties in the governing coalition. The old system of recruiting contractuals on a partisan basis and regularizing them later, appears still to be in full operation. The Camu procedure for recruitment of civil servants does not apply to these contractuals. The politicization drive, somewhat restrained in the regular ministries, has found a new outlet with the creation of many new semi-public agencies. Some observers point a finger at the Socialists who have been dominant in the successive Walloon governments and who are traditionally fairly sympathetic to the system of politicization. Perhaps Socialist politicians feel a greater need of civil servants they can trust as a counterbalance to a private sector they cannot trust. But this interpretation might stem from the partisan prejudice of their opponents.

Conclusion

Belgian observers are speculating about the staying power of the recent reforms of the federal administration. Certainly its objective of depoliticization was very ambitious. Much depended on the political will of a minister and the backing he enjoyed from a Prime Minister (and the NPM ideology). But that minister is now nearing the end of his political career and that Prime Minister is facing a general election with an uncertain outcome. Others will most likely take their place. In the meantime the opposition to the reform path chosen by these political leaders has not disarmed and is not likely to leave the field. It is true that nobody wants to return to the old ways of the party politicization era. The vicious spiral of that system had reached a nadir that almost all politicians and bureaucrats heartily deplored, not to mention many of the consumers of government services. However, which road should the successors to the present reformers choose? They have two alternatives.

The first one grants a good deal of autonomy to the top civil servants to select, appoint, and promote their subordinates. This autonomy to realize their function of personnel manager requires that they act as a board, with the help of staffers of their own, to offset attempts at undue political control by their ministers. The boards of SCS in charge of personnel management could not be prevented from taking party considerations into account and deals could still be made among them. But at least the impact of party politicians would be muted and the selection and promotion of civil servants would attain a higher level of legitimacy, especially if the preliminary screening were left to SELOR and other trusted consulting agencies. This was the road taken by the first wave of civil service reform in Flanders. However, in spite of much initial acclaim, this regime proved to be less stable than expected. The board of top civil servants did not succeed in closing the ranks against their ministers, who sought to reassert their control over their top SCS whose resistance, so they were tempted to assume, stemmed from their partisan biases.

Hence the road taken by the second wave of reform in Flanders and the Copernicus reform in the federal administration. Here too great care is said to have been taken to depoliticize personnel management. The emphasis was on the abolition of the cabinet staffers system and, even more than in the first wave of reform, on the introduction of a mandate system for all the SCS. However, the cabinet system proved remarkably resilient. It could be limited and mitigated but not abolished. In this area much will depend on the political will of the next government. The clock can be turned back quite easily in fact if not in principle. The mandate system, on the other hand, conceived as it is now is as a privilege of the ministers, tends to create too many frictions between the politicians and the top SCS/mandate holders, frictions that can easily be exploited by political opponents and the press. As a result this realization of the NPM reform is likely to prove uncomfortably unstable too.

It must be added that other achievements are questioned less frequently. If party political appointments and promotions still occur in the future, they will have to take the expertise of the candidates more into account. They will be less visible, better argued and less demoralizing for the civil servants in general. Even frankly political appointments of the top SCS will be reserved for an elite corps of civil servants who have passed the necessary tests of excellence. At lower levels the impact of political patronage in the recruitment and promotion of civil servants is even more likely to decrease. While the mandate holders may become more subject to a political spoils system, the lower-ranking career civil servants may be allowed to feel secure in a merit system. That is, they will feel secure from partisan pressure, not from competition with their colleagues.

Notes

1 Civil servants of level 2 could also take part in this examination without having a university degree, but then on specific conditions only.
2 For this research design we owe much gratitude to the German team of Hans-Ulrich Derlien and Renate Mayntz.
3 The ministries of Foreign Affairs and National Defence were excluded (Dierickx and Majersdorf, 1993). This study was part of an international comparative project. In some of the participating countries these two ministries were seen as atypical. They are perhaps so in Belgium too, the one being staffed largely by diplomats, the other by military.
4 As we shall see, most of the SCS have party loyalties too. And almost all of them were given party labels, at least at the time of the early study, whether they welcomed this or not, and whether they knew it or not.
5 To achieve party proportionality in the appointments and promotions of the SCS was not the only objective of these successive committees. Linguistic proportionality, or rather parity, had also to be respected. This meant that all top civil servants who had not mastered the other national language sufficiently well would get an assistant from the other language community. This measure can be seen as consociational since it comes down to protecting the Francophones who tend to know little Dutch, while the Flemish tend to be rather fluent in French. The promoters of the Copernicus reform of the federal administration have proposed that all top civil servants should be fluent in both languages. With regard to the appointment of cabinet staffers ministers would of course call mostly on candidates of their own (monolinguistic) party, but would also be careful to include some staffers who had mastered the other language.
6 These percentages are based on the dichotomy between technocratic and non-technocratic respondents. Only the percentage of 'technocrats' is shown.

7 A factor analysis suggested that these items could be seen as derived from a single underlying dimension and that aversion from one of these political actors went together with aversion from the other political actors. To get a feel of the semantic content of this scale we reproduce here the original items:

 1 The public interest of our country is under serious threat from the continuing strife between special interest groups.
 2 Political parties do play an important role in a democracy. However, they tend to unnecessarily exacerbate conflicts.
 3 The administrative apparatus, rather than the parties or the parliament, provides our country with a satisfactory government.
 4 People who enter a political career often think more about their own interest or that of their party than about the interests of their fellow citizens.

8 'Frustration with the job' is more frequent among rightists than among leftists (67 per cent versus 42 per cent). This suggests that ideology does also matter for the more emotional aspects of administrative attitudes.

9 The index is statistically not a very powerful one but a principal component analysis succeeds in finding a factor which explains 41 per cent of the total variance and the factor loadings are good enough for a first exploration of the data.

10 That does not mean that the former are completely non-partisan. Maybe they rely on the hidden bias of the bureaucratic structures. But consciously they try harder to differentiate their professional life from their party commitments as private citizens.

11 The new constitution stipulated e.g. that the recruitment of all civil servants of any public administration should, as before, be handled by the PRS. But most other aspects of civil service policy were left to the discretion of the governments (federal and regional).

12 It is true that the Walloon region and the Francophone community also started with a single ministry. Their cases show that centralization is a necessary, not a sufficient condition for reform.

13 The minister was a somewhat colourless personality who could hardly be expected to lobby his colleagues with startling new proposals. The fact that Van den Bossche, who had gained prestige as a reformer of the Flemish civil service, was called to head the federal Ministry of the Civil Service in 1999 suggests that the new federal government meant business. Indeed the new government led by the Liberal Verhofstadt made the reform of the federal civil sevice one of its top priorities.

14 The official good intentions were slow to take shape, however. In fact the board of Flemish secretaries-general has never yet functioned effectively as a partner to its government in matters outside its management concerns.

15 Very recently the federal government succeeded in filling the administrative top jobs created by the Copernicus project. The non-partisan screening procedure seems to have been quite successful as many of the appointees are civil servants with an opposition party label.

16 On the other hand some advocates of the 'management by objectives' approach would like to go futher and entrust more objectives to governmental or to frankly privatized enterprises. At least at the federal level, however, most reformers did not want to go that far yet. Co-ordination between these enterprises could prove difficult as the government is a coalition and the governance system is complex following the federalization process.

17 Belgium is a neo-corporatist, even pillarized country with strong linkages between parties and their respective following of interest groups. Some of these have appreciable research institutes of their own.

References

Aberbach, Joel D. and Rockman, Bert A. (2000), *In the Web of Politics: Three Decades of the U.S. Federal Executive* The Brookings Institution, Washington (DC).

Aberbach, Joel D., Putnam, Robert D. and Rockman, Bert A. (1981), *Bureaucrats and Politicians in Western Democracies* Harvard University Press, Cambridge (Mass.).

Aucoin, Peter (1990), 'Administrative reform in public management: paradigms, principles, paradoxes, and pendulums', *Governance* 115–37.

Bouckaert, Geert and Auwers, Tom (1999), *De Modernisering van de Vlaamse Overheid* Die Keure, Bruges.

Bouckaert, Geert, Hondeghem, Annie and Maes, Rudolf (eds) (1994), *De Overheidsmanager. Nieuwe Ontwikkelingen in het Overheidsmanagement* Vervolmakingscentrum voor Overheidsbeleid en Bestuur, Leuven.

Campbell, Colin and Szablowski, George J. (1979), *The Super Bureaucrats. Structure and Behavior in Central Agencies* McMillan of Canada, Toronto.

De Borger, Jozef (1988), 'Depolitisering van het openbaar ambt, een must voor een fatsoenlijke politiek', *Nieuw Tijdschrift voor Politiek* 3, 53–87.

Dierickx, Guido and Beyers, Jan (1999), 'Belgian civil servants in the European Union: a tale of two cultures', *West European Politics* 22, 3, 198–222.

Dierickx, Guido and Majersdorf, Philip (1993), *La Culture politique des fonctionnaires et des hommespolitiques en Belgique* Vanden Broele, Bruges.

Hondeghem, Annie (1990), *De Loopbaan van de Ambtenaar* K.U. Leuven, Vervolmakingscentrum voor Overheidsbeleid en Bestuur, Leuven.

Lijphart, Arend (1999), *Patterns of Democracy. Government Forms and Performance in Thirty-Six Countries* Yale University Press, New Haven and London.

Maes, Rudolf (ed.) (1997), *Democratie, Legitimiteit, Nieuwe Politieke Cultuur* Acco, Leuven-Amersfoort.

Molitor, André (1974), *L'Administration de la Belgique* CRISP, Brussels.

Peters, B. Guy and Savoie, Donald J. (1998), *Taking Stock: Assessing Public Sector Reforms* McGill-Queens University Press, Montreal.

Pollitt, Christopher and Bouckaert, Geert (1999), *Public Management Reforms: A Comparative Analysis* Oxford University Press, Oxford.

Savoie, Donald J. (1994), *Thatcher, Reagan, Mulroney: In Search of a New Bureaucracy* University of Pittsburgh Press, Pittsburgh (Pa.).

Stenmans, Alain (1999), *La Transformation de la fonction administrative en Belgique* CRISP, Brussels.

Stroobants, Eric and Victor, Leo (2000), *Beter Bestuur. Een Visie op een Transparant Organisatiemodel voor de Vlaamse Administratie* Vlaams Ministerie, Brussels.

Ziller, Jacques (1993), *Administrations comparées: les systèmes politico-administratifs de l'Europe des Douze* Montchrestien, Paris.

11 Dutch government reform and the quest for political control

Frits M. van der Meer

1 Introduction

Prior to the 1990s Dutch government experienced political–administrative conflict only on a limited scale and resulting cases were mostly dealt with in private. That changed in the 1990s. A series of parliamentary inquiries into highly publicised policy fiascos and some intense political–administrative conflicts triggered a more or less open debate on the design of Dutch political–administrative relations (De Vries and Van Dam 1998; Rosenthal 1999). For example, in 1994 a parliamentary inquiry into methods used to combat serious crime and drugs-related issues concluded that the police and the public prosecuting offices had employed illegal methods to achieve their objectives, namely allowing the import of hard drugs in order to infiltrate organised crime. In the lead-up to the inquiry, two ministers had to resign from office. The ministers of the Home Affairs and Justice departments disciplined the responsible commissioners of police and prosecutors. The prosecuting office again ran into controversy when the chief prosecutor became entangled in bitter conflict with the Justice Minister. It happened that both officials had the same party political affiliation. The Prime Minister accused the chief prosecutor of an open 'revolt' against cabinet. The chief prosecutor had to resign (1998) although he was more or less exonerated afterwards and appointed to head an independent agency. Likewise a parliamentary inquiry (1999) into the aftermath of the crash of an El Al Boeing into a block of flats in an Amsterdam suburb pointed to major frictions in political–administrative relationships. The high media profile of the secretary-general of the Ministry of Economic Affairs and his criticism of vital cabinet decisions led to his (semi-voluntary) resignation in 1999. Leading political pundits, scientists, professional politicians and senior civil servants viewed the rapid succession of incidents as a threat to the reputation of the government and public administration. It also produced serious unease within the civil service. In June 1999 four secretaries-general went public by complaining to a leading daily that the media and parliament had blamed the civil service unfairly for past policy incidents (*Volkskrant,* June 1999). Their opinion was indicative of a more general feeling in the civil service that it is being made to take on what should be ministerial responsibility.

Since then things have calmed down. Nevertheless it would be oversimplifying to explain things away by emphasising specific conditions at the time. Beneath the surface some more fundamental factors are at play. Since the 1970s there has been a growing awareness that permanent officials have taken a steadily increasing role in policy making and implementation. From the early 1980s a more proactive and entrepreneurial civil service has been emerging (De Vries and Van Dam 1998). Civil service power is said to have grown at the expense of ministerial and, in particular, parliamentary power. Regardless of the validity of these arguments, ministerial and civil service roles have become more complementary and overlapping. Although this conclusion is widely accepted in political science and public administration, a majority of politicians and experts in constitutional law disagree, particularly with respect to the normative aspects of this political-administrative osmosis. Many politicians still profess a formal 'Weberian style' doctrine of full ministerial responsibility and civil service loyalty.[1]

The political–administrative problems, together with awareness of the growing convergence of roles, have created a sense that it is urgent to sort things out. This implies that methods and instruments to reinforce political 'control' over the senior civil service are being discussed. This increased or reinforced political control is known as (top-down) politicisation. With respect to the Dutch case we will address the following questions. Are there any changes in the level of top-down politicisation in the Netherlands? Which methods of top-down politicisation are being used? How can (the changes in) the use of particular methods of top-down politicisation be understood?

Our analysis starts with a brief overview of the institutional arrangements governing the Dutch political and administrative system. These arrangements are important for an understanding of the changes in the Dutch level of top-down politicisation and the choice of methods to reinforce political control on the (senior) civil service. To examine the circumstances leading up to the increase in top-down politicisation, we have to return to the early 1980s, when economic and political conditions produced a watershed in post-war Dutch government and politics. The economic crisis, in combination with the European integration process and a number of fundamental changes in Dutch society, produced some profound challenges for the country's government. After discussing the changes in Dutch governance, we will look into their repercussions on the positions and roles of political official and civil servants. In the following section, attention is paid to initiatives to reformulate and redesign political–administrative relations. Peters and Pierre's perspective on top-down politicisation will be used as a guide-line (see Chapter 1 above). We focus on control mechanisms that are considered permissible, given the constraints of the Dutch institutional context, and that mainly imply the use of (new) management development instruments, a change in civil service ethics and a redefinition of the legal position of top civil servants. The analysis will show that party political nominations and manipulation of government structures (with the possible exception of agencification) are unusual as they are considered incompatible with the institutional arrangements described in section 2.1. The Senior Public Service (ABD) will be featured most prominently as a Human Resource Management-related 'allowable' control mechanism. Interestingly, ABD paradoxically diminishes the possibility of party political control but gives politicians a new HRM-related instrument to control the civil service.

2 Refounding Dutch governance: 1982 onwards

2.1 Institutional arrangements governing the Dutch political-administrative system

Dutch society is often characterised by its deep political, religious and regional cleavages (Lijphart 1968). Although these cleavages have become less noticeable since the 1960s, they have produced a lasting institutional mould governing public decision making. Likewise, the Dutch system of government harbours a fragmented political landscape, an emphasis on decentralisation and the involvement of societal groups in decision-making procedures. During the course of history, this model of co-operation has had different manifestations, e.g. pillarisation, the consociational model and more recently the so-called poldermodel.

This political fragmentation necessitates co-operation and negotiation between the various government organisations, (minority) parties and interest groups in order to ensure (central) government stability. From the nineteenth century on, that need for party political co-operation has manifested itself in the prevalence of coalition cabinets. Rarely has a single party ever held a dominant position in such a coalition. The Christian Democratic Parties (and from the 1980s the Christian Democratic Party) were able to stamp their imprint at times on coalition politics in some periods before 1994.[2] Positioned in the centre of the political spectrum, they were in office continuously from the beginning of the twentieth century till 1994. Nevertheless, even the Christian Democrats needed the support of at least one of the other major parties in order to secure a parliamentary majority. After the Second World War this meant making coalition agreements with the Labour Party (PVDA) or the (orthodox) Liberal Party (VVD). Sometimes smaller parties were invited in order to produce the necessary majority.

To limit the likelihood of 'political' accidents, parties devise so-called coalition programmes. In the post-war era the programmes have become increasingly elaborate and binding, consequently reinforcing executive dominance over parliament during a given term of office. Parliament wields its greatest influence during talks on the coalition arrangements although leaders (and sometimes senior spokespersons) of parliamentary coalition parties are consulted on crucial cabinet decisions.[3] The way parliament ties its own hands is a source of (backbench) frustration. Consequently parliament tends to concentrate on scrutiny of government action.[4]

The diffuse distribution of political power has prevented the development of a Prime Minister model in the Netherlands. The power of a Dutch Prime Minister depends on the individual's standing. As the largest party usually supplies the Prime Minister, the other coalition parties as a rule are allowed to 'nominate' a Deputy Prime Minister. Due to the existence of this heterogeneous cabinet system, cabinet ministers possess a considerable degree of autonomy although there are no 'super-ministers' with supra-departmental powers. Because of that same ministerial autonomy, ministers very much rely on their own ministerial civil servants. The personal 'weight' of the ministers and their experience in office determines whether that 'reliance' results in the minister 'going native'. Since the 1970s, nevertheless, ministerial autonomy has been somewhat curtailed under the influence of growing policy interdependencies. The Council of Ministers has increasingly developed into an important policy-making forum. Likewise, initiatives have been taken to decompartmentalise the civil service. These will be discussed in section 4. The emphasis on interdepartmental decision making has not meant a more limited role for top civil servants. On the contrary, the interdepartmental decision-making procedures has had the effect of increasing their importance. Civil Service Preparatory Committees (Ambtelijke Voorportalen) have been created and some top civil servants have access to the meetings of Ministerial Committees of the Council of Ministers. In these capacities, leading civil servants have had an important input in the redirection of Dutch government in the 1980s and 1990s.

2.2 The redirection of Dutch government in the 1980s and 1990s

From the early 1980s, Dutch politics and government experienced a profound change in structure and style. With the benefit of hindsight, the crucial turning point can be located in 1982, when a centre-right coalition (called Lubbers I, after the Prime Minister) came to power. It encountered severe financial and economic problems due to what proved later to be a structural crisis in the economy which had first become evident during the latter years of the left-wing Den Uyl cabinet in the mid-1970s. At that time employer organisations, economists and some leading civil servants warned against what they considered a fatal combination of an ambitious social security programme, extreme government intervention in the economy and excessive wage demands. The term 'Dutch disease' was coined. From 1977 to 1982 some feeble initiatives were taken to address the situation but these proved ineffective. In 1982 the centre-right coalition rejected the previous Keynesian-inspired economic policy in favour of a supply-side and monetarist policy.

Taking a neo-classical approach to government finance, with the support of political office holders and top civil servants alike, the Lubbers cabinet adopted a stringent fiscal policy resulting in cutbacks in expenditure and personnel. Senior civil servants in the areas of finance and economics in Civil Service Preparatory Committees and Ministerial Committees of the Council of Ministers took important roles as both initiators and supporters of the reforms.

Government and welfare reform and the reduction of civil service personnel and costs topped the political agenda. In addition to these cutbacks, the old bureaucratic approach was gradually overhauled with the introduction of a new managerial style of running government. In the then fashionable political jargon, the metaphor of the commercial enterprise BV Nederland was used to portray government as a dynamic entrepreneurial organisation. The political administrative language of those days shows some similarities with that of the Thatcher government in Britain. It differed to the extent that changes were not so much ideologically motivated as founded on pragmatic grounds: namely to avoid government bankruptcy and preserve the essentials of the welfare state.

The election victory in 1986 of the parties participating in Lubbers I helped to sustain the reform programme. In the 1980s and early 1990s a broad political and social consensus on the necessity of this new approach developed. Even the labour unions and trade unions agreed on the necessity of pay restraint, supplemented with employment and training schemes. A formal agreement known as the 'agreement of Wassenaar' was finalised in 1982 (Visser and Hemerijck 1997).

This 'new' approach was composed of an apparently curious blend of insights drawn from neo-classical economics, managerial-style (NPM) policies and the involvement of third sector groups. In the 1990s in the Netherlands it came to be called the 'poldermodel'. This 'poldermodel' basically involves a variation on the traditional neo-corporatist relationships in the social-economic policy areas between government and privileged interest groups such as trade unions and employers' organisations. The major break with the past is that relations were depillarised or, rather, 'deconfessionalised'. Diverse religious-based organisations merged into neutral federations. As the word 'neo-corporatism' was considered (at least by some) to be 'contaminated', the term 'poldermodel' was preferred. The poldermodel can be seen as the renaissance of a deconfessionalised neo-corporatist system in the social economic field but modified by a more vigorous and assertive government role (Visser and Hemerijck 1997).

Concentrating solely on the financial and economic roots of the major policy changes in the 1980s is misleading. Some parallel (and sometimes interrelated) societal processes were equally influential on the changing structure of the public sector and the mode of governance adopted by the Dutch government. The trend towards democratising internal relationships in society and the erosion of the pillarised society under the influence of the combined processes of individualisation and deconfessionalisation had already started to have their effects in the late 1960s. Depillarisation had the effect of fragmenting a seemingly transparent and stable societal structure. Under the influence of these processes the political landscape altered in a fundamental way. New parties were established and old parties, like the Labour Party, changed radically. Voters lost their traditional loyalties. The authority of central government could no longer be taken for granted but had to be earned by continuously justifying itself. Citizens were demanding a more active involvement in policy making and implementation. Decentralisation of central government tasks and powers again became an issue, and was considered an urgent priority in order to promote democratic decision making.

The radicalisation of both politics and society came to an end in the 1980s, partly owing to the persistent nature of the economic crisis. Further disenchantment resulted from the failure of the 'permanent quest for democratisation'. The lasting effects of this period of political and societal turmoil were the ending of the automatic acceptance of (central) government authority, an impetus for decentralisation, the depillarisation of societal counterparts to government and the inclusion of more transient pressure groups in decision-making arrangements (Bekke 1988). These effects placed an even heavier emphasis on negotiating and interactive styles of governance. New pressure and interest groups like the environmentalists gained access to (or were incorporated in) the policy-making arenas, together with the more traditional groups such as employers' organisations and trade unions.

In addition to the internal change processes, the Dutch society and economy became increasingly integrated into the international economy. Although the Netherlands traditionally has had a relatively open economy, the European integration process in particular has limited national autonomy. In the 1980s the on-going process of Europeanisation extended beyond the economic area to an increasing number of policy fields.

The changes described above are sometimes referred to, particularly in Anglo-Saxon literature, as the 'hollowing out of the state' (Rhodes 1994; Page and Wright 1999). In the Netherlands this process is usually referred to as the transfer or dislocation of politics, in accordance with the analysis of Ulrich Beck (Bovens *et al.* 1995; De Vries 1995). Although the dislocation of politics is based on a broader argument than the transfer thesis, both contain the same major characteristics.[5] A vertical and horizontal transfer of power from the traditional quarters of political decision making is seen in both. The vertical transfer goes in two directions. The powers and responsibilities of central government are moved in an upward direction by the on-going Europeanisation process and downward by the territorial decentralisation to municipalities and provinces.

In addition to this vertical transfer is a horizontal transfer involving, first, the creation of independent public (and even private) agencies for policy implementation and delivery of tasks (agencification), and, second, an increasing level of juridification. The use of framework legislation and 'vague' legal norms inherent to modern government legislation has increased the involvement of the legal system in issues of policy implementation. In response to appeals and complaints from citizens, the courts have become more assertive, intervening directly in (central) government decisions (Dijkstra 1996). Furthermore, new citizen-centred initiatives have been developed, often based on information technology. Finally these horizontal transfers are linked to the disappearance of (central) government tasks, responsibilities and powers due to privatisation and deregulation.

These transfers not only limit the scope of central government but also decrease the autonomy of the centre. In consequence of the increasing level of public sector fragmentation, a new system of co-ordination is needed. Although, as stated above, there is evidence of a vertical and horizontal transfer of power in the Dutch case, the 'hollowing out' and 'dislocation of politics' theses are somewhat crude and oversimplified. The idea of central government at the core of society can be considered a fabrication of political-administrative and sociological thinking of the late 1950s and 1960s, inspired by the expansion of government during this period. But even in the heyday of central government power, third sector involvement (resulting in an elaborate parastate) was a force to be reckoned with. In addition, the doctrine of the Dutch decentralised unitary state implied, at least in theory, a dispersion of tasks, powers and responsibilities over three levels of government that were in principle and to a certain extent autonomous. Territorial decentralisation was given a new impetus by the government reform programme in the 1980s. The same applies to a certain extent to agencification, which can be seen as a new element of functional decentralisation, reinforcing the already sizeable parastate. Traditionally, the Netherlands has had a wide range of functional decentralised or parastatal bodies, which have often had third party involvement. Some but not all of the new independent agencies were organised on the same lines, for example the Labour Mediation Service (Arbeidsvoorziening).

More fundamentally, the metaphors of 'hollowing out of the state' or 'dislocation of politics' suggest that tasks, responsibilities and power have disappeared. That is misleading as the horizontal and vertical transfer mechanisms have a reciprocal dimension. A transfer of tasks and responsibilities may imply a loss of autonomy but new strands of influence can be gained, either by taking a share in intergovernmental policy making (territorial and functional decentralisation) or by gaining supervisory power (privatisation and decentralisation) or by participating in a new compound organisation (the European Union) (Page 1997). The exact balance of wins and losses cannot be calculated overall but can only be determined when examining the situation in the various policy fields. The available literature is not very conclusive in this respect.

What is certainly true is that the Dutch system of government has become even more fragmented than before and central government has lost a fair degree of its (already limited) autonomy due to the developments described above. This has resulted in an even greater need to maintain and manage multiple linkages between the various actors involved in public policy making. These intricate external management tasks increase the vulnerability of the Dutch system to breakdowns.

3 The implications for the balance of power between political and administrative office holders

Attention has been drawn to the effects of the European integration process, privatisation, decentralisation, agencification, juridification, and increasing citizen and third party involvement on Dutch government. The repercussions of these changes on the balance of power between political and administrative office holders are difficult to determine. A loss or gain of central government power due to one or more of these processes does not necessarily mean a change in the balance of power between political and administrative office holders. At least in the Netherlands there is no hard evidence that any of these processes were instigated in order either to diminish or to enhance the power base of ministers or top civil servants. Both parties were quite eager to pursue the challenges involved.

The course and direction of Europeanisation are in the hands of neither Dutch political office holders nor civil servants, but both groups agree on the necessity of the integration process. Due to the institutional design of the European Union and the nature of its decision-making procedures, the loss of autonomy is to a certain extent compensated by political and civil service participation in European institutions such as the Council of Ministers, the intergovernmental policy negotiations and the working committees of the Commission in Brussels. In addition, the actual implementation of EU guidelines in national legislation is to a large degree performed in The Hague. The one category that could be defined as a loser in the process is parliament as supranational and international decision making tends to marginalise the parliamentarians.

In the downward transfer of power through territorial decentralisation, some ministries have certainly lost a considerable degree of power and responsibility to the municipalities and to a lesser extent the provinces. Although up to the 1980s decentralisation was seen as a vital concern to

214 Frits M. van der Meer

government, in reality the project was only supported by the Ministry of Home Affairs. The other departments, which were then really in charge of the major policy areas, only gave their support during the 1980s and 1990s when cutbacks had to be made in earnest. Decentralisation could help to solve their budgetary problems. In addition, in the early 1990s the idea took hold that ministerial departments should develop into strategic policy units. By decentralising policy implementation either by way of territorial decentralisation or functional decentralisation (agencification), the ministerial department could concentrate on these core (strategic) tasks. From the 1980s a great number of independent and later also ministerial agencies were created.[6] Two additional motives for furthering agencification initiatives are:

- decreasing the scope of ministerial responsibility and thus making it more effective;
- enhancing the efficiency and effectiveness of public service delivery by separating policy making and execution and by introducing NPM related policies.

On paper agencification can produce a win-win situation. Political office holders are made accountable for policy making in the ministerial (core) department, and are thereby protected against criticisms on implementation decisions as they are not directly involved in them. The managers of the agencies on the other hand gain considerable operational autonomy and run their organisations in a more business-like fashion. The loosening of the ministerial grip on these agencies can nevertheless produce some real political crises in the event of deficient interface relationships between the ministerial departments and the agencies. These relationships have in fact attracted severe criticism from, among others, the Algemene Rekenkamer (General Audit Office) and the Raad van Council of State for their defective financial and democratic accountability.

In spite of such criticism, the need for intergovernmental policy co-ordination has not harmed the position of the top civil service. In fact agencification was supported by many (top) civil servants, as the increased autonomy of the managers of the new independent agencies was considered a definite benefit, releasing managers of core departments of the often burdensome responsibilities of supervising the agencies. The same can be said of the privatisation initiatives and the programmes aimed at increasing the involvement of citizens and interest groups in (interactive) decision making. For instance, interactive policy making greatly increased the involvement of civil servants, as they have to manage these processes. Finally, juridification implies a loss to both political office holders and civil servants (unless judges are regarded as civil servants).

Two other important factors are influencing the changing balance of power between the political office holders and civil servants:

• increased self-awareness and professionalism among civil servants;
• diminishing party political profiles and a managerial approach to politics and government.

The origins of civil servants' new self-awareness and professionalism have to do with changes in their educational background and, at the senior level, growing involvement in public decision making. Government entered new policy domains after the Second World War. The increasing complexities of running government required a different type of civil servant. Gradually more economists and social scientists were engaged, at the expense of the traditional monopoly of law graduates (Van der Meer and Roborgh 1993). This meant that less emphasis was placed on the normative legal dimension of the function of the senior civil service and more on the specific knowledge and skills deemed necessary for each particular policy area. From the 1980s the preferred self-image of top civil servants changed even more from a 'classical' to a business and entrepreneurial model. The new proactive civil servant would meet the challenges of the new (reborn) government as it was being constructed in the 1980s and 1990s. A more business-like administration needed enterprising civil servants. At the same time the new ideology offered civil servants an escape route from the enduring popular criticism of the 'old-fashioned' bureaucratic way of running government. This new approach was not only promoted by politicians but was also heavily supported in the professional literature, by leading public administration experts and civil servants. NPM-style approaches were heartily supported by the civil service as the application of NPM was seen to enhance their general standing and their managerial autonomy.

In addition to this changing self-image, the roles of civil servants and politicians increasingly converged. From the 1980s ideological conflicts between the major parties on social-economic policy making were rapidly disappearing. As stated in section 2 above, a broad consensus both in politics and in administration developed on the preferred direction of reform. Both politicians and civil servants were considered to have a prime responsibility in managing the business of government internally and externally. The differences between political and administrative office holders became increasingly blurred. During the 1980s and 1990s top civil servants took part in national debates on important policy issues. Dutch top civil servants in general are not particularly secretive about their policy views, and they usually stayed within the confines of the political line of the cabinet.

4 Redesigning political–administrative relations in the 1990s

4.1 The issue of political control

Although the role convergence discussed above proved not to be problematic in normal government operations, the crises mentioned in section 1 above highlighted the potentially controversial issue of the demarcation of responsibilities. A debate ensued on how to redesign political–administrative relations while guaranteeing ministerial accountability to parliament. According to Peters and Pierre (Chapter 1 above) political office holders can choose from a limited repertoire of instruments for controlling civil servants. In a given institutional setting and tradition some instruments are permitted and others are not. In order to assess the significance for the Dutch case we examine the appointment of staff, the manipulation of structures, and the creation and adaptation of the ABD as an instrument for control.

4.2 Controlling the appointment of staff

There is much speculation about how far party politics plays a role in the nomination of candidates to the senior (administrative) posts in Dutch government. That appointment of top-level civil servants involves party political criteria is always denied by the cabinet, but members of the opposition parties are more doubtful. A look at the formal features of the Dutch appointment system shows that the merit elements are pre-eminent. Political criteria are not mentioned and a wide range of legal guarantees governs the recruitment and selection process. Thus the formal procedure looks Weberian enough. Nevertheless it is an open secret that the procedure leaves ample scope for the inclusion of informal (political) criteria. The appointment of chairmen and members of advisory boards, mayors of municipalities and Queen's commissioners of the provinces is far more political. Queen's commissioners have been political appointments since the nineteenth century. The appointment of mayors has become increasingly politicised since the Second World War (Van der Meer 1997). The same applies to the appointment of the chairpersons of central government advisory boards. An initial conclusion is that it is not customary to have (formal) party political appointments of permanent top officials (Van der Meer and Raadschelders 1998a). But two import caveats have to be made, involving the words 'formal' and 'party political'.

As stated, evidence relating to top-down politicisation of the senior civil service is circumstantial. Ministers and top civil servants are very secretive about this aspect of the appointment process. The general impression would seem to be that political affiliation plays a role at the top two grades in the civil service (Rosenthal and De Vries 1995; Van der Meer and

Raadschelders 1998b, 1999). The same applies to the unit that advises the secretary-general and the political office holders (secretary-general's bureau). Around 50 per cent of all top civil servants have a party political affiliation. This particular figure is not very indicative for the existence of party political nominations. Although the rate of party political member-ship among the general population is around 3 per cent, it is much higher in the senior levels of the civil service. It is well known that civil servants are relatively very active in political parties. For instance employers' organ-isations complain that parliament has become colonised by civil servants (VNO-NCW 1997). A more sympathetic explanation is that civil servants are, by nature of their occupation, more interested in public affairs. The recruitment of civil servants to parliament and political posts is not a recent phenomenon. Secker's (1991) historical analysis has shown it to be a traditional feature of Dutch politics. The appointment of politicians to civil service positions does happen but is less common. A more detailed analysis indicates that membership of political parties among top civil servants increases the hierarchy (Van der Meer and Roborgh 1993; Rosen-thal and De Vries 1995). For instance, almost all secretaries-general are affiliated to a political party, and the same is true of directors-general. Examining party political background reveals how rare it is for a secretary-general to be appointed with a party affiliation contrary to the political colour of the ruling coalition. On the basis of this evidence it can be con-cluded that the correct party political affiliation does no harm to the chances of an individual seeking to be appointed to the very highest civil service positions. Even so, there is no hard evidence that an immediate reshuffle of top civil servants takes place on party political grounds after a change of government.

Even if the possibility of party political nominations is taken for granted, it is the exception rather than the rule for there to be party polit-ical compatibility between political office holders and top civil servants. Changes in the make-up of coalitions and the practise whereby one party appoints a cabinet minister and another his/her junior minister(s) make it extremely rare for political office holders and the top civil servants to come from the same political party. In addition, the creation of the Senior Public Service (see section 4.4) has limited the discretion of individual ministers and even the cabinet.

When a new secretary-general or director-general is appointed, more often than not he or she has a different party political affiliation from the minister. With the exception of Geelhoed, the secretary-general of the Prime Minister's Office, all secretaries-general appointed by the Kok I cabinet had a different party political affiliation from the minister. Geel-hoed, a member of the Labour Party, was previously secretary-general of the Ministry of Economic Affairs and was appointed by a Christian Democrat Minister.

Far more important than the party political dimension is compatibility in policy views (Dijkstra and Van der Meer 2000). Candidates for particular top positions (in the independent agencies as well) are often selected because they are well known in and/or outside the civil service for policy views that are attractive to a minister and/or the top echelons in a ministry or the government as a whole. Before being appointed as secretaries-general, Geelhoed and Van Wijnbergen were university professors who actively participated in public debates.

More room for party political manoeuvre can be found in the recruitment and selection of appointees to the High Colleges of State (the Council of State, the Audit Chamber, the Office of the Ombudsman and the High Court). (The High Court is excluded from this practice, as are two colleges of minor importance, Nobility and Honours.) Likewise, chairpersons and (some of the) members of central government advisory committees are appointed according to political criteria. A prominent example is the appointment of the crown members of the Social Economic Council (Van der Meer and Raadschelders 1999), on which political leaders of the major parties are consulted. The same applies, as said, to the appointment of mayors and Queen's commissioners. The semi-political and administrative functions are divided according to an intricate system of political divisions and consultations. Before creating the image that Dutch politics indulges in a wave of patronage it should be stressed that the politicisation of appointments has two sides. The receiving organisation anticipates the political dimension of the nomination and often wants a member of the ruling coalition. The basic idea is that relations with central government are made easy by recruiting people who have open access to government.

4.3 The manipulation of decision-making arenas as an instrument of top-down politicisation

With the possible exception of agencification, the instrument of manipulating external decision-making arenas has seldom been used to increase political control over the civil service. Agencification was originally meant to enhance ministerial scrutiny of core departments and at the same time to retain ministerial grip on the independent agencies by developing clear interface relationships. But this was only one of the reasons. The new managerial perspectives on government and the wish to make implementation more effective and efficient have been far more influential factors. Agencification did in fact strengthen the autonomy of the managers in charge of the agencies to a greater extent than expected as that autonomy also had political implications. The majority of the recent policy crises creating political–administrative tension originated in defective implementation processes and often involved (independent) agencies. Agencification is thus seen rather to diminish than to increase political control over administration. As a result agencification is being re-examined. Although very few tangible results have been reached thus far, political initiatives have been made to limit the autonomy of the independent agencies by issuing new legal standards.

The European integration process, functional and territorial decentralisation, citizen and third party involvement in policy-making and the privatisation of government services have not been used as control instruments. With the exception of juridification these processes have reinforced the position of (senior) civil servants in government. The dispersal of public power over an increasing number of actors has increased central government demand for intergovernmental and intra-societal policy co-ordination. Civil servants are responsible for filling this gap.

As well as discussing, changing or manipulating external decision-making arenas, Peters and Pierre (Chapter 1 above) refer to the reorganisation of intra-organisational structures. We will concentrate here on the strengthening of interdepartmental decision-making forums such as the Council of Ministers and the introduction of ministerial cabinets. As explained in section 2.1, successive cabinets since the Second World War have taken initiatives to reinforce the position of the Council of Ministers in order to combat the compartmentalisation of politics and to address the growing interdependency of policies. Nevertheless, the balance of power is strongly tipped in favour of the individual ministries. Furthermore, in order to make the complex interdepartmental decision-making structure work, high-ranking civil servants participate in these bodies. No ministerial cabinets are found in Dutch central government, and have never been seriously contemplated apart from an abortive suggestion by a former education minister. Ministerial cabinets are not considered to be part of the Dutch political-administrative tradition. The concept of the loyal and party political neutral civil servant appointed on the basis of merit criteria is a treasured part of that tradition. Ministerial cabinets are rightly or wrongly regarded as a 'disreputable' feature of southern European administrative systems, since it is felt that they would enhance party political patronage. In addition, the coalition nature of Dutch politics constitutes a strong prohibition on the introduction of ministerial cabinets. As stated, the political apex of the Dutch ministries normally includes representatives of the different coalition parties. For this reason homogeneous ministerial cabinets would be difficult to attain. The idea of multiple ministerial cabinets goes against basic conceptions of government frugality. Finally, senior civil servants strongly resist (temporary) political superstructures in their departments. Besides trying to fence off competition in the area of policy advice, the neutrality doctrine mentioned earlier is an important explanatory factor.

These objections to ministerial cabinets have traditionally been raised against the appointment of political advisers as well. Although political advisers have occasionally been appointed since the Second World War, more of them were used by members of the centre-left Den Uyl cabinet.

These appointments gave rise to much controversy for a short period, at least in the civil service and political science literature. Only a limited number of political advisers are now appointed and they operate mainly as party political liaison and public relations officers for the ministers (Van der Meer and Raadschelders 1999). As a rule they are less directly involved in the policy-making process. Some are appointed on short contracts, others are recruited from their ministerial department. Apart from these (party) political advisers, ministers increasingly make use of permanent and personal policy advisers.

4.4 The creation of the ABD and changes in civil service legislation

The Algemene Bestuursdienst (ABD) or Senior Public Service dates from 1995. Its main purpose is to enhance civil service professionalism, to decrease compartmentalisation of central government by increasing interdepartmental mobility and to create a more unified civil service ethos. That mobility angle is quite interesting as functional mobility can be seen as a powerful instrument to erode the power base of top civil servants. The ABD was not originally or officially intended as an instrument to strengthen political control. The appointment mechanism in ABD even seemed at first to decrease the likelihood of party political appointments. Nevertheless some of its aims directly favour more civil service compliance (to use a negative description). By creating a unified civil service ethos the civil service can be made more responsive to political demands. More recently ABD has provided the possibility of more 'subtle' ways of controlling the senior civil service. The reform of the ABD procedures, announced in the programme of the Kok II cabinet (1998) and worked out in a policy document with the revealing title *Vertrouwen en verantwoordelijkheid* (Trust and responsibility) issued by the Ministry of Home Affairs in September 1999, greatly enhances the potential for political control over the civil service (Ministerie van Binnenlandse Zaken 1999). Coalition parties are said to have pushed for these changes in the programme discussions of the Kok II cabinet as a reaction to the political-administrative crises during the Kok I cabinet.

In order to understand ABD's potential for control, we have to examine its structure and background. Before the creation of ABD in 1995 ministries directly employed senior civil servants (secretaries-general, directors-general and directors). Secretaries-general and directors-general were appointed by the Council of Ministers on the recommendation of the minister involved. This left some scope for party political manoeuvring, as mentioned earlier. Directors were appointed by the minister involved. It is unknown whether party political considerations played a role here, but this is quite unlikely, given the level of party political affiliation cited by De Vries and Rosenthal (Rosenthal and De Vries 1995). The creation of a Senior Public Service meant a fundamental departure from the old job-oriented recruitment system. The senior civil servants taking part in ABD have a shared responsibility to guarantee the quality, professionalism and integrity of the public service (ABD 1996). The aims of professionalism and integrity can also be seen as placing an emphasis on making politics and administration more 'compatible'.

To run ABD, a 'bureau for ABD' has been set up, headed by a director-general. The ABD bureau serves as a personnel and management development office for this Senior Public Service, and is (organisationally) located in the Ministry of Home Affairs. In its first years the bureau concentrated on setting up an elaborate interdepartmental recruitment system, formulating management development instruments (for instance an ABD competency system), establishing career counselling initiatives and organising training and personal development programmes. The core task of the ABD bureau is to structure and operate the selection and recruitment process. If the ABD bureau is notified of a vacancy in a particular ministry, it selects a number of candidates from its database on the basis of the information supplied by the ministry involved, and presents these candidates to the ministry. Candidates are not limited to the existing membership of ABD in order to avoid a closed recruitment system. For instance in 1998 around 33 per cent of people appointed were from outside central government. People without any government experience are seldom selected. Normally candidates have either already held a position in central government or are recruited from other (levels of) governments. The ministry with the vacancy is in charge of the selection process (ABD 1999). Except in the case of the most senior personnel, the minister involved makes the appointment decision in agreement with the Minister of Home Affairs and in some cases the Prime Minister. The appointment of secretaries-general and directors-general is made by the Council of Ministers on the recommendation of the minister concerned and again in agreement with the Minister of Home Affairs and in some cases the Prime Minister.

ABD's original mobility targets were that around the year 2000 members would switch jobs every five years. Evidence from the ABD bureau indicates that from 1996 to 1998 about 10 per cent of senior civil servants changed positions each year.[7] Although it has to be said that the level of mobility in the Senior Public Service is much higher than in the general civil service, this figure suggests that the original target has been very difficult to achieve. An important reason for this failure is that hitherto changing jobs has not been compulsory. That has changed under new proposals issued in 1999. These include:

1 compulsory mobility for all ABD officials;
2 the extension of the ABD to all senior management officials in ministerial departments in 2001;
3 new appointment procedures for secretaries-general and directors-general;

4   specific result contracts between secretaries-general and directors-
     general and political office holders.

Points 3 and 4 merit special attention. All secretaries-general and
directors-general have to be selected in agreement with the minister of the
department involved, and appointed by the Minister of Home Affairs. The
position of the Minister of Home Affairs has thus been strengthened considerably. The director-general of the ABD bureau will make an initial
selection of suitable candidates. She/he has to consult a high-ranking
committee consisting of an external and independent chairperson and
two secretaries-general. In case of the recruitment of a director-general,
the secretary-general of the ministry with the vacancy will be included.
The Ministry of Home Affairs will employ all secretaries-general and
directors-general. From this ministry they will be posted to top-level positions in other ministries (after consultation with the relevant minister), in
principle for a period of seven years. After five years they will again be
available for a change of post. Under certain conditions an extension is
possible, but this is the exception rather than the rule.

In addition, a procedure has been developed for the removal of
secretaries-general or directors-general from their office before their term
has expired. This is meant to avoid legal conflicts and the payment of
costly severance deals in cases where a top official operates in a 'dysfunc-
tional' way or in cases of difficult (political–administrative) relations
within a ministry. During the yearly appraisal procedures these kinds of
problems can be anticipated in order to find a remedy at an early stage.
These procedures are potentially powerful (control) instruments in the
hands of the political office holders. They do not necessarily have to be
used, as the potential to use them may be sufficient.

Ministerial control of their top civil servants is reinforced by the introduction of so-called 'result contracts' concluded between top civil servants
and political office holders. These contracts are signed when a new top
civil servant is appointed or when a new minister comes to office (Ministerie Van Binkenlandse Zaken 1999: 34). The plans also mention that
these contracts will be linked to flexible payment schemes. The minister
decides whether merit payments are appropriate for these top-level officials and how large they should be. The exact mode has still to be
decided. These contracts can in theory be an additional instrument in the
hands of the political office holder. Whether these new plans prove effective in action remains to be seen. From a critical perspective it might be
argued that these schemes look like an attempt to return to the classical
'Weberian' control model.

5 Conclusion

The issue of political control over the civil service re-emerged in the early 1990s and gained momentum towards the end of the decade. Policy fiascos and some isolated but intense political–administrative crises formed the mechanism triggering this resurgence. Public ethics and the management of political–administrative relations are at present fashionable topics for debate. In fact, the public nature of government has been rediscovered or 'reinvented'. As argued, the roots of the political fear of losing control lie deeper than the crises themselves. The immediate causes and deeper origins have been discussed. The decline of clear party political profiles left ample scope for a managerially inclined mode of governance. This emphasis on managerial ideology and the more proactive role of top civil servants have diminished the differences in roles and perceptions of political and administrative office holders. One important difference still remains. A minister has a direct (responsibility) relationship with parliament. The old doctrines of full ministerial responsibility and civil service loyalty are still in force. These doctrines are considered fundamental to the survival of the democratic 'Rechtsstaat' and the parliamentary system.

In 'normal situations' few problems arise between ministers and their civil servants. Only in those cases when a minister and a civil servant have a personal conflict and/or parliament is asked to fulfil its control function in the case of a policy crisis do real problems arise as ministerial responsibility is invoked. This is now more likely to happen, as the likelihood of policy crises has grown since the 1980s. The changes in the system of government discussed earlier have increased its level of fragmentation and thereby its vulnerability. More linkages have to be made between different actors, organisations and policy arenas. The chance of failure (involving political office holders and civil servants) has consequently greatly increased. In those cases the role of, and actions taken by, civil servants in policy making and implementation come under scrutiny. The conflict between a more proactive and autonomous civil service and the old doctrine of loyalty and subservience will then become manifest. The quest for political control may then begin.

Peters and Pierre (Chapter 1 above) state that political office holders are limited in their choice of instruments to control civil servants. The argument is that in a given institutional setting and tradition, certain instruments are permissible, others are not. Top-down politicisation in the Netherlands is not so much sought in increasing or introducing party political nominations, changing existing structures or manipulating decision-making forums. The basic approach is to use the instrument of the Senior Public Service (particularly its management development policies and practises) and to change the legal position of top-level civil servants. Developing a (new) service-wide *esprit de corps*, changes in the appointment and exit system and new pay initiatives are some of the possibilities that the Senior Public Service offers to the political office holder to 'control' the civil service. Whether increasing the controls on the top civil service can reinforce ministerial supremacy and restore the formal fiction of ministerial responsibility can seriously be doubted as top civil servants are still expected to operate in a proactive way. As thus envisaged their role involves risk taking and autonomy.

Notes

1 A 'Weberian *style*' approach because the Dutch formulation of ministerial responsibility and civil service loyalty was developed well before the publication of *Wirtschaft und Gesellschaft* (Weber 1972). Furthermore, although the name of Weber is much invoked by all parties involved, they tend to overlook his use of an ideal type construction and the fact that Weber never argued that an absolute separation was in force or desirable. See Page's arguments (1992: 50–1). What certainly is true is that in recent (particular American) literature Weber has been interpreted through a Wilsonian and Science of Administration looking glass. It should finally be noted that Svarra (1999) argues that even in the United States the 'clear-cut' politics–administration dichotomy is really an invention of the late 1950s and 1960s.
2 In 1994 the Christian Democrats were left out of the new coalition government. The Dutch Labour Party (PvdA), the left-wing Liberal Party (D66) and the orthodox Liberal Party (VVD) were the coalition parties involved. This so-called 'purple' coalition was symbolic of the disappearance of the old ideological differences of the past.
3 There are nevertheless informal and incidental relations between some members of parliament and government ministries. Apart from the 'high-status' party leaders and spokespersons, the level of influence of members of parliament should not be overestimated.
4 During the parliamentary inquiry in 1998 (the Boeing disaster in Bijlmermeer in Amsterdam in 1998) members of the committee of inquiry received much criticism for overexposure in the media and 'showmanship' during the public interviews of witnesses. The last parliamentary inquiries were televised and attracted a large audience.
5 The dislocation of politics thesis also refers to the phenomenon that clear-cut geographical boundaries become less important for individuals as a point of reference for their sense of community. As the scale of societal life increases and diversifies the old territorial forms of government and democracy are challenged.
6 For instance garages licensed by government have to do the compulsory periodic safety checks on cars. They possess authorisation to issue safety permits.
7 The difference between independent public agencies and ministerial agencies is that the minister is still fully responsible for the latter, which are created to make a more business-like operation possible. As their work is still considered to have political implications, these agencies are not made fully independent.
8 Calculated on the basis of material supplied by Algemene Bestuursdienst and Verslag van Werkzaamheden (Annual Report of the Senior Public Service).

References

Algemene Bestuursdienst (ABD) (1996) *Plan van Aanpak*, The Hague.

Algemene Bestuursdienst (1997) *Verslag van werkzaamheden 1995/1996* (Progress report 1995/1996), The Hague.

Algemene Bestuursdienst (1999), *Verslag van werkzaamheden 1998* (Progress report 1998), The Hague.

Algemene Rekenkamer (1994–95) *Verslag over 1994. Part III: Zelfstandige bestuursorganen en ministeriele verantwoordelijkheid*, Tweede Kamer, Vergaderjaar 1994–1995, 24130, nr. 3 (General Chamber of Audit, independent agencies and ministerial responsibility).

Beck, Ulrich (1996) *Risikogesellschaft. Auf dem Weg in eine andere Moderne*, Frankfurt-am-Main, Edition Suhrkamp.

Bekke, A.J.G.M. (1988) *De betrouwbare overheid* (Reliable government), Alphen aan den Rijn: Samsom H.D. Tjeenk Willink.

Bovens, Mark, Wim Derksen, Willem Witteveen, Frans Backer and Paul Kalma (1995) *De verplaatsting van de politiek*, Amsterdam: Wiardi Beckman Stichting.

Dijkstra, Gerrit S.A. (1996) 'Juridisering en de veranderde verhouding tussen bestuur en burger', in Chr. L. Baljé, Th. G. Drupsteen, M.P.H. van Haeften and Th. A.J. Toonen (eds), *De ontzuiling voorbij*, Sdu.

Dijkstra, Gerrit S.A. and Frits M. van der Meer (2000) 'The Dutch civil service system', in Hans G.J.M Bekke and Frits M. van der Meer (eds), *Western European civil service systems*, Cheltenham/Aldershot: Edward Elgar.

Lijphart, A. (1968) *The politics of accommodation: pluralism and democracy in the Netherlands*, Berkeley: University of California Press.

Meer, Frits Van der (1997) 'Partijpolitieke benoemingen in Nederland. Een Belgianisering van het openbaar bestuur' (Party-political nominations in the Netherlands. A 'Belgification' of Dutch public administration?), *Overheidsmanagement*, June.

Meer, Frits M. Van der and Jos C.N. Raadschelders (eds) (1998a) 'L'entourage administratif du pouvoir exécutif', *Cahier d'Histoire de l'Administration*, no.5, Brussels: Ets Bruylant.

Meer, Frits M. Van der and Jos C.N. Raadschelders (1998b) 'Politisation ou practiques habituelles. Les Pays-Bas', *Revue Française d'Administration Publique*, 86, 281–92.

Meer, Frits M. Van der and Jos C.N. Raadschelders (1999) 'The role of senior officials in the Netherlands', in Vincent Wright and Edward C. Page (eds), *The role of senior officials in a service state*, Oxford: Oxford University Press.

Meer, Frits M. Van der and Renk J. Roborgh (1993) *Ambtenaren in Nederland. Omvang, bureaucratisering en representativiteit van het ambtelijk apparaat*, Alphen aan den Rijn: Samsom H.D. Tjeenk Willink.

Ministerie van Binnenlandse Zaken (1999) *Vertrouwen in verantwoordelijkheid* (Trust and responsibility), The Hague.

Nispen, F.K.M. van and D.P. Noordhoek (1986*) De grote operaties. De overheid onder het mes of het snijden in eigen vlees*, Deventer: Kluwer.

Page, Edward C. (1992) *Political authority and bureaucratic power: a comparative analysis*, New York: Harvester Wheatsheaf.

Page, Edward C. (1997) *People who run Europe*, Oxford: Clarendon Press.

Page, Edward C. and Vincent Wright (1999) 'Introduction', 'From the active to the enabling state', Oxford.

Rhodes, R.A.W. (1994) 'The hollowing out of the state. Changing nature of the public sector in Britain', *The Political Quarterly*, 65, 1138–51.

Rosenthal, Uri, (1999) 'De politiek-ambtelijke rechtsstaat. Over de tweezijdigheid van de politiek ambtelijke verhoudingen', *Liberaal Reveil*, 146–51.

Rosenthal, U. and J. De Vries (1995) Articles in *NRC-Handelsblad* (30–9, 6–10, 13–10, 20–10, 27–10 and 4–11).

Secker, Wilhelmina (1991) *Ministers in beeld. De sociale en functionele herkomst van de Nederlandse ministers, 1848–1990*, Leiden: DSWO Press.

Svarra, James H. (1999) 'Complementarity of politics and administration as a legitimate alternative to the dichotomy model', *Administration and Society*, 30, 676–705.

Thijn, E. van (1997) *Politiek en bureaucratie: baas boven baas* (Inaugural address, University of Amsterdam), Amsterdam: Van Gennep.

Thijn, E. van (ed.) (1998) *De sorry democratie. Recente politieke affaires en de ministeriele verantwoordelijkheid*, Amsterdam: Van Gennep.

Visser, Jelle and Anton Hemerijck (1997) *A Dutch miracle. Job growth, welfare reform and corporatism in the Netherlands*, Amsterdam: Amsterdam University Press.

VNO-NCW (1997) *Een democratie van leraren en ambtenaren*, The Hague.

Vries, Jouke de (1995) 'De dynamiek der departementen ministeries', *Beleid en Maatschappij*, 6.

Vries, Jouke de and Kutsal Yesilkagit (1999) 'Core executives and party politics. Privatisation in the Netherlands', *Western European Politics*, 2, 115–37.

Vries, J. de and M. van Dam (1998) *Politiek-bestuurlijk management*, Alphen aan den Rijn: Samsom.

Weber, Max (1972) *Wirtschaft und Gesellschaft*, Tubingen: J.C.B. Mohr (Paul Siebeck).

12 Politicisation of the Spanish civil service

Continuity in 1982 and 1996

Salvador Parrado Díez

1 Introduction

This chapter examines politicisation of the civil service after two government changes in Spain that involved alternation of political parties: 1982 and 1996.[1] In 1982, the socialist party (PSOE, Partido Socialista Obrero Español) entered government with an absolute majority after having been out of executive power for decades during Franco's dictatorship (1939–75). In 1996, the entry of the conservative party (PP, Partido Popular) meant the stabilisation of Spain's young democratic system. The first PP government replaced the PSOE government that had ruled the country from 1982 to 1996. The replacement of the Spanish political-administrative elite was quite substantial during the first PSOE government in 1982 (76.1 per cent of 231 posts eligible for political appointment at the rank of general director or higher; see below) and almost radical in 1996 (89.2 per cent of 270 similar posts).[2] The nature of the political system must be taken into account when considering these changes. While the Netherlands, Belgium, Sweden, Italy and Germany are all coalition governments, Spain, like Greece and Britain, has a democratic parliamentary regime with majoritarian principles. With few exceptions executive power is concentrated in periodically elected, single-party, majoritarian governments. Likewise, the national party system is quite polarised between the two parties, and although around five to seven parties gain parliamentary seats in elections, the two principal parties, the PSOE and the PP, together represent more than three-quarters of the electorate.

Most new administrative appointments were made in the first six months after the government was established, and the appointees for those offices constitute the focus of analysis. In both cases there was a need to ensure civil service loyalty while maintaining full ministerial responsibility. Both governments attempted to gain political control through top-down politicisation, in the terminology of Peters and Pierre in Chapter 1 above. On the one hand, the PSOE did not trust the cadres that had taken part in the previous transitional governments and in Franco's dictatorship. On the other hand, the PP mistrusted most political appointees from the previous socialist government. So, for the first time for many years, there was a high turnover of more than three-quarters of political appointments, whereas previously turnover after each change of government had been much lower, due to the continuity of the regime and, partly, the continuity of the transitional governments with the dictatorship.

By comparing both changes of government, this chapter tries to show the continuity (and change) of politicisation of the civil service. The title of this chapter might appear misleading as continuity (and change) are phenomena that can only be identified over a considerable time period. Derlien (1990c), for instance, explores the continuity and change in the West German federal executive elite for a considerable period of time between 1949 and 1984. Therefore, to search for patterns of continuity (or change) in two government changes only 14 years apart seems inadequate methodologically. However, I have been tempted to use the image of continuity for this chapter to challenge those views that consider the politicisation pattern in Spain after changes of government from different political parties to be distinct. I hope that this continuity (and eventual change) can be understood as a long evolutionary trend in which the transition from an authoritarian regime to a democratic one has taken place, and democracy is maturing.

According to Herzog (1982), recruitment as a means of controlling access to top positions stands out as one of the most relevant functions of the political system and allows two forms of scrutiny of the procedure through which some people reach the summit. The perspective of the individual makes it possible to understand the personal abilities required to reach the apex of the executive, while the structural perspective explains the restrictions and facilities that institutions offer for persons or groups determined to achieve the highest political-administrative posts. For the perspective of the individual, some social data of political appointees will be given (gender, age, place of birth, the city of the previous position before the new appointment, membership of a *corps* and university degree). For the structural perspective, I will provide an assessment of organisational evolution. Two of the definitions of politicisation offered in Chapter 1 above by Peters and Pierre will be used here: one regarding structures and the other concerning recruitment. Thus by politicisation of the civil service I understand the substitution of political criteria for merit-based criteria in the selection of members of the public service, with the objective of controlling policy and implementation. In this chapter, the structural analysis will relate to the summit of central administration (the prime minister's *entourage*) and to the ministerial apex (minister's *entourage*), while the examination of recruitment will focus on new political appointees.

There are three other aspects dealt with by Peters and Pierre that will not be covered in this chapter, either due to their lack of relevance for

this analysis or lack of evidence: the development of the parastatal administration, changing political arenas, and attitudes of civil servants and
politicians. Regarding the first aspect, the parastatal administration, this
chapter focuses on ministerial bureaucracy and non-departmental bodies
whose dependence on the government is high. There are a few exceptions: the National Tax Agency, for instance. The non-departmental
bodies included are similar to General Directions and similar units from
central ministries. Departmental and non-departmental organisations will
be treated together for two main reasons. On the one hand, the Spanish
public sector has not experienced a New Public Management (NPM)
movement parallel to countries like the UK, New Zealand or Australia, or
even the milder versions found in the Netherlands, Sweden and Denmark.
In both versions of NPM functional decentralisation and fragmentation of
the central bureaucracy have produced a large array of agencies responsible for implementing public services. A principal reason for this absence
of NPM reform comes from strong geographical decentralisation, with
regional authorities receiving control of implementation of most public
services. Therefore there was no reason to create agencies as these services
were going to be transferred to the regional level.

On the other hand, parastatal administration existed long before the
NPM reform movement, although the co-ordination mechanisms
deployed to ensure control over these bodies were based on the hierarchical model (instead of market mechanisms, contractual or network
models). In fact, unlike in Italy, recruitment to top positions in parastate
administration – either autonomous bodies or public corporations –
follows the same patterns as appointments to the level of general director
or above in the central administration. In this sense we cannot argue for a
degree of politicisation of appointments in the parastate sector, or at least
for a different version from that in a traditional bureaucracy. Finally, the
privatisation of public bodies since the mid-1990s has given government
the opportunity to control the public corporations by appointing chairpersons along partisan or clientelistic lines before transferring them to
private ownership. In this privatisation process, available evidence is only
illustrative and does not match the level of information available for top
positions of the traditional central bureaucracy.

Arenas for politicisation have been changing substantially (see Peters
and Pierre, Chapter 1 below) as the creation of the autonomous
communities (regional authorities) has decentralised many functions that
were previously the responsibility of the senior civil service in central ministries. It could not be argued, however, that this movement was politicisation in the sense that moving decisions to the regional level allows
solutions to be produced that are less likely to be ideologically more
aligned with the centre. The decentralisation process responds to the
demands of the newly established regional authorities in a context where
central government appears unwilling to devolve functions. The

geographical decentralisation nonetheless influences politicisation, as devolution of functions suggests a weakening of ministries in terms of their size, function and influence. Instead, power, responsibility and authority have been delegated to regional ministries accountable to regional parliaments. Nevertheless, the number of political appointments in central ministries does not seem to have decreased at the same rate, and the final stage of the political-administrative career of regional-level politicians seems to be Madrid. In March 2001, for instance, a president from a *comunidad autónoma* resigned from office in order to be appointed Minister of the Presidency. Finally, the lack of systematic data does not allow an enquiry into the third aspect of politicisation – attitudes about political involvement.

Having in mind the above three caveats, I would like to stress that an analysis of top ministerial positions does shed light on politicisation, as Spanish central administration is modelled quite closely on the Weberian model. In the Spanish case, where access and promotion within the civil service are achieved through fully meritocratic mechanisms – unlike other Mediterranean countries like Greece (see Sotiropoulos, Chapter 13 below) – politicisation has been increased through the duplication of administrative structures and the creation of political appointments in areas where traditionally apolitical technocrats held office. In any case, the extension of political appointments of this type is now considered appropriate, as it has been used lately as a means to control policy implementation by the bureaucracy. This dimension merits a complementary explanation, offered in the next section.

The following section begins with the literature for the period prior to 1982. A more thorough account of this period has been offered elsewhere (Baena 1999, Román 1997). For 1982 (see Parado 1996, 1998) and for 1996, the information was collected from official diaries, volumes of *Who's Who*, official reports and newspapers. The chapter has two main sections. In section 2, an analysis of the ministerial organisation and the premiership is offered. Section 3 focuses on the individual recruitment patterns.

2 The changing pool of political appointments and the civil service system

According to Aberbach and Rockman (1988a, 1988b), two factors characterise the development of executives in Western democracies. On the one hand, the development of the *administrative state* shows an increase of administrative rationality, which presupposes enhancement of values such as professionalisation, post continuity, administrative experience, and efficiency. On the other side, the increase of *political democracy* involves reinforcement of political rationality where responsibility and political leadership are valued. Although these two rationalities can produce divergent modes of behaviour at the top of the executive pyramid, research by

Aberbach *et al.* (1981) shows the tendency of convergence towards *hybrid actors* at the summit. Once they are in government, political leaders attempt to control the bureaucratic machinery in order to implement the most realistic aspects of the manifestos defended by the winning political party during its election campaign. If political leaders come from a different functional sector of society, they will probably mistrust professional administrators. This mistrust interferes with collaboration between the actors, and hinders the effectiveness of government. Whenever possible, incoming politicians will aim at controlling or influencing the recruitment of those who are going to play a major role in achieving their political objectives.

The existence of hybrid positions at the top of a bureaucracy helps to increase *political democracy* within the organisation, as well as intensifying control over the administrative machinery. Political appointments occupy this intersection. In Spain, political appointees are responsible for decision-making, implementation and/or political advice on public policies with nation-wide coverage. Their appointment to office is accomplished *pro forma* by a royal decree approved by the government. These political appointees totalled between 350 and 400 throughout the period 1982–2001. In fact, ministers nominate their close collaborators at the next hierarchical level on a personal basis and these select the next level of political appointments on the same basis. Thus, on the basis of the three reasons for political recruitment that Peters and Pierre give in Chapter 1 above, the selection and deselection of civil servants for political appointments are largely based on personal, in some cases almost clientelistic, loyalties, that transcend partisan allegiances. This was the story during the Francoist regime, repeated under socialist and conservative governments. This recruiting procedure does not dominate the whole career of civil servants but only those positions at the very top that are excluded from the civil service career. Thus, it appears that the meritocratic system remains largely untouched. It should, however, be noted that the administrative career of civil servants with university degrees is rather short and political appointments for civil servants have consequences for their careers. Therefore, the political appointment area belongs both to the realm of politics (incumbents come and go at the will of their superiors) and to the realm of administration (it offers career opportunities to civil servants) although appointments are also open to outsiders.

In order to understand the position of political appointments in the system, we need to understand the *corps* system and the civil career system. Traditionally, bureaucrats have tried to avoid political control by creating autonomous and self-regulating groups of civil servants – the *corps*. The *corps* constitute an organisational element of the Spanish civil service in several senses. They are the gateway for entry into public administration: administrative careers have historically depended on membership of the *corps*. The *corps* also operate as pressure groups within the public sector.

Their role as pressure groups depends, according to Gutiérrez-Reñón (1987), on their numbers, internal cohesion and access to power centres. While the origins of the *corps* and their primary goal was job security, the evolution of their objectives included increasing their administrative power by 'owning' sectors of the organisation, pursuing corporatist self-regulation, and controlling financing systems. The appearance of political parties and trade unions with the advent of full democracy in 1978, and with specific legislation in 1984, has not undermined the strength of the *corps* or their ability to dominate the administrative arena, although it has altered some rules of the game.

The current civil service system was formed after the 1984 Act of Parliament of the socialist government, with some amendments that have been added more recently. The main goal of the 1984 civil service reform was to undermine the power of the *corps*. Basically, three components of *corps* power can be identified during Franco's dictatorship: (a) they had a self-financing capacity through special taxes they charged citizens for the services they provided; (b) they had a self-governing capacity to protect their interests; and (c) they could veto proposals of politicians on personnel matters. *Corps* had an independent power and they used it to treat the administrative organisation as a part of their patrimony. In fact, the socialist government tried what previous governments had never dared: to challenge the *grands corps*, those whose members have a university degree. The 1984 reform was designed to establish an open system based upon recruitment to posts, in contrast to a closed system defined through an administrative career dominated by the *corps*. The reform clearly undermined the strength of the *corps*. Although they still monopolise the recruitment process, they no longer hold tight control over the filling of vacancies or the promotion and salary system. These aspects are now linked to holding a particular post and not to belonging to a particular *corps*. Since the 1984 legislation, entry to public administration is through an open competitive examination, and educational requirements have been established for entry into any *corps*. There are five educational groups, group A being for university graduates. Access to the civil service is conducted annually through the Public Employment Offer: ministries submit proposals on their staff needs and members of a single *corps* may not be in a majority in the commissions evaluating the examination. Only those posts placed at the lowest levels of the hierarchy could be made subject to labour contracts. Contracts for top executive positions are forbidden, although there were still 14 high-salaried contracts in 1999 that have somehow survived parliamentary scrutiny.

After passing the exam, a civil servant receives an initial grade (between grade 7 and 30 according to educational group A, B, C, D or E). These grades roughly match the 'post' system introduced in 1984. 'Posts' are grouped into levels (7 to 30) and educational requirements determine progress up the hierarchical ladder. Up to level 29, posts are filled through *merit concours*, while posts at level 30 are filled through a non-meritocratic process (see Figure 12.1). The incumbent of a post in level 30 must leave office at the will of a superior post-holder. The civil servant who holds an office at this level may be downgraded to an inferior post but still retains grade 30 status if he or she has been in the post for at least two years. The title for posts at level 30 is deputy general director, the top career post within the civil service.

Positioned above the civil service is a sphere occupied by political appointees. This area could also be considered part of the informal career of top civil servants – at least it was during Franco's period but is no longer. Top civil servants are currently rather disenchanted with the system because group A members normally enter at level 20, but in influential *corps*, such as civil administrators, diplomats and general attorneys, level 26 or 28 is usual for beginners. This means that a civil servant whose first post is at a high level will have a short career. In less than six years, a well-placed civil servant who has personal connections (not necessarily party political) could reach level 30 (to which promotion is achieved on a basis of personal trust and not through meritocratic criteria), the peak of his or her career. The appointment to level 30 posts is based on the discretionary powers of the general director (a politically appointed official), who will recruit the deputy general directors (level 30) from among civil servants. Since more than 80 per cent of general directors and under-secretaries (since 1996 all undersecretaries must have civil service status;

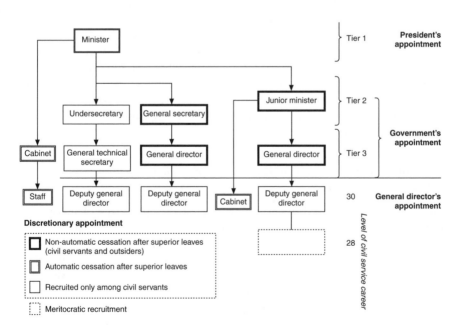

Figure 12.1 Typical ministerial organisation, 1996–2001.

see below) have belonged to a *grand corps* during the period of democratic government, and almost 98 per cent did during the dictatorship, these posts could be considered part of the informal career of civil servants, although technically speaking they are political appointments.

Political appointees could come from within the civil service or from outside. Three basic tiers make up this category: (a) appointments in the top tier, ministerial level, are made by the prime minister through a decree endorsed by the king; (b) appointments to the second (junior minister, undersecretary and general secretary) and (c) third (general director rank) (see Figure 12.1 in combination with Table 12.1) are made by degree of the government (prime minister and ministers), on the recommendation of the competent minister or junior minister. The differentiation between echelons will be used to analyse structural changes; all post holders will be categorised for the analysis of social data and information about individual careers. These political appointees, called *cargos de designación política*, are more like their American counterparts than German political functionaries (*politische Beamten*). But unlike American political appointees, almost 95 per cent of Spanish *cargos políticos* were traditionally civil servants, a proportion that has decreased to 75 per cent in the present democratic era in which political party patronage has begun to be important, along with previous experience in private enterprise. Unlike German *politische Beamten*, Spanish *cargos de designación política* are not part of the civil service although the job titles are the same (*Ministerialdirektor, Staatssekretär*) and most incumbents are civil servants.

The 'pool' of political appointments which altered radically in 1982 and 1996 is made up of a heterogeneous group of posts that have experienced qualitative and quantitative change over time. Some changes reflect the expansion of the public sector. Other changes involve a greater increase of political control in Peters and Pierre's terms (Chapter 1 above). I will now discuss two different evolutions: (a) the evolution of the organisational design at the top of the ministry; (b) the evolution of the *entourage* of the premiership.

2.1 Ministerial organisation: from the rule of professionals to the dominance of politicians?

Once they have entered government, one of the first tasks of incoming politicians is to reshape their organisation to suit themselves. Unless a specific commitment to reducing public expenditure by cutting political appointments has been made, executive politicians will try to expand the political sphere at the expense of the civil service. The expansion in numbers of politically appointed posts is an example of *structural politicisation*. The most obvious analysis is by quantification of the number of posts considered *spoils*. A more precise study should introduce a qualitative element, as some posts are more useful than others for controlling the

Table 12.1 Features of Spanish political appointments

Spanish name	English equivalent	Appointment and main functions
Presidente del Gobierno	Prime Minister (PM)	PM is the head of a strong executive empowered to monopolise the most important decisions of national policy.
Vicepresidente del Gobierno	Deputy Prime Minister	Assisting the PM through the co-ordination of the work of the executive or an area of it. Deputy prime ministers can also be departmental ministers.
Ministro	Minister	Guidance of a department. During democratic governments a minister without portfolio has been very rare.
Secretario de Estado	Junior minister (JM)	Management and guidance of subordinate General Directorates. Since 1993, participation in the General Committee of Junior Ministers and Undersecretaries (see below).
Secretario General	General secretary (GS)	Management and guidance of two or more subordinate General Directorates.
Subsecretario	Undersecretary (US)	Management of all ministerial common resources (human, budgetary and organisational). Since 1978, participation in the Commission of [Secretaries of State and] Undersecretaries (see below).
Director General	General director (GD)	Management of a specific area of the ministry.
Secretario General Técnico	General technical secretary (GTS)	Helping the US to manage all ministerial common resources (human, budgetary and organisational) and preparing the work of the Commission (see below).
Jefe del Gabinete del Ministro	Chief of the minister's *cabinet* (CMC)	Political advice to the minister. Relations with parliament and other *cabinets*.
Presidente de una empresa pública, organismo autónomo o agencia	Chief of a public enterprise, autonomous body or agency (PAB)	Management of an autonomous or quasi-autonomous body depending on a ministerial organisation.
Collective bodies		
Consejo de Ministros	Council of Ministers (it includes the PM, deputy prime minister, ministers)	Adoption of government decisions.
Comisión General de Secretarios de Estado y Subsecretarios	General Committee of Junior Ministers and Undersecretaries	Preparation of decisions taken in the Council of Ministers.

civil service. Thus, offices nearest to the core executive will be theoretically granted more decision-making power than the most junior posts. The prime minister and the minister constitute the locus of power in their respective domains. From a qualitative point of view, it is necessary to ask whether the expansion of the political sphere is achieved mostly at the top or at the bottom of the ministerial bureaucracy.

In each Spanish ministry there are seven different politically appointed posts, excluding the minister (see the job descriptions in Table 12.1, also Figure 12.1). The power relationship between these post holders has undergone some changes over time (see Figure 12.2). Three phases can be identified: Franco's regime (1939–75); the transitional period and governments of the centrist party UCD (1975–82); socialist and conservative governments (1982–2001):

1   Franco's regime (1939–75) was characterised by the rule of the minister and hierarchical simplicity. The administration was modest in numbers (see Table 12.2), due to the absence of a welfare state. Besides, the ministerial hierarchy was quite simple, although it was not arranged on the military model (see below).

The basic sectorial unit of a ministry and the lowest level for political appointments is the General Directorate (GD). At a higher level, the

Table 12.2 The growth of Spanish political appointments (1938–96)

	Second tier	Third tier	Total
Franco's regime (1938–75)			
1938	4	35	39
1941	5	19	24
1943	5	25	30
1951	11	59	70
1956	4	51	55
1957	12	89	101
1962	15	93	108
1965	18	100	118
1969	17	91	108
1973	12	76	88
Socialist governments (1982–91)			
1983	52	179	231
1986	64	206	270
1989	65	209	274
1991	78	227	305
Conservative government (1996)			
1996	53	217	270

Sources: Alba (1992) for the period (1938–75) (mimeo) and research sources (biographical data from 'Who's who' in Spanish publications, newspapers, government publications). There are no data available for the period 1976–81.

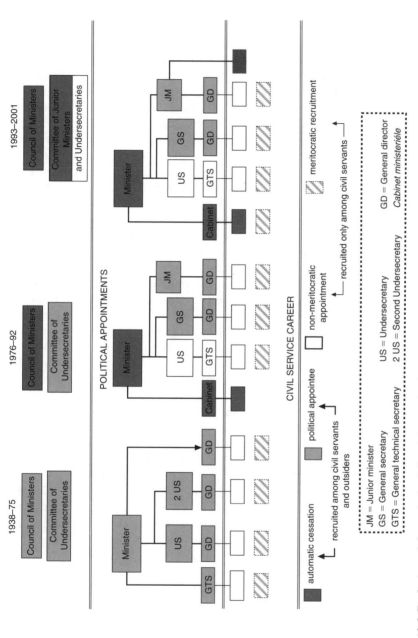

Figure 12.2 Evolution of the typical ministerial organisation.

Undersecretary (US) is responsible for all ministerial resources (human, budgetary and organisational). Besides these administrative functions, the US during Franco's time also enjoyed the capacity to influence the decision-making and implementation processes inside and outside the department (Baena 1992). Moreover, the US could directly control sectorial GDs that delivered policies. The increase of GDs in some ministries allowed the introduction of the 2nd undersecretary (2nd US), at an intermediate level between one or several GDs and the minister. Under the influence of the American managerialism of the 1940s, in 1957 the post of general technical secretary (GTS), with GD rank, was created as a direct adviser to the minister on technical and political matters. The difference between a military-ordered hierarchy and the administrative hierarchy of Franco's times can be seen in two aspects: (a) GDs depended on the minister either directly or indirectly through the US and the 2nd US; (b) although the rank of GTS was that of GD, the post holder had greater power because of having direct access to the minister, competing at times with the US (Baena 1992). In addition, civil servants filled most political appointments. In Franco's times, 91.9 per cent of USs and 90 per cent of GDs belonged to a *corps* of civil servants (Álvarez 1984). Likewise, most ministers were also bureaucrats from the most influential *corps* (Linz and De Miguel 1975, Baena 1977), so that all post holders came from the same *milieu*. Therefore, the Francoist state was labelled a bureaucratic state, and political power was basically bureaucratic power.

2   During the transitional period and centrist UCD governments (1975–82), a political-democratic element was introduced into the ministerial hierarchy. Three different organisational measures were launched or reinforced. First, the sectorial junior minister (JM) was placed close to the minister in 1977. This marked the beginning of the end of the political leverage of the US on the minister. The JM replaced the minister in outside relationships and was the chief of several GDs, like the 2nd US, but with a higher rank. The JM had a political profile and sometimes also a parliamentary seat.

In addition, another political unit was reinforced after 1977: the minister's *cabinet* (following the French style), with appointees who should automatically leave office at the end of the ministerial term. Although *cabinets* had existed in some ministries in Franco's time, they began to gain relevance as they lost their technical nature and acquired more political connotations in the new democratic spirit of party competition. The *cabinet* began to compete with the GTS as direct adviser to the minister, and constituted the interface between the executive, the parliament and the political party (Baena 1992).

Third, the introduction of two political offices (JM and the *cabinet*) did not imply that the battle against the US and the GTS had been won. A year later, in 1978, the Committee of USs, intended to prepare decisions taken at the Council of Ministers, was established in order to reinforce the collective nature of government. JMs were excluded from this Committee. The power of the GTSs increased as they helped the US prepare the work of the Committee. This means that those offices whose power was based upon administrative functions dealt with the sectorial matters of the ministry and sectorial JMs had to bargain with US to have their priorities placed on the ministerial agenda. Top civil servants opposed the appointment of outsiders to these positions, and the political party had little influence on recruitment to them. As top civil servants founded and occupied most leading positions in the centrist party, it could be argued that there was an osmosis between the political and the administrative elite.

3 During the socialist and the conservative governments (1982–2001), political actors' control over the administrative machinery increased. Three measures were taken before 1996. First, JMs were allowed to take part in the Committee that prepares the decisions of the Council of Ministers, and so were able to discuss the political agenda of the ministry, thus gaining in political importance, an opposite trend to the Dutch Civil Service Preparatory Committee (Ambtelijke Voorportalen) (see Van der Meer, Chapter 11 above). Second, the *cabinet* became institutionalised in 1982 and it was granted powers over policy formulation and co-ordination. Third, the post of general secretary (GS) was also institutionalised to replace the 2nd US and was granted US rank and lower status than JM.

Following socialist legislation, every GD depends directly on someone in the second tier and the direct link to the minister has been abolished. In the second tier, the struggle for power intensified as the JM and the US take part in the preparatory Committee of the Council of Ministers: each JM representing a sectorial area and the US in charge of all administrative resources of the ministry. Constant bargaining takes place among the sectorial JMs and the US in order to implement the ministerial programmes. Until 1996, civil servants and external candidates could fill all the political appointments mentioned above. The socialist government had tried to make civil service status a requirement for appointments to GD rank, proposing that they should be selected on non-meritocratic criteria from among civil servants, but this was not enforced. Since 1996, only US and GTS posts have to be filled by civil servants (see Figure 12.2). Currently, *cabinets*, the JMs and the GSs perform a political role, while the GTS and US are left with administrative matters, although their influence on decisions and, especially, implementation processes, remains strong.

The *cabinet*, which is similar to the French-style *cabinet ministériels*, has become, as in France, Belgium (see Dierickx, Chapter 10 above), Italy and to some extent in Germany, the key structural interface between elected politicians and the permanent civil service since democratisation. As in these countries, Spanish governments perceive a need for a strong policy staff to co-ordinate and prioritise the range of activity across their department, and to interact with other departments on policy issues and legislation, as well as with the prime minister's private office (*prime ministerial cabinet*) and with the parliament. Unlike in Italy, the *cabinet* is not exclusively composed of career civil servants from within the department, although the majority of its senior members belong to a *grand corps*. The most important development is that the ministerial *cabinet* tries to influence the management of line units besides giving advice to the minister. Although the evidence is rather anecdotal and has not been systematically gathered, there are examples of *cabinets* managing to co-ordinate the work of several general directorates.

In addition to the qualitative analysis of the organisation, a quantitative examination of political appointments between 1982 and 1996 will be given. Due to the principles of the democratic game between the executive and the legislative as well as the expansion of the welfare state, the socialist period (1982–91) witnessed a remarkable process of structural politicisation. Moreover, the entry, for the first time for more than 40 years, of a socialist party into government, which had not participated directly in the transition to democracy, explains the need for a large number of *spoils appointments*. Thus, the number of second-tier office holders was almost four times greater in 1982 (the first socialist government) than in 1973 (the last cabinet formed by Franco), while the increase in the number of GDs has been lower (see Table 12.2). The number of ministries also almost trebled between 1938 (when there were fewer than half a dozen) and the 1990s.

The expansion of political appointments occurred at the same time as the central administration was devolving many major functions such as education, health and many other smaller services to Autonomous Communities. The decrease of state functions should have involved a reduction in the national public sector in general and, specifically, in the number of political appointments. The decrease in political appointments during the 1996–2001 conservative government was also lower than expected. The PP strongly criticised the numerous political appointees who held office during the socialist period and they promised to reduce the numbers considerably, but once in office they could not keep the promise (see Table 12.2).

It is apparent that the (US) posts with administrative and political power derived from their control over administrative functions during Franco's time now have exclusive control over these functions, while sectorial control and relations with parliament, press, pressure groups and political parties are under the control of the JMs and the ministers' *cabinets*. On the other hand, the number of political appointments has remained relatively high during the democratic period, even though most public policy spheres have been transferred either to the European Union or to regional authorities. Regarding ministerial structure, most measures taken by the PSOE and PP governments followed a pattern of continued political control over the civil service.

2.2 The entourage of the premiership: from ministerial collegial rule to quasi-presidential guidance

One interesting organisational trend involving politicisation of the civil service can be seen in the entourage of the premiership. In the Spanish language, the word 'premiership' as *primus inter pares* is not used; instead, we have the label *Presidente*, which does not have the connotations of 'president' in the United States or France, as the Spanish political system is parliamentary. For this chapter, the translation 'premiership' has been preferred in order not to confuse the Spanish system with a presidential one. Although the prime minister plays an important role in policy-making and can influence decisions taken by the full Cabinet in its Friday meetings, the Spanish government in the democratic period is collective in nature, unlike the UK (see Sausman and Locke, Chapter 6 above), where the No. 10 Unit is present at all comprehensive policy reviews and takes many decisions outside full Cabinet meetings. Therefore, although the Spanish premiership seems to operate formally as a Cabinet model, it includes some prime-ministerial features.

The entourage of Franco was not highly developed, as the positions of head of state and head of government were institutionally embodied in the person of the dictator himself, except for a period during which the head of government was a military general. However, the administration in the executive summit has been increasingly institutionalised during the democratic period (Bar 1997). This 'quasi-presidentialisation' of the premiership has basically meant an increase in the number of political units in the entourage, along with tighter control on policy-making in order to yield tighter control on the decision-making of the traditional ministerial bureaucracy, but not on their implementation structures. Heywood and Molina (2000) argue that this entourage owes most of its power to political and administrative factors. Nonetheless, its substantial growth since 1982, seven years after Franco's death, is linked to the election of the PSOE and its distrust for the traditional ministerial bureaucracy dominated by the cadres who had held posts in Franco's regime and during the transition period. Three phases can be seen in the evolution of the premiership (see Figure 12.3).

1   Between 1975 and 1982, the core executive was comparatively weak. The Ministry of the Presidency was established and charged with responsibility for horizontal functions such as intergovernmental co-ordination and relations with parliament and other relevant public

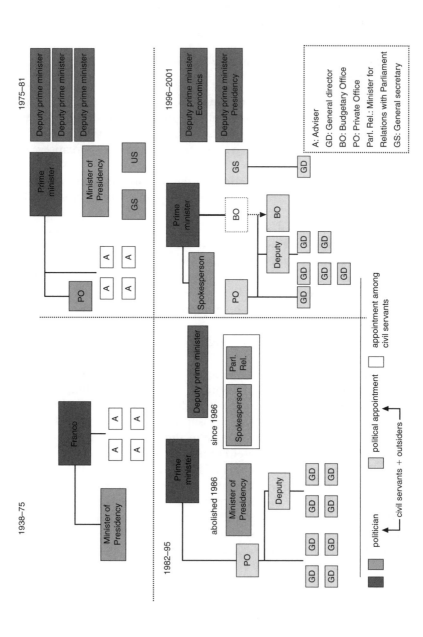

Figure 12.3 The entourage of the premiership.

bodies. Its most important co-ordination function is reflected in its presence at interministerial committees and chairing of the General Committee of Junior Ministers and Undersecretaries (Baena 1992). Besides the Ministry of the Presidency, the entourage of the core executive was composed of a group of civil servants, confidants and advisers to the prime minister and deputy prime ministers (numbering two or three).

2   Since 1982, the presidential entourage has been institutionalised in the immediate circle of support for the prime minister: the deputy prime minister (Vicepresidente del Gobierno), the General Secretariat of the Premiership (Secretaría General de la Presidencia del Gobierno), the Prime Minister's Private Office (Gabinete de la Presidencia del Gobierno), and the Government Spokesperson (Portavoz del Gobierno). There is no constitutional requirement for the position of deputy prime minister. At times this position remained vacant and at others there were three deputy prime ministers at the same time. Heywood and Molina (2000: 116) assert that the nature of the post has been highly dependent on the personality of its incumbent due to its lack of institutionalisation, but it could also be added that it has depended on the relationships of the incumbent with the prime minister and ruling political party. Since 1986 the deputy premier has been linked with intergovernmental matters through holding the presidency of the General Committee of Junior Ministers and Undersecretaries. In the period from 1996 to 2001, one deputy prime minister for political affairs was also head of the Ministry of the Presidency. If there are two deputy prime ministers, the second is responsible for the Ministry of the Economy, which gives it a 'super-ministerial' status. Both the Private Office (to control the flow of information among different political actors, to advise the prime minister and to monitor implementation and co-ordination of ministerial programmes) and the General Secretariat (involved in logistical co-ordination with security, protocol and IT tasks) have kept very similar functions since 1982 and are already institutionalised. They belong to the inner circle of the prime minister and control the basic links with political and administrative actors. Its role was and continues to be tied to control of the bureaucracy, although as Heywood and Molina (2000: 125) rightly point out, this mainly concerns decision-making, not implementation. The position of Government Spokesperson (co-ordinator of the government's information policy) has also changed since 1982, its status varying between minister and JM.

3   Since 1996, the minister of the presidency has been given the status of deputy prime minister and a Budget Office (Oficina Presupuestaria) has been established, whose director, with junior minister rank, was directly subordinated to the prime minister. With the first measure, a political deputy premiership was established, responsible for the

co-ordination of government at the highest level. With the second measure, the prime minister was trying to balance power over economic policy between the Ministry of the Economy and the premiership, because of the new challenges of the European Union. In 1998 the chief of the Budget Office was placed under the Prime Minister's Office, with the economic deputy premiership having a monopoly on monitoring the budget.

Most high-ranking members of the premiership are politically appointed. In the Private Office, appointees must resign automatically on the termination of a prime minister's mandate. Moreover, the Private Office's role of mediator between the premiership and other actors – ministries, parliament, press and pressure groups – has increased its importance. The functions of the cabinet and the entourage of the premiership depend on the priorities of the prime minister. Thus, the activities of the premiership during the transition period focused on the transition itself and on approval of the Constitution. The premiership of the PSOE government was more concerned with infrastructures and social matters, while the PP government is concerned with compliance with the Maastricht criteria and relations with Basques and Catalans (Heywood and Molina 2000). Resembling the parallel nature of the Private Office, this unit is divided into departments, reflecting the ministries, in order to monitor the policies delivered by each ministry (on the comparable trend in Germany, see Schröter, Chapter 4 above). By establishing private offices for both the premiership and the ministries, political executives tried to work around public servants searching for responsiveness. They thus intended to duplicate the career service with a cadre of political officials, as in the *cabinet* systems in France, Germany, Italy and Belgium.

There was a quantitative increase of political appointments at the top of the ministerial bureaucracy during the socialist period, while the entry of conservatives meant a decrease of such appointments. More important than this growth was the strength that the ministerial and the presidential private offices acquired. At the top of the whole system, it seems that the former collegial rule is slowly being replaced by the primacy of the premiership which has increasing capacities to exert control on decisions taken in central administrations. In comparative terms, the entourage of the premiership is stronger than in other parliamentary systems like Germany and resembles the French system, for example, especially outside *cohabitation* periods.

3 Individual patterns of recruitment

Before examining the influence that *corps* of civil servants exercise upon political appointments, a brief analysis of social data will be offered.

Whenever possible, continuities and discontinuities between the PSOE government of 1982 and the PP government of 1996 will be highlighted.

3.1 Age and regional origins: convergences and divergences

There are multiple relationships between the age and attitudes of elites. Some scholars believe that attitudes change with age (Wildenmann *et al.* 1982); others relate age to political party sympathy (Putnam 1975), and others claim that an older elite group impedes recruitment of younger generations (Zapf 1965, Keller 1968). While political appointees during the Franco era were aged 53 to 55 on average (Alba 1984), each change of government since 1982, associated with a change of political party, has brought younger cohorts to office.

In comparative terms, the political appointees of 1982 and 1996 are fairly young. In 1982, political appointees were 41 years old on average, and 46.1 in 1996. This comparative youth could be contrasted with the following data: if a democratic transition had not taken place, the administrative elite would have averaged around 50 years of age in the government of 1982, according to a forecast based on the data of Alba (1984). The change of age shows that a new generation has replaced the old one. Elsewhere, it has been shown that this decrease in the average age did not happen under the transitional governments (Parrado 1996). In international comparative terms, the German political functionaries were between 51 and 54 years old on average in the period 1949–84 (Derlien 1988: 68).

Similar reasons could be identified on the micro level for the reduction of the average age of political appointees in both cases. It is not that there was a change in the average age of society as a whole, rather that younger generations in the political party managed to control the organisation from the top. In 1982, this change was linked to Felipe González, the PSOE prime minister. In normal conditions, the political appointees of the 1996 conservative government should have averaged 55 years, like their German counterparts. However, they averaged 46.1 years. This difference is related to changes in the political party that supported the government. The conservative party (PP) was founded from the AP (Alianza Popular), whose cadres had served under Franco. Besides the ideological connotations, the relatively old age of AP cadres must be considered. The founding of the PP in 1988 brought new generations into power. Aznar, the party secretary and president of the government, surrounded himself with young political appointees of his own generation, instead of appointing persons of 55 years old, as former party leaders did. The change in the conservative party with Aznar has meant that both party leaders and appointees are younger, and closer to him in age. The party that wins the elections in the year 2004 will appoint cadres in the administration with an average age of between 51 and 55 (if the conservatives win) and between 40 and 44 (if the socialists win, as there is a new party leader of a much younger generation). The relative youth of political appointees implied lack of administrative experience not only in the first PSOE government but also in the case of some USs and GDs in the 1996 government who were only 32 years old when appointed.

The regional origin of political appointees demonstrates that the Spanish system still has a very centralised political recruitment despite the fact of having almost a federal status. Table 12.3 shows the regional distribution of new political appointees according to three dimensions: the region of their birth, the region where they obtained their degree, and the region in which they held their position immediately prior to the political appointment in 1982 or in 1996. The following findings should be stressed.

A majority of political appointees from all over the country (with more weight for the Madrid region) studied and worked in Madrid before their political appointment. There are no remarkable differences between the appointees of 1982 and 1996 in this regard. As for the place of birth, the appointees of 1982 are more evenly distributed among all regions than those of 1996 when there were eight regions with under 1 per cent representation. Apart from Madrid, in 1996 a considerable proportion of appointees came from Andalucía (11.9 per cent) and from Castilla-León (14.4 per cent), where the prime minister was also regional president. Political appointees form a relative homogeneous group in terms of age and geography, and were comparatively young in both 1982 and 1996. In terms of geographical stages of their life (birth, university studies and job), strong centralisation of the system can be observed in both cases. In these dimensions, continuity has been the rule.

3.2 Civil servants' control over appointments

The political party that forms the government and the *corps* have distributed the spoils of government since the arrival of democracy. In general terms, civil servants have exerted *patronage* on appointments, while the political party played a secondary role, at least in appointments from 1982 to 1991 (Parrado 1996). Although information of this type is quite limited, as most office holders do not divulge their party membership, it seems that although carrying a party card is not a requirement for political appointment, having the wrong political label could have a negative effect (contrast with the Belgian case; see Dierickx, Chapter 10 above). Personal relations established through membership of the same *corps* are an important factor for nominations, however. In this section, the relationships between *corps* and appointments for 1982 and 1996 will be analysed.

The control of bureaucrats over political appointments depends highly on how civil servants are grouped (classes, *corps*, specialists and generalists,

Table 12.3 Distribution of new appointments among regions at different stages of a candidate's life (1982 and 1996) (%)

	Place of birth		Place of university studies		Place of last position before the political appointment	
	1982	1996	1982	1996	1982	1996
Does not apply	–	–	1.5	0	–	–
Andalucía	6.5	11.9	2.2	5.3	2.9	3.7
Aragón	2.6	3.4	–	1.8	–	0.7
Baleares	2.6	0.8	–	–	0.6	–
Canarias	2.0	–	0.7	–	1.2	–
Cantabria	0.7	0.8	–	–	–	0.7
Castilla-La Mancha	5.2	5.1	–	–	0.6	0.7
Castilla León	7.2	14.4	–	4.4	–	1.5
Cataluña	9.8	5.9	9.7	7.9	5.8	2.2
Comunidad de Madrid	29.4	34.7	70.9	71.9	78.4	73.5
Extremadura	1.3	–	–	–	–	–
Galicia	6.5	2.9	2.2	2.6	1.2	5.9
Navarra	3.3	–	–	2.6	–	–
País Valenciano	6.5	5.9	2.2	0.9	–	2.9
País Vasco	5.2	5.9	3.0	–	0.6	0.7
Principado de Asturias	6.5	0.8	3.0	0.9	1.8	–
Región de Murcia	1.3	0.8	2.2	1.8	–	–
Rioja (la)	0.7	–	–	–	–	–
Abroad	5.2	2.5	2.2	–	7.0	6.6
N = 100%	153.0	118.0	134.0	114.0	171.0	136.0
No information	51.0	121.0	70.0	125.0	33.0	103.0

and so on). The creation of an informal unit of civil servants with strong ties among its members, a small group who work together to improve their quality of life within the public agency, with a capacity to influence personnel policies, and having close contacts with political appointees of the top echelons, facilitates the recruitment of civil servants for political posts through informal channels. Spanish *corps* have traditionally enjoyed considerable power to colonise not only political but also administrative posts. For example, diplomats have always been quite reluctant to allow members of other *corps* to be eligible for a political appointment in the Ministry of Foreign Affairs or even in an administrative office in commercial legation.

During the authoritarian regime, in the absence of political parties, *corps* of civil servants monopolised political recruitment. *Corps* not only monopolised most political appointments (Alba 1981, Álvarez 1984, Alba 1984) but also had a large percentage of seats in the non-democratic parliament (Linz and De Miguel 1975, Bañón 1978, Baena and García-Madaria 1979) and in many executive bodies of public and private enterprises (Baena 1977). Consequently, the history of Franco's regime is restricted to the history of the bureaucracy and the Spanish political system was labelled the Francoist bureaucratic state. During the period of the first two presidents from 1978 until October 1982, who belonged to the Unión de Centro Democrático (UCD), a left-centre political party, civil servants not only monopolised most political appointments, but also controlled the political party which has since disappeared (Román 1997, Baena 1999).

This situation started to change slowly from 1982 and again from 1996 as the PSOE had a longer tradition and the PP had a basis outside the bureaucracy. The PSOE intended to nominate candidates who had not been involved in Franco's regime, but party membership was not a requirement as the basis for nomination was personal ties. The PSOE had to compete with the *grands corps*, which were composed of civil servants who had completed a degree as a requirement to enter office, for monopoly over political recruitment. There are differences in recruitment patterns between 1982 and 1996. While 17.5 per cent of newly appointed top officials in 1982 came from outside, in 1996 almost 25 per cent of new appointments were external candidates (Table 12.6). These *outsiders* were normally appointed to second-tier offices and many had connections to parts of the public sector that had been privatised. The predominance of strong *corps* helps to explain the low proportion of external appointments, but economic reasons also play a part. When outsiders cease to work for the civil service they do not receive indemnification, whereas civil servants who work for at least two years in the rank of GD or above will obtain a salary complement bringing them to the level of GD for life (even if they are administratively downgraded) and, most important, they may continue to work in the civil service, while outsiders leaving office have restricted access to jobs linked to the ministry where they worked due to the law of incompatibilities. Therefore, it is difficult to see how the budget could stand a rate of 80 per cent of outsiders. If the *corps* play a significant role in promoting political appointments, it will be interesting to distinguish which particular ones are best able to provide access to the top. Although there are more than 200 *corps* in Spain's central administration, only a dozen of them are influential in political decisions and recruitment. Table 12.4 shows the evolution of *corps* control over political recruitment since 1938. Although this chapter focuses on the 1982 and 1996 governments, data from the Franco period are given for comparison.

The dominant *corps* in political recruitment during the period 1938–75 were those based in the legal profession and their members came from law faculties. Consequently, *corps* related to law and order, diplomats and professors (from law disciplines) occupied most political appointments. Economists were not appointed to top posts and the military accounted for the majority of the category 'Other'. The different 'governments' of the Franco period after the early 1960s did not contain a high proportion of military (no more than 7.5 per cent; see Alba 1984), and they were in charge of only the three military ministries, while the civilian ministries were occupied by technocrats from Opus Dei.

Table 12.4 Distribution of *grands corps* in new appointments, 1982 and 1996 (comparison with 1938–73) (%)

	Governments under Franco (1938–82)[a]					Socialist government 1982[b]	Conservative government 1996[b]
	1938	*1943*	*1951*	*1962*	*1973*	*1982[b]*	*1996[b]*
Law[c]	12.9	25.1	26.9	24.1	18.8	7.4	11.4
Diplomats	35.5	12.5	30.4	13.8	6.3	10.4	13.7
Professors	19.4	16.7	21.4	14.9	18.8	18.5	13.1
Engineer	9.7	12.5	1.8	11.5	7.8	5.9	8.6
Fin.-comp.	–	8.3	3.6	16.0	10.9	17.8	10.3
Soc.-comp.	–	–	–	–	–	–	1.7
Civ.-adm.	–	–	–	–	–	19.3	7.4
Com.-tec.	–	–	–	–	–	8.9	5.7
Other	22.6	25.0	–	18.4	37.5	8.8	28.0
N = 100%	39.0	30.0	70.0	108.0	80.0	135.0	175.0
No information	–	–	–	–	–	69.0	64.0

Notes
a Alba (1984: 234). All political appointments are included (old and new).
b Only new appointments.
c Law: includes public prosecutors, attorney general, judge, notary.
   Engineer: Civil, industrial and forestry engineers.
   Fin.-comp.: Finance comptrollers.
   Soc.-comp.: Social security comptrollers.
   Civ.-adm.: Civil administrator (social security technicians are included).
   Com.tec.: Commercial technicians and economists.

The predominance in political appointments of *corps* members with legal backgrounds is compatible with the state elite's main goal during the dictatorship. The main objective of the 'government' during this period was to ground the non-democratic state on administrative law that preserved the most important rights of citizens as administered subjects. The conservative values of these *corps* members can also help to explain their predominance. Engineering *corps* replaced economic *corps* at the top levels as engineers were able to create employment through great civil works projects (roads, bridges and ditches). Engineers could also manage the economy in an autarchy of a non-complex system.

The distribution of *corps* at the upper levels changed after 1982, a year when the *corps* of civil administrators had the largest share of political appointments (19.3 per cent in Table 12.4). The *corps* related to law and order diminished considerably in 1982 and after, while professors and diplomats maintained an important share of power in both 1982 and 1996. *Corps* that require economics studies increased their share of political appointments during the socialist period. The increasingly complex economic situation of the Spanish state resulted from the double territorial dynamic of applying for entry to the European Community in 1986 and the 'quasi-federalisation' of the state after 1978. In these processes knowledge of economics began to be very valuable. As most political issues are bound by highly complex economic decisions, the nature of political appointments changed. Spanish governments of the 1980s and 1990s focused on the international crisis and its effects on the national economy, once the democratic framework had been agreed during the late 1970s.

In 1996, in a rather more complex state, the increase in lawyers and engineers might be considered surprising. It can be explained by the proximity of the members of these *corps* to the values of the conservative government, and there was a revival of *corps* that were strong during Franco's dictatorship. This assertion is relevant inasmuch as the *corps* devoted to law and order are smaller than the others (see also Table 12.5 for the first degrees of new political appointees). In Table 12.5, the proportion of law specialists remains the same while economists with political appointments are fewer in number. Unlike the Dutch case study and more in line with the German political functionaries, the top civil servants whom politicians preferred were not the entrepreneurial but rather the classical variety. This trend is not surprising if we take into account the fact that the NPM reform failed in Spain and the main concern has continued to be intergovernmental relationships in a highly legalistic system. Civil administrators closer to the PSOE saw their influence reduced in the new political appointments in 1996 (7.4 per cent).

So far, bureaucrats have controlled access to political appointments. The political masters have taken into account that public programmes could be jeopardised if civil servants were excluded from government.

Table 12.5 Distribution of first degree in new appointments, 1982 and 1996 (%)

	Socialist government 1982	*Conservative government 1996*
No degree	1.1	–
Law	43.5	46.6
Economics	24.2	15.0
Engineering/ Architecture	12.9	19.5
Natural and exact sciences	8.6	6.8
Humanities	4.8	6.8
Political and social sciences	3.8	1.5
Military school	1.1	3.8
N = 100%	186.0	133.0
No information	18.0	106.0

There has been a slight movement towards more external recruitment during the democratic phase, but it is not envisaged that outsiders will totally replace bureaucrats in political appointments. The civil service culture is too strong to be excluded from the political appointments. Appointments are based upon personal relations and the *corps* has been and continues to be a traditional channel of personal ties in spite of the fact that political parties also compete for patronage and regardless of the loss of status of the *corps* within the civil service.

The data in Table 12.6 allow a complementary analysis. As already mentioned, the number of successful external candidates for new appointments increased slightly in 1996 (24.1 per cent) in comparison with 1982 (17.5 per cent) (for similar data for Germany, see Derlien 1989: 176, 1988: 63 although the implications are slightly different). The internal distribution of percentages also shows some differences between organisations within the public sector. In 1982, there was a relatively high percentage of new appointees who had held office in previous governments (11.5 per cent, adding rows 1 and 2), but this decreased to 2.2 per cent (only row 2) in 1996. On the other hand, diplomats working abroad were favoured by the PP government for new appointments more than by the PSOE government. Finally, the expansion of the regional authorities explains why a greater share of new political appointments came from the regional level in 1996 than in 1982. In both years, the rotation from the political to the administrative arena is similarly rather small (8.1 per cent in 1982 and 8.7 per cent in 1996).

252 Salvador Parrado Díez

Table 12.6 Distribution of last position prior to new appointments, 1982 and 1996 (%)

Previous position	Socialist government 1982	Conservative government 1996
1 Political appointment of 2nd tier (JM, US, GS)	2.7	0.0
2 General director	8.8	2.2
3 Civil service career (high-flyers)	28.0	25.5
4 Foreign service	4.3	13.9
5 Public enterprise and autonomous agency	2.2	0.7
6 Justice	2.7	2.2
7 University education (professors)	11.0	10.9
8 Military cadres	1.6	1.5
9 Others (central administration)	6.6	0.8
10 Minister of autonomous regional government	0.0	2.2
11 Regional administration	2.2	5.1
12 Local councillor	2.2	2.2
13 Local administration	2.2	0.0
14 PUBLIC ADMINISTRATION (total of 1–13)	74.5	67.2
15 National parliament	6.0	2.9
16 Regional parliament	0.5	2.2
17 Executive of political party or trade union	1.6	3.6
18 Politics (15 + 16 + 17)	8.1	8.7
19 Liberal profession	2.2	0.7
20 Private enterprise/bank	12.6	21.9
21 Others (private sector)	2.7	1.5
22 PRIVATE SECTOR (19 + 20 + 21)	17.5	24.1
N = 100% (14 + 18 + 22)	182.0	137.0
Information not available	22.0	102.0

4 Concluding remarks

Recruitment to political office has been addressed in this chapter in order to show the tools that Spanish political executives have deployed to control the bureaucratic machinery. Two main aspects have been examined: the evolution of the organisational design and the individual recruitment patterns.

First, two main organisational trends can be observed during the democratic era: a reinforcement of the premiership by enlarging its entourage and strengthening control of the work of the ministerial bureaucracy, and a shift of power relationships in favour of political appointees who can be either external or internal candidates (JM, GS, GD) over political appointees selected exclusively from the administration. The same developments occurred under both socialist and conservative governments. In this sense, a strategy of continuous political reinforcement has taken place. At the end of the day, democratic politics is eroding the bureaucratic politics of previous times, as far as organisation is concerned.

A few *corps* monopolised political appointments under the Franco regime, with exclusive control of non-meritocratic recruitment. In the absence of political parties, civil servants could control the nomination of the political masters. Bureaucrats occupied the political executive, almost to the exclusion of outsiders. Moreover, top civil servants had parallel control of the big public and private corporations and parliamentary seats in the non-democratic Cortes, as there was no law preventing public servants also holding offices in private business. It was a power elite in the terms argued by Mills (1956). The ministries were small, but large enough to manage an internationally isolated system. During the transition period between 1975 and 1981, evidence shows that replacement of cadres from the former authoritarian regime was incremental rather than radical and, in the absence of a strong political party, *corps* still could control non-meritocratic recruitment and be present in other entrepreneurial positions.

The expectations of radical change were high with the election in 1982 of the PSOE, a party which had not taken part in the transitional process within the state structures, and in 1996 of the PP, as the right wing had not ruled democratically for decades. In order to implement their programme, socialist leaders replaced the top cadres through a radical substitution of political appointments, whereas the predominant informal rules until 1982 had favoured a gradual rotation of these appointments. The entry of the conservative government in 1996 also entailed replacement of political appointees. Thus, the Spanish system of political appointments became very similar to the American one. Although both socialist and conservative governments replaced a great number of political appointments, it seems that the conservative strategy has been more radical (affecting 89.2 per cent of appointments) than the socialist (76.2 per cent). The continuity of some appointees from previous governments shows that there is not always a political party identification between political appointees and the government. Those appointees are apolitical technocrats who occupy politically appointed offices with low visibility or low profile in the ministry (like the general director for legal affairs). There are also differences in the destiny of political appointees with civil service status after leaving office. While the socialist government provided these appointees from previous governments with relatively good post-positions, the conservatives got rid of ex-socialist appointees by placing them in non-relevant posts away from decision-making.

There are many elements of continuity in the individual patterns of recruitment. Political appointees of both governments were relatively young, although for different reasons: in 1982 political appointees were younger as a consequence of the transition from dictatorship to democracy; in 1996, the procedure was linked to restructuring in the PP. In both cases, there has been a strong centralisation in geographical terms of the different stages of life (birth, university studies and position previous to political appointment). Madrid is still a focus for would-be political appointees in spite of the quasi-federal nature of the system. Finally, there is a growing tendency to appoint outsiders: their numbers have risen from around 10 per cent during Franco's time to 17.5 per cent in 1982 and 24.1 per cent in 1996. The rest are controlled by less than a dozen *corps*. While civil administrators and finance comptrollers controlled numerous political appointments in 1982, *corps* based in law and order and diplomats dominated in 1996. It seems that there has been a return to the *corps* distribution of Franco's times. This could be considered an element of change.

The enlargement of the reserve pool of political appointments, the acceptance of more outsiders in recent government and the redesign of the organisational summit favour the increase of political executive control over bureaucracy and show the tendency towards *political democracy* depicted by Aberbach and Rockman (1988a). It seems that the removal of civil servants from top positions is not related to any suspicion that they are not sufficiently responsive to changes in the priorities of their political leadership. There is no reason to believe they would not be responsive, but it is preferred that they come from the circle closest to the leadership. On the other hand, public servants are selected for political appointment not only on the grounds of their 'responsive competence', so that they implement basic changes within the administrative system, as Peters and Pierre point out at the outset of Chapter 1 above, but also because there are not enough resources to hire and attract private managers for public offices.

Notes

1 In what follows, I use the methodology applied by Professor Derlien (1985, 1989, 1990a, 1990b, 1990c). I am very grateful for his help which is always available to improve my research. I also thank Professor Olmeda for the help he has provided me in dealing with the *entourage* of the presidency. Mistakes and errors are entirely mine.
2 Appointments of ambassadors, government delegates in provinces and the like are not included.

References

Aberbach, J. and B. Rockman (1988a) 'Mandates or Mandarins? Control and Discretion in the Modern Administrative State', *Public Administration Review*, 48, pp. 608–12.
Aberbach, J. and B. Rockman (1988b) 'Image IV Revisited: Executive and Political Roles Governance', *Governance*, 1, 1, pp. 1–25.
Aberbach, J. D., R. D. Putnam and B. A. Rockman (1981) *Bureaucrats and Politicians in Western Democracies*. Cambridge (Mass.), Harvard University Press.
Alba, C. (1981) 'The Organization of Authoritarian Leadership: Franco Spain', in R. Rose and E. N. Suleiman, *Presidents and Prime Ministers*. Washington, American Enterprise Institute for Public Policy Research, pp. 256–83.

Alba, C. (1984) 'Bürokratie und Politik. Hohe Beamte im Franco-Regime (1938–1975)', in P. Waldman, W. L. Bernecker and F. López-Casero (eds) *Sozialer Wandel und Herrschaft im Spanien Francos.* Munich, Ferdinand Schöningh, pp. 211–35.

Alba, C. (1992) 'Investigación sobre los cargos designación política de la dictadura franquista', mimeo.

Álvarez, J. (1984) *Burocracia y poder político en el régimen franquista.* Madrid, INAP.

Baena, M. (1977) 'El poder económico de la burocracia en España', *Información Comercial Española*, 522, pp. 12–21.

Baena, M. (1992) *Instituciones administrativas.* Madrid, Marcial Pons.

Baena, M. (1999) *Elites y conjuntos de poder en España (1939–1992).* Madrid, Tecnos.

Baena, M. and J. M. García Madaria (1979) 'Elite franquista y burocracia en las Cortes actuales', *Sistema*, 28, pp. 3–50.

Bañón, R. (1978) *Poder de la burocracia y Cortes franquistas 1943–1971.* Madrid, INAP.

Bar, A. (1997) 'Spain. A Prime Ministerial Government', in J. Blondel and F. Müller-Rommel (eds) *Cabinets in Western Europe.* London, Macmillan, pp. 102–19.

Derlien, H.-U. (1984) 'Einstweiliger Ruhestand politischer Beamter des Bundes 1949 bis 1983', *Die öffentliche Verwaltung*, 17, pp. 689–700.

Derlien, H.-U. (1985) 'Politicisation of the Civil Service in the Federal Republic of Germany. Facts and Fables', in F. Meyer, *La Politisation de l'administration.* Brussels, Institut International des Sciences Administratives, pp. 1–39.

Derlien, H.-U. (1988) 'Repercussions of Government Change on the Career Civil Service in West Germany: The Cases of 1969 and 1982', *Governance*, 1, 1, pp. 50–78.

Derlien, H.-U. (1989) 'Die Regierungswechsel von 1969 und 1982 in ihren Auswirkungen auf die Beamtenelite', in Heinrich Siedentopf (ed.) *Führungskräfte in der öffentliche Verwaltung.* Baden-Baden, Nomos Verlag, pp. 171–89.

Derlien, H.-U. (1990) 'Keeping the Balance between Political Appointments and Professional Careers in the Case of the FRG (Research Committee N1 3)', *Deutsche Sektion des Internationalen Instituts für Verwaltungswissenschaften*, 1, pp. 36–44.

Derlien, H.-U. (1990a) 'Wer macht in Bonn Karriere?', *Die Verwaltung*, 8, pp. 311–19.

Derlien, H.-U. (1990b) 'Die administrative Elite', *Der Bürger im Staat*, 40, pp. 32–5.

Derlien, H.-U. (1990c) 'Continuity and Change in the West German Federal Executive Elite 1949–1984', *European Journal of Political Research*, 18, pp. 349–72.

Derlien, H.-U. (1991) 'Regierungswechsel, Regimewechsel und Zusammensetzung der politisch-administrativen Elite', in B. Blanke and H. Wollmann (eds) *Die alte Bundesrepublik. Kontinuität und Wandel.* Opladen, Westdeutscher Verlag, pp. 253–70.

Gutiérrez-Reñón, A. (1987) 'La carrera administrativa en España: evolución histórica y perspectivas', *Documentación Administrativa*, 210/211, May–September, pp. 29–70.

Herzog, D. (1982) *Politische Führungsgruppen.* Darmstadt, Wissenschaftliche Buchgesellschaft.

Heywood, P. and I. Molina (2000) 'A Quasi-Presidential Premiership: Administering the Executive Summit in Spain', in B. G. Peters, R. A. W. Rhodes and V.

Wright (eds) *Administering the Summit. Administration of the Core Executive in Developed Countries*. London, Macmillan, pp. 110–33.

Keller, S. (1968) *Beyond the Ruling Class. Strategic Elites in Modern Society*. New York.

Linz, J. J. and J. M. de Miguel (1975) 'Las Cortes españolas: 1943–1970', *Sistema*, 8, 9, pp. 85–110.

Mills, W. R. (1956) *The Power Elite*. New York, Oxford University Press.

Parrado, S. (1996) *Las élites de la Administración estatal (1982–1991). Estudio general y pautas de reclutamiento*. Sevilla, Junta de Andalucía, Instituto Andaluz de Administración Pública.

Parrado, S. (1998) 'Controlling the Access to the Spanish Summit (1938–1991)', in J. C. N. Raadschelders and F. M. Van der Meer (eds) *L'Entourage administratif du pouvoir exécutif/Administering the Summit*. Brussels, International Institute of Administrative Sciences, pp. 115–31.

Peters, B. G., R. A. W. Rhodes and V. Wright (eds) (2000) *Administering the Summit. Administration of the Core Executive in Developed Countries*. London, Macmillan.

Putnam, R. D. (1975) 'The Political Attitudes of Senior Civil Servants in Britain, Germany, and Italy', in Mattei Dogan, *The Mandarins of Western Europe*. New York, Sage, pp. 87–127.

Román, L. (1997) *Funcionarios y función pública en la transición española*. Madrid, Centro de Estudios Políticos y Constitucionales.

Wildenmann, R., U. Hoffmann-Lange, M. Kaase, A. Kutteroff and G. Wolf (1982) *Führungsschicht in der Bundesrepublik Deutschland*. Mannheim.

Wilson, G. K. (1993) 'Counter Elites and Bureaucracies', *Governance*, 6, 3, pp. 426–37.

Zapf, W. (1965) *Wandlungen der deutschen Elite. Ein Zirkulationsmodell deutscher Führungsgruppen 1919–1961*. Munich, Piper.

13 Two faces of politicization of the civil service

The case of contemporary Greece

Dimitri A. Sotiropoulos

The dominant hypothesis in the literature on the Greek civil service is that it has been and continues to be over-politicized, mainly on account of the constant efforts of political elites to use the state mechanism as a source of generating votes rather than as an instrument of policy implementation (Lyrintzis, 1984; Makrydemetris, 1999; Mouzelis, 1986; Sotiropoulos, 1993, 1996, 1999, 2001; Spanou, 1992, 1996, 1998, 2001; Tsekos, 1986; Tsoucalas, 1986). The hypothesis assumes that the Greek political elites are acting in a structural context which lends itself to extreme politicization. This is the context of a polarized party system, in which parties dominated by personalities have fought for power between 1949 and 1967 and again since 1974 (Mouzelis, 1978; Legg, 1969; Clogg, 1987), and of an equally polarized political culture (Diamandouros, 1983; Demertzis, 1990). This culture, is the outcome of the political socialization of several generations of Greeks in successive periods which included a very destructive civil war (1946–1949), a disciplined parliamentary democracy imbued with anti-communism and systematic monitoring of the Left (1949–1967), military dictatorship (1967–1974), and the intense rivalry between the Greek socialist party (PASOK) and the conservative New Democracy party (ND) from 1974 until today. One cannot understand politicization in Greece without grasping the political significance of these two parties, which together represent more than two-thirds of the electorate. PASOK, the socialist/populist party, was founded in 1974 by the charismatic Andreas Papandreou. It managed to win an astonishing 48 percent of the vote in the elections of 1981 and has ruled with an absolute majority ever since – with a short interval in 1990–1993 when it was out of power mainly due to the protracted illness of its leader and the involvement of several of its ministers in financial scandals. ND was founded by Constantine Caramanlis, another charismatic leader who masterminded the transition from authoritarian rule to democracy in 1974. His party enjoyed an absolute majority in the Greek parliament between 1974 and 1981 and again between 1990 and 1993 (under the leadership of Constantine Mitsotakis).

The polarized political system and political culture have been conducive to the penetration of the civil service by successive incoming governments ("top-down politicization") and to the involvement of civil servants in party politics ("bottom-up politicization"). In this context, "top-down" politicization (or politicization "from above") of the civil service in Greece can be analyzed by addressing the most relevant elements of the comparative study of politicization (Peters and Pierre, Chapter 1 above). As Peters and Pierre suggest, the analysis may focus, on the one hand, on politicization of the structures of the civil service and the creation of new arenas of decision-making, and, on the other hand, on political control of the bureaucracy through new appointments, influencing the behavior of existing civil service personnel or changing their attitudes and culture. In the Greek case, politicization "from above" has been promoted through the duplication of administrative structures, efforts to change the behavior of civil servants, waves of new appointments in the civil service and politicization of promotions to the top of the civil service hierarchy.

At this point, a note on "bottom-up" politicization (or politicization "from below") is pertinent, in order to underscore the dynamics of the process of politicization "from above." It would be wrong to conclude, in a voluntaristic manner, that politicization is the outcome of the needs and activities of politicians, as some Greek observers have done (e.g. Athanassopoulos, 1983). It would also be false to conclude that the civil service has been the innocent bystander, if not the victim, of the misuse of the state by the political class. "Bottom-up" politicization has been fueled by the mobilization of political party-led labor unions within each ministry and public enterprise. One does not have to overstate the impact of PASOK's rule on the organization of the wider Greek public sector and on the behavior of the occupants of public sector positions (Mavrogordatos, 1997) to accept that civil servants have not really been passive observers of the situation. They have themselves been protagonists, albeit in a supporting role due to their weakness as a collective actor, in the shaping of the contemporary Greek public administration. To that effect, it suffices to note the pressure by civil servants for additional income, faster promotions, expanded competences, exclusive rights for their own sectoral associations granted by individual ministries and public agencies, and preferential treatment of their kin in the recruitment of new personnel and in career advancement. Without these pressures from civil servants, the phenomena of politicization described in this chapter would be much less acute.

In order to show the meanings of the above modes of politicization, first, the historical evolution of the modern Greek state as an administrative mechanism will be breifly sketched, followed by a short evaluation of its current situation; second, an important characteristic of the case under study, namely clientelism, will be described in detail; and, third, recent developments will be discussed; a conclusion follows. The main argument of this chapter is that the two processes, politicization from below and politicization from above (or top-down politicization), are two sides of the same coin.

The extent of politicization in the Greek civil service

The Greek civil service has always been heavily politicized, probably to a greater extent than in any other West European nation-state. Politicization, which does not mean over-politicization, can probably be shown by reference to the "political–electoral cycle," which involves an upswing in public spending and hiring in the public sector on the eve of general elections and a downswing between elections (see Table 13.1; also Spanou, 1990; see Thomadakis and Seremetis, 1992 on fiscal aspects). Over-politicization is more difficult to prove by citing figures showing the size of the public sector. It can only be demonstrated by interpreting the existing legal provisions which facilitate the penetration of the bureaucracy by party politics. Subjective perceptions are therefore involved.

Some degree of politicization is common in modern public bureaucracies. But the over-politicization of the Greek civil service is often manifested in the manner in which personnel are hired and promoted. While officially all relevant procedures are standardized and meritocratic,

Table 13.1 Percentage change of size of civil service by type of organization in Greece, 1980–1998

	Central government	Public bodies	Public corporations	Local government
1980	–	–	–	–
1981	1.3	1.6	–	–
1982	−0.8	0.6	2.1	−0.1
1983	3.9	1.2	2.1	4.9
1984	2.0	3.6	2.0	2.6
1985	7.0	5.1	1.0	12.1
1986	−4.2	5.3	10.7	−1.0
1987	1.6	16.9	4.6	2.2
1988	0.7	10.4	4.3	8.0
1989	0.2	9.1	12.7	1.6
1990	−3.9	0.2	−1.6	28.2
1991	−1.6	4.5	−1.6	1.2
1992	−4.3	−5.9	−36.2	11.6
1993	3.4	−1.4	−7.7	−1.3
1994	−4.3	4.3	2.6	0.5
1995	1.3	2.4	4.8	1.4
1996	1.1	2.7	−0.3	−0.5
1997	−3.4	0.1	−1.6	−1.1
1998	−2.4	1.1	−0.8	0.0

Sources: Anthony D. Makrydemetris and P. Livierakos, "How Many Are the Civil Servants?," *Oeconomicos Tachydromos*, 9 May 1996, Table 3, reprinted in Makrydemetris (1999: 254); Ministry of the Interior (YPESDDA), *Bulletin of Statistical Data on Sector Personnel*, Athens: National Printing Office, 2000: 33–34.

Note
The years in *italics* are years of general elections.

unofficially it is widely admitted that politicization is quite extensive. Two sample surveys of Greek civil servants, conducted in 1989 and 1995, support this claim in regard to both recruitment to and promotions in the civil service (Sotiropoulos, 1991; Mylonopoulou-Moira, 1998). As far as recruitment is concerned, almost 50 percent of the civil servants who responded in the 1995 survey admitted that they had used patronage either to be recruited to the civil service without undergoing any competition for entry or to pass the competitive examinations required for entry to the civil service (Table 13.2). More precise and indicative data show the extent of politicization in promotions (Table 13.3). Among the respondents of the 1995 survey, 25 percent simply said that political party connections carry most weight in the selection of new heads of administrative units and an additional 45 percent said that objective criteria (e.g. merit, job experience) combined with party connections determine the selection. This attitude is corroborated by how political appointees, such as advisors to ministers and governing party cadres, saw the selection

Table 13.2 Attitudes of Greek civil servants to the politicization of the mode of their own recruitment (1995)

Mode by which respondents were recruited to the civil service	%
By entrance examination	45.9
By entrance examination and patronage	18.6
By patronage	30.7
By graduation from the National School of Public Administration	0.4
By other mode	2.0
No answer	2.4
Total	100.0
	(N = 1270)

Source: Non-random sample survey of 1270 civil servants in nineteen Greek ministries, conducted in 1995 by Polyxeni Mylonopoulou-Moira (1998: 183).

Table 13.3 Attitudes of Greek civil servants to the politicization of criteria of promotion in the civil service (1995)

Prevalent criteria	%
Objective criteria	16.6
Personal patronage criteria	3.3
Party patronage criteria	25.4
Party patronage *and* objective criteria	45.0
Other criteria	6.9
No answer	2.8
Total	100.0
	(N = 1270)

Source: Non-random sample survey of 1270 civil servants in nineteen Greek ministries, conducted in 1995 by Polyxeni Mylonopoulou-Moira (1998: 208).

process in the late 1980s (Table 13.4). While the seniority and professional capacity of the candidates played an important role, their political opinions and personal contacts mattered as much, if not more.

Although comparative claims on such matters across time and space are bound to be unreliable, Greek politicization seems to have longer and deeper roots than in other European cases. For instance, the widespread belief that the Greek civil service is very politicized does not only concern PASOK's first terms in power (1981–1985 and 1985–1989). In the 1989 survey, very few senior civil servants and political appointees claimed that the career of a civil servant was not affected at all by party affiliation either under ND, in 1974–1981, or under PASOK, in 1981–1989 (Table 13.5). It has been argued that in the early 1980s the politicization of the Greek civil service by PASOK was more blatant than the comparable cases of the Spanish and the French civil service by the socialists of the PSOE and PS respectively (Bodiguel, 1986). Although comparisons across different political regimes are often not warranted, it is significant that Greek top civil servants surveyed in 1989 believed that political opinions mattered in promotions; comparable surveys of French top civil servants in the Fifth Republic (1974) and of Spanish top civil servants serving under Franco (1968, Table 13.6) show opposite findings.

What is the ideological color of politicized civil servants? Do they lean toward the Left or the Right? The evidence is very thin, but there is some

Table 13.4 Attitudes of high-ranking Greek civil servants and political appointees to the principal criteria affecting nomination of heads of directorates in the civil service (1989) (%)

Criteria	Top civil servants	Advisors to minister	Party cadres
Seniority	9	28	25
Hard work	4	3	6
Initiative and original ideas	6	3	6
Political opinions	16	28	25
Professional capacity	39	5	28
Personal contacts	5	13	3
Prestige in the ministry	8	3	3
Other criteria	2	0	3
No response	11	20	3
Total	100	100	100
	(N = 76)	(N = 40)	(N = 40)

Source: The non-random sample survey of 76 high-ranking civil servants and 76 political appointees (i.e. ministerial advisors and political party cadres employed in headquarters of ministries) conducted by the author in four ministries in Athens, 1989 (Sotiropoulos, 1991: 361).

Note
Percentages may not add up to 100 due to rounding.

Table 13.5 Attitudes of Greek civil servants and political appointees to the relative influence of affiliation of a civil servant with the governing political party for career advancement in the civil service, under different governments (%)

Relative influence	Top civil servants	Advisors to ministers	Party cadres
Civil servant supporting ND would be promoted more in 1974–1981, under ND government	28	33	50
Civil servant supporting PASOK would be promoted more in 1981–1989, under PASOK government	25	25	25
Civil servant supporting the governing party would be promoted the same in both periods	31	18	17
Career of civil servant would not be affected at all by party affiliation in either period	5	8	3
No response	11	18	6
Total	100 (N = 76)	100 (N = 40)	100 (N = 36)

Source: Non-random sample survey of 152 high-ranking civil servants and political appointees (i.e. ministerial advisors and party cadres) conducted by the author in four ministries in Athens, 1989 (Sotiropoulos, 1991: 367).

Note
Percentages may not add up to 100 due to rounding. The precoded question was "In practice, do you think that the career of a civil servant in this ministry would have been promoted the same, if that civil servant was a member of the governing political party in the years 1974–1981 (i.e. a member of the ND, when this party was in power) or of the other governing party (i.e. a member of PASOK, when that party was in power) in 1981–1989?"

indication that, at least in the late 1980s, Greek top civil servants leaned toward the Center, as might be expected, but also to the Center-Left, to a greater extent than the Greek population as a whole (Table 13.7 and Figures 13.1 and 13.3; positions 5 and 6 for the Center, 3 and 4 for the Center-Left, 7 and 8 for the Center-Right). Also in the 1980s, the self-definition of political appointees, such as general secretaries of ministries and advisors to ministers, was further to the Left (Figure 13.2). If data on the ideological self-definition of civil servants are dubious, data on their political party affiliation are notoriously unreliable. Yet, in the same small-scale survey of 1989, 21 per cent of the top civil servants admitted to being card-carrying members of one of the two major Greek political parties, PASOK and ND (Table 13.8).

Table 13.6 Attitudes of Greek, Spanish, and French top civil servants to the main factors influencing the nomination of directors in the civil services of Greece (1989), Spain (1968), and France (1974) (%)

Main factor	Greek civil servants	Spanish civil servants	French civil servants
Seniority	9	19	1
Hard work	4	8	NA
Initiative and original ideas	6	20	NA
Political opinions	16	NA	1
Professional capacity	39	23	54
Personal contacts	5	11	3
Prestige in the ministry	8	NA	3
Belonging to a corps	NA	8	36
Other criteria	2	11	2
No response	11	NA	NA
Total	100	100	100
	(N = 76)	(N = 843)	(N = 90)

Sources: For Greece, the non-random sample survey of 76 high-ranking civil servants conducted by the author in four ministries in Athens, 1989 (Sotiropoulos, 1991: 354). For Spain, see Gómez-Reino and Orizo (1968: 291); and for France, Suleiman (1974: 147).

Note
NA means not available. Percentages may not add up to 100 due to rounding. The Spanish respondents were members of the civil service elite corps but not necessarily directors of ministries.

Table 13.7 Self-placement of Greek high-ranking civil servants, political appointees, and the general population along the ten-point Left–Right scale (survey conducted in 1989; non-response not included) (%)

	Civil servants	Political appointees	General population
1	0	2	4.2
2	7	3	5.6
3	4	34	8.5
4	25	43	9.7
5	24	11	24.9
6	19	8	14.8
7	15	0	8.2
8	4	0	9.8
9	0	0	4.9
10	0	0	9.5
Total	100	100	100.0
	(N = 67)	(N = 65)	(N = 1597)

Sources: The data for the general Greek population are taken from the May 1989 research of the Greek Center for Social Research (EKKE) on political culture and electoral behavior (Voulgaris, 1990: 255). The data for the first two columns come from the non-random sample survey of 76 high-ranking civil servants conducted by the author in four ministries in Athens, 1989 (Sotiropoulos, 1991: 230).

Note
Percentages may not add up to 100 due to rounding.

FREQUENCY

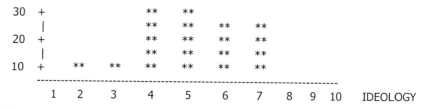

CIVIL SERVANTS

```
30  +                        **      **
    |                        **      **      **      **
20  +                        **      **      **      **
    |                        **      **      **      **
10  +          **      **     **      **      **      **
    -----------------------------------------------------------------
          1    2    3    4    5    6    7    8    9   10   IDEOLOGY
```

Figure 13.1 Self-placement of high-ranking Greek civil servants on the ten-point Left–Right scale (survey conducted in 1989, N = 67).

Sources: See Table 13.7.

FREQUENCY

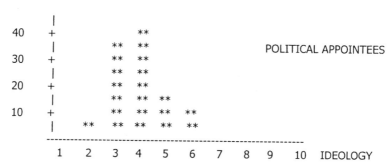

```
       |
40  +           **
       |     **   **                    POLITICAL APPOINTEES
30  +       **   **
       |     **   **
20  +       **   **
       |     **   **   **
10  +       **   **   **   **
       |   **   **   **   **   **
    -----------------------------------------------------------------
        1    2    3    4    5    6    7    8    9    10   IDEOLOGY
```

Figure 13.2 Self-placement of Greek political appointees on the ten-point Left–Right scale (survey conducted in 1989, N = 65).

Sources: See Table 13.7.

FREQUENCY

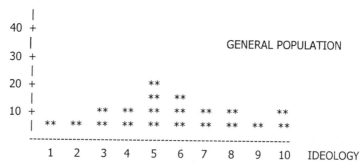

```
       |
40  +                                   GENERAL POPULATION
       |
30  +
       |
20  +                **
       |             **   **
10  +        **   **   **   **   **   **        **
       |   **   **   **   **   **   **   **   **   **   **
    -----------------------------------------------------------------
        1    2    3    4    5    6    7    8    9   10   IDEOLOGY
```

Figure 13.3 Self-placement of Greek population on the ten-point Left–Right scale (survey conducted in 1989, N = 1597).

Sources: See Table 13.7.

Table 13.8 Distribution of political party membership of Greek civil servants and political appointees (1989) (%)

Political party	Civil servants	Political appointees
PASOK party member	17	47
ND party member	4	0
Left party member	0	14
Not party member	58	25
No response	21	13
Total	100	100
	(76)	(76)

Source: Non-random sample survey of 76 high-ranking civil servants conducted by the author in four ministries in Athens, 1989 (Sotiropoulos, 1991: 326).

Note
Percentages may not add up to 100 due to rounding. Left parties were KKE and EAR which participated together in the elections of 1989 in a coalition called *Synaspismos tes Aristeras kai tes Proodou* (Coalition of the Left and Progress).

The social and historical roots of Greek over-politicization

What are the sources of Greek over-politicization? They can be traced – to some extent – by looking at the Greek state from a macro-historical perspective. The historical path of uneven and dependent development that Greece has followed in the last two centuries has formed the context within which its bureaucratic structure is still contained. The Greek state mechanism bears traits of the legal-rational bureaucratic model, combined with elements of patrimonial bureaucracy. While this mechanism fulfills all the typical requirements which Max Weber set forth in his description of the ideal type of modern bureaucracy (Weber, 1958), it may be better understood as a borderline case. This is mainly due to the historical origins of the public administration, which emerged after the Greek War of Independence from the Ottoman Empire (1821–1827). For one thing, the social and economic conditions which, according to Weber, are conducive to the emergence of modern bureaucracy did not exist in early modern Greece of the nineteenth century, or at least had not taken the full-blown capitalist industrial form that they had in other Western democracies. Modern Greece exhibited an early parliamentarism, commonly found in industrialized states, but with no corresponding extensive industrialization. In the nineteenth century and the first half of the twentieth century, Greece had an agricultural economy, with very few small industrial enclaves. Major industrial activity did not take place before World War I. Yet Greece was an early democracy because universal male suffrage was introduced in the mid-nineteenth century, that is earlier than in many core Western democracies (Mouzelis, 1986: xiii–xvi).

Between the mid-nineteenth century and the late twentieth century, Greece experienced economic mis-growth and political turmoil, which inhibited its administrative modernization. This delay of modernization can be attributed to many factors, including the lack of a strong industrial class which would have pressed for administrative reform, and the emergence of political party competition and factionalism prior to the building of an administrative elite and of administrative structures capable of withstanding government change (Sotiropoulos, 1993).

Today, as is well known, Greece is a member of the European Union, has already joined the European Monetary Union, and has an economy which enjoys steady growth. It has a democratic regime with majoritarian rule, i.e. executive power is concentrated in periodically elected, mostly single-party, majoritarian governments. Governments are durable, although there are frequent reshuffles of the same political personnel (especially in the 1980s), and the number of ministerial positions is quite large (Cabinets may have over forty or even fifty members). The executive is more powerful than the legislature. Although until 1986 the Presidency of the Republic enjoyed strong powers, the constitutional revision introduced by the PASOK government in that year made Greece a clearly parliamentary regime. The strength of the executive can be attributed to the two-party system and to the electoral law of reinforced proportional representation. ND and PASOK have dominated the party system, and the parties of the Left have not influenced the composition of government (with the exception of the two post-PASOK, short-term, coalition governments between June 1989 and April 1990). The electoral law which was implemented with various modifications in all the elections from November 1974 to June 1989 favored the largest parties and particularly whichever was the governing party. The same holds today, but there are guarantees that minor parties are represented in the parliament if they surpass the electoral threshold of 3 percent of total votes. Finally, Greece has a rigid constitution, a unicameral parliament and an executive branch of government which is very centralized and unitary (Lijphart *et al.*, 1988).

In spite of the above improvement of the political system as a whole and of the gradual Europeanization of the Greek administration (Hlepas, 1999), the politicization of the Greek civil service is still pervasive and is related to a major consequence of the specific historical development of the state. This is the enduring clientelism in the central public administration and the wider public sector. Clientelism is apparent in many arrangements of hiring, transfer, and promotion of personnel which benefit those civil servants who side with the governing party and which characterized the Greek civil service throughout the twentieth century.

Clientelism

In the nineteenth century voters and, in particular, civil servants used to forge bonds of patronage with political party representatives in their region and with party notables, who would thus develop a personal clientele. These bonds were based on the exchange of votes for personal favors and involved a personal and diffuse relationship between the voter and the politician. In the manner of a typical spoils system, at each change of government, civil servants could be and, indeed, often were fired by the new administration, which employed its own political supporters. Tenure for civil servants was introduced in 1911, when a new constitution was passed by the Liberal party of Eleftherios Venizelos. However, its relevant provisions were breached five times between 1911 and 1950 (Flogaites, 1987: 214; Papadopoulou, 1990). So while formally tenure of civil servants was constitutionally guaranteed, in practice, informally, it was often cancelled by extenuating political circumstances, such as the inter-war National Schism between Liberals and Royalists and the post-war civil war between the government's army and the army of the Left (1946–1949). Throughout the post-war period, the Greek civil service was regulated by the Civil Service Code, passed in 1951. This law reflected both the mentality of the Cold War era and the hegemony of the conservative and center political parties, which had joined forces to win the civil war against the Communist party and its allies. The law, imbued by anti-communist ideology, allowed for close monitoring of the recruitment, promotions, and transfers of civil servants by the political party in power, i.e. by the conservative party which governed for most of the period between the end of the civil war and the breakdown of Greek democracy in 1967. As is well known, a military *coup d'état* occurred in that year. It was staged by right-wing colonels, who controlled the civil service even more closely than the previous political regime. While the deposed democratic governments used to control left-wing voters and civil servants, mostly by excluding them altogether from the political system, the colonels suppressed everyone from the Left, the Center or even the Right who resisted their authority.

Since the fall of the colonels' military regime (which lasted from 1967 to 1974), a political party system of "limited but polarized pluralism" has flourished within the confines of the Greek democracy (Mavrogordatos, 1984). Compared to the pre-1967 "disciplined" democracy, the current democratic regime is open, solid, and successful. However, the state mechanism is still a tool in the hands of the alternating governments, although the form of politicization has evolved. For instance, in the first two terms of PASOK governments (1981–1985 and 1985–1989) personal patronage was replaced by party patronage in the form of bureaucratic clientelism (Lyrintzis, 1984). Indeed, this form of clientelism is systematically organized and employed by the bureaucracy of whichever political party is in power. In its traditional form, clientelism was more personal, linking voters to individual politicians. In its more modern, bureaucratic form, voters turn for help, not to individual politicians, but to the local bureaucratic organization of the political party which they support, or else they go directly to the central headquarters of the party of their preference. If the shift from personal to bureaucratic clientelism is a marked change, there are also remarkable continuities. Despite recent efforts at privatization, the Greek state's intervention in the economy is still heavy but inefficient, while alternating political parties still bend the state machine to their own needs (Mouzelis, 1980; Tsoukalas, 1986). Clientelism is also associated with the lack of interpersonal trust which Eisenstadt and Roniger have found in south European societies (Eisenstadt and Roniger, 1984: 80–81). In Greece, the lack of trust may be related to particular structures of the past, such as the unstable and weak economy and the lack of durable bourgeois culture.

An example of clientelism is the pattern of recruitment of new administrative personnel. In 1974–1981, while the ND was in power, the primary means of recruitment of new administrative personnel was the offer of contracts for a limited period to temporary employees and the conduct of entrance examinations for permanent (more precisely, tenure-track) civil servants. The examinations for tenure-track jobs were separately overseen by the staff of the hiring ministry or public agency, but, importantly, the list of finalists was allegedly drafted by the ministers or political managers of the public agencies themselves. This political intervention from above undermined the legitimacy of the formal recruitment procedure. What undermined it even more was the fact that among the successful candidates who appeared in the lists of finalists only a small number were finally hired by the state. The rest of the finalists were dubbed "successful" applicants but had to wait to be hired until the next round of recruitment. They had either to form separate labor unions and press for employemnt in the public sector, something they often did, or to take new entrance examinations. Once recruited, they pressed their political supervisors (i.e. their patrons) for preferential treatment, favorable transfers, and, above all, promotions. Political supervisors, such as ministers, deputy ministers, and general secretaries of ministries, easily gave in to such pressure because, by doing so, they were able to politically control the civil service. The above patterns were also observed under the rule of PASOK, which, however, chose additional means to politicize the civil service on a massive scale. These included the mobilization of civil servants in the framework of party-dominated labor unions and a few "waves" of hiring new temporary personnel. Further differences in the politicizing practices of the two parties are highlighted below in a historical account of the post-authoritarian period.

The nuts and bolts of politicization

As Peters and Pierre note, politicization may take the form of influencing the appointments and the behavior of civil service personnel as well as the form of structural change, if incumbent civil servants do not give in to political pressure and cannot be removed without breaking the constitution (Peters and Pierre, Chapter 1 above). In contemporary Greece between the mid-1970s and the early 1990s, such types of politicization were attempted by both major parties, the ND and PASOK, albeit in a different fashion.

First, after 1974 the ND government took steps to eliminate pro-junta higher officials from the public administration and was quite successful in this task. The passage of a law codifying all the legislation concerning the status of civil servants had little effect on the Greek civil service, as most relevant regulations were given in the original Civil Service Code voted in the immediate post-war era (in 1951). However, toward the end of the 1970s the ND passed a law which severely limited the right to strike in the public sector. This piece of legislation and other practices of the ND government received heavy criticism from the opposition. Such widely disputed practices involved political patronage in hiring practices and promotions in the civil service and the wider public sector as well as sporadic police surveillance of voters of the Left. According to the government's critics, the regime change of 1974 did not mean the overthrow of the post-war Greek state, which had traditionally been labeled "The State of the Right" by parties of the Center and the Left.

For most of the 1980s (1981–1989), PASOK ruled on its own with a comfortable parliamentary majority and attempted an ambitious administrative reform program. In 1982, soon after this party came to power, it abolished the civil service post of director general, fired all the directors general from the top echelons of the Greek public administration and recruited its own political appointees en masse (Law 1232/1982). Scores of political advisors and party cadres formed the entourage of each minister and deputy minister. Such political appointees staffed the offices of the ministers and overshadowed top civil servants. Most of these political appointees were more left-wing than the civil servants, identified with PASOK, and believed the ND had already politicized the civil service before PASOK came to power (Figure 13.2 and Tables 13.5 and 13.8).

This change of the arena of decision-making inside the ministries was followed by a second change of arena at the level of central government. PASOK passed legislation (in 1982 and again in 1985) reorganizing the Cabinet by increasing the powers of the Prime Minister and aggrandizing his political office which became a sort of Greek White House, increasing the number of ministries and ministers, and introducing collective governing bodies to coordinate various ministries (Laws 1299/1982 and 1558/1985).

In contrast to the above attempts at heavy political control of the bureaucracy, PASOK also took steps to modernize the civil service and make it more professional. In the mid-1980s, it created a professional school for pre-service and in-service training of civil servants. The school, which was modeled on the French Ecole Nationale d'Administration, was founded in 1983 and started functioning two years later (Law 1388/1983). It soon met with resistance from the judiciary and the senior civil servants of major ministries, such as the Ministry of Foreign Affairs, which always operated their own recruitment system. (Although this ministry was more of a typical Weberian bureaucracy, it was also heavily politicized. Before 1981 diplomats generally came from very politically conservative family backgounds. After PASOK came to power, the ministry was gradually penetrated by the new governing party.)

Professionalization was not attained through this training system or through the new "points system" used for the recruitment of new lower- and middle-rank civil servants. This system was based on a standardized evaluation of a candidate's social and academic qualifications (Law 1320/1983). The new recruiting system, introduced in 1983 but applied only once, in 1984, favored the recruitment of socially disadvantaged candidates into the civil service, to the detriment of young, highly educated candidates. The system was amended in 1987 (Law 1735/1987) and then was silently abandoned.

What were the main characteristics of the above developments and how can the obvious contradiction between political control and modernization of the bureaucracy be explained? After 1981, state structures were characterized by great organizational fluidity, evident in the constant reshuffles of PASOK's Cabinets and new governing organs. This fluidity can be explained by a general pattern in PASOK's administrative legislation by which it oscillated between the three goals of professionalization of the civil service, use of the state apparatus for electoral purposes, and exercise of social welfare and labor policies through the making of administrative policy (instead of limiting administrative policy to the goal of administrative reform). According to Spourdalakis (1988) the competing goals of PASOK's general political strategy reflected divisions between the party's internal factions. While a general dichotomy of populism versus modernization may convey the two poles between which PASOK had navigated since its inception as a new party in 1974, the numerous internal divisions within it reflected ideological and generational differences. Three factions, technocrats, old parliamentarians, and leftists, espoused different policies in major domains, including the public sector. The outcome of internal party disputes over policy matters was usually an inefficient compromise, forged by Andreas Papandreou himself, who sided more often than not with the parliamentarians and the leftists against the technocrats. Thus, the administrative policy of PASOK included contradictory goals because it reflected the party's competing material and ideal interests. The goal of professionalization of the civil service reflected the party's ideology of reform; the goal of capturing and using the state served the party's electoral strategy; and the goal of implementing social and labor policy through public employment policies both reflected the ideology of PASOK and served its electoral interests. From another viewpoint, the contradictory nature of the party's administrative policy can be explained by the uneasy compromise between it's populist ideology of grass-roots participation and social egalitarianism and the government's realist strategy of prolonging its mandate by transforming the state into a useful tool for attracting votes.

After PASOK's fall from power in 1989, the ND party, which won the decisive elections of 1990, failed to bring about any significant change to the above administrative tradition of the post-authoritarian Greek state. The ND government reestablished the rank of director general in the civil service and reintroduced competitive entrance examinations for recruitment (Laws 1892/1990 and 1943/1991). However, as in the case of PASOK, two lines of action, supported by two corresponding groups comprising both party cadres and government ministers, were in conflict inside the ranks of the ND in 1990–1993: the modernizers, seeking to trim the public sector and introduce modern methods of management in the administration without completely forgoing the political benefits of patronage practices, and the traditionalists, who favored the continuation of heavy monitoring of the public administration by the governing party in order to reap the electoral benefits of clientelistic appointments and exclude segments of the civil service politically associated with the rule of PASOK.

Civil service, political parties, and society

Politicization "from above" does not take place in a social vacuum. It involves different collective actors and reflects pressures from below. In Greece of the 1980s, civil servants, PASOK Cabinet ministers, and PASOK party cadres constituted three different groups interacting in the Greek state apparatus. They also interacted with society in a manner evident in the increase of the size of the public sector. According to an OECD source, in 1988 approximately 289,700 people were employed in the central government (i.e. in the civil service) of Greece (OECD, 1990: 23). The number is relatively low but it was lower at the beginning of the 1980s and increased substantially in 1985, a general election year. Between 1981 and 1988 there was a net increase of 2 percent in the Greek labor force as a whole but of 12 percent in the civil service personnel. Thus while PASOK was in power, employment in the civil service grew six times as fast as total employment (Sotiropoulos, 1991: 400), although the net increase in personnel of the wider public sector was much larger (Table 13.1).

Throughout the 1980s and particularly during its second term in power (1985–1989), PASOK used the wider public sector as a depository of labor power and as a political machine for attracting votes. For the 1985–1989 period, this is indicated by data on the number of personnel in public bodies (e.g. hospitals, social security funds) and public corporations (see Table 13.1). As noted at the beginning of this chapter, the data show that the "political-electoral cycle" has been prevalent in Greece.

This cycle was at work for most of the post-dictatorship period: with a few exceptions, the years of general elections coincide with peaks in the size of the public sector, obviously due to extensive recruitment the last few months before each election. Such practices were not new in modern Greek politics: conservative governments had done the same in the past. PASOK simply extended the traditional function of the Greek state as a safety valve. In the post-war period this state grew in size under conditions of pressing unemployment in the rural areas, rising internal migration to the Greek cities, and increasing unrest among segments of the electorate.

PASOK was able to achieve the above results among other reasons because it encountered relatively little resistance from either the society or the state. The civil society and political institutions of modern Greece had never been allowed to acquire a fully independent existence. Their tutelage was complete during the long rule of conservative party governments and the short, intermittent rule of authoritarian regimes throughout the twentieth century and especially after World War II. In the post-war era, the parliament, the judiciary, local authorities, and the civil service were almost always subservient to the government. The bureaucracy was particularly weak compared to the political parties alternating in power and its autonomy of action vis-à-vis the government was circumscribed (Sotiropoulos 1993: 49). Thus, the conservatives had prepared the way for the unhindered conquest of the state by PASOK. In short, the diachronic situation described above indicates the weakness of the Greek civil service as well as the inability of civil society to resist the intrusion of successive political regimes and majoritarian party governments into the state and society.

The outcomes of politicization of the Greek civil service by the socialist and the conservative parties

However, these intrusions did not always bring about exactly the same results. The different effects on the bureaucracy brought by PASOK's rule in 1981–1989 and ND rule in 1974–1981 are threefold: first, in the type of politicization of the civil service, whether through the use of the party apparatus or through loose circles of party notables; second, in the organized fashion with which PASOK built and consolidated its hegemony over the state, making the separation between political and administrative (i.e. executive) functions more pronounced than before, as will be explained below; and third, in the centralization and concentration of authority in the hands of the Prime Minister in the first PASOK period. The different kinds of politicization of the civil service resulted from the different types of party that PASOK and the ND represented. In brief, PASOK was already a mass party in the first post-dictatorship period (1974–1981), whereas the ND, from being a party of notables, was transformed into a mass party after it fell from power in 1981.

One outcome of PASOK's administrative reforms (already discussed above) was the politicization of the top echelons of the central public administration, but of a different order from the politicization that had taken place under the conservative governments before 1981. The prime conceptual distinction here is that between a political party of notables, accustomed to draw on the state for the resources needed to preserve its power, which was the case of the ND before 1981, and a mass party without access to any organizational resources other than its own, which was the case of PASOK before 1981 (Kaler-Christofilopoulou, 1989). The different history and organization of these two parties should account for their different approaches to the problem of controlling the state, the prize of so many social contests in modern Greek history.

Under the 1974–1981 ND governments, the top echelons of the civil service were occupied by tenured officials, i.e. the directors general, who were selected by the whole Cabinet. This was only one of the techniques for controlling the state that the conservatives had been using since the end of the Greek civil war. Other such practices were the surveillance of new recruits to the public administration, the government monopoly over the mass media and the subordination of state-funded labor unions. Briefly, these were the ways in which the conservatives preserved their hegemony over opposition from the Center and the Left. On the basis of the above considerations, it can be claimed that in the post-war era the Greek conservatives employed means of domination that are often found in authoritarian regimes as well as in democratic ones whose legitimacy is undermined by bitter legacies of intense strife (e.g. civil war).

The separation of political and administrative functions within the bureaucracy became more pronounced under PASOK, although this party continued and extended the politicization of the Greek civil service. Indeed, PASOK proved a very good disciple of the conservatives in the matter of controlling the state, because it also used the public administration, the mass media, and the labor unions to promote its own causes. Still, PASOK's politicization was different in the sense that as a result of the massive and organized reform of the top of the hierarchy of the state, the political echelons of the public administration became more clearly distinguishable from the civil service than under the ND. The division of labor between formulation of policy by politicians and execution of policy by bureaucrats was more clear-cut under PASOK than under the ND. This is because under PASOK when major policy decisions were at stake, top civil servants were kept at bay, except in the case of those who were card-carrying members of PASOK and who influenced ministers and often became their personal advisors. Yet, as an unintended consequence of the occupation of the state, PASOK, an officially anti-liberal party, ironically strengthened one of the principles of liberal democracy: the separation of politics from administration, in the sense that even highly experienced top civil servants had very little say over policy matters. It was not infrequent for top civil servants of important ministries to complain, during interviews with researchers, that they only learned about major bills introduced to the parliament by their own minister by reading the daily press.

The politicization of appointments to the Greek civil service in the 1990s

Given the over-politicized past of the Greek civil service in the 1970s and the 1980s, what was the situation in the 1990s? As already noted, the practices of recruitment to the Greek civil service have traditionally oscillated between formalist rigidity and informal laxity. Since 1994, Greek governments have pledged to fight patronage and to control the budget deficit and the public debt, which, among other problems, have been inflated through patronage practices and have inhibited the full integration of Greece into the EU. The above pledges have had organizational effects on the process of recruitment. In the past, particularly between 1974 and 1990, ministers and directors of public enterprises were able to recruit new personnel, often on a temporary basis or on fixed-term contracts. In doing so, they sought to satisfy specific needs of their ministry or enterprise, to promote their personal political career by creating a personal clientele, or to enhance the electoral chances of their political party by appointing new public employees just before general elections. This practice has affected some (but not all) quarters of the Greek public sector. Over time, recruitment has gradually become very centralized and rigid, to the point of making the state's personnel policy very inefficient (Spanou, 1992). As a result, as we have mentioned above, a parallel process of hiring temporary personnel (exempted from the normal examination routines) has been going on for a long time. Perhaps this long-time practice was intensified after 1994, since the law passed in that year (Law 2190) imposed very rigid rules on hiring new tenure-track personnel and, as an unintended consequence, opened up space for experimentation with various forms of temporary personnel.

In early 2001, recruitment to the Greek civil service was still regulated by Law 2190/1994, while the status of the recruited civil servants was regulated by the new Civil Service Code passed in February 1999 (Law 2683/1999). The first law is widely known as the "Peponis Law," after Anastasios Peponis. He was an old party cadre of the Center Union party of George Papandreou and served several times as minister in the PASOK governments of Andreas Papandreou. Mr Peponis drafted this law in 1994 when Minister of the Presidency of Government. This legislation has created a new context, which allows for less politicization in the processes of recruitment and promotions in the civil service and more politicization in the exercise of political rights of civil servants. The latter is associated with the expansion of politicization "from below," which has been going on since the early 1980s.

The aforementioned law of 1994 sought not only to reform the process of appointments but also to remedy what PASOK perceived as injustices done to the party's supporters in the civil service in the three years of ND government (1990–1993). Under the same law, ND sympathizers who had been recruited to the public sector on short-term contracts just before the October 1993 elections (when the ND fell from power) were made redundant, as were employees whose fixed-term contracts had been renewed by the ND government within the last month before these elections.

As noted above, governing parties have traditionally tried to hire new personnel on the eve of general elections, bypassing the typical recruitment procedures. This issue became very explosive because of a special provision of Law 2190/1994 which laid off all the 5500 employees of the state-run electric power company (DEI) who had been hired by its conservative managers less than thirty days before the October 1993 general elections. After winning the elections, the new PASOK government accused the ND of extending the contracts of temporary personnel and of recruiting new, unnecessary personnel to the DEI just before the election with the aim of trading public jobs for votes in the traditional clientelistic manner. The new government adopted an austerity policy to reduce the public debt and fired the company's 5500 unnecessary employees. These petitioned the Greek Supreme Court, asking to be reinstated, and won the case two years later, in March 1996 (Sotiropoulos, 1996: 140). The decision to lay off the 5500 DEI employees in a time of rising unemployment may be interpreted as signs of political revenge on the part of PASOK and a new policy of fiscal austerity in response to EU pressures on Greece.

Despite the above developments, PASOK's return to government in 1993 did not result in as far-reaching a politicization of the civil service as the first time it had come to power. For instance, the second time PASOK did not remove incumbent directors general, unlike its practice in its first government of 1981. The new government gradually sought to replace the top administrative officials through changing the composition of "service councils," the administrative bodies in charge of promotions, whenever a position of head of directorate, division, or section became vacant. In the meantime, the same law allowed pro-PASOK employees to return to the civil service if they could show that their resignation at any time in 1990–1993 was due to political manipulation by the ND.

The law of 1994 replaced the grade scale which had been introduced only two years before, in 1992, by the ND government, which in turn was a substitute for the grade scale introduced by PASOK in 1986. (The ND law was 2085/1992, while the earlier PASOK law was 1586/1986.) The range of political appointments was enlarged by the new 1994 PASOK law, as was the case with some of the ND laws passed between 1990 and 1993. But there were some meritocratic appointments, most important among them those made to a new independent public authority (ASEP, Higher Council for Personnel Selection). According to the same law, ASEP was made responsible for all personnel recruitment to the civil service. The creation of ASEP was first criticized for allowing the Minister of the Presidency of Government a free hand in the appointment of its eleven-member managing board. However, in 1994 PASOK appointed two retired magistrates to the positions of president and vice-president of ASEP and the new authority has conducted all entrance examinations since 1994 with impartiality.

Originally ASEP supervised the recruitment of employees to work in the central government. The politicization of the wider public sector has been more intense than that of the central administration. This pattern holds for the periods of rule of both political parties. Let us give a few examples. Between 1991 and 1994, while the ND was in power, parliamentary deputies, again regardless of political party, each had the right to employ two individuals from outside the public sector as personal assistants. The two assistants, after working for two years in the deputy's office, could be rewarded by being hired by the public sector. The former employees of each deputy had the right to choose in which ministry or public organization they wanted to be hired with tenure. (The measure was introduced by Law 1943/1991, under the ND, and abolished by Law 2190/1994, under PASOK.) The law of 1994 allowed general managers of public enterprises, who were themselves politically appointed, to recruit three political appointees each, for as long as they remained in office (article 22 of Law 2190/1994). Also, in a case of political patronage by quota, for some time all parliamentary deputies, regardless of political party, had the habit of asking the Ministry of Public Order to hire several new policemen, recommended by each deputy. In an attempt to curtail the largess shown in hiring by individual general managers of state-run companies, in 1997 the PASOK government extended ASEP's remit to include the public sector (Spanou, 1998: 248).

The new Civil Service Code

This rather inchoate legislation on recruitment and promotions has been modified and rationalized by the new Civil Service Code which was passed in February 1999, after at least five years of incubation. At first glance, the Code seems to allow ministers and other political managers less room for maneuver in hiring, transferring, and promoting civil servants.

Civil servants can only be hired on the basis of an annual program coordinated by the Ministry of the Interior. Someone may be appointed a civil servant after passing written entrance examinations organized by the independent public authority of ASEP. No hiring can be done without the prior consent of the competent government bodies and confirmation of the availability of necessary funds (articles 11, 12, 13, and 14 of Law 2683/1999).

As regards the political rights of civil servants, the new Code confirms the new, more open exercise of freedoms already in existence since PASOK came to power in 1981 and first recognized in 1987 (Law 1735/1987). Civil servants enjoy freedom of expression of their political, philosophical, and religious beliefs as well freedom of technical criticism of administrative actions in the ministry or other public organization or enterprise in which they are employed. They are free to establish labor unions, to become members of such unions and to strike to protect their collective interests. Civil servants' labor unions have the right to negotiate with the government on salaries and conditions of employment (articles 45 and 46 of Law 2683/1999), a freedom which until 1999 had been granted only to unions of the private sector.

The transfer of a civil servant is possible only when there is a vacancy in another service and is effected on the basis of a system of points. The system primarily inhibits the transfer of older, married employees with many years of experience and enhances the horizontal mobility of younger, unmarried employees with few years of experience. Promotion of civil servants to the position of director general is decided by an autonomous special service council, which is not located in any particular ministry and was first established in 1990, when, as mentioned above, the ND government reintroduced the rank of director general which had been abolished by PASOK in 1981 (Law 1892/1990). The seven-member special service council consists of a high-ranking judge as president and three university professors, one director general of the Ministry of the Interior, one director general of the Ministry of Finance, and the president of the confederation of the labor unions of civil servants (ADEDY) (articles 158, 160, and 161 of Law 2683/1999). These members are nominated by their respective services and organizations, a provision that prevents government interference in the composition of the special service council. This safety valve is lacking in the local service councils which function in each ministry or public body, and are responsible for internal promotions, transfers, and disciplinary matters. With a two-year mandate, they are composed of five members, three of whom are directors, i.e. permanent top civil servants, selected by the minister or general manager of the public body, while the remaining two are elected representatives of all civil servants working in the relevant ministry or body (articles 160, 161, and 162 of Law 2683/1999). The three directors who are hand-picked by the minister are often supporters of the governing political party, while one of the two elected representatives usually comes from the pro-government labor union. As a consequence, four out of the five members of the service council usually belong to the same political faction within the ministry and support the government.

While such provisions seem to reproduce the political leverage of the governing party, to which ministers and general managers belong, the new Code at least curbs the older practice of rotating top civil servants among positions of head of directorate, division, or section. While each promotion is made for three years, civil servants who have been selected as heads of units twice running may keep their post without an additional, third evaluation. The selection of the best candidate by the service council should be made on specific criteria, cited in the law, with special emphasis on merit and experience (articles 83, 84, and 85 of Law 2683/1999). More demanding meritocratic criteria are applied by the special service council in the selection of directors general, who are not rotated.

Not all of the provisions, which clearly mean progress compared with past legislation and practices in the Greek civil service, have been implemented. In the past, throughout the rule of PASOK and the ND, it was not rare for formal legal provisions to bear no relation to what was actually taking place in each ministry or public body in regard to hiring, transferring, and promoting civil servants. Despite strict formal regulations, which emphasized transparency and the application of principles such as merit and equity, informal constellations of interests of political officials, trade union leaders, and well-connected civil servants repeatedly made it possible to bypass the spirit and the letter of the law. Since the passage of the new Code such tendencies have reappeared. For instance, in a few ministries the ministers appoint at will temporary heads of directorates and heads of sections wherever there are vacancies, notionally until the local service councils convene to fill the vacancies. But the councils are never convened, even though the six-month period allowed for such temporary appointments may elapse. As a result, the hand-picked heads of units become permanent since the minister tolerates this illegality which he or she has created.

Concluding remarks

Two principles, political favoritism and meritocracy, have coexisted in tension for some time now in the legislation and practices pertaining to the Greek civil service. A third principle, the strength of which has fluctuated over time, is egalitarianism. In the context of the Greek civil service, egalitarianism meant that 'equality of result' in terms of salary and/or authority was deemed more important than 'equality of opportunity' combined with meritocratic standards. This trend was particularly important in the early 1980s. Since the mid-1980s there has been a gradual attenuation of the social criteria (family status, age, financial need) which predominated in past legislation on recruitment to the civil service (e.g. Law 1320/1983). Some pieces of legislation (e.g. Law 1735/1987 and particularly Law 2527/1997) have favored educational, i.e. meritocratic, credentials over social need as criteria in the recruitment process. This tendency is associated with another tendency to establish quantifiable and standardized critieria in order to avoid political interventions in the appointment of civil servants. The cost of the latter tendency is the decrease in the capacity of selection committees to make substantive evaluations of candidates. This, in turn, reflects a general spirit of corporatism and egalitarianism which, in conjunction with populism, has permeated the attitudes of both major political parties, the public labor unions, and the mentality of individual civil servants since at least the early 1980s (Spanou, 1998: 250).

An ideal which is still dominant in many social strata is that as many citizens as possible should have an equal opportunity to become public employees and later tenured civil servants. This egalitarian vision is complemented by another widespread ideal whereby positions of authority should in principle be open to all candidates, almost regardless of credentials, and differentiation among them should be minimal. This is already reflected in the rather small differences between the salaries of junior and senior civil servants (with the exception of directors general who are compensated well, but are relatively few). A final, related trend, which is more recent and needs further research, is towards interparty clientelism. Political parties may come to behind-the-scenes negotiations and compromises in some cases when there are enough vacant positions in a committee or an administrative body for affiliates of the governing party and the opposition parties to be appointed. This has occurred at administrative levels or sectors where the opposition parties have a strong presence (prefectures, municipalities, federations of labor unions).

Of course, trends such as those presented in this chapter exist in many other modern public bureaucracies. If there is anything specific about the Greek case, it is the pervasiveness, persistence, and strength of clientelistic practices, combined with an egalitarian spirit, which make the country somewhat different from other core Western democracies. The conclusion is that in Greece politicization is entrenched and that, if practiced by all parties, in and out of power, it may have started losing its conflictual nature and inflammatory character as a style of governance. Finally, politicization might not have taken the hold that it has had had it not been for the reluctant collaboration of an insecure civil service with a political class that uses the state at will.

Note

1 The author would like to thank professors Nikos K. Hlepas, B. Guy Peters, Jon Pierre, and Calliope Spanou for their comments on this chapter, as well as two higher administrative officials, Tina Minakaki and Leonidas D. Antonopoulos, for data.

References

Alivizatos, Nicos (1979). *Les Institutions politiques de la Grèce à travers les crises, 1922–1974.* Paris: Pinchon.

Athanassopoulos, Demetrios (1983). *He Hellinike Dioikese: Anepikaires Skepseis gia Mia Dioiketike Metarrythmise* [Greek Administration: Untimely Thoughts for Administrative Reform]. Athens: Papazeses (in Greek).

Bodiguel, Jean-Luc (1986). "The Political Control of Civil Servants in Europe: Some Aspects," *International Review of Administrative Sciences,* Vol. 52, No. 2, pp. 187–199.

Clogg, Richard (1987). *Parties and Elections in Greece: The Quest for Legitimacy.* Durham, North Carolina: Duke University Press.

Demertzis, Nicos (1990). "He Hellenike Politice Cultura ste Dekaetia tou '80" [Greek Political Culture in the 1980s], in Christos Lyrintzis and Elias Nicolacopoulos, eds., *Ekloges kai Kommata ste Dekaetia tou '80: Exelixeis kai Prooptikes tou Politicou Systematos* [Elections and Parties in the 1980s: Evolutions and Prospects of the Political System], pp. 70–96. Athens: Themelio (in Greek).

Diamandouros, Nikiforos P. (1983). "Greek Political Culture in Transition," in Richard Clogg, ed., *Greece in the 1980s,* pp. 43–69. London: Macmillan.

Eisenstadt, Shmuel N. and Luis Roniger (1984). *Patrons, Clients, and Friends: Interpersonal Relations and the Structure of Trust in Society.* New York: Cambridge University Press.

Flogaites, Spyridon I. (1987). *To Helleniko Dioiketiko Systema* [The Greek Administrative System]. Athens: Ant. Sakkoulas (in Greek).

Gómez-Reino, M. and Francisco A. Orizo (1968). "Burocracias Publica y Privada," in Centro de Estudios Sociales, ed., *Sociologia de la Administracion Publica Espanola.* Madrid: Centro de Estudios Sociales.

Hlepas, Nikolos-Komninos (1999). "Wandel der griechischen Verwaltung und europaeische Integration" in Mary Papaschinopoulou, ed., *Griechenland auf dem Weg zur europaeischen Waehrungs- und Wirtschaftsunion,* pp. 186–206. Schriftenreihe des Europa Kollegs, Hamburg: Nomos/Athens: Ant. N. Sakkoulas Verlag.

Kaler-Christofilopoulou, Paraskevi D. (1989). "Decentralization in Post-Dictatorial Greece," Ph.D. dissertation. London: The London School of Economics and Political Science.

Legg, Keith (1969). *Politics in Modern Greece.* Stanford, California: Stanford University Press.

Lijphart, Arend, Thomas C. Bruneau, P. Nikiforos Diamandouros and Richard Gunther (1988). "A Mediterranean Model of Democracy? The Southern European Democracies in Comparative Perspective," *West European Politics,* Vol. 11, No. 1 (January), pp. 7–25.

Lochak, Danielle and CURAPP, eds. (1986). *La Haute Administration et la politique.* Paris: Presses Universitaires de France.

Lyrintzis, Christos (1984). "Political Parties in Post-Junta Greece: A Case of 'Bureaucratic Clientelism'?," *West European Politics,* Vol. 7, No. 2 (April), pp. 99–118.

Lyrintzis, Christos and Elias Nicolacopoulos, eds. (1990). *Ekloges kai Kommata ste Dekaetia tou '80: Exelixeis kai Prooptikes tou Politicou Systematos* [Elections and Parties in the 1980s: Evolutions and Prospects of the Political System]. Athens: Themelio (in Greek).

Makrydemetris, Anthony D. (1999). *Dioikese kai Koinonia* [Administration and Society]. Athens: Themelio (in Greek).

Mavrogordatos, George Th. (1984). "The Greek Party System: A Case of 'Limited but Polarized Pluralism'?," in Stefano Bartolini and Peter Mair, eds., *Party Politics in Contemporary Western Europe*, pp. 156–169. London: Frank Cass.

Mavrogordatos, George Th. (1988). *Metaxy Pytiokampti kai Prokrousti: Oi Epaggelmatikes Organoseis sten Hellada* [Between Pityokamptes and Prokroustes: Professional Organizations in Greece]. Athens: Odysseas (in Greek).

Mavrogordatos, George Th. (1997). "From Traditional Clientelism to Machine Politics: The Impact of PASOK Populism in Greece," *South European Society and Politics*, Vol. 2, No. 3 (Winter), pp. 1–26.

Mouzelis, Nicos P. (1978). *Modern Greece: Facets of Underdevelopment*. London: Macmillan.

Mouzelis, Nicos P. (1980). "The Greek State and Capitalism," in Richard Scase, ed., *The State in Western Europe*, pp. 241–273. London: Croom Helm.

Mouzelis, Nicos (1986). *Politics in the Semi-Periphery: Early Parliamentarism and Late Industrialization in the Balkans and Latin America*. London: Macmillan.

Mylonopoulou-Moira, Polyxeni (1998). *Oi Demosioi Ypalleloi* [The Civil Servants]. Athens: Ant. N. Sakkoulas (in Greek).

OECD (1990). *Economic Survey of Greece 1989/1990*. Paris: OECD.

Papadopoulou, Olga (1990). "Les garanties du fonctionnaire dans la Constitution Hellénique," Ph.D. dissertation. Paris: Université de Paris II-Sorbonne.

Psomiades, Harry J. and Stavros B. Thomadakis, eds. (1993). *Greece, the New Europe and the Changing International Order*. New York: Pella Publishing Co.

Samatas, Minas (1986). "Greek Bureaucratism: A System of Sociopolitical Control," Ph.D. dissertation. New York: New School for Social Research.

Sotiropoulos, Dimitri A. (1991). "State and Party: The Greek State Bureaucracy and the Panhellenic Socialist Movement (PASOK), 1981–1989", Ph.D. dissertation. New Haven, Connecticut: Yale University Press.

Sotiropoulos, Dimitri A. (1993). "A Colossus with Feet of Clay: The State in Post-Authoritarian Greece," in Harry J. Psomiades and Stavros B. Thomadakis, eds., *Greece, the New Europe and the Changing International Order*, pp. 43–56. New York: Pella Publishing Co.

Sotiropoulos, Dimitri A. (1994). "Bureaucrats and Politicians: A Case Study of the Determinants of Perceptions of Conflict and Patronage in the Greek Bureaucracy Under PASOK Rule, 1981–1989," *British Journal of Sociology*, Vol. 45, No. 3 (September), pp. 349–365.

Sotiropoulos, Dimitri A. (1996). *Populism and Bureaucracy: The Case of Greece Under PASOK, 1981–1989*. Notre Dame, Indiana: The University of Notre Dame Press.

Sotiropoulos, Dimitri A. (1999). "The Greek Higher Civil Service," in Edward C. Page and Vincent Wright, eds., *Bureaucratic Elites in Western European States*, pp. 13–31. Oxford: Oxford University Press.

Sotiropoulos, Dimitri A. (2001). *He Koryfe tou Pelateiakou Kratous* [The Peak of the Clientelist State]. Athens: Potamos Editions (in Greek).

Spanou, Calliope (1990). "Ekloges kai Demosia Dioikese: He Eklogike Energopoiese ton Endodioiketikon Pelateiakon Mechanismon" [Elections and Public Administration: The Electoral Mobilization of Intra-administrative Patronage Mechanisms], in Christos Lyrintzis and Elias Nicolacopoulos, eds., *Ekloges kai Kommata ste Decaetia tou '80: Exelixeis kai Prooptikes tou Politicou System-*

atos [Elections and Political Parties in the 1980s: Evolutions and Prospects of the Political System], pp. 173–179. Athens: Themelio (in Greek).

Spanou, Calliope (1992). "Les politiques de recrutement dans l'administration hellénique: Une modernisation impossible?," *Revue Française d'Administration Publique*, No. 62 (April–June), pp. 325–334.

Spanou, Calliope (1995). "A la recherche du temps perdu: La modernisation de l' administration en Grece," *Revue Française d'Administration Publique*, No. 75 (July–September), pp. 423–439.

Spanou, Calliope (1996). "Penelope's Suitors: Administrative Modernization and Party Competition in Greece," *West European Politics*, Vol. 19, No. 1 (January), pp. 97–124.

Spanou, Calliope (1998). "Les sirènes de la politisation: Fonction publique et politique en Grèce," *Revue Française d'Administration Publique*, No. 86 (April–June), pp. 243–254.

Spanou, Calliope (2001). "Re-shaping the Politics – Administration Nexus in Greece: The Decline of a Symbiotic Relationship," in B. Guy Peters and Jon Pierre, eds., *Bureaucrats, Politicians and Administrative Reform*, pp. 106–115. Basingstoke and London: Taylor & Francis.

Spiliotopoulos, Epaminondas (1983). "L'administration dans le débat politique en Grèce," in Charles Debbasch, ed., *Administration et politique en Europe*, pp. 255–265. Paris: Editions du CNRS.

Spourdalakis, Michalis (1988). *The Rise of the Greek Socialist Party*. London: Routledge.

Suleiman, Ezra N. (1974). *Power, Politics and Bureaucracy in France*. Princeton, New Jersey: Princeton University Press.

Thomadakis, Stavros B. and Dimitris Seremetis (1992). "Fiscal Management, Social Agenda and Structural Deficits," in Theodore C. Kariotis, ed., *The Greek Socialist Experiment: Papandreou's Greece 1981–1989*, pp. 203–255. New York: Pella Publishing,

Tsekos, Theodore (1986). "Changement politique et changement administratif: La haute fonction publique en Grèce avant et après 1981," in Danielle Lochak and CURAPP, eds., *La Haute Administration et la politique*, pp. 165–206. Paris: Presses Universitaires de France.

Tsoukalas, Constantine (1986). *Kratos, Koinonia, Ergasia ste Metapolemiki Hellada* [State, Society, Labor in Post-war Greece]. Athens: Themelio (in Greek).

Voulgaris, Yannis (1990). "Allages sto Eklogiko Soma tes Aristeras kai Kommatikos Antagonismos, 1985–1989" [Changes in the Left-Wing Electorate and Party Competition, 1985–1989], in Christos Lyrintzis and Elias Nicolacopoulos, eds., *Ekloges kai Kommata ste Dekaetia tou '80: Exelixeis kai Prooptikes tou Politicou Systematos* [Elections and Political Parties in the 1980s: Evolutions and Prospects of the Political System]. Athens: Themelio (in Greek).

Weber, Max (1958). "Bureaucracy," in Hans Gerth and C. W. Mills, eds., *From Max Weber: Essays in Sociology*, pp. 196–244. New York: Oxford University Press.

14 Conclusion

Political control in a managerialist world

B. Guy Peters and Jon Pierre

Most of the discussion of public administration for the past several decades has been focused on administrative reform and especially on the "New Public Management" (NPM) that has emphasized the importance of effective management in controlling public programs. The definitions of "effective management" in NPM have been derived largely from the private sector and have tended either to ignore the role of politics or to consider politics and politicians as barriers to making "government work better and cost less." While those managerialist recommendations for reform have not been anti-democratic *per se*, they certainly have considered politics as at best a necessary evil and at worst a serious barrier to effectiveness and efficiency in the public sector.

Some politicians have themselves been active participants in implementing and institutionalizing the managerialist changes in the public sector. The first major thrust of such changes occurred during the 1980s, and were driven almost equally by the political right (Savoie, 1994) and the political left (Boston, 1991), but definitely had a political basis. Politicians motivating the first rounds of reform tended to consider that the public bureaucracies they had inherited when coming to office were major barriers to policy change. Those political leaders wanted to deinstitutionalize the existing bureaucratic systems in order to be able to alter fundamentally the manner in which government made and implemented public policies. In almost all of these cases the simple solution offered was to implement practices derived from the private sector.

Since the initial rounds of euphoria about managerialism as a solution to the problems facing government and politicians, political leaders have found that these changes have in fact made their lives even more difficult. Managerialism in administration has enhanced the autonomy of organizations and managers within government. Autonomy has been promoted structurally through partial privatization of previously government-owned enterprises, and through the creation of numerous autonomous and quasi-autonomous organizations (Bouckaert *et al.*, 2003). The desired managerial autonomy has been enhanced procedurally by eliminating a number of operational constraints on the behavior of public managers, and by the recruitment of many new administrators (often from the private sector) working on performance contracts. These newcomers to government were committed to fulfilling the conditions of their contracts and tended to resist intervention from politicians whom the managers regarded as amateurs in running government.

Paradoxes of politicization

Confronted with retaining the political responsibility for what happens within government but having fewer levers available to control what might occur, political leaders began to search for means of influence and control that could reassert their power over the public sector. The politicization described in this volume was one of the more important of the strategies adopted to achieve that end of control. The ubiquity of increased politicization in these countries coming from different political traditions and facing different policy and administrative strategies indicates the importance that politicians have attached to being able to control what is happening within their organizations.

Increasing politicization by enhancing managerialism

The increased level of politicization in the industrialized democracies represented in this volume can be characterized by a number of paradoxical outcomes. Governing is far from an exact science and despite the best efforts of reformers their interventions may result in unintended consequences, some exactly the opposite of those intended. The most fundamental of these paradoxes is that reforms meant to weaken the role of political leaders have resulted in greater political intervention in the day-to-day management of government, and a weakening of depoliticized, professional managers within the public sector. The original reformer in the NPM tradition apparently underestimated the capacity of political leaders to utilize their resources, most notably their legitimate position in government, to alter the personnel system in government.

This failure to understand the power and priorities of political leaders may reflect the misunderstanding of the public sector shared by many of the individuals involved in these reforms. Their commitment to the managerialist ideas, and the assumptions of the superiority of private sector management, may have produced some improvements in the efficiency of delivery of public services, but this efficiency may have been purchased at the price of diminished capacity of political leaders to shape *what* is happening in government, as well as *how* it happens. Reforms that may have appeared technical and at worst benign can be thought by some political leaders to be significant threats to their roles and prerogatives.

Another way of putting this point is that although the contributors to this volume have been focusing on the politicization of bureaucracies, many individuals in government have been more concerned about the increasing bureaucratization of policy decisions. There is an apparent conflict between demands to make government more efficient and effective and demands to make government more responsible to political demands. Further, demands for greater efficiency may not themselves be politically neutral, given that some programs are more difficult than others to make efficient in a strictly economic sense, and hence may be disadvantaged in a political world that focuses on managerial performance rather than political responsiveness.

Managerial methods can be used for political ends

Another of the paradoxes of the politicization reported in this volume is that the same managerialist changes that made this counterattack by politicians necessary provided some of the opportunities for their success in reasserting control. The most obvious example of the role that managerialist reforms made to politicization is that the demise, or at least the weakening, of the civil service system allowed politicians greater latitude in the selection of officials. While the purpose of open recruitment had been to attain greater management capacity in government the same tool could as easily be used to recruit *committed*, qualified managers. This consequence of managerialism may be seen most clearly in several of the Westminster systems which have been very active in deinstitutionalizing their civil service systems (see Sausman and Dargie, Chapter 6 above; Gregory, 1995).

Likewise, the creation of a number of autonomous and quasi-autonomous organizations has provided additional opportunities for politicization. In particular, these organizations have generated a number of boards and other control bodies that could be filled with people of the appropriate political persuasion (Skelcher, 1998).[1] In addition, in some cases the personnel employed by these organizations are removed from the civil service system and at least partially privatized. Further, the separation of these organizations and the services they provide from the usual lines of ministerial accountability has provided a great deal of motivation for politicians to find the means of ensuring that these organizations comply with the wishes of the sitting government, and politicization is one of the standard repertoire of these reactions to enhanced autonomy.

The opportunities for politicization of these agencies and similar organizations are increased because of their relative lack of identification among the citizenry as public sector organizations. Although quasi-autonomous organizations are performing public functions these entities may fall into the "twilight zone" of government (Seidman, 1999)[2] so that the people are unsure whether they are public or private, and hence the political pressures to maintain the dominant values of the public sector, e.g. depoliticization, may be less important. While the people may be clear about the public nature of the services rendered, for example railways or water or sports facilities, they may be extremely vague about, and uninterested in, the organizational details, and hence provide fertile ground for the use of political appointment.

Performance and politicization

The simple need of politicians to reassert their control over increasingly autonomous public organizations does not, however, appear to be the sole consequence of managerialism for the politicization of the public service. Again, somewhat paradoxically, the growing emphasis on performance management in the public sector has tended to increase the level of politicization of action within government. For some of the same reasons cited above the individuals responsible for attaining superior performance may want to have people who are "on their side" if they are to be judged by results. To some extent ministers and other political officials have always been judged by the performance of their organizations but as that measurement becomes more overt then the need to control becomes more pressing.

The performance movement in government has focused on both individual levels and organizational levels of performance. Both of these forms of management may enable political leaders to have greater control over their administrative staffs. The relationship is perhaps clearest for the personal level, given that politicians are being given the opportunity to define what is good and bad performance on the job as they rate their immediate subordinates; and if they wish, political reliability and affinity can be among the criteria, whether overtly or covertly.[3] Likewise, to the extent that performance management cascades down through the organization each echelon may have some, albeit a declining level of, political influence.

The linkage with organizational performance may not be quite so overt, but may still be present, and still be important. As implied above, an emphasis on organizational performance places pressures on all the members of an organization, but perhaps especially the leadership, to make that organization perform better.[4] Given that they will be responsible for outcomes, the leaders of an organization will tend to want people they trust, meaning almost certainly that they will want colleagues with whom they share some political affinity. That pressure for performance is generally felt in situations in which, as described above, many of the constraints on more politicized personnel practices have been weakened, if not eliminated entirely.

Weaker parties but stronger politicization

Another of the paradoxes of the contemporary pressures for politicization has been that although politicization apparently has been increasingly important in government, political parties themselves are of declining importance for citizens. One might argue that this paradox is not so surprising. First, politicization is primarily an elite phenomenon, while the declining identification with parties has been observed primarily at the mass level. In addition, if there is a declining identification of the public with political parties then it may make sense for the parties to provide some tangible benefits for membership in the form of jobs; if parties cannot attract members with policy, they can at least offer jobs.

Although we might find some counter-arguments it does appear somewhat paradoxical that with parties finding it difficult to attract and retain members, and with many people find it easier to move from party to party (Dalton and Wattenberg, 2000), party allegiance is perceived as important for the people who implement policy. It is perhaps all the more paradoxical given the emphasis on management and performance that has been dominating government for the past several decades. Indeed, what is perhaps most paradoxical in this shift toward more politicization is that it is strongest where managerialism has been strongest, and rather weak where NPM has made few incursions into the culture of governing.

In order to understand what drives politicization we also need to look at the principal agents of this phenomenon, namely the political parties. While there are several systemic sources of politicization, as we have seen, and although politicization seems to be primarily a strategy among politicians as a collective to enhance their control over the civil service, the basic ideological objectives of politicization can be found inside the political parties. In this perspective, politicization sits at the nexus of state–society relations and serves to increase bureaucratic compliance with the policies of the government of the day.

That said, political parties in the advanced industrial democracies have become less creatures of civil society and more creatures of the state (Katz and Mair, 1995). Parties are becoming increasingly dependent on the state for financial reasons as their membership declines while the professionalization of the party organizations increases, with all that entails in terms of organizational expenditures. These interests of political parties in the state cut across the ideological cleavages of the party systems; indeed, so much so that some observers now suggest that the political parties have more interests that unite them than set them apart. If political parties are becoming in essence a "cartel" of parties at the top of government (Katz and Mair, 1995), with political elites to some extent becoming more alike and becoming increasingly distanced from the voting public, then politicization may make somewhat more sense. Again, this becomes part of a job machine for these activists. Further, it is a means of solidifying control of the party activists over the government, and it actually may make less real difference for policy than it does for the maintenance of the elite. This may also help to explain the finding of Geddes (1991) and others that politicians do not reform civil service systems when they have the opportunity, even if they might be able to blanket some of their own appointees into permanent positions.

Overt politicization

The final paradox that is revealed through these examinations of politicization is that overt politicization appears more successful, and more
tolerable, than the more covert forms of political involvement in administration. Two of the clearest examples of politicization in the cases
reported here – Germany and the United States – have been very open
about political appointments of a number of top officials. In both cases
(see Schröter, Chapter 4 above; Peters, Chapter 7 above) it is widely
known and accepted that a change in government means a change of a
number of important administrative figures in government. In the United
States these are not conceptualized as civil service posts but they are the
functional equivalent of civil servants in other countries.

   For politicization, success may be defined as the capacity to make political appointments, or to force career civil servants to think about their
actions in more political terms, without undermining the capacity of
government to govern effectively. It is in fact rather remarkable how little
overt opposition there has been to the increasing use of political criteria
in the selection and dismissal of public officials. Such acceptance of political involvement can be found even in countries with long histories of a
neutral, professional public service (see Christensen, Chapter 2 above).
In some cases the public servants appear to have accepted the inevitable
and begun to resign when there are changes in government, thus height-
ening the appearance of influence. Likewise, the public appear in most
cases to have accepted these changes with little or no resistance, or even
notice.[5]

Conclusion

The fundamental point that emerges from this comparison of politicization of the public service is that in any political system some positions
will be political. The real question is how many will be political, and which
ones. The dividing line between the political and the apolitical has been
shifting in the direction of the political, and more positions that once
would have been off limits for political tampering are now clearly subject
to political pressures and appointments. We may well debate the desirabil-
ity and efficacy of this change, but it does appear to have become a reality
of modern government.

   These chapters also point out how fragile a career professional public
service may be under political pressures. All the countries studied here
have such professionalized systems, or have made serious attempts to
establish them, and all have experienced some slippage away from that
standard. We have pointed to the paradoxes involved in these movements, but it is also clear that in government politics is still trumps and if
political leaders have the desire to impose their will over the public

sector it is very likely that they will win; they may win by covert strategies but they will win.

The long-term consequences of politicization have yet to be determined. On the one hand we might expect that once politicians are given these new powers over personnel they will find it difficult to refrain from using them, and politicization will continue, and perhaps even expand. On the other hand, the neutral career systems that have been under some attack from politicization themselves emerged in most cases from even more politicized, if not overtly corrupt, administrative systems. This may be one of the many cyclical changes one can observe in government – centralization/decentralization as a classic example – and there will be before very long a new set of reforms that will reinforce the principles of a depoliticized public service.

Notes

1 These positions have had the additional advantage for political leaders of being a source of numerous patronage positions. In an era in which political parties have been of declining interest to citizens, having "jobs for the boys and girls" has been very helpful for party officials as well as government officials.
2 Birkinshaw *et al.* (1990) refer to this as government by "moonlight."
3 Contracts may be used to define performance but at the upper echelons of government the tasks and hence the standards may be so subjective – what is good policy advice? – that political criteria can be introduced rather freely.
4 The linkage between individual and organizational performance in government is not clearly established, but that does not prevent attention focusing on those at the top of failing organizations.
5 While we may become very exercised about these changes the average citizen appears to be concerned primarily with the delivery of services, and not particularly concerned with all the details of personnel systems.

References

Birkinshaw, P., I. Harden, and N. Lewis (1990) *Government by Moonlight: The Hybrid Parts of the State* (London: Unwin Hyman).
Boston, J. (1991) *Reshaping the State: New Zealand's Bureaucratic Revolution* (Auckland: Oxford University Press).
Bouckaert, G., B. G. Peters, K. Verhoerst, and B. Verschuere (2003) "The Study of Organizational Autonomy," Paper prepared for IRSPM VII, Hong Kong, April 5–6.
Dalton, R. J. and M. P. Wattenberg (eds) (2000) *Parties without Partisans: Political Change in Advanced Industrial Democracies* (Oxford: Oxford University Press).
Geddes, B. (1991) "A Game Theoretic Model of Reform in Latin American Democracies," *American Political Science Review* 85, 378–91.
Gregory, R. (1995) "Post-Reform Attitudes of New Zealand's Senior Public Servants: A Follow-Up Study," *Political Science* 47, 161–90.
Katz, R. and P. Mair (1995) "Changing Models of Party Organization and Party Democracy: The Emergence of the Cartel Party," *Party Politics* 1, 5–28.

Savoie, D. J. (1994) *Reagan, Thatcher, Mulroney: In Pursuit of a New Bureaucracy* (Pittsburgh, Pa.: University of Pittsburgh Press).

Seidman, H. (1999) *Politics, Power and Position*, 5th edn (New York: Oxford University Press).

Skelcher, C. (1998) *The Appointed State: Quasi-Government Organizations and Democracy* (Buckingham: Open University Press).

Index

Page numbers in *italics* refer to tables